THE ELEMENT ENCYCLOPEDIA OF FAIRIES

THE ELEMENT ENCYCLOPEDIA OF FAIRIES

Lucy Cooper

HARPER element

HARPER element

ISBN 978-1-4351-5116-1

Typeset by Palimpsest Book Production Limited
Falkirk, Stirlingshire
Printed and bound in China

2 4 6 8 10 9 7 5 3 1

Contents

Acknowledgments

Many thanks to everyone who has helped along the way in making this book a reality. Thank you to Susannah Marriott for sparking this project into life, to Caitlin Doyle at HarperCollins for forbearance and support, and to my family and friends for putting up with (and on occasions accompanying me on) my long sojourns in fairyland, especially Viktoria Heard, Clive and Françoise Cooper, Frances Ford, and Jon Levine.

Introduction

Boggles, Bloody Bones, brownies, black dogs, Shellycoats, barguests, Robin Goodfellows, hags, hobgoblins, dobies, hobthrusts, fetches, kelpies, mumpokers, Pans, sirens, nymphs, imps, incubuses, Kit with the Cansticks, Melsh Dicks, knockers, elves, Rawheads, Padfoots, pixies, dwarves, changelings, redcaps, colt pixies, Tom Thumbs, boggarts, shag foals, brags, wraiths, waffs, gally-trots, Peg Powlers, Pucks, fays, selkies, Cauld Lads, sylphs, nixies, cluricaunes, kobolds, leprechauns, banshees, *Lhiannan Shees*, Gabriel Ratchets hounds, trows, sprites, and spunkies . . .

Welcome to the wonderful and diverse world of fairies.

These are just some of the fairy creatures listed in a series of nineteenth-century folklore pamphlets by a Yorkshire tradesman named Michael Denham, later published as *The Denham Tracts*, edited by James Hardy (London: Folklore Society, 1892–1895).

This snapshot of the fairy realm in the British Isles of the not-so-distant past introduces us to a world in which nursery bogies, such as Bloody Bones, lurked in the cupboard under the stairs, and mischievous pranksters Puck and Robin Goodfellow cavorted in the countryside, likely to transform at any moment into flickering lights and lead unwary travelers on a merry dance through briars, ditches, bogs, and streams. Dobie, the helpful household fairy, lent a hand

around the home, while the troublesome boggart delighted in upturning dishes, snatching bread and butter, and teasing members of the household with his tricks.

This brief peek into fairyland reveals a colorful cast of denizens, wildly different in appearance and characteristics, before we have even ventured further afield than the British Isles. Fairies have appeared in various guises in cultures around the world since ancient times, from the dryads and nymphs of ancient Greece to the noble *Sidhe* of Ireland, and from the Australian *arawotya* to the *zinkibaru* of Africa. Traditionally, fairies have assumed a number of different roles, as guardians, guides, gatekeepers, muses, and messengers, exerting an influence over human lives that may be by turns benevolent, malevolent, or mischievous, which makes pinning them down to definitions a tricky task.

TOWARD A DEFINITION

Definitions are slippery things in the fairy world. Hard and fast rules have a habit of bending, blurring, or evaporating into thin air when applied to the capricious denizens

of fairyland. The harder you try to pin down a fairy, the more likely it is to wiggle out of your grasp and vanish with a mischievous poke of the tongue.

As a rule of thumb, it is generally said that fairies belong to a race of supernatural beings possessing magic powers who sometimes meddle in the affairs of humans.

C. S. Burne, in *The Handbook of Folklore* (1914), describes fairies as beings somewhere between gods and men, not quite human yet not quite divine. They share the Earth with humans more or less invisibly. They may be messengers for higher powers or operate independently but interact in some way with the lives of humans.

In Native American folk beliefs, every aspect of the natural world is imbued with the universal life force, which goes by many names, including *manitou*, *orenda*, and *wakanda.* Fairies in the form of nature spirits are found in many other cultures, too.

Under these broad definitions we find fairies of all shapes and sizes. The ant-sized *abatwa* of South Africa are small enough to hide behind a blade of grass, while the Cornish spriggans, generally no taller than a person's bootlaces, can rapidly increase to the size of giants to frighten away would-be thieves who attempt to steal their treasure. The German household spirit King Goldemar is invisible, but makes his presence known by the touch of his thin, froglike hands.

Shapeshifting is a common fairy attribute, and looks can be deceptive—a wizened old hag is likely to be a beautiful princess in disguise. Swan maidens and selkies transform from human to animal form and have been known to interbreed with humans—though unions between mortals and fairies seldom run smoothly. Other fairies manifest as animals in the shape of cats, dogs, birds, or hybrid creatures, part-human, part-animal, such as mermaids, merrows, and Lamia, or in humanlike form, whether tiny or larger than life.

The denizens of fairyland are eclectic, beautiful, beguiling, and often downright bizarre. The *hebu* of South America has a glowing posterior and eyebrows so bushy that she must stand on her head if she wishes to look at the sky. The Matshishkapeu, or "Fart Man," of the Innu people in Canada is the source of much amusement, but also wields great power and serves a serious function in having dominance over animal masters as well as human behavior. In the fairy world, sometimes wisdom is found in the most unlikely of places. Grave seriousness mixes with playfulness and humor.

Already we have glimpsed many fairy creatures and there is hardly a pair of wings in sight. The winged fairies of children's picture books are a relatively new addition to the fairy world, popularized during the Victorian era. The fairies you will find here are drawn from the folk beliefs of cultures around the world.

SOURCES

The work of folklorist Katharine Briggs provides a rich store of reference for fairy lore of the British Isles, while Thomas Keightley's *The Fairy Mythology* (1828) brings together fairy lore from many different cultures around the world. These, along with many other sources, have provided starting points for investigation. Where possible, the oldest sources of accounts have been tracked down. Material has been drawn from anthropological texts, journals, periodicals, encyclopedias and dictionaries of mythology, collections of folklore, folk tales, superstitions, customs, and letters.

In 1881, the Cornish folklorist Robert Hunt wrote that even then:

> *. . . old-world stories were perishing like shadows in the mist before the rising sun. Many wild tales which I heard in 1829 appear to have been lost in 1835 . . . I drank deeply from the stream of legendary lore which was at that time flowing, as a well of living waters . . . and longed to renew my acquaintance with the wild tales of Cornwall which had either terrified or amused me as a child.*

How many more wild tales from around the globe must have been lost as the old stories were swept away by the march of progress? And yet the fairies are still with us. With a little digging, it is possible to unearth old tales and beliefs. In some places fairies still inhabit the here and now. Elsewhere the stream of legendary lore is buried deep underground and one must dig deep to find it. Yet still it flows.

Inevitably, there is not room here to include the many thousands of denizens of fairyland, and apologies are extended to those who do not appear between these pages. However, it is hoped that the fairies here, representing many cultures around the world, will spark interest for further exploration of the fairy realm.

A NOTE ON SPELLINGS

As beliefs have passed down the generations through oral tradition and spread to different locations, fairy names have taken on the dialects of different places. This means there are often many spellings of the same name, none of which is "correct." Here, effort has been made to list the most commonly used names, along with common alternative spellings.

USING THIS BOOK

The A–Z listings contain entries for hundreds and hundreds of individual fairies, alongside some of the folklorists and fairytale collectors, such as the Brothers Grimm, whose work has contributed to what we know about fairy lore today. Words in **bold** cross-reference related entries, allowing you to hopscotch your way through the world of fairy.

You'll find more information on specific aspects of fairy lore in the various sections. "What are Fairies?" (*p.1*) explores theories on the origins of fairies, from a conquered pygmy race to fallen angels.

Fairyland has always exerted an irresistible pull on humans and "Where is Fairyland?" (*p.11*) delves into the realms of fairy. Here you will discover entrances to fairyland, but tread carefully, for the path is often beset with danger, and that glittering pile of fairy gold is likely to turn into a handful of withered leaves in the light of day. Yet those who approach fairyland with a pure heart might be rewarded with a peek behind the veil of the everyday at the curious wonders of the fairy realm.

Fairies are well known for their capricious nature. Those wishing to make their acquaintance would be wise to ensure they have a protective piece of iron in their pocket before peering through a self-bored stone or picking a four-leafed clover. "Connecting with

Fairies" (*p.159*) looks at traditions and customs concerned with seeing fairies—and how to ward off unwanted attention from pernicious or mischievous fairies. Here you will also find tales of fairy encounters, a calendar of the times of year when fairies are at their most active, and information on fairy music and art.

One of the most commonly held beliefs about fairies, still widespread today, is that they are nature spirits, identified with flowers, trees, lakes, rivers, mountains, and other features of the natural landscape. "Elementals and Flower Fairies" (*p.299*) traces ideas about the connection between fairies and the elements of nature, from the alchemist Paracelsus via the Theosophists to Mary Cicley Barker's flower fairy illustrations. Here you will find a rich variety of fairies of the earth, water, fire, and air from cultures around the world, as well as flowers and trees of fairy lore.

From larger-than-life magical heroes of Celtic legend to Shakespeare's Oberon and Titania and J. M. Barrie's Tinkerbell, fairies have undergone many transformations through the ages. "Fairies in Literature and Legend" (*p.407*) takes a look at the changing face of fairies in English literature, from the mouths of storytellers via the quills of poets and playwrights right up to the present, as well as flits through some of the earliest-recorded fairy tales, from *The Thousand and One Nights* of Arabia to those related in the fashionable French *salons.*

Are you ready to begin your adventure in fairyland? Pick an entry at random, follow the trail of breadcrumbs, and see where you end up. Be warned, though: many who enter the land of fairy are never quite the same afterward.

After two years immersed in the world of fairies while compiling

Italian Folktales (1956), the Italian writer Italo Calvino wrote, "The world about me gradually took on the attributes of fairyland, where everything that happened was a spell or metamorphosis."

Capricious, amusing, fearsome, and delightful, the topsy-turvy world of fairies invites us to take a look beyond the surface, to rediscover the magical in the everyday and glimpse the extraordinary in the ordinary. Prepare to venture into the fairy realm, where nothing is ever quite as it seems . . .

PART 1
What are Fairies?

WHAT ARE FAIRIES?

Quite simply, the answer to this question will depend on whom you ask. It's like the story of the lady and the vicar, viewing the moon through a telescope, who see two shapes inclined toward each other. "Methinks," says the lady, "they are two fond lovers, meeting to pour forth their vows by earth-light." "Not at all," says the vicar, taking his turn at the glass, "they are the steeples of two neighboring churches."

What is seen is often determined by who is doing the looking.

So, what are fairies? Memories of a conquered race of pygmy people? Feared and venerated spirits of ancestors? Remnants of ancient mythology? Nature spirits? Depending on whom you ask, fairies are bound up with all—or none—of these things.

A PYGMY PEOPLE

Some folklorists and anthropologists, mostly nineteenth-century ones, have suggested that fairy beliefs sprang from memories of conquered races of dwarvish people who lived in caves or mounds and used flint arrows. Stories about fairies, according to this theory, were the result of a clash of cultures. In Britain, this race of small people was conquered by the ancestors of the modern British, who had iron weapons. The conquered people retreated to the hills, or were driven into remote areas such as mountains and swamps, as the larger, more powerful, better-armed race advanced. Some hold this to be why iron is still used as protection against pernicious fairies today.

John Webster, writing in the same era as Shakespeare, expressed a view that was popular at the time:

> *. . . fairies are pigmy creatures which really exist in the world, and are and may be still in islands and mountains that are inhabited, and that they are not real daemons. But that either they were truly of the human race, endowed with the use of reason and speech, or, at least, that they were some kind of little apes or satyrs, having their secret and recesses and holes in the mountains.*

Jakob Grimm, best known as one half of the Grimm brothers, who famously collected fairy tales throughout Germany and Europe, theorized that once there had been a widespread dwarf population

across Europe, which had given rise to many traditions associated with supernatural elves and fairies.

David MacRitchie, a Scottish folklorist and antiquarian, popularized the "pygmy theory" in his controversial book *The Testimony of Tradition* (1890). In *Fians, Fairies and Picts* (1893), he used the science of archeology, which was then just developing, to provide evidence for his theory of an ancient dwarflike people. He argued that the Fians, the people preceding the Scots, and the Picts, of Irish and Scottish history, had been skilled in medicine, magic, music, and masonry, and had lived in hidden underground earth houses, which were later known as fairy hills or fairy forts, such as the chambered mounds of Maes-Howe in the Orkneys and New Grange at Boyne in Ireland. The fires that could be glimpsed at night through the tops of their underground dwellings were the "fairy lights" that appeared in folklore across Britain as lights that led humans astray. Stories of women, men, and children taken away by the "fairies" were in fact the result of stealthy raids carried out by the defeated race as acts of retaliation against their oppressors.

This belief was found in other Celtic regions too. In Cornwall around the end of the nineteenth century, the local secretary for the Society of Antiquarians believed the original inhabitants of the area to have been "a strange and separate people" who still lived in the Cornish wilds. Once thought to be witches and wizards, they were, he believed, really the descendants of the Pictish tribes, and thus the Picts had become pixies, or "piskies," as the Cornish called them.

SPIRITS OF THE DEAD

W. Y. Evans-Wentz, an American anthropologist and folklorist of Celtic descent who went on to translate *The Tibetan Book of the Dead*, explored the Celtic lands of Ireland, the Highlands of Scotland,

Wales, Cornwall, the Isle of Man, and Brittany at the turn of the nineteenth century, collecting fairy stories, experiences, and beliefs from the people he met. He discovered a strong connection between fairies and the dead.

In Ireland, there was a belief that fairies were the spirits of the departed, returning with wisdom, warnings, or messages. The dead of the ancient tribes of Ireland are known as the Gentry. In Wales, the *Tylwyth Teg*, or Fair Folk, are ancestor spirits, often envisaged as being 6 feet (nearly 2 meters) tall. In Scotland, distinction was made between the Host, or *Sluagh*, and the *Sith* (*Shee*). The *Sluagh*, "hosts" of the spirit world, are the spirits of mortals who have died. According to one account in Evans-Wentz' *The Fairy-Faith in Celtic Countries* (1911), "they fly about in great clouds, up and down the face of the earth like starlings, and come back to the scenes of their earthly transgressions. No soul of them is without the clouds of the earth, dimming the brightness of the works of God, nor can any win heaven, till satisfaction is made for the sins of the earth." The *Sith*, literally "people of the hills," were fairy beings believed to dwell in the hollow hills or fairy mounds of Scotland. They were known as the *Sidh*, or *Daoine Sidh*, in Ireland.

Fairy ancestor spirits bestowed flags, banners, and gifts on Scottish clans, such as the famous "fairy banner" of the MacDonalds, the "fairy flag" of the MacLeods of Skye, and the Luck of Edenhall, a glass beaker decorated with enamel, now in the Victoria and Albert Museum, which is said to have been crafted by the fairies and gifted to the Musgrave family of Edenhall in what is now Cumbria. "If this cup shall break, or fall/ Farewell the luck of Edenhall" goes the famous saying. As yet, the glass remains intact.

In Cornwall, the story of *The Fairy Dwelling of Selena Moor* explains that fairies are the spirits of the dead not good enough for heaven, not bad enough for hell.

They are shapeshifters and can take the form of beasts or birds, but every time they return to their proper shape, they are a little bit smaller than they were before. Over time, their senses and emotions dull, and they live on the memories of past feelings.

It was said, too [of the Fair Folk], that those who take animal forms get smaller and smaller with every change, till they are finally lost in the earth as muryans (ants) and that they pass winter, for the most part, in underground habitations, entered from cleves or carns. And it is held that many persons who appear to have died entranced are not really dead, but changed into the fairy state.

"The Fairy Dwelling of Selena Moor" in William Bottrell, Traditions and Hearthside Stories of West Cornwall *(Vol. II, 1873)*

FALLEN ANGELS

Folk and religious beliefs, including beliefs about fairies, became intermingled with the coming of Christianity, and in *Carmina Gadelica* (1900), a collection of charms, incantations, prayers, poems, and songs from Gaelic-speaking regions of Scotland gathered by folklorist Alexander Carmichael (1832–1912), there is a vivid account of the belief in the Scottish Highlands and Ireland that fairies are fallen angels.

According to this, when the Angel Michael threw the Hosts of Satan out of Heaven, they were followed by an almost endless stream of angels who had been seduced by Satan's cunning wiles. Seeing that the Shining Hosts of Heaven were rapidly diminishing, the Son cried: "Father, Father, the City is being emptied!" and God raised his hand and the gates of Heaven closed. The seduced angels stopped, bewildered, and remembered themselves. Some had already descended into Hell, and they became demons. But others were in the sky, on the mountains, in the woods, or in the sea, and they became the fairies of the air, the earth, the forests, the seas, and the rivers.

THE HIDDEN PEOPLE

In Scandinavia, there is a belief that fairies are the hidden children of Eve. The story goes that after the Fall, Adam and Eve settled down and had many children. One day when God was walking through the world He came to call on Eve and asked her to present her children to Him. Caught unawares, she had time to wash only half of them. Ashamed, she sent the unwashed ones to hide and brought out only the ones she thought presentable. But God wasn't deceived. "Let those who were hidden from me," He said, "be hidden from all Mankind." And this was the beginning of the *huldre*, the "hidden people."

In another version of the tale, the *huldre* were the offspring of Adam and his first wife, Lilith.

According to these stories, fairies were not creatures of another order, like angels, but were half human.

DIMINISHED GODS

Some believe that fairies were once important deities, worshiped in pagan times as gods and goddesses of nature. With the coming of Christianity, these spirits were reduced, or tamed, and consequently reduced in stature from powerful beings to the status of folklore.

In Ireland, the *Tuatha de Danann* were once believed to be the children of the goddess Don, otherworldly beings with supernatural powers. Conquered by the invading Milesians, they took to the hollow hills and became the *Daoine Sidh* (pronounced *Deeny Shee*). They battled and mated with the warriors of the Fianna Finn and over the years dwindled in stature. Originally the same size or larger than humans, down through the generations they shrank to the size of children, or smaller.

This theory overlaps with ideas of the vanquished race, driven to live in the hills. As with all beliefs surrounding fairies, the boundaries are blurred and we are left to draw our own conclusions. Suffice to say, belief in supernatural beings, in various forms, who are neither gods, nor strictly speaking ghosts, and who can intervene in human lives is widespread across many ancient cultures and peoples, from the Far East, where they have long played a role in romances and stories, to the ancient Hindu tradition, where they inhabited Earth long before the creation of humanity, to Persia, where the *peris* lived in enchanted palaces and castles and fought the malevolent forces of the *divs*.

Nowadays it's common to think of fairies as small or even tiny winged creatures. However, that hasn't always been the case. In earlier times, they were often life-sized, or larger. The Irish *Sidh* were as tall or taller than humans. An Irish "seer," one for whom fairies are visible, once described opalescent beings of about 14 feet (over 4 meters) in stature and shining beings of about human height, or a little taller.

FROM THE FATES TO THE FAIRIES

The word "fairy" has been through nearly as many transformations as beliefs about the creatures themselves. It originates from the Latin root *fatum*, meaning "destiny" or "fate." *Fata*, the plural of *fatum*, was the name given to the classical Greek and Roman female deities said to be present at a baby's birth and to determine the future course of that life. These *Fata*, or Fates, the three daughters of the night, were Clotho, Lachesis, and Atropos. Clotho spun the thread of each individual life. Lachesis shaped and twisted the thread. Atropos took her shears and cut the thread at the appointed time. In Spain, they were known as the *Hadas*, and in France as the *Feés*. In Albania, the *Fatit* rode in on butterflies three days after a birth to determine the course of the child's life.

The belief in the Fates as guardian spirits who watch over us, especially at times of transformation such as birth and death, has endured over time and they have entered into popular fairy tales, such as the story of *Cinderella*, in the form of fairy godmothers.

From this root, we get the French verb *faer*, or *fĕer*, meaning "to enchant." From that we get *faerie*, or *fĕerie*, which originally referred to a state of enchantment, but which also came to apply to the "enchanter" as well. By the seventeenth century, a whole host of names, including "fairfolks," "farie," "fairie," "fairye," "fairy," and "faery," seem to have been in use.

FAIRY OR FAERY?

Today "fairy" and "faery" are most commonly used to talk about fairy creatures, and "fairyland" or "faery" or "faerie" to talk about the place where fairies live (which goes by many other names in different cultures too).

Some use "fairy" to refer to the small, winged creatures most associated with the Victorians and flower fairies, and "faery" to talk about the wider group of beings with roots that originate in ancient times and places, and reach out to include nature spirits—mermaids, hobgoblins, brownies, elves, and a whole host of related beings. There is no one "correct" use. Here, "fairy" is used to refer to the many wonderful and varied creatures that make up the diverse fairy world.

Names have always been a slippery issue when it comes to fairies. Out of deference, or fear of causing offense, humans have traditionally referred to them by other names and euphemisms, such as the little people, the good folk, the fair folk, or the good neighbors. There are many names for them in the British Isles alone. The *Ad-hene* Manx on the Isle of Man, meaning "Themselves," is a name humans must get right and never take in vain. The *Daoine Sidh* in Ireland, the *Sith* in the Scottish Highlands, the piskies in Cornwall—the names go on and on.

Folklore gives us many examples of where finding out a fairy's true name can bring power over the creature, such as in the tale of *Rumpelstiltskin,* where a girl must guess the name of her mysterious helper to gain power over him and avoid a curse. The same is true in the Cornish and Scottish tales "Tarraway" (or "Duffy and the Devil") and "Whuppity Stoorie." Here you will learn the names of many hundreds of fairies.

Many attempts have been made to categorize fairies. Thomas Keightley, the author of *The Fairy Mythology* (1828), divided the beings into "Fays or Fairies of Romance" (human-sized beings endowed with special powers) and "Elves or Popular Fairies" (diminutive beings). Characteristically, fairies have defied categorization—and you will find them all here.

PART 2
Where is Fairyland?

WHERE IS FAIRYLAND?

Invisible lands across the sea, hollow hills that raise themselves up on legs at full moon, revealing the twinkling lights of the fairy homes within, underwater palaces and castles in the sky, streams, lakes, mountains, forests, woods, trees, and flowers, under a rock or at the bottom of the garden—fairyland, like fairies themselves, comes in many different guises.

In the county of Cornwall alone, descriptions of fairyland and fairy dwellings range from the fantastical to the everyday. In "The Lost Child" in Robert Hunt's *Popular Romances of the West of England* (1865), a little boy who follows the sound of exquisite music into the woods describes being led by a beautiful lady into a fabulous palace with glass pillars and glistening multi-colored arches hung with crystals. In contrast, another account states that one of the favorite haunts of the fairies are simply "places frequented by goats."

From otherworldly palaces to mundane hillsides, fairyland is elusive, remaining always just around the corner—glimpsed briefly, disappearing in the twinkling of an eye.

Celtic tradition abounds with tales of mythical enchanted isles located somewhere across the western sea, visible only briefly to mortal eyes before disappearing again into the mists. *Tir Nan Og*, Land of the Ever Young, is where the *Tuatha de Danann* are supposed to have resided since being chased from the mainland by the Milesians. In Manx folklore, it is the Isle of Emhain, Land of the Women. To the Britons, the Isle of Man was a magical land. In "The Magic Legs" in *Fairy Tales of the Isle of Man* (1963), Dora Broome tells of the mist-hidden island that Mannanon, Son of Lir, could make invisible at will. In Wales, sailors told tales of isles of enchanted green meadows off the coast of Pembrokeshire and Carmarthenshire.

The land of Avalon is one of the

most famous of the fairy lands across the sea. This is where some believe King Arthur lies sleeping, awaiting the hour when he will return to rule again.

In Old Norse mythology, there are Nine Worlds which are home to the various types of beings, including humans, elves, gods, and goddesses, that make up the Old Norse worldview. These worlds are held in the branches and roots of Yggdrasil, the World Tree. Alfheim is the world of the elves. Asgard is the world of the Aesir tribe of gods and goddesses, located in the sky, invisible to human eyes but linked to the human realm by the rainbow bridge Bifrost. Midgard is the name given to the human world.

"Gard" is derived from the old Germanic idea of *innangard* and *utangard.* Literally meaning "inside the fence" and "outside the fence," the terms applied to the physical or geographical location of a place as well as the mindset of its inhabitants. The human world's name of Midgard, or "Middle Enclosure," implied that humankind sat somewhere between the ordered, *innangard* world of the gods of Asgard, and the chaotic, *utangard* world of the giants of Jotunheim.

IN-BETWEEN PLACES

Just as fairies are often connected with thresholds and transitions in human lives, such as birth and death, so too fairy worlds are located at thresholds and borders. Woods and forests that mark the separation of a town or village from the wilderness of nature, seashores and mountaintops at the point between sea and land, land and sky—all of these are in-between places where fairies dwell. Domestic fairies traditionally make the hearth their home, which sits at the point of intersection between the cosy world inside the household and what lurks outside. Twilight, midnight, Samhain (Halloween), the times favored by fairies, are all in-between times, on the cusp of night and day, light and dark, summer and winter.

THE PASSAGE OF TIME IN FAIRYLAND

In many accounts of visits to fairyland, time operates differently there from in the human world. In some accounts, it takes on a dream-like quality, expanding so that a year spent with the fairies is a mere few minutes in the mortal world. One such story is that of the Welsh boy who entered a fairy ring to dance and was transported to a glittering palace in a beautiful garden, in the middle of which was a well in which fish of gold and silver swam. His fairy hosts told him he could live in their realm as long as liked, providing he kept to one rule: he must never drink from the well. After a time, the desire to drink from the well grew until it became so strong, the boy could no longer resist and he cupped his hands and drank. Immediately, a cry shook the garden and he found himself standing back on the chilly hillside among his father's sheep. Though it had seemed to him that weeks had gone by, hardly an hour of human time had passed.

More common are the tales of time passing so swiftly in fairyland that a person who thinks they have been away for only three days returns to find that 300 years have passed in the mortal realm. In the Japanese story of Urashima Tar, a fisherman who rescued a turtle was rewarded with a visit to the underwater realm of the dragon god, Ryūjin. He was a guest at his palace, Ryūgū-jō, but after three days, he asked to return to his village on land to visit his ageing mother. He arrived there only to discover that 300 years had passed. Then he opened a *tamatebako*, a special box, a gift from the underwater realm, which he had promised to keep shut, and released a cloud of white smoke. Instantly, his back bent, his beard grew long and gray, and old age and death fell upon him.

ADVENTURES IN FAIRYLAND

The theme of old age and death coming to those who return from the fairy realm to the mortal one is common. The legends of Oisin and Bran are examples of two heroes who lived to tell the tale of their visits to fairyland. One was strong enough to survive the return to the human realm; the other had a lucky escape back to fairyland.

Oisin and Tir Nan Og

In Irish folklore, the story of Oisin is a famous example of how mere days or months in the fairy realm can add up to years in the human world.

Oisin was the son of Fionn mac Cumhaill and a fairy woman of the *Sidhe.* With fairy blood in him, it was no surprise that he was a great singer, poet, and warrior, and he lived through many great battles. The fairy princess Niamh of the Golden Locks invited him to go with her to *Tir Nan Og*, the mythical Land of the Ever Young that lay across the sea to the west of Ireland. There they lived happily together for what seemed to him a few months.

Oisin wished to see his father and his people, the Fianna Finn, to tell them that all was well with him. Niamh was reluctant to let him leave, but in the end gave him a white horse to ride back across the sea. She told him not to touch the earth of Ireland, for if he did, he would not be able to return to *Tir Nan Og.* He promised and rode away across the waves.

When Oisin arrived back in Ireland, however, he found everything changed. The hills seemed small, the forests and woodlands had shrunk, and the great fort of Tara was reduced to nothing more than a hill. There wasn't even a single voice or face anywhere that he recognized.

In despair, Oisin turned his horse to return to *Tir Nan Og*, but came across a group of men, who seemed to belong to a smaller, less mighty race than the Fianna Finn. They were struggling to move a stone. Even though they tried with all their might, they could not shift it. Feeling compassion for their weakness and courage, Oisin stopped to help them. Remembering his promise, he didn't dismount from his white charger, but bent down and lifted the stone with one hand. The men regarded the shining golden warrior with amazement. But at that moment, the saddle slipped and he fell to the ground. The white horse thundered away to the sea.

Where the great warrior had fallen, there lay an old man, the weight of hundreds of years heavy upon him.

Unlike many returning from the fairy realm, Oisin did not crumble to dust on mortal soil, however, but lived on and told the new Irish race about the heroic days of the Fianna Finn.

Bran and the Land of Women

The passage of time works in a similar way in Emhain, the Land of Women. It is related in the story of Bran mac Febail, as told by Lady Gregory in *Gods and Fighting Men* (1904).

One day the Irish king Bran mac Febail heard the sweetest music. It lulled him to sleep and when he awoke he held in his hand a silver branch covered in white blossom. He brought it to the royal house, where a woman appeared in strange clothes and began to sing:

I bring a branch of the apple-tree from Emhain, from the far island around which are the shining horses of the Son of Lir.

A delight of the eyes is the plain where the hosts hold their games; curragh *racing against chariot in the White Silver Plain to the south.*

She went on to describe a shining, many-colored land of blossoms, birds, and sweet music, without grief, sorrow, sickness, or death. When she had finished her song, the silver branch leaped from Bran's hands into hers and she vanished.

Next morning Bran set out with a fleet of *curragh* boats to row across to the sea to find the Isle of Emhain.

After two days and two nights, he and his men encountered Mannanon, Son of Lir, in his golden chariot. He told Bran he would reach the Land of Women before sunset.

Sure enough, it wasn't long afterward that they reached the Isle of Emhain, where the chief woman welcomed them and pulled them ashore with a ball of thread. They went to a grand house where there was a bed for every couple and food and drink without end. There Bran and his men lived happily for what seemed to them a year.

Despite the beauty and delights of the Isle of Emhain, one of the company, Nechtan, grew homesick for Ireland and begged to return, just for an hour. The chief woman was loath to let them go and told Bran they must not touch the soil of Ireland and must talk to only their company on the boat. Bran promised, saying he would stay only a short while and return quickly.

They rowed away to Ireland, where the people gathered on the shore asked who they were. Bran asked if they had heard of Bran of Febal, but they replied that no such man was alive now, although their old stories told of a man who had rowed away to the Land of Women many hundreds of years before. On hearing that, Nechtan leaped from the *curragh* and waded to shore. As soon as his foot touched the soil, he turned to a heap of ash, as if he had been in the earth for hundreds of years.

Cautioned by his fate, the other men stayed aboard the *curraghs.* Bran rested long enough to tell of his voyage, then turned his fleet around and rowed back to the joys of the Isle of Emhain.

Oissin and Bran were lucky to escape the fate of death on returning to the human world. Like Nechtan, many who return from fairyland crumble to dust on touching human soil. This raises comparisons between fairyland and the Underworld, or the land of the dead.

FAIRYLAND, THE UNDERWORLD, GLAMOR, AND TABOOS

As in many stories of the Underworld, often there are taboos placed on eating and drinking in fairyland, and visitors would be wise to refuse any food or drink offered to them, no matter how appealing it appears. Fairies are known for using their glamor, or magic, to conceal the real nature of things.

The Legend of Innis Sark

Lady Wilde's *Legend of Innis Sark* (1887) provides a cautionary tale against consuming fairy food and a lesson that all may not be as it seems in fairyland.

One November Eve (soon after Halloween), exhausted after a hard day's work, a young man fell asleep under a haystack. He awoke to find himself in a fairy kitchen where, to his horror, he saw an old hag being chopped up and boiled to serve to the dinner guests.

The next thing he knew, he was being seated at a banquet table and a prince sitting on a throne at the head of the table was inviting him to eat. He looked around at the beautiful ladies and noblemen seated at the table, and then at the banquet. Fruit, chicken, turkey, butter, freshly baked cakes, and glasses of bright red wine filled the table.

Again, the prince invited the young man to eat. But, the scene from the kitchen still fresh in his mind, he declined. The prince persisted, insisting the young man taste the wine. Unable to resist the bright red liquid winking in a crystal cup offered to him by one of the beautiful ladies, the lad gave in and drank it down in one gulp. No sooner had he set down the empty glass than a clap of thunder shook the table, the lights went out, and he found himself alone in the dark night lying beneath the haystack.

Cherry of Zennor

In another tale, it is not food and drink but a special ointment that is taboo. This is a Cornish tale, "Cherry of Zennor," collected by Robert Hunt in *Popular Romances of the West of England* (1865).

A few generations ago there lived a man known as Old Honey, such was the sweetness of his nature. He had a wife and several children and together they lived in a humble two-room cottage set on the cliffs at in the far west of Cornwall in a place called Trereen. Despite a simple diet of winkles and whelks and potatoes, they were a healthy, handsome family, and none more so than one of their daughters, Cherry.

When the miller's boy visited to collect corn for the mill and left his horse tied to a furze bush, Cherry would climb onto its back and gallop off across the rugged cliffs and up onto the rough, rocky cairns that rose behind the little village.

Inevitably, this lively young lady soon became frustrated with the simplicity of her daily life and longed for a pretty frock to wear to the fair, or the church, or even to the preachings at the nearby villages of Morva or Nancledry. When one of her friends did just this and boasted of all the young beaus who had walked her home, she decided that she must leave home and look for work in the "low countries," as the adjacent parishes were known. Her mother wanted her to go no further than Towednack, so she might still see her occasionally. But Cherry said, "No! I'll never go where the cow ate the bell rope, and where they eat only fish and tatties and conger pie on Sundays."

Old Honey saw that his daughter was determined and so one bright spring morning, Cherry put a few things in a bundle, waved goodbye to her family, and set off over the moors, heading south in the direction of Gulval and Ludgvan.

The path was steep and hard, and by the time she came to the crossroads at Lady Downs, she had to sit down to rest on a hard granite rock. She was tired and hungry and thirsty and began to regret her hasty decision. She hadn't met a single soul on her journey, but now, quite suddenly, a gentleman appeared before her.

"Good morning," he said. "Could you direct me to Towednack?"

Cherry pointed to the east and explained that she had left home to look for service, but was now resolved to return to Zennor.

"What great fortune smiles upon us both," said the gentleman, "for I am looking for a good, clean girl to keep house for me, and here you are!"

He explained that his wife had died and he needed someone to look after his little boy, milk the cow, and tend to some light housework. He seemed a very kind gentleman and Cherry agreed to go with him.

They walked down from the moors and before long Cherry found herself in beautiful, gentle countryside such as she had never known before. Soft green trees shaded the lanes and pretty flowers carpeted the verges. The scent of honeysuckle and sweetbriar filled the air and ripe red apples hung from the trees.

Soon they came to a crystal-clear stream of water. Uncertain as to its depth, Cherry paused, not knowing how to cross. The gentleman lifted her and carefully carried her to the other side.

The lane became ever darker and narrower, almost like a tunnel through the trees, and they seemed to be going rapidly downhill, but Cherry felt safe in the company of this kindly man.

They came to a gate and when the master opened it, Cherry thought she must have entered into heaven. The garden was filled with flowers, fruit hung from the trees, the air was alive with birdsong, and a bright light shone everywhere, although the sun itself could not be seen. Cherry was reminded of the fairylands of which her granny had spoken, but here was the gentleman standing tall beside her and at that moment a little boy came running down the path crying, "Papa, Papa!" so, surely, these could not be fairies.

Before Cherry could greet the child, whose eyes were bright and direct, a bent and bony old woman appeared and took the boy back into the house. As she did so, the old hag stopped in the doorway and gave Cherry such a look that it felt as though a dagger was piercing her heart. However, when they entered the house, the old woman, who was called Aunt Prudence, laid the table with good food and drink, and Cherry soon recovered her good spirits.

Next, Aunt Prudence gave Cherry her instructions. She was to sleep in a bedchamber at the top of the house, where the child would also sleep. She was never to open her eyes at night, nor to speak to the boy. At daybreak, she was to take him to the spring in the garden to wash him and anoint his eyes with a special ointment that she would find in a crystal box beside the water. She was never to touch her own eyes with the ointment. After dealing with the child, she was to call the cow to get some milk for breakfast.

The next morning Cherry did all these things, then Aunt Prudence gave her a good breakfast and explained her household duties. Most of these were scrubbing and washing dishes and utensils and churning the butter and scalding the milk. She was warned not to wander about the house.

The following day, the gentleman asked Cherry to help him in the beautiful garden, picking apples and pears and weeding the leeks and onions. She enjoyed the work and the master gave her a kiss to show his appreciation of her diligence.

The days passed happily in this way and Cherry was quite content. Then, one day, Aunt Prudence took her into the rest of the house, which seemed dark and forbidding. She was told to remove her shoes and enter a room that had a floor as smooth as glass. All around it were stone statues of figures large and small, some distorted or limbless but all disturbingly lifelike despite their stony appearance. Cherry was frightened, but when Aunt Prudence insisted that she polish a wooden box as hard as she could, she did as she was told.

Suddenly, there came a terrible groaning from the box and poor Cherry fainted to the floor.

The master heard the noise and came angrily into the room. He gently carried Cherry down to the kitchen, where she soon revived. Aunt Prudence was dismissed from the house for taking Cherry into forbidden corners of the building.

Cherry recovered her vitality and curiosity and continued to live happily with the little boy and her master.

A year drifted by, but despite her contentment, Cherry could not help wondering about the boy, who she often thought saw more than she did with his bright, strange eyes, and even about her master, who sometimes disappeared for days on end or vanished into the depths of the house where Cherry was afraid to go.

One day, she could not resist touching some of the special ointment to her own eyes. Immediately, she felt a terrible burning sensation and splashed water from the spring to cool her eyes. As she did so, she was astonished to see hundreds of little people all dancing and playing in the pool. Among them was her gentleman, as tiny as the rest, dancing with the ladies. Cherry looked around the garden and everything was sparkling and bright, with tiny fairies and elves cavorting among the flowers and bushes and trees. She spent the rest of the day gazing at them in a trance of delight.

At dusk, her master rode up, restored to his normal self. He went to the enchanted room where Aunt Prudence had taken Cherry, and Cherry heard the sound of beautiful music floating on the soft night air.

Days passed and the master spent more nights in the private room. One night, Cherry's curiosity overcame her fears and she crept to the door of the magic room and peered through the keyhole. What a sight met her eyes! The master was singing with many ladies in attendance; one in particular was dressed like a queen and playing on the wooden box that Cherry had polished. Cherry was filled with jealousy when she saw her master kissing this beautiful lady.

The next day the master stayed at home and asked Cherry to help him pick fruit in the orchard. After a time he bent to kiss her, but she drew back and slapped him, saying, "Keep your kisses for the fairy people!"

Realizing that she must have used the magic ointment, sadly the master told Cherry that she would have to go. That same night he called her and gave her a bundle of good clothes as payment for her services, and with a lantern to light the way, they set off into the lanes by which they had come so long ago. But now they were steep and dark and narrow and they only came onto the Lady Downs as the gray light of dawn slowly drove away the darkness.

The gentleman kissed Cherry goodbye and said he was sorry to leave her, but she had broken her word and he could no longer keep her in his service.

The sun rose over the moors and Cherry made her way back to Old Honey and her family. When they first saw her, they thought she must be a ghost, as they feared she had died. To begin with, they weren't convinced by her story, but as time went by and she didn't change a single word of it, they all came to believe her.

But Cherry longed for the life she had left behind, and on moonlit nights they say that you still may see the lonely figure of Cherry Honey wandering the Lady Downs in search of her long-lost fairy master.

FAIRY TREASURE

Humans have long been drawn to fairyland by tales of treasure and untold riches. But where fairy treasure is concerned, it is wise to tread carefully, for the path is often beset with glamor, curses, and taboos.

"The Old Wandering Droll-Teller of the Lizard, and his Story of the Mermaid and the Man of Cury," collected by William Bottrell in *Traditions and Hearthside Stories of West Cornwall* (1870), is a reminder of the old adage that all that glitters is not gold—especially when it is fairy gold.

In the story, a mermaid attempts to entice a mortal man, Lutey, into her underwater kingdom with promises of glittering treasures. Her description of the merpeople's grottoes mixes the wondrous with the macabre, and reveals the fate that lies in store for many who are tempted to enter the fairy realm in search of riches:

"In our cool caverns we have everything one needs," said she, "and much more. The walls of our abodes are encrusted with coral and amber, entwined with sea-flowers of every hue, and their floors are all strewn with pearls. The roof sparkles of diamonds, and other gems of such brightness that their rays make our deep grots in the ocean hillsides as light as day."

Then, embracing Lutey with both her arms round his neck, she continued, "Come with me, love, and see the beauty of the mermaid's dwellings. Yet the ornaments, with which we take the most delight to embellish our halls and chambers, are the noble sons and fair daughters of earth, whom the wind and waves send in foundered ships to our abodes. Come, I will show you thousands of handsome bodies so embalmed, in a way only known to ourselves, with choice salts and rare spices, that they look more beautiful than when they breathed, as you will say when you see them reposing on beds of amber, coral, and pearl, decked with rich stuffs, and surrounded by heaps of silver and gold for which they ventured to traverse our domain. Aye, and when you see their limbs all adorned with glistening gems, move gracefully to and fro with the motion of the waves, you will think they still live."

In some cases, it is possible for the pure of heart to elude death and reap the reward of fairy treasure, providing specific conditions are met. In *The Science of Fairy Tales* (1891) Edwin Sydney Hartland describes the fairy island of Rügen in Germany, where long ago a king amassed piles of gold and jewels in the chambers beneath his castle. It is said that he still keeps watch over his treasure and occasionally he is seen wearing a golden crown and riding a gray horse around the lake, or glimpsed in the forest at night, wearing a black fur cap and carrying a white staff. At other times, he appears in the form of a black dog. The only way to get past his enchantment and win the fairy treasure is for a pure virgin on St. John's Eve between 12 and 1 o'clock to:

. . . venture naked and alone, to climb the castle wall and wander backward to and fro amid the ruin, until she light upon the spot where the stairway to the tower leads down into the treasure chamber. Slipping down, she will then be able to take as much gold and jewels as she can carry, and what she cannot carry herself the old king will bring after her, so that she will be rich for the rest of her life. But she must return by sunrise, and she must not once look behind her, nor speak a single word, else not only will she fail, but she will perish miserably.

According to one tale, a princess whose chastity had been brought into question ventured to claim the treasure and prove her virginity. When she entered the vault the king bestowed the treasure upon her and sent servants after her laden with more riches. All went well until she turned to see if the servants were following behind her. At that point the king transformed into a black dog that leaped at her with a fiery throat and glowing eyes. The door slammed shut and she fell into the vault, where she has remained for 400 years. She awaits a pure youth who must find his way to her on St. John's night, bow to her three times, and silently kiss her. The enchantment that keeps her there thus broken, he may then take her hand and lead her forth to be his bride—and they will inherit untold riches.

In Hungary, too, there are tales of buried fairy treasures that can be obtained only under a specific set of circumstances. It is said that although the Hungarian fairies have disappeared from the surface of the Earth, they continue to live in caves under their castles, where their treasures lie hidden. According to *The Folk Tales of the Maygars* (1886), these subterranean habitations are:

. . . no less splendid and glittering than were their castles of yore on the mountain peaks. The one at Firtos is a

palace resting on solid gold columns. The palace of Tartod, and the gorgeous one of Dame Rapson are lighted by three diamond balls, as big as human heads, which hang from golden chains. The treasure which is heaped up in the latter place consists of immense gold bars, golden lions with carbuncle eyes, a golden hen with her brood, and golden casks filled with gold coin. The treasures of Fairy Helen are kept in a cellar under Kovaszna Castle, where the gates of the cellar are guarded by a magic cockerel. This bird only goes to sleep once in seven years, and anybody who could guess the right moment would be able to scrape no end of diamond crystals from the walls and bring them out with him. The fairies who guard the treasures of the Poganyvar (Pagan Castle) in Marosszek even nowadays come on moonlight nights to bathe in the lake below.

In Brittany, at the Castle of Morlaix, there is no need to slip past a sleeping magic cockerel or wait until the guards are bathing beneath the moon. Thomas Keightley, in *The Fairy Mythology* (1828), states that:

. . . a number of little men, not more than a foot high, dwell under the castle of Morlaix. They live in holes in the ground, whither they may often be seen going, and beating on basins. They possess great treasures, which they sometimes bring out; and if any one pass by at the time, allow him to take one handful, but no more. Should any one attempt to fill his pockets, the money vanishes, and he is instantly assailed by a shower of boxes on the ear from invisible hands.

As is often the case with fairies, the modest, pure, and well-intentioned are rewarded, while the greedy are punished.

ENTRANCES TO FAIRYLAND

In spite of—or maybe sometimes because of—the dangers, glamor, and taboos, fairyland has always exerted an irresistible pull on humans. While careless trespassers may face retribution from disgruntled fairies, those who approach and observe fairyland with respect may be rewarded with a glimpse beyond the veneer of the everyday world and into the curious wonders of the fairy realm.

Fairy Hills

In Celtic lore in particular, tales of fairy hills abound. Fairies are said to dwell beneath or within the mounds and hills in the countryside of Ireland, Scotland, and Wales. Circular ring forts, known as *raths,* are a favorite haunt of the Irish little people. In Scotland, the people of peace make their homes beneath hills or knolls called *knowes.* The Irish name for fairies is *Daoine Sidh. Daoine* means "folk" or "people," and *sidh* means "hill" or "mound," so *Daoine Sidh* is literally "people of the mounds." This is often shortened simply to *sidh.*

There are many tales in which people have accidentally stumbled upon these fairy mounds and into the realm of fairy. It is said that walking nine times around the hill at full moon will reveal the secret entrance to the fairies' abode.

In the British tale "Childe Rowland," the eponymous hero enters Elfland via a hill to rescue his sister, Burd Ellen, from the Elf King's Dark Tower. He circles a terraced green mound three times "widdershins"—in the opposite direction to the sun—saying, "Open, door! Open, door! And let me come in." This grants him entrance to fairyland.

In Scandinavia, there are tales of fairy mounds being raised up on red pillars, so that the occupants can feast with their neighbors. In one Danish account, a lad named Hans saw three hills raised on pillars, with much merriment and dancing going on beneath. In Scotland, Robert Kirk recorded a similar belief about Scottish fairy mounds. According to Kirk, every quarter-year, with the changing of the season, the inhabitants of the Scottish hills moved from one place to the next. It was considered dangerous to walk about at night at these times, for the entrances to fairyland were open and the little people were abroad. The "fairy paths," the well-trodden routes running in straight lines between fairy hills, were especially to be avoided at these times.

In America, the Sioux believe that dangerous spirits reside in a mound near the mouth of the

Whitestone river, named the Mountain of Little People or Little Spirits. Humans are wary of visiting this hill, for the little people are said to be armed with sharp arrows, which they are skilled in using to defend their abode from human incursions—a reminder that human visitors are not always welcome to enter fairyland, and any attempts to do should be made with caution.

Fairy Rings

Circles of grass known as "fairy rings" mark the fields and meadows where fairies dance and cavort during their moonlit revels. In some places, these appear as bright, lush patches of grass, in others as bare circles of earth. Sometimes circles of mushrooms, known as *Marasmius oreades,* sprout from fairy rings, some of which are believed to be hundreds of years old. In Orkney, one such ring appears as a patch of bright green on bare moorland, which mushrooms sprout from at certain times of year.

Many are the tales of individuals who have stepped into a fairy ring, lured by the sound of pipes, harps, or fiddles and the irrepressible urge to kick up their heels and dance. Once inside the ring, one is swept up into the wild dance of the fairies, unable or unwilling to leave. Time takes on a different dimension and when a mortal stumbles out into the human world after what seems a single night of dancing, it is not unusual to find that many years have passed.

A Welsh tale collected in Thomas Keightley's *The Fairy Mythology* (1828) relates the dangers of stepping into the fairy ring to dance:

Rhys and his friend Llewellyn were farm laborers who worked in the mountains. One day they were returning to the farmhouse with their ponies when Rhys stopped and asked Llewellyn if he could hear music. Llewellyn could not, but Rhys insisted that he could and was eager to stay. He urged his friend to take his pony back to the farm so that he might linger a while and listen.

Llewellyn put the ponies in their stable, ate his supper, and went to bed. The next morning Rhys had not returned and Llewellyn informed their master of what had happened.

A search of the countryside ensued but to no avail: Rhys had vanished.

Suspicions grew that Llewellyn was responsible for his friend's disappearance and he was put in jail, though there was no evidence of any wrongdoing.

An old farmer, well versed in matters of the fairy world, suspected he knew what had happened and asked whether Llewellyn and several others could accompany him to the spot where Rhys had vanished.

On arrival, they saw a circle of grass and Llewellyn heard sweet music. The old farmer asked the group to place one foot on the edge of the fairy ring and be sure to keep the other outside the circle.

As they did so, the music grew louder and, to their astonishment, they saw dozens of little people, the size of three or four-year-old children, dancing round and round. Rhys was among them. Llewellyn grabbed him by the collar and dragged him out of the circle. He pleaded to be allowed to finish the dance, convinced he had only been there five minutes. His friends managed to pull him back to the farm, but he took to his bed in a state of melancholy at leaving the revels and a couple of days later he faded away.

Barrows and Megaliths

Ancient standing stones, barrows, and cairns the world over have fairy portal associations. In Brittany, near Carnac, Ti Goriquet (House of the Gories) is composed of more than 4,000 large standing stones. According to local folklore, the ancient monument is the work of the *crions* or *gories*—little men between 2 and 3 feet (nearly a meter) high, who, despite their small stature, possess the strength of giants. Every night they are said to dance around the stones. Any traveler within their reach is forced to join in the dance, where he is whirled about until, breathless and exhausted, he falls down, amidst peals of laughter from the little people. In this instance, the visitor is offered only a brief glimpse of fairyland, for the fairies vanish with the break of day.

In India, some megalithic remains are also believed to be gateways to the realm of the little people. According to some accounts, certain stone cairns and tombs in southern India are believed to be the work of a race of bearded dwarves known as the Pandayar, who, like their European cousins, could move and handle the huge stones easily. It is said that the Pandayar built the monuments for the purpose of hiding their treasure and placed spells upon them to guard against marauders.

Fairy Rocks

In America, the Iroquois people summon spirits by knocking on a special stone. In Somerset, England, a fairy rock touched with the correct number of primroses opens the way to fairyland, but the incorrect number of flowers angers the fairies.

In the Scottish Borders, Habetrot, a spinning fairy, lived beneath a "self-bored" stone—a stone with a naturally formed hole through the middle. At sunset, she allowed visitors to enter via a hidden door in the side of the stone.

Caves

From the cavernous entrance to the Underworld of Greek and Roman mythology to humble holes in the cliff, caves repeatedly appear in folk tales as portals leading to other worlds and fairy realms.

In the classical tale of Psyche and Cupid, Psyche must enter the Underworld and bring back a box containing the beauty of the goddess Proserpine in order to win back her lover, Cupid. It is through a cave that she gains entrance to the Underworld to carry out her task.

In England, the legendary King Herla entered the fairy realm via a cave in a high cliff that led to a dwarf's splendid palace. Returning to the mortal world, he discovered that hundreds of years had passed. According to a taboo placed upon them by the dwarf, he and his men were prevented from dismounting from their steeds and went on to roam the land as the wild hunt.

A down-to-earth account in William Bottrell's *Traditions and Hearthside Stories of West Cornwall* (1873) tells of a Cornish cliff cave as an entrance to fairyland:

A few days since, a woman of Mousehal told me that not long ago troops of small people, not more than a foot and a half high, used – on moonlit nights – to come out of a hole in the cliff opening onto the beach, Newlyn side of the village, and but a short distance from it. The little people were always dressed very smart; and if anyone came near them they would scamper away into to the hole. Mothers often told their children that if they went under the cliff by night, the small people would carry them away into 'Dicky Danjy's holt.'

Wells

In folk beliefs from around the world, wells and springs traditionally represent an entranceway to the spirit world. People from many different cultures have gone to such places to petition gods, spirits, or fairies, perform divination rituals, and make offerings. The idea of a "wishing well," where a wish is granted in exchange for the offering of a coin, has roots that stretch back to ancient times.

Trees growing near a well or spring are often believed to possess special healing properties. "Cloutie trees" are still found in the British Isles today. Clouties—pieces of cloth—are tied to the tree to bring luck or good health. Traditionally, a piece of clothing was torn from the afflicted area of the body, for example to cure a bad back a piece of cloth was ripped from the back of a shirt or a dress. As the rag disintegrated, health was restored.

Wells that were once shrines to water fairies and water spirits have now often been rededicated to Christian saints, continuing the tradition of wells as portals to the spirit world.

Trespassers in Fairyland

Entranceways to fairyland tend to be rooted in the natural world—and sometimes humans have, unwittingly or otherwise, meddled with the territory of the little people. In such cases, the fairies have usually been quick to make their displeasure known and to demand that trespassers rectify their transgressions or face a punishment.

In Ireland, houses built blocking fairy thoroughfares have been subjected to fairy disturbances. In some cases, it is said that fairies have levitated buildings that blocked their path and moved them to a new position. So dwellings are now often built with the front and back doors opposite one another, and the doors are left open to facilitate the easy passage of fairy traffic. In recent years, a bypass was re-routed to avoid a thorn bush said to be frequented by fairies.

In Iceland, a member of parliament saved a 24-ton boulder from being buried during work on the national highway. Believing it to be home to three generations of elves, he had it and its inhabitants shipped to his own home, where it would be out of harm's way.

The message here is for humans to be mindful of the impact of their interactions with the environment and to approach the fairy world with respect.

FAIRY PLACES TO VISIT

In Welsh tradition, fairyland was once located in the Vale of Neath, in Glamorganshire. A certain steep and rugged crag there, Craig y Ddinas, bears a distinctly awful reputation as a stronghold of the fairy tribe. Its caves and crevices are said to have been their favorite haunt for many centuries, and some believe the last fairy court in Wales was held upon this rock before the Welsh fairies vanished.

Other fairy places include:

Silbury Hill in Wiltshire, where King Sil is said to be buried, wearing his golden armor and sitting astride his steed.

Bryn Yr Ellyllon, "Hill of the Goblins," near Mold in Clyd Flint, Wales, where an apparition clad in golden armor is said to haunt the hillside. An archeological dig here in the 1800s unearthed a skeleton and gold corselet.

The Rollright Stones in Oxfordshire. The Oxfordshire fairies were last said to be seen here before they vanished.

Glastonbury Tor, Somerset, where St. Collen saw through the fairy glamor of Gwyn ap Nudd's fairy palace.

Maes-Howe in the Orkneys and New Grange at Boyne, chambered mounds once home to Fians and Picts and later known as fairy mounds or forts.

Tomnahurich Hill, a round, tree-covered hill on the outskirts of Inverness, in Scotland, has long been famed as a haunt of the fairies. In *Popular Superstitions and Festive Amusements of the Highlanders of Scotland* (1823), Grant Stewart recounts the tale of two fiddlers enticed into the fairy hill.

Two traveling fiddlers came to Inverness one Christmas seeking work. A strangely dressed old wizened gentleman requested that they perform at a gathering that evening and offered them handsome pay. They set out in high spirits, but when they arrived at their destination it appeared more like a rough tower than a fine castle. However, their host reassured them and persuaded them to enter.

Once inside, all misgivings vanished, for never had they seen a more sumptuously furnished hall or a more elegant assembly of guests. They played all night, never growing tired and performing a succession of jigs and reels for the eager dancers.

When morning came, they only wished the night had lasted longer, such was the revelry that they had enjoyed. Their host paid them well, thanked them, and bid them farewell.

But when the fiddlers left the great hall, outside everything was changed. To their consternation, they found that the great tower they had exited was no more than a low hill. When they made their way into Inverness, there were buildings where once there had been trees and fields, and the inhabitants of the town, dressed in strange, fantastical clothes, poked fun at their old-fashioned rags.

A crowd gathered around the

musicians and an old man hobbled up and questioned them.

"I know who you are," he declared, "you are the two men who lodged with my great-grandfather and who, it was supposed, were decoyed by Thomas the Rhymer to Tomnahurich Hill. Sore did your friends lament your loss, but a hundred years have passed since then, and your very names are forgot."

The fiddlers believed the old man's story and were glad to have come out from the fairy hill alive. The church bells began to ring and they went to church to give thanks for their safe return. However, when the minister uttered the first word of scripture, they crumbled to dust.

Some say that Thomas the Rhymer (*see p.506*), the mortal musician whisked away by the Queen of Elfland, still lives, or sleeps, beneath Tomnahurich Hill.

Rusalka Lake in the Czech countryside, near the town of Pribram, was the inspiration for the composer Dvorak's opera *Rusalka.* Based on folk beliefs about the water sprite Rusalka, it tells the story of her unhappy love affair with a mortal man. The composer's house, Vysoka mansion, is nearby, and is now a museum.

Yoro waterfall, located on the slopes of the Tagi mountain in Mino province, Japan, is known as a magical Fountain of Youth. According to Japanese legend, a woodcutter discovered the waterfall's youth-giving properties.

The woodcutter lived with his elderly father the mountains. One cold winter's day he was out looking for wood when he came across a golden waterfall. He drank from it and was surprised to discover that it was not water, but *sake* (rice wine). He filled his gourd and took it back to his elderly father, who drank it with delight and immediately felt many years younger.

News of the magical waterfall reached the Empress, and she journeyed to Mino to drink from it. She named it Yoro—water of life, or regeneration.

Other fairy places include the forest of Paimpont in France, which is all that remains of an ancient woodland thought to have once covered much of inland Brittany. Legend has it that it is home to Brocéliande, Forest of King Arthur, the Fountain of Youth, and the *Val sans Retour* (Valley of No Return), where Morgan le Fay enchanted her victims.

Transylvania is usually associated with vampires; however, in Hungarian folk belief it was inhabited by fairies. Transylvania, now part of Romania, and Csallóköz, now part of Slovakia, were traditionally identified as the Hungarian fairyland. Almas cave near Baraolt in central Romania is reputed to be a fairy haunt. The cold wind known as the Nemere is said to blow when the fairy in the cave feels cold. In one tale, when plague was raging in the neighborhood, the people ascribed it to the cold blast emanating from the cave, so they hung shirts before the cave mouth and it is said the plague ceased. Some say this is also the cave from which the children led away by the Pied Piper of Hamelin re-emerged.

The fairy mountain Ngongotaha stands on the North Island of New Zealand, overlooking the big blue lake of Rotorua. The peak is known as Te Tuahu a te Atua (the Altar of the God) and was said to be one of the principal homes of the *patupaiarehe*, the fairy people of New Zealand. The tribe that lived on Mount Ngongotaha were known as the Ngati-Rua, their chiefs were named Tuehu, Te Rangitamai, Tongakohu, and Rotokohu.

It is said that the Maori ancestor Ihenga became thirsty while exploring the mountain and a *patupaiarehe* woman offered him a drink from a calabash, which he accepted. However, when the fairy people began to crowd around him, curious at seeing a mortal, he became scared that they might attempt to capture him. Smearing himself with *kokowai*, a mixture of shark oil and red ochre, the stench of which offended the *patupaiarehe*, he repelled the inquisitive creatures and ran away down the mountain. Later, he went on to be on friendly terms with the *patupaiarehe* and named the mountain Ngongotaha, meaning "drink from a calabash."

The Majlis al Jinn in Oman, "Meeting Room of the Spirits" or "Gathering Place of the *Djinn,*" is the second-largest cave chamber in the world. The colossal chamber is large enough to house over a dozen Boeing 747s or a 50-story skyscraper. Its name comes from the belief on the Arabian peninsula that *djinn* inhabit caves.

Trollkyrka (Troll's Church) in Sweden is located in the heart of Tivden National Park. A trek up the trail to the "tower" of the church reveals a rocky outcrop where pagan fairy rituals took place in years gone by. A poem by folklorist Carshult describes the procession up into the troll hills, where a secret password was uttered, a fire was lit, and spirits summoned.

A

Abatwa

This race of tiny fairies from South Africa dwells with the ants. Small enough to ride an ant or hide behind a blade of grass, in all respects other than size, the *abatwa* resemble humans from the Zulu tribe. They are shy, elusive creatures, only occasionally seen by humans, most often wizards, children, or pregnant women. It's believed that if a woman spies an *abatwa* in the seventh month of pregnancy she is sure to give birth to a boy.

Abbey Lubber

From the fifteenth century onwards, many British abbeys and monasteries gained a reputation for luxury and wantonness. Folk satires were spread about them, including stories of the abbey lubbers, mischievous spirits who tempted the monks and nuns into drunkenness, gluttony, and lasciviousness. They were most often to be found in the abbey wine cellar.

Absinthe

See **Green Fairy, the**.

Acalica

These Bolivian weather fairies have powers over the sun, wind, and rain. They live underground

in caves and are rarely seen by humans. When they do appear, it is often as wizened old men.

Ad-hene

Manx name for the fairies, meaning "Themselves"—a name humans must get right and never take in vain.

Adlet

This mythical race is found in legends from Greenland and from Inuit tales of Labrador and northern Canada relating the union of a girl with a dog, from which the resulting ten offspring are five dogs and five Adlet, a creature half-dog, half-man.

In some legends the Adlet are sent inland for their safety and become the Native American tribes.

Adlivun

See **Anguta**, **Sedna**.

A. E.

"A. E." was the pseudonym of George William Russell (1867–1935), an Irish poet, artist, and "seer"—one who had the "second sight" and was able to see fairies. A lifelong friend of **W. B. Yeats**, he was also an expert on agriculture and an eminent economist. His accounts of fairies in paintings and prose describe them as radiant, shining beings.

Aedh

In Irish mythology, Aedh was one of the sons of **Dagda** of the ***Tuatha de Danann***.

Aeval

See **Aibell**.

Afanasyev, Aleksandr *(1826–1871)*

A Russian folklorist and collector of fairy tales.

After studying law at Moscow

University, Afanasyev became a journalist and wrote about many of the literary figures of the seventeenth century. From 1850, he turned his attention to traditional folk tales and began making a systematic collection from oral testimonies as well as from the few publications available. He was familiar with the work of the **Grimm** brothers and applied the same methodology as they had done. Unlike the Grimms, however, he did not rework or embellish the tales and was committed to faithful reproductions of the original versions.

Narodnye russkie skazki (*Russian Fairy Tales*) was published in eight volumes between 1855 and 1863. Comprising 600 tales from various regions of Russia, it is one of the world's largest collections of folk tales gathered by a single collector. *Russian Fairy Tales for Children*, which followed, contained a selection of humorous and magical tales from his collection suitable for children. Afanasyev's collection of legends, *Russian Folk Legends*, was banned by Russian censors, who deemed the material to be blasphemous. The banned tales were eventually published anonymously in Switzerland under the title *Russian Forbidden Tales*.

Afanasyev's work influenced many writers and composers, and is still in print today in numerous languages.

Agricultural Spirits

Traditionally, household spirits often watch over fields, crops, and animals as well as hearth and home, helping to gather the harvest or feeding up favorite beasts, especially cattle, although those of a more mischievous disposition have also been known to frighten cattle, causing their milk to dry up until placated with gifts of the finest cream or food. The Russian ***domovoi*** is particularly fond of cows that match his coloring. The Swedish ***tomte*** is a farm spirit who rewards farmers who show kindness to their animals and good husbandry. The Cornish **pisky threshers** help with the threshing of the grain in return for new suits of clothes.

Aguane

Shapeshifting female fairies of Italian and Austrian folklore who dwell in the hills and streams of the Alps. Described as beautiful women with bewitching voices and cloven hooves, they are guardians of streams. Those who try to harm them or enter the waters without their permission may meet with a watery end.

Aibell

(Also Aoibheall or Aeval.) The Irish fairy queen of north Munster, County Clare, part of the ***Tuatha de Danann***, and guardian spirit of the O'Brien clan. Her name probably derives from the Gaelic *aoibh*, meaning "beauty," or the proto-Celtic *Oibel-a*, literally meaning "burning fire." She lived at Craig Liath (Gray Rock), where she held a midnight court to determine if husbands were satisfying their wives' sexual needs. If found to be lacking, the man in question would be ordered to overcome his prudishness. The lover of Dubhlainn Ua Artigan, a young warrior from Munster, Aibell played a magic harp and it was said that whoever heard its music would not live long afterward. She appears in many works of Irish literature, including the eighteenth-century comic poem *Cúirt an Mheáin Oíche*, or "Midnight Court," by Brian Merriman.

Aigamuxa

Demons in the Saan mythology of Namibia and South Africa. Cannibalistic and with eyes on the soles of their feet, they inhabit sand dunes and chase the unwary.

Aiken Drum

A name best known in the Scottish nursery rhyme:

There cam' a man to oor toun
To oor toun, to oor toun,
There cam' a man to oor toun
An' his name was Aiken Drum.

In more recent versions, the words have changed to "There was a man lived in the moon . . ." and Aiken Drum wears edible clothes: a cream cheese hat, a roast beef coat, and penny loaf buttons.

Aiken Drum is also the name given to the "Brounie [**Brownie**] of Blednoch" in the ballad by William Nicholson (1878). This fairy is naked except for a kilt made out of green rushes.

Aitahqa-a-Nukumaitore

(Or *Nuku-mai-kore.*) Tree fairies of Maori mythology, whose name means "Not inclined this way." Described variously as having large chests and waists and small heads, having no head at all and very short arms and legs, or as all hands, elbows, and shoulders, they dwell in trees and parasitical plants such as *wharawhara* and *kiekie* and are said to subsist on uncooked food, namely *kumara*, a type of sweet potato, and whale meat.

Aitvaras

A fiery household spirit in the folklore of Lithuania. The *aitvaras* is a shapeshifter who manifests in different forms according to his environment. He appears as a cockerel when inside the house and as a dragon when outside. Sometimes only his fiery, comet-like tail is visible. He brings prosperity to his owner, often at the expense of the neighbors, from whom he steals gold, milk, and food. In exchange for his endeavors, he requires only to be fed on a diet of omelets. However, employing the services of an *aitvaras* comes at a price: it is said that an *aitvaras* is obtained from the Devil, hatched from the egg of a seven-year-old cockerel, in exchange for one's soul.

Here is one tale of an *aitvaras*:

A newly wed bride was given the task of grinding corn for her mother-in-law. No matter how much she ground, the corn basket remained full and her work was never done.

By the light of a consecrated candle from the church, she saw an aitvaras *in the form of a cockerel spewing forth a constant stream of grain into the basket.*

However, the *aitvaras* perished in the holy light of the candle, much to mother-in-law's horror, for she not only lost her source of wealth but her soul went to the Devil in exchange for the loss of the "luck-bringer."

Aka

(Or Akari.) According to Carib folklore in Guyana, Akari resides in the head and is one of many spirits inhabiting the body. Dreams and nightmares are considered to occur when the hairy bush spirit Yurokon captures Akari from the head of a sleeping person and takes him for a walk into the forest. As long as he remembers to return Akari to his rightful place, the person will experience it as a dream; if he forgets and leaves Akari in the forest, the person will die.

Akari

See **Aka**.

Akakasoh

Tree spirits, or ***nats***, in Burmese folk beliefs. Similar to the hamadryads of Greek mythology, the *akakasoh* dwell in trees. They inhabit the uppermost branches and their presence can be detected by the rustling of a tree's leaves.

Other types of tree-dwelling *nat*, such as the ***shekkasoh*** and the ***boomasoh***, make their homes in other parts of the tree.

Alan

Part-bird, part-human spirits in the folklore of the Tinguian people of the Philippine Islands. Described as a human–bird hybrid with backward-facing fingers and toes, the alan dwell in the jungle, where they hang, batlike, from the trees to rest. When not suspended from the trees, they reside in houses made of gold.

According to Mabel Cook Cole

in *Philippine Folk Tales* (1916), the Tinguian people often slighted or mistreated lesser spirits such as the alan.

In one tale, two hunters enlist the help of an alan to provide them with a fire over which to cook a swine. When the alan asks one of them to take the swine's liver to feed her baby, he eats it on the way and throws the alan's baby into a cauldron of boiling water.

The two hunters hide up a tree. When the furious alan comes looking for them, she tries to climb up a vine, but they slash it and she falls to her death.

The hunters then go to the alan's house, where they find a jar of beads and jar of gold and return to the village with their bounty.

Alven

Also known as *Otteermaaner*, *Alven* are water sprites who dwell in the river Elbe. Light and wingless, they wrap themselves in bubbles in the water to move around. As the name *Otteermaaner* suggests, they are sometimes said to show themselves as otters. They are believed to be the protectors of night-blooming water flowers.

Alp Luachra

(Also Alp-luachra or Alpluachra.) Also known as Joint-eater or Just-halver, an Alp luachra is a greedy fairy from Irish mythology. When a person falls asleep beside a stream or a spring, the Alp luachra appears in the form of a newt and crawls into their mouth, feeding on the food that they have eaten.

In **Robert Kirk**'s *Secret Commonwealth of Elves, Fauns and Fairies* (1691), the Joint-eater is described as a kind fairy that sits invisibly next to its victim, sharing their food, thus accounting for how someone with a large appetite—a Great-eater—can remain skinny:

They avouch that a Heluo, or Great-eater, hath a voracious Elve to be his attender, called a Joint-eater or Just-halver, feeding on the Pith or Quintessence of what the Man eats; and therefore he continues Lean like a Hawke or Heron, notwithstanding his devouring appetite.

Douglas Hyde's *Beside the Fire* (1890) tells of how one poor soul was infested by a pregnant Alp luachra and her children. To get rid of the mother and her brood, he ate a large quantity of salted meat without drinking anything, then lay down by a stream with his mouth open. After a while the Alp luachra were forced to leap out into the water to quench their salt-induced thirst.

Amesha Spentas

The "Bounteous Immortals" in the Zoroastrian belief of Iran. They are the attendants of the Creator, Ahuru Mazda. Similar to the **Muses** of Greece, each of the six *amesha spentas* spirits ruled over a specific earthly quality: achievement, inspiration, wisdom, intellect, sensitivity, and love.

The six spirits are: Ameretat, "Long Life," guardian of the Earth's plants and trees, spirit of immortality; Aramaiti, "Holy Harmony," guardian of the Earth's fruitfulness; Asha, "Righteousness," "Truth," guardian of earthly fire and the sun; Vohumanah, "Good Thought," guardian of the Earth's benign creatures, especially the cow; Kshathra, "Rulership," "Dominion," symbol of the triumph of good over evil, guardian of the Earth's metals; and Haurvatat, "Wellbeing," "Wholeness," guardian of the Earth's water and the afterlife.

Ana

Queen of the Fairies in Romany gypsy folklore.

Ana lived in a mountain castle with her entourage, the *keshalyi,* the benevolent Romany fairies, until the king of the *loçolico,* evil earth-dwelling spirits, fell in love with her. When she spurned his advances, he sent his horde of minions to devour the *keshalyi.*

In order to save them, Ana agreed to marry him. She suffered many years of degradation and gave birth to a succession of monstrous offspring.

Eventually, she succeeded in negotiating her freedom. The *loçolico* king set her free on the condition that whenever a *keshalyi* reached a certain age, she must be given to his minions.

It is said that Ana retreated to her castle in shame, only occasionally venturing out in the form of a golden toad.

Andersen, Hans Christian *(1805–1875)*

Best remembered for his fairy tales, the Danish author Andersen was also a prolific writer of novels, plays, poems, and accounts of his many travels.

He was born in Odense to a family of meager means. He was to remain an only child. His father was keen to give him an education that nurtured the imagination and read many books to him, including *The Arabian Nights.* When his father died in 1816, Andersen's formal education, albeit basic, was disrupted due to the need to find work to support himself and his mother. Ever since his first visit to the theater, aged seven, he had been hooked on the world of the stage, and at the age of 14 he traveled, alone, to Copenhagen, looking for employment as an actor. He was successful in the Royal Theatre as a soprano singer until his voice broke, and the theater's director, Jonas Collins, took him under his wing and funded his university education.

Andersen wrote a few plays and novels, without much success to begin with, but soon his writing career took off. His first book of tales, *Fairy Tales, Told for Children,* was published in 1835. It was a compilation of tales from his boyhood memories and stories of his own invention. Further books followed and, as their popularity gradually grew, they were translated into numerous languages.

Among the most famous of Andersen's tales are "The Little Mermaid" (possibly inspired by the sad love story of the water sprite **Undine**), "The Emperor's New Clothes," "The Princess and the Pea," "The Wild Swans," and "The Red Shoes."

Angus Mac Og

A Celtic god of youth, love, and poetic inspiration. One of the sons of **Dagda** of the ***Tuatha de Danann***.

Anguta

The father of **Sedna**, Inuit sea goddess ruling the undersea Otherworld, Anguta is responsible for conveying souls from the land of the living to his daughter's underworld realm of Adlivun, where he metes out punishment for their previous sins until they are purged.

Ankou

A personification of death in Breton mythology, the Ankou also appears in Cornish, Welsh, and Irish folklore. Also known as the grave watcher, he is a fairy version of the Grim Reaper and often appears as a skeleton wearing a black robe and carrying a scythe. In Ireland he is known to ride a black coach pulled by four black horses to collect the souls of those recently passed over.

According to Breton folklore collector Anatole le Braz (1859–1926), "the Bard of Brittany," "The last dead of the year, in each parish, becomes the Ankou of his parish for all of the following year. When there has been, in a year, more deaths than usual, one says about the Ankou: '*War ma fĕ, heman zo eun Anko drouk.*' (On my faith, this one is a nasty Ankou.)"

In a short story by Wyndham Lewis, *The Death of the Ankou* (1927), a tourist in Brittany perceives a beggar to be the embodiment of the Ankou. In fact, it is the tourist who acts as Ankou to the beggar, who subsequently dies.

Anthropophagi

From the Greek for 'people-eater', an anthropophage (plural anthropophagi) belonged to a mythological race of cannibals first described by Herodotus (*c.*440 B.C.). The word first appeared in English around 1552.

William Shakespeare brought these cannibalistic fairies into British public awareness in his plays *The Wives of Winsdor* and *Othello.* In *Othello* (Act I, scene iii), he famously described them as follows:

And of the Cannibals that each other eat,
The Anthropophagi, and men whose heads
Do grow beneath their shoulders.

In popular culture, anthropophagi are often described as headless, with their mouths in the center of their chests. This is likely due to a misinterpretation of the line about men whose heads grow beneath their shoulders, which in fact refers to a separate mythical race called Blemmyes. However, the popular picture of the anthropophagi as headless cannibals with faces on their torsos has endured. According to *Naturalis Historia,* one of the world's earliest encyclopedias, the anthropophagi were in the habit of drinking out of human skulls, and placing the scalps, with the hair attached, upon their breasts, "like so many napkins."

Aoibheall

See **Aibell**.

Appletree Man

A guardian of the orchard, Appletree Man dwells in the oldest apple tree, where the fertility of the orchard is supposed to reside. He chases away fruit raiders, but may also take umbrage with genuine harvesters. In the traditional English cider counties such as Somerset, apple-pickers could harvest the fruit only at certain times of day. Customs such as wassailing, involving singing to the apple tree and pouring cider at its roots, are still performed in parts of Somerset to placate the Appletree Man in the hope of bringing about a good harvest.

See also **Old Roger**.

Apsaras

(Also *apsarasa.*) From Buddhist and Hindu mythology, a female spirit of the waters and clouds. English translations of the Sanskrit name include "**nymph**." *Aspsaras* are described as beautiful, supernatural female beings. Known for their ability as dancers, they are often the youthful wives of the ***gandharvas***, the court musicians of **Indra**, leader of the **Devas** and lord of Svargaloka, or heaven, in the Hindu religion. They dance in the palaces of the gods to the *gandharvas'* music, entertaining, and sometimes seducing, gods and men. Sometimes compared to the **muses** of ancient Greece, each of the 26 *apsaras* at Indra's court represents a specific area of the performing arts.

Like the **Valkyries** of Norse mythology, *apsaras* are the carers of fallen heroes. They are also associated with fertility rites. Sky-dwelling ethereal beings, they are often depicted taking flight and can be compared to angels, as well as to the nymphs, **dryads**, and **naiads** of ancient Greece, due to their association with water. Said to be able to shapeshift at will, they also rule over gambling and gaming. The best known are Rambha, Urvasi, Tilottama, and Menaka.

Apuku

A forest spirit in the folk beliefs of Suriname. Described as a short, dark figure with backward-facing feet, he dwells in shrubs deep within the forest. He falls in love with human females and is prone to jealous outbursts if a woman he has developed an attachment to is pursued by other men.

In local tradition, if a man is unsuccessful in wooing a woman, he prepares a special herbal bath to "tame the *apuku*" of the woman he desires.

Árák Sruk

Guardian or tutelary spirits in Cambodian folklore. Residing in the family home, or in a nearby tree, the *árák sruk* was regarded as an ancestor spirit whose advice could be sought in curing sickness. An annual festival honors the *árák sruk* spirits.

ARAWOTYA

A spirit of the sky in the mythology of the Wonkamala people who inhabited the Lake Eyre region in South Australia. According to A. W. Howitt's *The Native Tribes of South-East Australia* (1904), the *arawotya* was originally a spirit of the earth who created deep springs and other sources of water in the otherwise arid regions of southern Australia and parts of western Queensland.

ARIANHOD

A magical female in Welsh mythology, daughter of the goddess **Don**. The fourth branch of the *Mabinogion*, the ancient epic stories of Wales, relates the story of Arianhod, her son, **Lleu Llaw Gyffes**, and **Blodeuedd**, the Flower Maiden.

Arianhod dwells in a palace named Caer Arianhod, which today is associated with a rock formation off the coast of Gwynedd, northwest Wales.

Math, King of Gwynedd, has to have his feet held by a virgin when he is not in battle. Arianhod's brother, Gwydion, proposes her for the task, but when Math places his magic rod on the floor for Arianhod to step across in a test of her virginity, she fails the test and immediately gives birth to two sons.

The first is named Dylan, "Ocean Wave." Arianhod refuses to name the second son, but Gwydion tricks her into naming him Lleu Llaw Gyffes, "Light or Fair One with the Sure and Steady Hand." Arianhod proclaims that he shall have no bride of this Earth, so Gwydion and Math construct a bride for him out of oak, broom, and meadowsweet, and she is named Blodeuedd, or "Flower Face."

Lleu and the beautiful flower

maiden are married and live in wedded bliss for a short time, but Blodeuedd falls in love with another man, Gronw Pebyr. The lovers decide that they must murder Lleu before he discovers their affair. Blodeuedd knows Lleu to be almost invincible, but on the pretext of concern for his safety, she discovers that he can be killed with a spear made over the duration of a year, thrust into him when he is bathing with one of his feet touching a billy goat.

Despite the complicated conditions, the flower maiden and Gronw conspire to bring about Lleu's demise. However, he transforms into an eagle and escapes.

Hearing of all that has happened, Math and Gwydion seek out Lleu in eagle form. Gwydion puts his wand to the bird and returns him to his human form. Gwydion turns Blodeuedd into an owl.

Her lover, Gronw, offers compensation to Lleu, but Lleu deems it fair that the blow that was meant for him should be returned. Gronw is permitted to hide behind a rock for protection, but Lleu throws his spear so hard that it passes through the rock and pierces the adulterer's back.

Lleu Llaw Gyffes goes on to become Lord of Gwynedd.

Arianhod is remembered in the name of a constellation of stars. The *Corona Borealis*, or Northern Crown, constellation is known in Wales as *Caer Arianhod.*

Arkan Sonney

Pronounced *erkin sonna,* Arkan Sonney, or "Lucky Piggy," is the fairy pig of the Isle of Man. It is a beautiful little white pig believed to bring good luck to those who can catch it. Dora Broome's *Fairy Tales from the Isle of Man* (1963) describes the Arkan Sonney as white, with red ears and eyes, like most fairy animals, and able to alter its size, but not its shape.

Asbjørnsen, Peter Christen, and Moe, Jørgen Engebretsen *(1812–1885), (1813–1882)*

The Norwegian folktale collectors Asbjørnsen and Moe became friends as teenagers and shared an interest in folklore. As young adults, they collected various tales from different parts of Norway and embarked on a collaborative work. Their first collection of tales, *Norske Folkeeventyr* (*Norwegian Folk Tales*), was published in 1841 to great acclaim. A further edition, containing additional stories and published in 1852, proved to be equally successful.

One of the challenges Asbjørnsen and Moe faced was that of language and style. The Norwegian dialects used by oral storytellers were too localized to be understood by a wide audience, while the Norwegian literary style of the time was strongly influenced by Danish, making it unsuitable for a collection of national folklore. Adopting an approach similar to the **Grimm** brothers, Asbjørnsen and Moe opted to tell the tales using simple language in place of dialects, while retaining the national uniqueness of the tales. This helped form the basis for the Norwegian language as it is known today.

Between 1845 and 1848 Asbjørnsen published another collection of tales, *Norwegian Fairy Tales and Folk Legends.* George Webbe Dasent, a translator of folk tales and scholar of Norse studies, translated the first volume into English as *East of the Sun and West of the Moon.*

Asbjørnsen and Moe's work is regarded as part of Norway's national heritage and remains popular today.

Ashray

See **Asrai**.

Askafroa

The "Wife of the Ash Tree" in Scandinavian and Teutonic folklore. The guardian of the ash tree, she was considered to be a pernicious spirit. Regional variations include the Danish *Askefrue* and the German *Eschenfrau.*

Askefrue

See ***Askafroa***.

Asojano Babaluaye

An **orisha** in Yoruba beliefs, a disfigured, pestilent outcast inspiring fear, a formidable presence inflicting plagues and disease, Asojano is a representation of all the world's ills. In more modern times, his powers of destruction are tempered by an ability to heal and among other qualities he is a beneficient guardian of those suffering from AIDS.

ASRAI

Asrai or ashrays are water fairies. In some accounts they appear as beautiful maidens, tall and lithe with translucent skin, although they are in fact hundreds of years old.

Two almost identical tales from Shropshire and Cheshire in England tell of a fisherman dredging up an asrai, which seems to plead to be set free, but its language is incomprehensible. In one tale, the fisherman binds the asrai, and the touch of its cold, wet hands burns him, marking him for life. In both stories, the fisherman covers the asrai with wet weeds while it lies moaning in the bottom of the boat, but its moans grow fainter, and by the time the fisherman has reached shore it has melted away, leaving only a pool of water behind.

AUGHISKY

Pronounced *agh-iski*, this is the Irish **water horse**. In the Scottish Highlands it is known as ***each uisge***.

According to **W. B. Yeats** in *Fairy and Folk Tales of the Irish Peasantry* (1888), *aughisky* were once common. They would come out of the water and gallop across the sands or fields, particularly in November. If you could manage to saddle and bridle them, they made the finest horses. However, you had to ride them inland, for at the first glimpse of salt water they would gallop headlong into it, taking their rider deep into the sea to devour them. It was also said that untamed *aughisky* devoured cattle from the fields.

AVELINE

In **Andrew Lang**'s story of the Princess Minon-Minette in *The Pink Fairy Book* (1897), Aveline is an industrious fairy godmother to the princess, unlike **Girouette** in the same tale, who carelessly neglects her prince's upbringing. It is due to the ever-vigilant and ingenious magic of Aveline that the prince and princess survive and literally rise above their ordeals, finally finding each other once again as they float through the air.

Aziza

This forest-dwelling African race of fairies is from the kingdom of Dahomey, in the present-day Republic of Benin. The Aziza are benevolent, providing help and magic to hunters. Playing a role similar to that of Prometheus in Greek mythology, they are said to have imparted practical or spiritual knowledge to humans, including the use of fire. Living in anthills and silk-cotton trees, they are usually described as being hairy little people.

Awd Goggie

In Yorkshire, England, children were warned to keep away from orchards for fear that Awd Goggie, a wicked sprite who protected woods and orchards, would "get them."

See also **Appletree Man**, **Nursery Bogies**.

B

Baba Yaga

In Slavic mythology Baba Yaga is an ambiguous supernatural entity, residing deep in the forest in a hut supported by giant, yellow chicken legs. The hut has no windows or visible entrance until the phrase "Turn your back to the forest, your front to me" is uttered, when it revolves to reveal the door. Surrounding the hut is a fence on which skulls are impaled.

In Russian folk tales Baba Yaga is described as an ugly and deformed old hag with a long nose, iron teeth, and bony legs, who takes delight in frightening, and possibly devouring, children. Her bed is the enormous oven in which she supposedly cooks the children and she travels in a mortar, steering this strange craft with a pestle and sweeping away all traces of her passage with a silver birch broom.

The ambiguous nature of Baba Yaga is emphasized in some tales in which her wise words and helpfulness are sought. She is also portrayed as one of three sisters, all bearing the name of Baba Yaga. An altogether mysterious and controversial being.

Babi Ngepet

A demon boar in Javanese folk tales who is the manifestation of a human involved in the practice of the black arts, specifically in seeking to become rich by purloining the goods of neighbors in the guise of a pig.

The superstition is still current, as is evident in a recent news report on an Indonesian website concerning the arrest of a pig in Jompang, East Java, on suspicion of it being a *babi ngepet* (*sindonews.com*, June 2013). Discussion ensues on how to distinguish between a pig and an "imitation," concluding that only by killing it can its identity become clear: if it transforms into another creature, it is certainly a *babi ngepet.*

Bacalou

A Loa, or Haitian Voodoo spirit, much to be feared.

Bäckahäst

A Scandinavian water creature manifesting as a beautiful white horse in folk tales. The comeliness of his appearance lures unsuspecting victims to jump onto his back and then, unable to escape, they are pitched into the nearest water to drown.

Badalisc

A mythical creature of the Lombardy region of northern Italy. The *badalisc* is a bad-tempered, gossipy monster with a large head and big mouth. Each year at Epiphany he is "captured," with much drum-banging and a cast of traditional characters to accompany the procession. Afterward, he is led around the village and a speech is read out on his behalf in which the sins and misdemeanors of the locals are laid bare.

Badb

(Also *badhbh.*) A collective name for the three Irish goddesses of war—**Nemen**, **Macha**, and **Morrigu**—possessing magical powers to create confusion, stir fury, and bestow courage to aid their chosen victors in battle. In *The Fairy-Faith in Celtic Countries* by **W. Y. Evans-Wentz** (1911), the *badb* are described thus:

> *. . . this Irish war-goddess, the* bodb *or* badb, *considered of old to be one of the* Tuatha De Danann, *has survived to our own day in the fairy-lore of the chief Celtic countries. In Ireland the survival is best seen in the popular and still almost general belief among the peasantry that the fairies often exercise their magical powers under the form of royston-crows; and for this reason these birds are always greatly dreaded and avoided. The resting of one of them on a peasant's cottage may signify many things, but often it means the death of one of the family or some great misfortune, the bird in such a case playing the part of a* bean-sidhe *[banshee].*

Badhbh

See **Badb**.

Bakru

In South American tradition a *bakru* is a tiny, childlike creature formed from wood and flesh, with a very large head. Protected by its wooden body, and with no brain of its own, it is a spirit to be feared for its ruthlessness. In Suriname there are several varieties of *bakru*, one of which is created by evil magicians to bring harm and even death to its victims.

Ballybog

(Or peat fairy.) Protectors of the peat bogs in Ireland, these little creatures are extremely unprepossessing in appearance, with bulgy, no-neck bodies supported on spindly legs, a froglike mouth full of long, pointy teeth and, due to their location, unsurprisingly covered in mud.

Balor of the Evil Eye

See **Fomorians**.

Bannik

In Slavic folklore the *bannik* is the spirit of the *banya*, or bathhouse, an entity to be treated with the utmost respect and caution due to his violent tendencies if he and his demonic friends are angered or offended.

Banshee

(Or *Bean-Sidh.*) An Irish omen of death in the form of a weeping, wailing spirit, described, in the seventeenth-century *Memoirs of Lady Fanshawe*, as "a woman in white . . . with red hair and pale and ghastly complexion: . . . to me her body looked more like a thick cloud than substance. I was so much frightened, that my hair stood on end, and my night clothes fell off . . ." Lady Fanshawe was recounting her experience while staying with an old Irish family.

Tales of the Scottish banshee depict the banshee as deformed. In *Popular Tales of the West Highlands* (4 vols, 1860–1862), **J. F. Campbell** describes an old mill that is haunted by a banshee:

She was sitting on a stone, quiet, and beautifully dressed in a green silk dress, the sleeves of which were curiously puffed from the wrists to the shoulder. Her long hair was yellow, like ripe corn; but on nearer view, she had no nose.

See also **Bozaloshtsh**, ***Caoineag***, ***Caointeach***, ***Cyhyraeth***.

Baobhan Sith

A beautiful but evil fairy in Scottish folklore, a succubus whose purpose is to seduce her victim and suck their blood until they die.

Barbegazi

Mountain-dwelling, white-bearded **gnomes** of French and Swiss tradition, whose element is ice and snow. Their extremely large feet are advantageous for gliding over the snow-covered terrain. Their name is derived from *barbe-glacée*, meaning "frozen beard."

Barguest

A hellish black hound of the northern English moors, eyes afire, on the hunt for its next victim. Only those doomed to die can hear the howl of the barguest and their only escape is to cross running water, for the hound cannot follow.

Bariaua

Benevolent nature spirits in the folklore of the Tubetube and Wangawga people of Melanesia. These intensely shy beings dwell in trees and dread being seen by humans. However, they have been known to borrow canoes belonging to mortals, for it is said they are not able to build their own seagoing craft.

In one account, two *bariaua* borrowed a canoe one night to go fishing. Returning to shore in the early hours of dawn, they were surprised by an early-riser, a man named Burea. They disappeared immediately, leaving their catch of fish and their net in the canoe.

Burea shared the fish with the other villagers and hung the net up in the *potama*, or clubhouse.

The next morning the net had gone, claimed back by the *bariaua*, but the kindly spirits did not inflict any punishment upon Burea for eating their haul of fish.

Baron Samedi

Depicted as a top-hatted, formally dressed corpselike figure in the Haitian Voodoo tradition, Baron Samedi has great powers over life and death, and represents both the hedonism and enjoyment of life and the inevitability of death.

Basile, Giambattista (c.1575–1632)

Born in Naples, Giambattista Basile was an Italian soldier, poet, writer, and collector of fairy tales. He is best known for his collection of Neapolitan tales, *La Cunto de la Cunti* (*The Story of Stories*) (1634, 1636), also known as *Il Pentamerone*, a collection of 50 stories based on traditional Italian folk tales. It was published posthumously by his sister under the pseudonym Gian Alesio Abbatutis. It includes the earliest recorded versions of many tales that are still familiar to readers today, including "Puss in Boots," "Rapunzel," "Snow White," "Beauty and the Beast," and "Cinderella."

Basile's collection influenced

later fairytale writers and collectors, including **Charles Perrault** in France and the brothers **Grimm** in Germany.

BATHING FAIRIES

The curious phenomenon of a troop of fairies discovered bathing in the health-giving waters of Ilkley Wells in the north of England is recounted in the 1878 edition of the *Folk-Lore Record.* A local resident asks the villagers what kind of things these fairies were, and they usually maintain that they are active little beings and resemble the human form, that they are "lill folk, and always dressed in green, but so agile that no-one [can] ever come up to them." The bathman, William Butterfield, who looks after the Wells, further describes how he came to open up the baths one morning and had great trouble with the door, until:

. . . with one supreme effort, he forced it perfectly open, and back it flew with a great bang! Then whirr, whirr, whirr, such a noise and sight! all over the water and dipping into it was a lot of little creatures, all dressed in green from head to foot, none of them more than eighteen inches high, and making a chatter and jabber thoroughly unintelligible. They seemed to be taking a bath, only they bathed with all their clothes on. He shouts, 'Hallo there!' then away the whole tribe went helter skelter, toppling and tumbling, heads over heels, heels over heads, and all the while making a noise not unlike a disturbed nest of young partridges.

The water is left "still and clear" and William Butterfield never sees them again.

BAUCHAN

(Or Bogan.) In Scottish folklore a type of **hobgoblin**. One example is described in **J. F. Campbell**'s *Popular Tales of the West Highlands* (1860–1862) as the protector of a family on the Island of Skye, but otherwise as a violently hostile spirit. He appeared only in the hours of darkness, "and any stray man who passed was sure to become a victim, the bodies being always found dead, and in the majority of instances mutilated also . . . He was seldom, if ever, seen by women, and did no harm to either them or to children." He was eventually caught and tucked under the arm of his captor, who wanted to see him in daylight. The *bauchan* had never been heard to speak, but began begging to be set free, swearing "on the book, on the candle, and on the black stocking" to be gone. He was liberated after this promise and flew off singing a mournful refrain.

Baumesel

Literally, "Ass of the Trees," the *Baumesel* is a tree-dwelling **goblin** in the folklore of Germany.

Baykok

(Or *Bakaak.*) In the Ojibwe nation's traditional beliefs, the *baykok* manifests as a malevolent skeletal presence who eats the liver of its victims. In Longfellow's *The Song of Hiawatha* it represents death.

Bean Nighe

Another guise of the **banshee** in Scottish and Irish folklore is as the *bean nighe*, or washer woman, who is to be found beside lonely streams washing blood from the clothes of those soon to die.

On the Island of Skye the *bean nighe* is said to be "squat in figure and not unlike a small pitiful child," according to **J. G. Campbell**'s *Superstitions of the Highlands and Islands of Scotland* (1900).

Bean-Sidhe

See **Banshee**; also ***Bean Nighe***.

Bediarhari

Malaysian term for fairies, or the "good folk."

Bela

A tree spirit in the folk beliefs of the Kolarian people of India. When the

Kolarian people made a clearing in the jungle it was customary to leave a solitary tree standing for the spirits to take refuge in. These trees became shrines to the nature spirits of the jungle.

According to an account in the *Annals of Rural Bengal* (1868), a jungle shrine in Bengal consisted of a bela tree, where the spirit resided, along with a kachmula tree, and a saura tree. The Kolarian left earth, rice, and money at the foot of the bela tree as offerings to the tree spirit.

Belliegha

A Maltese water monster inhabiting, and controlling, wells and water sources; *belliegha* translates as "whirlpool."

Bendith y Mamau

"The Mother's Blessing," the local name for fairies in Glamorgan, Wales, where, according to **Sir John Rhys**' *Celtic Folklore: Welsh and Manx* (1901):

> *. . . the parish was then crammed full of* Bendith y Mamau, *and when the moon was bright and full they were wont to keep people awake with their music till the break of day. The fairies of Llanfabon were remarkable on account of their ugliness, and they were equally remarkable on account of the tricks they played. Stealing children from their cradles during the absence of their mothers and luring men by means of their music into some pestilential and desolate bog were things that seemed to afford them considerable amusement.*

Further accounts of their tricks include details of the underground secret passages leading to their dwelling and to caverns of stored gold where:

> *They have, they say, a gold ladder of one or two and twenty rungs, and it is along this that they pass up and down. They have a little word; and it suffices if the foremost on the ladder merely utters that word, for the stone to rise of itself; while there is another word, which it suffices the hindmost in going down to utter so that the stone shuts behind him.*

A farmhand accidentally gains access to the passage but is discovered by the fairies who take him to live with them and ". . . at the end of the seven years he escaped with his hat full of guineas." However, he passes on the secret to a farmer, who accumulates great wealth:

. . . thrice the fill of a salt-chest of guineas, half-guineas, and seven-and-sixpenny pieces in one day. But he got too greedy, and like many a greedy one before him his crime proved his death; for he went down the fourth time in the dusk of the evening, when the fairies came upon him, and he was never seen any more.

Bendigeidfran

See **Bran the Blessed**.

Ben Varrey

"Woman of the Sea," or **mermaid**, in Manx folklore, which has many tales of the half-fish, half-woman's beauty enchanting young men and luring them into the sea. Mermaids from the Isle of Man are also portrayed as benevolent toward deserving mortals, warning fishermen of impending storms and thereby averting disaster.

One account of a mermaid who is captured by shore-dwellers and attended for three days with the utmost care tells of her eventual liberty and reunion with her own kind, whereupon she expresses her puzzlement as to why mortals should throw away the water in which they have boiled eggs.

Berkhyas

In ancient Persian folklore as retold in **Thomas Keightley**'s *The Fairy Mythology* (1828), Berkhyas is described as a ***div*** (or demon) of enormous stature with eyes like pools of blood, a hairy body, and boar's tusks for teeth. Pigeons nest in the serpentine tendrils of his hair.

Bertha, Frau

In *Notes on the Folklore of the Northern Counties of England*

and the Borders (1866), William Henderson writes:

German Folk-lore connects unbaptised infants with the Furious Host or wild hunt . . . the mysterious lady Frau Bertha is ever attended by troops of unbaptised children, and she takes them with her when she joins the wild hunstman, and sweeps with him and his wild pack across the wintry sky.

BHOOT

An unsettled, wandering spirit caused by a violent death, taking on the appearance of an animal or human in Indian mythology. Clothed in white and with backward-facing feet, it casts no shadow.

BIASD BEULACH

In *Witchcraft and Second Sight in the Highlands and Islands of Scotland* (1902), **J. G. Campbell** relates a tale from the Island of Skye describing the malignant spirit of the Pass of Odail, which was "more awful that its character was not distinctly known." It appeared in the dead of night sometimes in the shape of a deformed man and sometimes as a roaming beast, uttering unearthly howls and shrieks. It ceased to appear after the body of a man was found, with two wounds piercing his side and his leg, each bearing the imprint of a hand. It was considered impossible that these wounds could have been inflicted by a human.

BILLY WINKLER

A Lancashire nursery spirit similar to Wee Willie Winkie, who sprinkles magic dust or sand into the eyes of children to get them to sleep. In the 1908 novel *The Blue Lagoon: A Romance* by H. de Vere Stacpoole, Billy Winker is invoked as a similar figure to the **Sandman**: "'Shut your eyes tight . . . or Billy Winker will be dridgin' sand in them.'"

However, in a traditional folk song from Lancashire in John Trafford Clegg's *Sketches and Rhymes in the Rochdale Dialect* (1895), Billy Winker is a drayman a little too fond of drinking the contents of the barrels of ale he delivers.

Biloko

(Also *eloko.*) Malevolent **dwarves** in the folklore of the Nkundo people of central Zaire. *Bilokos* used bells to bewitch humans, placing spells upon them that could result in death. These malignant creatures dwelled in hollow trees and subsisted on a diet of human flesh. They are described as having beards of grass and wearing garments of leaves.

In one tale a wife stays behind at the hut while her husband goes hunting. As he leaves, he warns her that if she hears the ringing of a bell she must pay no attention to it, for it portends death. However, later that day, when the woman is alone in the silence of the forest, she is charmed to hear the ringing of a little bell and invites the owner of the bell to join her at the hut.

A *biloko* dwarf emerges from the forest and joins the woman. She offers him some food cooked over her fire, but he tells her he eats only human flesh. By now the woman is under his spell and she offers him the flesh of her arm.

The next day, the bell rings again and this time the bewitched woman offers the *biloko* the flesh of her buttocks.

On the third day, suspecting some evil is afoot, the husband does not go hunting, but instead hides behind the hut. When the dwarf appears and holds a knife to the woman's side, proclaiming he wants to eat her liver, the man fires an arrow at him.

Struck by the blow, the *biloko* falls down, driving his knife into the woman's side, and killing her.

The husband drives his spear into him and beheads him, then invites the people from the village to see the vanquished dwarf.

Biriir ina Baroqo

A Somalian folk tale recounts the battle of two **giants** who each ruled half of the country. Habbad was cruel and wicked, but the benevolent giant Biriir ina Barqo came to hear of his despotic ways and defeated the oppressor in a battle, thus uniting the country under his peaceful rule.

Bisimbi

Nature spirits associated with waterfalls, pools, and also rocky outcrops, who are described in traditional Central African folk legends. They take on diverse names and attributes in other areas of the continent. Generally benevolent toward humans, they can be troublesome if generous offerings are not forthcoming and downright malevolent in their attempts to penetrate the brains of children. Mothers have devised a simple foil to this endeavor by placing a wooden sliver across the fontanelle on their babies' heads.

Black Annis

A poem by Leicestershire poet John Heyrick, who lived in the eighteenth century, describes Black Annis thus:

Tis said the soul of mortal man
recoil'd,
To view Black Annis' eye, so fierce
and wild;
Vast talons, foul with human flesh,
there grew
In place of hands, and features livid
blue
Glar'd in her visage; while the
obscene waist
Warm skins of human victims close
embraced.

This flesh-eating, blue-faced hag lived in a cave in the Dane Hills near Leicester. She was supposed to have excavated it with her bare hands, using only her long, claw-like iron nails. She was partial to a diet of children and lambs, and when she had devoured them, their skins were spread over the branches of the giant oak tree at the mouth of the cave.

Black Dogs

See **Barguest**, **Capelthwaite**, ***Cù Sith***, ***Cwn Annwn***, **Yeth Hound**.

Blodeuedd

Literally, "Flower Face," taking her name from the Welsh *blodeu*, "flower" or "blossom," and *gwedd*, "face" or "appearance," Blodeuedd is one of the main female figures in the fourth branch of the *Mabinogion*, a collection of ancient epic Welsh stories, which relates how she was made from oak, broom, and meadowsweet as a magical bride for **Lleu Llaw Gyffes**, "Lleu the Fair of the Steady Hand," son of **Arianhod**.

Bloody Bones

See **Rawhead and Bloody Bones**.

Blud

A malevolent fairy in Slavic mythology who causes confusion and disorientation.

Blue Burches

A folk tale from Somerset describes the pranks of Blue Burches (breeches), a **hobgoblin** of a mischievous but harmless disposition whose tricks were endured with forbearance by the cobbler in whose house he lived. In time, the local clergymen heard of the hobgoblin and came to the conclusion he was an incarnation of the Devil, whereupon they set out to exorcise him. The cobbler's son unwittingly betrayed Blue Burches in the guise of an old white horse grazing nearby and the parsons cried out, "Depart from me, you wicked—!" The hobgoblin dived into the duck pond and was gone.

Blue-Cap

A spirit of the mines in the north of England, manifesting as a small, flickering blue flame. The diligent blue-caps expected and received their modest wages in a far-flung corner of the mine and were helpful to respectful miners, warning them of prospective dangers.

See also **Coblynau**, **Knockers**, ***Kobold***.

Blue Men of the Minch

"The Blue Men of the Minch," a tale relating particularly to that stretch of water in the Hebrides between Lewis and the Shiant Islands, is related in **J. G. Campbell**'s *Superstitions of the Highlands and Islands of Scotland* (1900), in which an eyewitness "who was very positive he had himself seen a one" describes his encounter: "A blue-coloured man with a long grey face and floating from the waist out of the water, followed the boat he was in for a long time, and was occasionally so near that the observer might have put his hand upon him."

The Blue Men were held responsible for the stormy waters of the Minch, leaving their undersea cave-dwellings to swim toward passing ships to wreck them and only being thwarted in their intent by canny captains who could outwit them with rhyme and a sharp tongue. They are variously described as fallen angels or, as in D. A. Mackenzie's *Scottish Folk-lore and Folk Life* (1935), as being based on historical accounts of captured Moors in Ireland, called "Blue Men," who were abandoned in the ninth century by Norse seafarers.

Bodach

Literally, "old man" or "specter," this name is found in numerous place names in Scotland. *Tigh nam Bodach* or "House of the Specter," is an example of an ancient pagan site in a remote glen, where a "family" of curiously shaped stones bears the names of the *Bodach*, his wife *Cailleach*, and their children. These supernatural beings, as folk tales relate, were responsible for the fertility of the area and, being treated kindly by the local population, left the stones to be moved out of the shelter each year during the summer to ensure continuing abundance.

However, a different creature altogether, the *Bodach Glas*, or Dark Gray Man, is described in *Waverley* by **Sir Walter Scott** as being a gray specter warning of impending death or catastrophe.

Bodachan Sabhaill

A helpful barn **brownie**, the Little Old Man of the Barn "will thresh with no light in the mouth of the night" while the old farmer sleeps, according to a verse in D. A. Mackenzie's *Scottish Folk-lore and Folk Life* (1935).

Bogan

*See **Bauchan**.*

Bogeyman

Tales of the Bag-man, or Man with the Sack, are told in many cultures to frighten children into good behavior. They generally portray him as a nebulous, threatening spirit carrying a bag or sack on his back in which he puts children who misbehave.

Boggart

There are many local tales of this mischievous, sometimes malevolent, **brownie**, either in the guise of a household spirit who steals the food from the table and torments the family or as a tricksy field-dweller.

In an old Lincolnshire story the boggart is described as "a squat hairy man, strong as a six-year-old horse, and with arms almost as long as tackle poles" who declares he is the rightful owner of the land a farmer has purchased; however, the farmer is cunning and agrees that they should share the disputed field, asking the boggart to choose whether he will take what lies above or below the earth. The boggart chooses to take what grows above ground, and the farmer promptly sets potatoes. Whichever choice the boggart makes, the farmer thwarts him, until the boggart leaves in disgust, telling the farmer he wants nothing more to do with his land. "And off he goes and nivver comes back no more . . ."

BOGIES

A name encompassing a variety of troublesome spirits such as bug-a-boos, bugbears, **boggarts**, and **bogles**, whose aim is to sow discord and mischief among humans, although as in the tale of the boggart (*see above*), they can sometimes be outwitted by a quick mind and clever tongue.

See **Awd Goggie**, **Churnmilk Peg**, **Gooseberry Wife**, **Jack in Irons**, **Jenny Greenteeth**, **Melsh Dick**, **Mumpoker**, **Nursery Bogies**, **Padfoot**, **Shellycoat**, **Rawhead and Bloody Bones**.

BOGINKI

Supernatural female water spirits in Polish mythology, "little goddesses" who sometimes steal human babies, replacing them with **changelings**.

BOGLES

In *Notes on the Folklore of the Northern Counties of England and the Borders* (1866) by W. Henderson, bogles are described in one tale as possessing a rather better nature than most **goblins**, only bedeviling wrong-doers in a retributive manner; however, in another account a bogle haunts a household and can only be got rid of with the aid of a Bible, whereupon he hastily departs in the form of a gray cat. After many years he reappears as a death omen just before the man of the house is killed in the mines.

Another haunting tale is of Berry Well, in a village in Yorkshire, where a bogle takes on the shape of a white goose.

BOKWUS

A Native American wild forest spirit of the Pacific northwest coast. Masks portray him as beetle-browed and with a beaklike nose, and he lures the spirits of the drowned to live with him in his forest dwelling.

Bongas

Spirits in the folklore of the Santal people of India. *Bongas* permeate every area of life in the form of ancestor spirits, household spirits, and nature spirits dwelling in hills, trees, and rocks. They are propitiated by elaborate ceremonies that often culminate in dances and the drinking of rice beer. Like their European fairy counterparts, they are capricious, choosing either to bring good or ill fortune to the humans whose affairs they take an interest in. They can assume human form, and there are many tales of *bonga* girls or maidens wedded to human grooms, who bring either happiness or torment to their mortal husbands.

The *kisar bonga* is a household spirit; similar to a Scottish **brownie**, he brings prosperity to his master if treated with due respect, but is quick to take offense and withdraw his help.

Booman

In the northern isles of Orkney and Shetland, the Booman **hobgoblin** is variously described as a "good fairy," by Edmonston in the nineteenth century, or in other folk tales as a frightening presence haunting lonely roads. Today he is remembered mainly in a traditional game which involves enacting a funeral while singing "Booman is dead and gone" and in other folk songs.

Boomasoh

Tree spirits, or ***nats***, in Burmese folk beliefs. They reside among the tree's roots. Other types of tree-dwelling *nat*, such as the ***akakasoh***

and the ***shekkasoh***, make their homes in other parts of the tree.

Bottrell, William (1816–1881)

Writer and folklorist William Bottrell was born near St. Levan, a few miles from Land's End in Cornwall, England. He was educated at Penzance Grammar School until 1831 and later at Bodmin School. His grandmother told him traditional Cornish stories from a young age and was a great influence on his future writings. These stories had been handed down for generations.

Bottrell traveled extensively and bought some land in the Basque region of Spain, where he gathered more traditional folk tales. The land was later confiscated and he returned, ruined, to Cornwall. He settled on a smallholding near Lelant where he gathered more stories from the tin miners of the area. He recounted these tales to **Robert Hunt**, who used them in his own publications. Bottrell was encouraged by the editor of the *Cornish Telegraph* to write and publish the tales himself and the first of these writings appeared in that newspaper in 1867. He also wrote for the periodicals *One and All* and the *Reliquary*.

Bottrell's tales tell of **giants**, **mermaids**, witches, and Cornish fairies such as ***buccas***, **knockers**, and **spriggans** (apparently he had a black cat named Spriggans). The tales were compiled into three volumes, the first of which was *Traditions and Hearthside Stories of West Cornwall* vol. I (1870); the second volume was published in 1873, and the third, *Stories and Folklore of West Cornwall*, in 1880.

Bozaloshtsh

Literally, "God's Plaint," a **banshee**-like spirit in Wend folklore of eastern Germany. Like the Irish banshee, she is an omen of impending death and weeps in lament beneath the window of those about to die. In some accounts she is described as a small woman with long hair; in others she is associated with the elder tree and is described as a red-eyed woman clad in white with long, braided hair.

Brag

Described in folk tales from Northumberland and northern Britain, the brag is an irksome **goblin** taking on the appearance of a horse, a calf, or a headless man among others.

An old tale relates the misfortune that befell the wearer of an ill-fated white suit: meeting the brag in the form of a horse, the white-suited man unwisely leaped onto its back for a ride home and was promptly tossed into a pond, the horse laughing and neighing noisily as it galloped away.

Bran the Blessed

(Also Bendigeidfran.) Son of the Welsh sea god **Llyr** and brother of **Branwen**, Bran the Blessed, whose name means "**raven**" or "crow," is featured in the ancient Welsh stories of the *Mabinogion.* He is described as a sea deity, a **giant** of such massive proportions that no house can accommodate him, a king of Britain, and the keeper of the magical cauldron of regeneration, which restores fallen warriors to life.

One of the most famous stories of Bran tells of his struggles with the Irish.

One day the Irish king Matholwch came to Bran the Blessed to make an alliance. Bran and his brother, Manawydan, agreed to grant the king their beautiful sister Branwen's hand in marriage to forge a lasting peace between Britain and Ireland.

Branwen consented and a great wedding celebration was held in the open air, for no building was big enough to contain the godlike proportions of Bran. There was much rejoicing, until Bran's half-brother, Efnisien, arrived back to discover that the wedding had taken place without his knowledge. Flying into a rage because he had been left out of the proceedings, he attacked and mutilated King Matholwch's horses. This act of cruelty was intended as an insult and Matholwch was greatly offended.

In an attempt to make peace and appease his Irish guests, Bran offered various gifts of horses, silver, and gold, and eventually won them over when he promised to give them the magical cauldron of regeneration. King Matholwch accepted the gifts and returned to Ireland with his bride.

At first all was well. Branwen was well received in Ireland and bore Matholwch a son, Gwern. However, as time passed, anger at Efnisien's insult grew among Matholwch's people. Matholwch himself took his resentment out on Branwen, banishing her from his chamber to work in the kitchen. No Briton who visited Ireland was allowed to return home lest Bran hear how badly his sister was being treated. But while chopping wood in the yard, the resourceful Branwen tamed a starling and, after years of patient teaching, trained it to carry messages for her. She tied a message to the bird's leg to take to Bran, telling him of her plight.

When the news reached Bran, he summoned a great fleet of ships and men to invade Ireland and rescue his sister. Too large to fit aboard any ship, he himself waded through the sea.

The Irish were confounded when they saw what looked like a huge forest and strange mountain moving through the sea toward them. When Matholwch asked Branwen about this strange vision, she knew it was her brother coming to save her. When she told Matholwch that the forest was a fleet of ships and the great mountain behind it was her brother, the people of Ireland were afraid. They retreated across the River Shannon, destroying the bridge behind them, but when Bran reached the river he stretched his great body across it, allowing his men to cross over his back like a bridge.

Backed into a corner, Matholwch sought to make amends. He offered his kingdom to Branwen's son, Gwern, and proposed to construct a building large enough to house even Bran, where the Irish and British could meet to celebrate a lasting peace.

Finally, Bran agreed and the great meeting-house was built. But Matholwch wasn't true to his peace offer and hid armed men in sacks that were hung up inside the mighty house.

When the two sides entered the house for the supposed peace meeting, Efnisien enquired what was inside the sacks. On being told they contained flour, he proceeded to squish the contents of each sack until all of the warriors were dead.

Matholwch had been caught out by his own sly trick and had no choice but to continue with the peace talks. Gwern was crowned king and was popular with both sides, except for Efnisien, who jealously thrust the boy onto the fire, shattering the peace and provoking an outbreak of fighting.

In the morning, the dead Irish warriors were placed in the cauldron of regeneration and rose to fight again.

Seeing the bodies of his kinsmen scattered dead on the ground, in an act of remorse Efnisien threw himself down among the bodies of his enemies. As he was thrown into the cauldron, he stretched out his body, rupturing the cauldron and bursting his heart in the process.

Once the cauldron was broken, Bran's men gained the advantage, until the giant king was struck by a poisoned spear and mortally wounded. His dying wish was that his kinsmen cut off his head and bury it under the Gwyn Fryn, the White Mound or Tower near London, whence it would guard the land from invasion.

When Branwen set foot back in Britain, her heart burst at the thought that she had been the cause of so much sorrow and destruction and she dropped dead.

In Ireland, there were only five survivors, said to be pregnant women who gave birth to the five provinces of Ireland.

Seven warriors remained on the Welsh side and they carried out Bran's request, but it took them many years to reach their destination. Eventually arriving at Gwyn Fryn, they buried the head of the giant king facing the European mainland, where some say it remains as a protective spirit guarding the land of Britain from attack.

Some believe that the Tower of London was built over the head. Today a legend that is sometimes associated with Bran's remains is that as long as there are ravens in the Tower of London, the kingdom of Britain will not fall.

BRANWEN

Daughter of the Welsh sea god **Llyr**, sister of **Bran the Blessed** and Manawydan. Branwen, the "white **raven**," is featured in the ancient epic stories of the *Mabinogion*, where she is described as one of the most beautiful women in the Isle of Britain.

When the Irish king Matholwch

took her as his bride but subsequently maltreated her, much fighting ensued between the Irish and the Britons, and Branwen died of heartbreak at the death and destruction that she believed she had caused.

BRIGGS, KATHARINE *(1898–1980)*

English folklore scholar Katharine Mary Briggs is best known for her numerous and comprehensive collections of fairy lore and folk tales of the British Isles. She was born in Hampstead, London, the daughter of Edward Briggs and Mary Cooper. The family originated from Yorkshire, where they had invested, with success, in coal mining. Her father was a watercolorist who particularly enjoyed painting Scottish scenery, and in 1911 the family moved to Perthshire.

Briggs' interest in stories began at an early age, possibly catalyzed by her father's fondness for storytelling. She also heard many traditional tales recounted while living in Scotland. In 1918 she moved to Oxford, where she studied English at Lady Margaret Hall. She obtained her PhD after the Second World War with a thesis on folklore (*Folklore in Jacobean Literature*). She wrote extensively on the topic of folklore and her works remain among the most esteemed sources on British folklore and fairy lore today. Her publications include *The Personnel of Fairyland* (1953), the *Anatomy of Puck* (1959), *Folktales of England* (1965), the four-volume *Dictionary of British Folk Tales in the English Language* (1970–1971), and her comprehensive *A Dictionary of Fairies, Hobgoblins, Brownies, Bogies and Other Supernatural Creatures* (1976).

Briggs served as president of the British Folklore Society for three years; an award was named in her honor after her death in 1980.

Brighid

See **Brigit**.

Brigit

(Or Brighid.) In Celtic mythology Brigit is a daughter of the ***Tuatha de Danann*** in Ireland, a pagan goddess of poetry and smithcraft, possessing the powers of divination and healing.

Legends of her birth say she was bathed in milk and would take only pure milk from a fairy cow with white skin and red ears as her sustenance. Her birth is celebrated on the ancient Celtic festival of Imbolc in February when, in Scotland, the old woman of winter, *Cailleach*, drinks from the Well of Youth and metamorphoses into Bride, who, with her white wand, heralds the growth and regeneration of spring. By the hearthside a bridie doll of corn is left with offerings of bread and milk to ensure protection and abundance.

Brolga

In the Dreamtime Aboriginal myths of Australia, Brolga was a girl who was famous for her graceful dancing. A malicious sorcerer desired her as a wife, but he was rejected. As she danced alone one day she was engulfed by a whirling dust storm, which left behind no trace of her—the spurned magician had exacted his revenge and changed her into a beautiful silver-gray bird whose dance imitated the elegant movements of her arms. The Brolga bird dances to this day in northern Australia.

Brollachan

In *Popular Tales of the West Highlands* (1860–1962), **J. F. Campbell** describes the *brollachan*, from the Gaelic for a shapeless, deformed being, as having eyes and a mouth but no discernible shape and only the two words "myself" and "thyself" at his command.

The story tells of a lame young miller boy lying beside his fire in the mill when the *brollachan* enters and keeps him company. As the fire burns low, the boy throws on another peat and an ember jumps out onto the *brollachan*, who shrieks and howls loudly. His mother, a *fuath* (*see* **Fuathan**), bursts into the room and demands to know who is responsible for burning him. The *brollachan* can only reply, "Myself and thyself," with which she has to be content, while the crippled boy hides beneath a sack and prays for his own safety. The *fuath*, not satisfied, chases a lone woman to her home and, just as she enters the door, tears off her heel in revenge. The woman is left lame for the rest of her life.

Broonie

In Shetland the tale is told of the King of **Trows**. His name was Broonie and he was responsible for guarding the corn. Farmers were glad of his benevolent spells as he sped from farm to farm, but Broonie liked to be left alone and would scatter the corn stooks hither and thither if he was disturbed. As the nights became colder, the good folk decided to make him a gift of a cloak and hood, and placed them so he would find them. But Broonie scorned the kind gift and left the neighborhood forever.

Brother Mike

In a Suffolk tale, a tiny "frairy" (the local dialect word for fairy) is caught in a farmer's barn and cries out the name of Brother Mike in despair while struggling to escape.

Brown Man of the Muirs

A **dwarf** dwelling near the Keeldar Stone on the lonely moors of Northumberland. He is dressed all in brown and of a squat and stocky appearance, with a head of wildly curling red hair and glowing eyes. He is a jealous guardian of wild creatures and fiercely defends his territory from huntsmen trespassing on his land.

Brownie

A household spirit in the folklore of Scotland and northern England, generally described as a shaggy-haired little man about 3 feet (1 meter) tall, sometimes dressed in shabby brown clothes and sometimes naked. **Meg Mullach**, or Hairy Meg, is an example of a female brownie, but in most accounts they are male.

Brownies attached themselves to a particular household or farm. They came out at night to complete tasks left unfinished by servants or farm laborers, tending to livestock, threshing grain, reaping crops, cleaning the house and barns, churning butter, and taking care of numerous other chores. In return, housewives left out treats, placing a bowl of cream, or a tidbit of freshly baked bread or cake where the brownie was likely to find it by chance. It was important not to offer a brownie direct payment for his services, as this invariably led to his departure. Some say this was because brownies were only bound to work until considered worthy of payment; others that the brownie was too much of a free spirit to accept the bondage of human clothes or wages. The **Cauld Lad of Hilton** is one of many examples of a brownie who ceased his services when he was given the gift of clothing. In Cornwall, a **pisky** sometimes performed a similar role to a brownie, helping with the threshing of the corn. But when the **pisky threshers** were given new clothes, they vanished, never to return. In one unusual case a Lincolnshire brownie was annually given a linen shirt. One year the farmer substituted a shirt of coarse hemp and the brownie took offense at the poor quality of the garment and left.

Criticizing a brownie's work was another sure way to cause offense and turn him from an industrious helper into a troublesome, mischievous **boggart**. However, when treated with respect, a brownie was very loyal to the master or mistress of the household, chiding and scolding lazy servants and laborers, and even fetching the midwife when his mistress went into labor.

See also **Aiken Drum**, ***Bodachan Sabhaill***, **Boggart**, ***Bongas***, **Brownie-Clod**, ***Bwbachod***, ***Bwca***, **Tom Cockle**, **Dobbs**, **Dobie**, **Fenodoree**, **Gruagach**, ***Haltija***, **Hob**, **Hobgoblin**, ***Kaboutermannekin***,

***Killmoulis*, *Kobold*, *Kodinhaltia*, Korrigan, *Niagriusar*, *Nisse*, *Phouka*, Portunes, Puddlefoot, Redcaps, Silkies, Urisk, Wag-at-the-Wa'.**

Brownie-Clod

A **brownie** of the Scottish Highlands with a frolicsome temperament, always playing tricks and with a tendency to throw grass clods at passing strangers, hence his name. A simple being, he was tricked into taking on the task of threshing as much corn as two men for the whole winter by the promise of a cape and hood. The tricksters eventually relented when they saw how hard he worked and gave him the clothes, whereupon Brownie-Clod stopped work in a flash and made off with his gift.

Bucca

A Cornish spirit inhabiting the shoreline between high and low tide, to whom fishermen left offerings of fish in order to ensure a good catch in their nets.

The Cornish tales of **William Bottrell** in *Traditions and Hearthside Stories of West Cornwall* (2 vols, 1870–1973) name two *buccas*, Bucca-dhu (Black Spirit) and Bucca-gwidden (White Spirit) and Bucca-boo as a corruption of the former, meaning "Old Nick, or one of his near relations."

Buggane

The Buggane is described in *Manx Fairy Tales* by S. Morrison (1911) as "a great big ugly beast" with a "thick gruff voice of a giant" who is so mad with rage at a woman baking after sunset that he captures her and carries her at great speed toward a waterfall. Just as she fears her end is nigh, she remembers the knife she carries, cuts the strings of her apron, and tumbles to the ground, while the Buggane's headlong flight pitches him into the roaring waterfall instead.

Bugul-Noz

Described as "a colossal spirit called Teus or Bugelnoz, who appears clothed in white between midnight and two in the morning" in *Legends and Romances of Brittany* by Lewis Spence (1917), the

Bugelnoz's task is "to rescue victims from the devil, and should he spread his mouth over them they are secure from the Father of Evil." However, later depictions of this Breton "Night Shepherd" portray him as so exceedingly ugly that he hides away in deep forests, a lonely and unhappy spirit.

Bullbeggar

In *The Discoverie of Witchcraft* by R. Scot, first published in 1584, bulbeggars are described as "terrifying goblins." Elsewhere in old texts the bullbeggar is depicted as a cautionary bugbear, an ugly or deformed man useful as a threat with which to control misbehaving children.

See also **Nursery Bogies**.

Bunyip

A malevolent water spirit in Aboriginal mythology, taking many forms and haunting waterholes and rivers, and feared because of its huge size and predatory nature. A description in *The Geelong Advertiser* newspaper of 1845 says:

The bunyip, then, is represented as uniting the characteristics of a bird and an alligator. It has a head resembling an emu, with a long bill . . . Its body and legs partake of the nature of the alligator. The hind legs are remarkably thick and strong, and the fore legs are much longer, but still of great strength.

Ancient fossilized bones found by anthropologists and shown to Aborigine elders in the nineteenth century were instantly identified by them as bunyip bones, and drawings and cave paintings exist depicting the many fantastical embodiments of the bunyip.

Bushyasta

A *daeva* (demon) in Zoroastrian texts, a spirit of indolence and lethargy, who attempts to thwart the good energy of mortals by exhorting them to sleep away their lives.

Buttery Spirits

The fattest fairies, found in inns and taverns where the landlord is deceiving his customers by using inferior meat and watered-down beer. The only food the insatiable buttery spirits devour is either stolen or dishonestly presented as fine fare; in this way the portly spirits inadvertently prevent the landlord from profiting from his duplicity.

Bwbach

See ***Bwbachod.***

Bwbachod

Also known as the *bwca* or *bwbach,* the *bwbachod* is a Welsh household spirit that belongs to the same family as the **brownie**.

The *bwbachod* rewards tidiness. To enlist the help of one, traditionally Welsh maids would sweep the kitchen, set a good fire last thing at night, leave the churn filled with cream on the whitened hearth, and leave a basin of fresh cream on the hob. In the morning, if she was in luck, she would find that the *bwbachod* had emptied the basin of cream and plied the churn-dasher so well that she had only to give a thump or two to bring out the butter in a great lump.

Bwbachod have a dislike of teetotallers and like to harass them. In *British Goblins* (1880), **Wirt Sikes** relates the story of a *bwbachod* who took an especial dislike to a preacher who was much fonder of his prayers than of good ale. Being in favor of people who sat around the hearth with a drink and a pipe, the *bwbachod* took to pestering the preacher, knocking the stool from beneath his elbows when he was praying, jangling the fire irons, or frightening him by grinning in at the window. He finally succeeded in frightening the preacher away by appearing as his double, which was considered to be an omen of death. The preacher mounted his horse the next day and rode away, looking back over his shoulder at the *bwbachod,* who was grinning from ear to ear.

Bwca

(Pronounced *booka.*) An industrious Welsh **brownie**, working at night on household tasks such as spinning, washing, and ironing in return for bread and milk. He is happy to work without being seen, or his name being known, but if he is spied on he will immediately depart, never to return.

See also **Bwbachod**.

C

Cabyll Ushtey

A Manx **water horse** said to frequent the banks of lakes after dark. There is some debate as to whether it is as dangerous as its Scottish counterpart, the greedy ***each uisge***, but it is believed to seize cattle and occasionally steal children.

A pale gray water colt was reportedly sighted at Ballure Green in the Isle of Man in 1859.

It is said Glen Meay, a small village on the west coast of the Isle of Man, is haunted by a man who rode a *cabyll ushtey* and was drowned at sea. His ghost is now said to roam the wooded glen beneath the waterfall.

Some say the *cabyll ushtey* is one guise of the shapeshifting ***glastyn***.

See also ***Aughisky***.

Caillagh ny Groamagh

Manx weather spirit. *Caillagh ny groamagh* means "old woman of gloominess." On St. Bride's Day, February 1st, the Manx *Caillagh ny Groamagh* appears as a giant bird carrying sticks in her beak. If it's dry, she comes out to collect sticks to keep her warm through the summer. If it's wet, she stays in and in it's in her interest to make the summer warm and dry. Therefore, a dry St. Bride's Day portends a wet summer to come, while a wet St. Bride's Day is a sign of a fine summer ahead.

See also ***Cailleach Bera, Cailleach Bheur***, **Jimmy Squarefoot**.

Cailleach Beara

See ***Cailleach Bera.***

Cailleach Bera

(Pronounced *kill-ogh vayra.*) (Also *Cailleach Beara.*) Irish hag, similar to the ***Cailleach Bheur*** of Scotland. She lived in the mountains and carried stones in her apron for building. When her apron string broke, the stones fell out, creating rocky peaks and crags.

The Hag's Chair and the megalithic tomb Slieve na Calliagh are situated on top of Hag's Mountain, Sliabh na Caillí, at Loughcrew in County Meath.

See also ***Caillagh ny Groamagh.***

Cailleach Bheur

(Pronounced *cal'yach vare.*) Blue Hag, a weather spirit of the Scottish Highlands. The Blue Hag is the personification of winter. She is the daughter of Grianan, the winter sun. In the old Celtic calendar there were two suns. The "big sun" shines from Beltane (May Day) to Samhain (Halloween). The "little sun" shines from Samhain to Beltane. The *Cailleach Bheur* is reborn each Samhain, when she smites the earth with her staff to fight off spring. When Beltane comes, she throws her staff under a holly tree or gorse bush and turns into a stone.

She is the guardian spirit of deer, which she herds, milks, and protects from hunters. She is a friend to wild cattle, swine, and wolves, and sometimes assumes the shape of a wild boar. She is also a guardian of wells and streams.

One story concerning the creation of Loch Awe in Scotland, recounts how, tired after a long day herding her deer, *Cailleach Bheur* fell asleep while watching over a well. The well overflowed and water poured down the mountains and flooded the valley below, forming first a river and then the loch.

Cait Sith

(Pronounced *cait shee.*) Fairy cat of the Scottish Highlands. Believed by some to be a witch transformed into a cat rather than a fairy, the *cait sith* is described in **J. G. Campbell**'s *Superstitions of the Highlands and Islands of Scotland* (1900) as being black with a white spot on its breast, the size of a dog. When angry, it arches its back and bristles its fur.

After a death, Scottish Highlanders would keep watch over the body to prevent the *cait sith* from coming near it. They believed that the fairy cat could steal the soul from a corpse by jumping over it before the burial. Games, riddles, music, and wrestling took place at the watches, called Feill Fadalach (Late Wakes), which were designed to distract the *cait sith* and protect the soul of the recently deceased.

Campbell, John Francis (1821–1885)

Author of one of the most famous collections of Scottish folk tales, John Francis Campbell was born in Edinburgh, but brought up on the island of Islay (Inner Hebrides). The island had belonged to his family since the eighteenth century; he was also known as Campbell of Islay. His upbringing was unusual in that he was allowed to mix with the local children. This was rather unconventional at a time when social etiquette required everyone to keep to a strict code of conduct and "know their place." He said of his education:

As soon as I was out of the hands of nursemaids I was handed over to the care of a piper. His name was the same as mine, John Campbell, and from him I learned a good many useful arts. I learned to be hardy and healthy and I learned Gaelic; I learned to swim and to take care of myself, and to talk to everybody who chose to talk to me. My kilted nurse and I were always walking about in foul weather or fair, and every man, woman, and child in the place had something to say to us. Thus I made early acquaintance with a blind fiddler who could recite stories. I worked with the carpenters; I played shinty with all the boys about the farm; and so I got to know a good deal about the ways of the Highlanders by growing up as a Highlander myself.

He was educated at Eton and at Edinburgh University, where he studied geology and photography. He later invented an instrument to record sunshine hours that is still in use today.

His interest in local folk tales was rekindled when one of his close friends returned from Stockholm, having met **Jakob Grimm** there. He was persuaded to collect tales from the Highlands and islands of Scotland and trained a team of Gaelic speakers who collected 800 stories. His *Popular Tales of the West Highlands, Orally Collected* (in four volumes) was published between 1860 and 1862.

Campbell, John Gregorson

(1836–1891)

A collector of tales and traditions from the Scottish Highlands, J. G. Campbell pursued the same method of collection as **J. F. Campbell**, recording tales directly from Gaelic speakers, which were later translated into English.

Campbell was born in Argyllshire, Scotland, and was first educated at the local school in Appin, where the family moved when he was three years old. His further schooling was in Glasgow, where he later attended the Andersonian University. While at university his passion for traditional tales grew and he met many storytellers and committed their tales to memory.

Campbell continued his studies and read law, but his inclination was toward the Church and he was licensed by the Presbytery of Glasgow in 1858. He continued to be a keen collector of stories. These were eventually compiled in *Superstitions of the Highlands and Islands of Scotland* and *Witchcraft and Second Sight in the Highlands and Islands of Scotland* and were published posthumously in 1900 and 1902 respectively.

Canotila

Native American tree spirits, literally meaning "they live in a tree." From the mythology of the Lakota of North and South Dakota.

Caoineag

(Pronounced *konyack.*) Meaning "weeper," *caoineag* is one of the names of the Scottish **banshee**. Her wail, heard in the darkness at a waterfall, heralds catastrophe for the clan. She is heard, but never seen. Unlike the ***bean nighe***, she can't be approached to grant wishes.

*C*AOINTEACH

(Pronounced *kondyuch.*) Meaning "wailer," the *caointeach* is another version of the *caointeag*, the Scottish **banshee**. She is local to Argyllshire, Skye, and the neighboring islands. She has a particularly lamentable and loud cry that rises almost to a scream. In appearance, she has been described as a very little woman or child wearing a high-crowned white hat, short green gown, and petticoat. She sometimes beats clothes on a rock, like the ***bean nighe***.

James Macdougall and George Calder's *Folk Tales and Fairy Lore* (1910) relates the story of the *caointeach* who followed the MacKay clan. When a death was going to take place, she would call at the sick person's house with a green shawl around her shoulders and warn the family by wailing sadly outside his door. When the friends and family heard her lament, they lost all hope of the sick person getting better, for it was proof that the end was near.

The *caointeach* has ceased to give warning to the MacKays since one wet, cold, winter night, when she stood softly wailing outside a house and a member of the family took pity on her and offered her a plaid (blanket). She accepted the gift, but in the same way as when a **brownie** accepts a gift of clothes his spirit is "laid," or set free, so too the *caointeach* has never come back to mourn for the MacKays.

CAPELTHWAITE

In Westmorland, northwest England (now part of Cumbria), there was once a barn called Capelthwaite Barn, in which the Capelthwaite made its home. He was said to be able to assume any form at will, but his preferred shape was that of a black dog the size of a calf. He was friendly toward the owners of the barn, and helped them by rounding up their sheep and cows.

However, when it came to strangers, he showed a mischievous and spiteful streak. In the end, the vicar of Beetham performed a ceremony and "laid" this supernatural black dog in the river Bela. It was not seen again, except for in one tale related in William Henderson's *Notes on the Folklore of the Northern Counties of England and the Borders* (1866), when a man returning from the local fair somewhat disheveled, without his cap or coat, persisted in blaming the Capelthwaite for his misadventure, telling his wife that the Capelthwaite had chased him and thrown him into the hedge.

Carmichael, Alexander (1832–1912)

A writer, antiquarian, and folklorist, Alexander Carmichael was born on the island of Lismore, Inner Hebrides, Scotland. He attended local schools and later became a civil servant in various locations in Ireland and Scotland. It was while he was on the Isle of Skye that he became a collector of stories for **J. F. Campbell**.

The strict methodology that was Campbell's approach did not suit Carmichael's artistic temperament, but nonetheless he learned to take notes on everything that interested him. He left Scotland and lived in Cornwall for two years before taking up a post in the Uists (the central group of islands of the Outer Hebrides). Here he continued collecting ballads, hymns, anecdotes, incantations, poems, and songs. From 1873 some of his lore was printed in the newspaper the *Highlander*.

He went on to work in various locations in Scotland and retire to Edinburgh, by which time he was considered by many to be a pillar of the Gaelic intellectual community. He then embarked on a more ambitious work and compiled *Carmina Gadelica* (1900), a treasure trove of culture, lore, and traditions from various Gaelic-speaking regions of Scotland.

Cauld Lad of Hilton, The

A domestic spirit, half-**brownie**, half-ghost. His story is as follows.

Long ago at Hilton Hall in Northumbria, there lived a contrary spirit called the Cauld Lad of Hilton. Some say he was the spirit of a stable boy who had been killed by one of the past Lords of Hilton. Now he could be heard at night clattering about in the kitchen after the servants had gone to bed, putting sugar in the salt cellar, upturning chamber pots and setting everything topsy-turvy. If the servants left him a bowl of cream or a cake spread with honey, he would clean and tidy. Sometimes he could be heard sadly singing, lamenting that the person who would "lay" him to rest, or exorcise his spirit, was yet to be born:

Woe's me! woe's me!
The acorn's not yet
Fallen from the tree,
That's to grow the wood,
That's to make the cradle
That's to rock the bairn,
That's to grow to the man,
That's to lay me.
Woe's me! Woe's me!

However, the servants knew that the way to lay a brownie was to pay for its services in non-perishable goods such as clothes. So they left out a green cloak and hood for the Cauld Lad of Hilton. He dressed in them at midnight and frisked about in them until dawn, singing:

Here's a cloak and here's a hood,
The Cauld Lad of Hilton shall do no
more good!

As the sun rose, he vanished, never to be seen again.

Ceasg

(Pronounced *keeask.*) A Scottish **mermaid**. Half-woman, half-grilse (a young salmon), she is also known as *maighdean na tuinne,* "maiden of the wave." Her top half is that of a beautiful woman, while below the waist she has the tail of grilse. She may grant three wishes to anyone who catches her.

There are stories of marriage between *ceasgs* and humans. The male offspring of these unions are said to grow up to be excellent sea captains.

Like most sea maidens, the *ceasg* is also believed to have a darker, dangerous side. This is described in a story in **J. F. Campbell** and George Henderson's *The Celtic Dragon Myth* (1911), in which the hero is swallowed by a *ceasg*.

An idea common to tales from the Scottish Highlands is that of the separable soul. *Ceasgs* are believed to keep their souls separately from their bodies, hidden in an egg or in a box. To destroy a *ceasg*, one must find and destroy her soul.

Ceni

See **Zemi**.

Changeling

In fairy lore throughout Europe and other parts of the world one of the fairies' favorite tricks was to steal a human child, or sometimes a nursing mother, and take them away to fairyland. They replaced the human either with one of their own kind, known as a changeling, or with a **stock** or **fetch**, a "doll" representing the stolen child or woman, which by means of fairy glamor was given the semblance of life. The stock or fetch could take the form of a piece of wood or a bundle of grass and sticks, fashioned in the likeness of the abducted human.

Fairy changelings were sometimes sick or weak fairy children whom the fairies placed in the care of a human family so that they might have a better chance of survival. At other times they were elderly fairies who were being given the opportunity to live out their old age in comfort, cosseted and doted on by their new "parents."

Typically, changelings were described as sickly, wizened, or otherwise abnormal in appearance, either never gaining the power of speech or displaying unsettlingly advanced language skills. In many tales, they had insatiable appetites and cried constantly. Occasionally, there were tales of parents who treated the changeling kindly in the hope that their own child would likewise be cared for. More often, suspected changelings were subjected to cruel tests and ordeals in an attempt to drive away the fairy and secure the return of the healthy human child. In many tales, these included dunkings in holy wells, beatings, or leaving the supposed changeling unattended in the woods, on a hillside, beneath a church stile, on a manure pile, or in an otherwise inhospitable environment. Sadly, many human children born with physical abnormalities or wasting diseases or who otherwise did not fit the norm endured sometimes fatal cruelties at the hands of parents and communities who labeled them as changelings.

Various reasons are given as to why fairies coveted human babies, ranging from the sinister to the benign. At the darker end of the spectrum, it was said that fairies had to pay a tithe or tribute to hell (as in the ballad of **Tam Lin**) and rather than spill fairy blood, they paid in the blood of humans. Alternatively, humans were taken to fairyland as slaves and put to work as servants or smiths. Beautiful golden-haired children were most prized by the fairies. Some said that they were sought after to improve the fairy stock; others simply that fairies thought these fair-haired children were particularly attractive and doted upon them like pets.

Nursing mothers were frequently sought to suckle fairy offspring. According to some tales, it seems that fairies wanted human milk to give their fairy children a human soul. An account in R. H. Cromek's *Remains of Galloway and Nithsdale Song* (1812) relates the case of a nursing mother who was blessed and rewarded by a fairy for allowing her child to feed on human milk.

Various methods were employed to trick a changeling into revealing its identity. In many tales across Europe it is the mother's unusual use of eggshells that compels the changeling to give itself away. In a German tale the mother cracks an egg in half and sets it on the stove to boil, forcing the changeling to exclaim from the cradle, "Well, I am as old as the Westerwald, but I've never seen anyone cooking with an eggshell!" As the changeling laughs, it shoots up the chimney and the human child is restored to the cradle.

Many Celtic changeling tales involve the "brewery of eggshell," in which eggshells are set upon the hearth on the pretext of brewing beer in them. This strange behavior prompts the changeling to pass comment, uttering words to the effect: "I remember seeing an acorn having an oak, and I remember see-

ing a hen having an egg, but I don't remember seeing anybody brew beer in the shell of a hen's egg."

Variations on this theme include an Icelandic tale in which a woman constructs a spoon handle out of twigs that is so long it pokes out of the top of the chimney, and a Danish tale in which the mother makes black pudding using an entire pig. This prompts the changeling to remark, "A pudding with hide! And a pudding with hair! A pudding with eyes! And a pudding with bones in it! Thrice have I seen a young wood spring upon Tiis Lake, but never yet have I seen such a pudding! The Devil will stay no longer!" It runs away, never to return.

In other tales, it is an old fairy changeling's desire for music, merriment, and dancing that gives it away. There are many Celtic tales in which a traveling tailor plays an integral role in unmasking the changeling. Typically, the father goes out to work and the mother goes out on an errand, leaving the tailor to watch the "baby" as he works. When the two of them are left alone, the tailor begins to whistle as he stitches, at which the creature in the cradle jumps up with a glint in its beady eyes and demands that the astonished tailor strikes up a tune on the fiddle or pipes so that it might dance. In some versions it is the changeling itself who takes up an instrument and plays a lively tune, sometimes insisting on a dram of whisky to accompany the revels. When the parents return, the little creature returns to the crib, where it resumes its crying and wailing. The tailor informs the parents of their child's true identity and they drive out the changeling by building a blazing fire and placing it upon it so that it is sent up the chimney and the true human baby returned in its place.

Throwing the changeling on the fire isn't always sufficient to bring back the human child, however. In a Scottish tale collected by **J. F. Campbell**, "The Smith and the Fairies," a 14-year-old boy, the son of a smith, is taken by the fairies and a changeling left in his place.

A wise old man, a friend of the smith, set about brewing beer in eggshells. The changeling burst out laughing, exclaiming, "I have lived 800 years and I have never seen the like of that before!" The smith threw it on the fire and it flew through the roof, but the boy wasn't immediately returned.

The wise man instructed the smith to visit the fairy hill on a full moon, when the entrance would be open.

Taking a Bible, a cross, a dirk (dagger), and a cockerel, the last of which he hid in his coat, the smith went to the fairy mound, where he heard the sound of pipes, dancing, and merriment. Sticking his dirk in the earth as he crossed the threshold, he ventured inside, to find the fairies enjoying their revels while his son was slaving away at a forge.

The fairies became very agitated with the smith for intruding on their festivities, but couldn't approach him because he carried the Bible and cross. When he demanded they return his son, they shouted and made such a noise that the cockerel crowed.

The smith grabbed his boy and they left through the door wedged open by the dirk just as the fairy mound closed and all became dark once more.

At first the boy was silent and pale and wouldn't go about his work, but a year and a day after his rescue he made a rapid recovery, took up his tools, and went on to prosper as one of the land's finest smiths.

The metal dagger, Bible, cross, and cockerel in this tale are common examples of items used as protection against malicious fairies. The Bible and cross are allied with Christian beliefs that equate fairies with demons. The crowing of the cockerel is a sign that dawn is imminent and therefore that fairy revels must end, for fairies are believed to be afraid of the light. Metal, specifically iron, was widely used to ward off the unwanted attention of fairies. Metal objects were often placed in babies' cradles as protection against the children being snatched by the fairies. An open pair of scissors or a pair of tongs was considered particularly effective. They had the added benefit of forming the shape of the cross—considered a protective symbol even before the advent of Christianity. An item of the father's clothing such as a waistcoat or a pair of trousers served the same function. According to E. S. Hartland's *The Science of Fairy Tales* (1891), a right shirt sleeve or a left stocking was particularly favored, though quite why this should be so is not clear.

In Sweden it was said that the fire must be kept burning in the room of a baby who had not yet been baptized—unbaptized children being particularly at risk from the incursions of fairies was a common theme across many cultures. As protection, a piece of steel such as a needle should be attached to the child's swaddling—the preferred color of which was red, to simulate fire—and the water the child was washed in should not be thrown out. In China, the ash of dried banana skin was used to draw the sign of a cross on an infant's forehead and a fisherman's net placed over the cradle to guard against evil spirits. In Egypt, it was widely believed that a human child left unattended was at risk of being swapped with a ***djinn*** child.

Many tales across cultures stated that babies were particularly at risk of being taken by fairies during the first six weeks of life and were most vulnerable during the first three days. It was advocated that a fire be kept lit near the child at all times and that the parents keep constant watch. This had obvious practical benefits in safeguarding the child against accident, injury, and disease. Of course, in modern-day childcare it is still important to keep a baby warm and under the watchful gaze of its parents—not for fear of fairies, but to ward off illness and because infants cannot conserve heat for the first four weeks of life.

Accounts of changelings continued to be reported into the late nineteenth century. In 1895 in Ireland a woman named Bridget Cleary was killed by her husband, family, and neighbors, who claimed that she was a fairy changeling. The ordeals she was subjected to in order to cast out the fairy and return the "real" Bridget resulted in her death.

Though reports of this type are thankfully a thing of the past, changelings continue to capture the imagination and appear in many works of art and literature. A famous example is Shakespeare's *A Midsummer Night's Dream*, which revolves around a squabble between **Oberon** and **Titania**, King and Queen of the Fairies, over a changeling boy. **W. B. Yeats**' poem "The Stolen Child" was inspired by Irish tales of children spirited away to fairyland. More recently, Maurice Sendak, children's author and illustrator and creator of *Where the Wild Things Are* (1963), drew on changeling lore in his book *Outside Over There* (1981), in which Ida's baby sister is taken by **goblins** and replaced with a changeling made of ice. Ida must go the goblin realm and rescue her sister by playing her horn. Jim Henson's film *Labyrinth* (1986), developed in conjunction with renowned fairy artist Brian Froud, acknowledges Sendak as an influence. Featuring David Bowie as Jareth the Goblin King, it tells the story of Sarah, who must rescue her baby brother from the domain of the goblin king.

Changeling stories deal with themes that continue to resonate, such as panic when a child goes missing, the fear that a child is sick or weak, or—from the point of view of the changeling—the feeling of not fitting in. Perhaps this is why changelings continue to be a source of inspiration for films, art, and literature today.

Chin Chin Kobakama

Japanese fairies. A Japanese fairy tale, written down by T. Hasegawa in *Chin Chin Kobakama* (1903), tells the story of a lazy little girl who ate plums and hid the stones under the matting on her bedroom floor. Eventually this angered the fairies and they punished her. Every night at 2 a.m., known in Japan as the Ox Hour, the fairies rose up from the matting as tiny women dressed in bright red robes, singing:

Chin-chin Kobakama,
Yomo fuké soro,
Oshizumare, Hime-gimi!
Ya ton ton!

"We are the Chin-chin Kobakama, the hour is late, sleep, honorable noble darling!"

Though the words were kind enough, they were sung to taunt the little girl and the fairies pulled faces as they sang.

After many nights of this, the girl became tired and frightened. So, one night her mother sat up with her to see the fairies. When the little women appeared, she struck at them and they fell to the floor—as plum stones. So, the girl's laziness and naughtiness were discovered. After that she was a very good little girl and never dropped plum stones on the floor again.

Churnmilk Peg

Guardian of Yorkshire nut thickets and orchards, she disapproves of laziness in humans, but takes a fairly laid-back approach to her duties, passing the time by smoking her pipe while protecting nuts and fruit from human hands. **Melsh Dick** carries out the same task.

Cipenapers

Welsh version of the word "kidnappers," sometimes used to talk about fairies.

Clap Cans

Lancashire **bogie** that can be heard but not seen, so-called because of the sound it makes, like that of banging together cans or pots. It is one of the less frightening of the bogies.

Cloud Master, the

See **Nuberu, El**.

Cloud People, the

Spirits of the clouds in the mythology of the Pueblo peoples of North America. According to Hopi legends, the Rain Cloud clans performed ceremonies to the Cloud People to bring rainfall. They sang songs until a mist began to form, then heavy rains fell and frightful bolts of lightning came from the sky. After this display of power, the Rain Cloud clans were invited to join the Hopi pueblo.

The Cloud People were expert basket-makers. They introduced this skill to the Hopi people and were the originators of the basket dance, which is still performed at certain ceremonies.

The Hopi continue to perform rituals at the winter solstice and in the spring to ask to the Cloud People to bring rainfall to ensure a good harvest. In these ceremonies the Cloud People are represented by ***kachina*** masks.

Cluricaune

(Pronounced *kloor-a-cawn.*) Irish cellar-dwelling fairy, similar to a **leprechaun**. Irish folk-tale collector Thomas Crofton Crocker described him as wearing a red nightcap, a leather apron, long pale blue stockings, and shoes with silver buckles. In some tales he acts like a **buttery spirit**, beleaguering drunkards and frightening unscrupulous servants stealing from the wine cellar. If the victim attempts to escape the cluricaune's taunts by moving house, the cluricaune hops into a cask and accompanies them.

Coblynau

(Pronounced *koblernigh.*) Welsh mining fairies, similar to the Cornish **knockers** and English **bluecap**. In *British Goblins* (1880), **Sikes** describes them as grotesquely ugly, about 18 inches (45 centimeters) tall, and dressed like miners. They helped miners by indicating where to find good lodes of ore. In Germany, these mine spirits were known as ***Kobolds***.

Tom Cockle

An Irish household **brownie** who stayed with the same family for generations. When the family relocated to America, they were sad to bid farewell to their helper. But on arriving in their new home, they were delighted to find food set out and a fire already burning brightly in the hearth, for Tom Cockle, their loyal brownie, had come with them.

Coco, El

A bogieman in many Spanish and Portuguese-speaking countries. The myth of *El Coco* is thought to have originated in Portugal and Galicia and spread to Latin American countries such as Mexico, Argentina, and Chile with Spanish and Portuguese colonization. The name "*Coco*" is related to the Portuguese and Spanish for "skull" and the bogieman is sometimes represented as a coconut or a carved pumpkin. Like a dark counterpart to a guardian angel, he is said to take the form of a dark, shadowy figure, often sitting on the roof, where he watches over a child, ready to pounce at any sign of disobedience or bad behavior and spirit them away.

Coleman Grey

A little **pisky** boy who was adopted by humans, as related in **Robert Hunt**'s *Popular Romances of the West of England* (1865).

Colepexy

Pexy or colepexy are the names of a Dorset **pixy**. In Dorset, an area of southern England renowned for its fossils, belemite fossils are known as colepexies' fingers, and fossilized sea urchins are also called colepexies' heads.

Sometimes described as a fairy horse, the colepexy haunts woods, and coppices, acting as a guardian of orchards, leading travelers astray, and occasionally luring unsuspecting folk into mounting him, whereupon he embarks on a wild ride across the Dorset downs, through thorny thickets and wetlands before bucking off his rider, leaving them stranded in a stream or ditch.

William Barnes, in *Poems of Rural Life, in the Dorset Dialect* (1844), describes the colepexy's activities thus: "To beat down the few apples that may be left on the trees after the crop has been taken in; to take as it were, the fairies' horde."

See also **Colt Pixy**.

Colt Pixy

Fairy horse of Hampshire whose neighing tricks other horses and travelers into losing their way, leading them into bogs, similar to a **brag** or **dunnie**.

In Somerset, the colt pixy is an orchard guardian who chases away scrumpers (apple thieves), and may be a variant of the **colepexy**.

See also **Lazy Lawrence**.

Corrigan

See **Korrigan**.

Cottingley Fairies

When two girls in Bradford borrowed a camera to take photos of the fairies at the bottom of their garden, neither of them could have imagined the sensation that was about to follow. When the resulting images attracted the attention of Sir Arthur Conan Doyle, the eminent writer with a keen interest in the supernatural, the Cottingley Fairies phenomenon had everybody talking. The excitement and speculation have rippled down through the years, sparking the idea for two films released in 1977, *Photographing Fairies* and *Fairy Tale: A True Story*, and the story continues to attract interest today.

It all began when cousins Elsie Wright, aged 16, and Frances Griffiths, aged 10, got into trouble for getting wet playing in the stream at the bottom of the garden at the Wrights' home in Cottingley. The girls loved playing in the stream, not least, they said, because they saw fairies there. When their parents laughed at the notion of fairies at the bottom of the garden, dismissing it as fanciful, or merely an excuse for splashing in the stream, the girls set out to prove the grown-ups wrong. They persuaded Elsie's father, a hobbyist photographer, to let them borrow his camera and set off for the stream. They returned triumphantly, in great excitement.

When Elsie's father developed the photographs in his darkroom, he dismissed the initial picture—of Frances watching four fairies dancing on a bush—as the girls fooling around with paper cut-outs. However, a couple of months later the girls went on to produce a second photograph, of Elsie sitting on the lawn with a **gnome**.

In 1919 Elsie's mother showed the photographs at a meeting of the Theosophical Society at a lecture on "Fairy Life." A few months later, the photos were displayed at the Society's annual conference, where they caught the eye of Edward Gardner, an eminent member. His interest was piqued and he sent the images and the glass-plate negatives to a photography expert, who was of the opinion that the photographs were genuine. Gardner then used enhanced negatives to reproduce the images, which he used to deliver illustrated lectures around the country.

The editor of the Spiritualist magazine *Light* drew the photos to the attention of renowned author and Spiritualist Sir Arthur Conan Doyle. He had been commissioned to write an article on fairies for the Christmas edition of the *Strand* magazine. He contacted Gardner to find out who had taken the photos and subsequently got in touch with the Wrights to ask for permission to use the two photos to illustrate his article. Impressed that such an eminent figure as Conan Doyle was interested, Elsie's father agreed that the photos could be used, but refused to accept any money for them, stating that if they were in fact genuine, then they shouldn't be sullied by the exchange of money.

Conan Doyle was preoccupied preparing for a lecture tour of Australia, so Gardner went to meet with the Wright family. Elsie's father told him that he been convinced there was some trick involved in the photographs, but when he had searched the girls' room for evidence—scraps of pictures or cut-outs—he had found nothing incriminating. As further verification of the photographs' authenticity, Gardner returned to Cottingley with two cameras and some photographic plates, which had secretly been marked to reveal any tampering. Frances was invited to stay to see if the girls could repeat their feat and again take pictures of the fairies.

Insisting that the fairies would not show themselves if other people were watching, the two girls set off alone to the stream, where they took several photos, three of which appeared to show fairies. "Frances and the Leaping Fairy" showed Frances in profile looking at a winged fairy sitting on branch; in "Fairy Offering a Posy of Harebells to Elsie," a fairy is offering Elsie flowers. The final photo, "Fairies and their Sun Bath," showed the fairies, without either of the girls, frolicking in the sunshine.

Packed in cotton wool, the plates were sent back to Gardner, who wrote to Conan Doyle in Australia expressing his joy that the experiment seemed to have worked.

The Christmas edition of the *Strand* in which the original photos were published sold out in two days. Elsie and Frances' names were changed to protect their privacy and they were referred to as Iris and Alice Carpenter. Conan Doyle concluded his article by writing he hoped that if the photographs helped to convince people of the existence of fairies it would jolt the materialistic twentieth-century mindset out of its rut and into acknowledging the glamor and mystery of life. It was his hope that the images would encourage people to open up to other psychic phenomena too.

Initial reactions to the images were mixed. Skeptics noted that the fairies conformed to the images in traditional nursery tales and sported suspiciously fashionable hairstyles, while others took the girls and their photos at face value, welcoming the images as evidence of the existence of supernatural beings.

Conan Doyle used the second batch of photographs to illustrate another article in the *Strand* in 1921. This article went on to form the basis of his book, *The Coming of the Fairies*, published in 1922.

In 1921 Gardner made a final visit to Cottingley, this time accompanied by a clairvoyant named Geoffrey Hodson. On this occasion neither Frances or Elsie claimed to see fairies; however, Hodson professed to observe many of the winged creatures. Frances and Elsie later denounced him as a fake.

Public interest in the Cottingley Fairies phenomenon gradually died down after 1921. Elsie and Frances married and lived abroad for many years. It was not until

1966 that the fairies—and Frances and Elsie—found themselves once again in the limelight, when a reporter for the *Daily Express* tracked down Elsie, now living back in England. In an interview, she admitted that the fairies might have been figments of her imagination, but said that what she saw in her mind had somehow been captured on the photographic plate. The article triggered more media interest and scientific investigations into the photographs, most of which concluded that they were fakes.

In 1983, in an article in the *Unexplained* magazine, the cousins admitted that the photos had been fabricated. However, they maintained that the fairies *were* real and they had genuinely seen them. Elsie, a skilled artist from a young age, had copied out illustrations of fairies from *Princess Mary's Gift Book* (1914), a popular children's book, which they had then made into cardboard cut-outs, being careful to dispose of all traces of anything that could be used as evidence. However, a question mark remains over the fifth and final photograph, "Fairies and their Sun Bath." Both girls claimed to have taken it, and Frances always maintained that it was genuine.

In an interview on Arthur C. Clarke's *World of Strange Powers*, Elsie explained that she and Frances had been too embarrassed to say anything after the highly esteemed Arthur Conan Doyle had championed the pictures as genuine evidence of fairies. What had started out as an attempt to prove their parents wrong had taken an unexpected turn that they could never have predicted. They had never thought of it as fraud, Elsie said, just two cousins having a bit of fun. She couldn't understand how so many people—and very highly regarded figures at that—were taken in. She believed they had *wanted* to be taken in.

Prints of the photographs, two of the cameras the girls used, and watercolors of fairies painted by Elsie are displayed at the National Media Museum in Bradford.

Co-walker

An apparition of one's double or doppelgänger. In the north of England it is known as a **waff** and portends death. In *The Secret Commonwealth of Elves, Fauns and Fairies* (1691), **Robert Kirk** believes it to be a type of fairy that can be seen by those with second sight. This double resembles a person in every way, like a twin or shadow, and can be seen before and after that person is dead. It is often sighted eating at funeral banquets or bearing the coffin to the grave.

See also **Fetch**, **Swarth**.

Cowlug Sprites

In the villages of Bowden and Gateside, on the border between England and Scotland, the cowlug sprites haunt the villages on Cowlug Night. These strange sprites are aptly named, with ears said to be shaped like the ears of cows.

Crimbil

Welsh for **changeling**.

Crodh Mara

Scottish sea-dwelling fairy cattle. These hornless cattle sometimes bestow the gift of their milk on humans.

One story tells of the Hero of Clanranald, who lived with his wife and their cow. The cow gave very little milk. One day the hero's wife saw three *crodh mara* and went to milk them. That night she heard a voice that told her to spill some milk on the fairy hill. She did, and from that day on the cows appeared for her to milk every day. When she died, they never returned.

In another tale, a couple spotted *crodh mara* on an island at Lochmaddy. The milk from the fairy cattle supplied the couple with butter and cheese for half a year.

Croker, Thomas Crofton *(1798–1854)*

The antiquarian and folktale collector Thomas Crofton Croker was born in Cork, Ireland. After a sporadic local education, he joined a mercantile firm in 1813, but soon became more interested in artistic pursuits and developed an interest in the folk and fairy traditions of Ireland. In 1819 he obtained the position of clerk at the Admiralty in London, where he continued to work until his retirement.

His writings were influenced by visits to the province of Munster in the south of Ireland where he collected legends, folk songs, and tales. He wrote the first volume of *Fairy Legends and Traditions of the South of Ireland* in 1825. The book proved to be very successful; it garnered praise from **Sir Walter Scott** and was translated into German by **Jakob Grimm**. The second and third volumes were published in 1828. Croker's wife, Marianne, was a painter and provided the illustrations for the books. Croker himself is regarded as the first field-collector of folk tales in Ireland.

Croquemitaine

French bogeyman, literally, the "cruncher of mittens." When French children misbehave, their parents threaten to send them to the *croquemitaine*, who will gobble them up.

Cú Chulainn

See **Cuchullin**.

Cú Cuchaind

See **Cuchullin**.

Cù Sith

(Pronouced *coo-shee.*) Scottish fairy dog. His dark green color marks him out as distinct from other Celtic fairy hounds. Other fairy dogs are generally described as either white with red ears, or black; the most common type in England are black dogs. As described by **J. G. Campbell** in *Superstitions of the Highlands and Islands of Scotland* (1900), the *cù sith* is the size of a young bull, with a shaggy coat and a long tail coiled or plaited on his back; his huge footprints can often be seen in the mud or the snow. He runs silently, gliding along in a straight line. Three loud barks, which can be heard by sailors far out at sea, are the signal that the *cú sith* is out hunting.

See also **Yeth Hound**.

Cuachag

(Pronounced *cooachack.*) A Scottish river sprite or *fuath.* It haunted Glen Cuaich and takes its name from this place. Like all ***fuathan***, it is a pernicious spirit.

Cúchulainn

See **Cuchullin**.

Cuchullin

(Also Cú Chulainn, Cú Cuchaind, or Cúchulainn.) Hero of the *Ulster Cycle*, one of the first collections of Irish heroic legends, he also appears in Manx and Scottish folklore. Cuchullin was born a mortal, his name was Sétanta, but he was the son of the god Lugh of the Long Arm and even as a child he displayed great strength. When he was seven years old he killed Culain the Smith's fierce hound, who guarded the King of Ulster's court. To make amends he offered to guard Ulster until his death. He was given the name Cuchullin, "Culain's Hound."

From the outset, Cuchullin's striking appearance set him apart as different. He had seven toes on each foot, seven fingers on each hand and seven pupils in each eye. His red shock of hair was dark brown at the roots, light blond at the tips. He wore 100 strings of gems on his head, his chest glittered with a hundred brooches, and he had many admirers.

However, he was prone to fits of battle frenzy. During such fits, he transformed into a monster, turning himself around inside his skin, so that his feet and knees faced backward and his calves and heels faced forward. Each strand of his hair stood up on his scalp with rage, a flame leapt from his mouth, and a jet of black blood spouted from the top of his head. His eyes displaced themselves, one to his cheek, the other the back of his skull. He fought from his chariot, driven by Laég, his faithful charioteer, drawn by his gray and black horses Liath Macha and Dub Sainglend. In this fevered, crazed state, he had to be dipped into three vats of ice-cold water to return him to normal temperature.

When he was 17 years old, he single-handedly defended Ulster against Queen Medhb in the epic battle of the Cattle Raid of Cuailane. Eventually it was Queen Medhb who brought about his demise. Cuchullin bound himself to a pillar or standing stone so that he might stand up and fight his enemies to the very end and thus he died a hero.

See also **Lug**, **Raven**.

Curupira

Brazilian guardian spirit of the forest. In Brazilian mythology he is most often depicted as a red-headed boy, with the distinguishing feature of backward-facing feet. The name comes from *curu*, meaning "boy," and *pira*, meaning "body," in the language of the Tupi people of the Brazilian rainforest. Curupira safeguards trees, plants, and animals from the destructive activities of humans, using his backward feet to confound hunters who try to follow his tracks.

Cutty Soams

A mischievous coal-pit **bogle** from the north of England, also known as Old Cutty Soams. Putters were mine workers—sometimes girls—

responsible for pushing the wooden wagons that transported coal or ore out of the mine. "Soams" were the ropes that attached the putter to the wagon. Cutty Soams was known for severing these ropes. According to an account in the *Monthly Chronicle* (1887), when the men went down to work in the morning, it was not uncommon for them to find that Cutty Soams had been busy during the night, and every pair of soams in the colliery had been cut to pieces. Though fond of causing mischief, Cutty Soams was also known to bring about good, at times pouncing upon an unpopular overseer to give him a sound thrashing, much to the delight of the miners.

Cwn Annwn

(Pronounced *koon anoon.*) Welsh hell hounds. Similar to the **Gabriel Ratchets**, the wish hounds, and the **Seven Whistlers**, they are harbingers of death. To hear them is a sure sign that someone's time is up. Their howls are said to grow softer as they approach; close by, their yelping sounds like the cries of small beagles, yet far away their growling is a loud wild lament.

See also **Yeth Hound**.

Cyhyraeth

(Pronounced *kerherrighth.*) Welsh form of the Scottish ***caoineag***, the "weeper." She is rarely seen, most often manifesting as an invisible, disembodied voice. Her groaning is an omen of death, especially multiple deaths that are the result of a disaster or an epidemic. Like the Irish **banshee**, she wails for locals who have died in foreign lands away from home. Accompanied by a corpse light or **will o' the wisp**, her cries have been heard on the sea off the Welsh Glamorganshire coast before shipwrecks, foretelling the path a corpse would take to the churchyard.

In **Wirt or W. Sikes**' *British Goblins* (1880), her wailing is described as doleful and disagreeable, like the groaning of a dying person. As well as foretelling death, it is often a portent of foul weather. First it is heard at a distance, then closer, then near at hand, offering three warnings of death. "It begins strong, and louder than a sick man can make; the second cry is lower, but not less doleful, but rather more so; the third yet lower and soft, like the groaning of a sick man almost spent and dying."

D

D'Aulnoy, Marie-Catherine (c.1650–1705)

French countess and writer who published *Les Contes de Fées* (Fairy Tales) in 1697 and *Contes Nouveaux ou les Fées à la Mode* (New Tales or Fairies in Fashion) in 1698. She was one of the most influential writers in the French *salons,* fashionable gatherings of literary and artistic figures popular in the seventeenth century.

Like many of her contemporaries, such as **Charles Perrault**, Madame d'Aulnoy drew on tales from oral folk tradition and retold them in a literary style. Her tales include "Le Prince Lutin," translated into English as "The Imp Prince," "**Yellow Dwarf**," and "The White Cat" among others.

Dagda

King of the ***Tuatha de Danann***, the immortal fairy people of Ireland.

Human invaders known as Milesians forced the Dananns to hide under "hollow hills" or mounds. However, they still controlled the natural growth of wheat and grass, essential for bread and milk, and so persuaded the Milesians to make a treaty with their king, Dagda.

Dagda had four great palaces underground and he gave two of these to his sons Lug and Ogme, keeping the other two for himself, the greater of these being Brugh na Boinne. A third son, Angus Mac Og, returned from his travels and was angry to find he had been left out. He asked Dagda if he could have the Brugh for a day and a night, and this was agreed. But at the end of that time Angus claimed the Brugh forever, as a day and a night following on from one another represented all time. Although a great warrior, Dagda wasn't the sharpest knife in the box and could be conquered by cunning, and he allowed Angus his claim.

Dagda then took his fourth son, Aedh, to his last palace, near Tara. There they were visited by Corrgenn of Connacht and his wife. Corrgenn suspected Aedh of adultery with his wife, and promptly killed him. In turn it was expected that Dagda would kill him. However, feeling that he had been to some extent justified in his actions, instead he laid upon him a *geasa*, or curse: Corrgenn had to carry the body of Aedh with him until he found a stone of the exact size to cover it.

After many miles, eventually Corrgenn found a suitable stone on the shore of Loch Feabhail. He dug a grave on a hill and laid the body in it before carrying the stone up to cover it. All this was too much for him, however: his heart burst and he died. Dagda had a wall built around the tomb and this place has been called the Hill of Aileac, or Hill of Sighs, ever since.

Daji

See ***Huli Jing***.

Dame Hirip

A child-stealing fairy woman of Hungarian folklore, one of the ***tündér***, the Hungarian fairies.

According to an account in *The Folk Tales of the Magyars* (1889), Dame Hirip lived in a castle on the Varoldal mountain in Gyergyószentmiklós. She had two sons whom she sent down the mountain to rob travelers passing through of their gold and silver, and to kidnap human girls. She herself would stand on the tower of the castle, clutching a wreath in anticipation of her sons' return.

One day, the sons encountered the sweethearts of two of the girls they had kidnapped. The two heroes, clad in mourning for their brides-to-be, fought the sons and were victorious, whereupon Dame Hirip, stationed at her lookout on the castle tower clutching her wreath, faded away.

Dame Rapson

A fairy woman of the ***tündér***, the Hungarian fairies. The *tündér* were said to dwell in mountain castles that they inherited from **giants** or constructed themselves, often with the assistance of magical helpers. *The Folk Tales of the Maygars* (1889) relates how Dame Rapson enlisted the help of a magical cat and cock to construct her mountain abode.

The cat and cock carried materials to dizzying heights up a sheer-sided mountain face with which to build Dame Rapson's castle.

To construct the road leading to the castle, the fairy enlisted the help of the Devil, who demanded as payment a valley of silver and a mountain of gold.

After the road had been built, the Devil demanded his wages. The cunning fairy presented him with a gold coin, which she held between her fingertips, and a silver coin, which she placed on her palm, explaining that the gold coin was the mountain and the coin was the valley.

The Devil flew into a rage at being outwitted and destroyed the road. It is said that remnants of it are still visible in the snow-clad Gorgeny mountains near Paraja where it is still known as Dame Rapson's Road.

Dana

(Pronounced *thana.* Also Danu.) One of the great mother goddesses in Irish mythology. Particularly associated with the ***Tuatha de Danann***, she was also worshiped in other countries under different names. As mother of the gods, she has similarities with the mother figure **Don**, who features in the Welsh *Mabinogion* stories. In Lady Gregory's account of how the *Tuatha de Danann* came to Ireland, in *Gods and Fighting Men* (1904), special mention goes to Dana, whose power goes beyond that of all the other great queens.

Danu

See **Dana**.

Daoine Mainne

See ***Daoine Sidh***.

Daoine Sidh

(Pronounced *theena shee* or *deeny shee.*) (Also *Daoine Mainne.*) The fairy people of Ireland. They are said to dwell in hollow hills and the name literally means "people of the mounds." They are often referred to by euphemistic names such as the Little People, the **Gentry**, the **Wee Folk**, the Good People, or the People of that Town, so as not to cause offense. They are generally supposed to be the diminished gods of the ***Tuatha de Danann***, the early inhabitants of Ireland. Celtic legends tell of fairy ladies and heroic fairy knights who spent their time hunting, fishing, riding, and dancing.

Daphne

According to Greek myth, she was a beautiful mountain nymph who attracted the attention of the great god Apollo. But she rejected him and so that she could escape his pursuit, her mother, Gaea, the Earth Goddess, transformed her into a laurel tree.

At the Pythian Games, held every four years at Delphi in honor of Apollo, a wreath of laurel gathered from the Vale of Tempe in Thessaly was given as a prize. The laurel wreath is still regarded as a symbol of success.

Nay, Lady, sit. If I but wave this wand,
Your nerves are all chained up in alabaster,
And you a statue, or, as **Daphne** *was,*
Root-bound, that fled Apollo.

Milton, Comus *(678–681)*

Deevs

See ***Divs***.

Dennison, Walter Traill *(1826–1894)*

Walter Traill Dennison was a farmer, antiquarian, and folklorist. He was a native of the Orkney island of Sanday, where he collected local folk tales. He published these, many in the Orcadian dialect, in 1880, under the title *The Orcadian Sketch-Book*. His collection of Oracadian tales includes an account of an encounter with the fearsome **Nuckelavee**.

Derrick

Fairies in the folklore of Devon and Hampshire. In Devon they are considered to be ill-tempered, while in Hampshire they are regarded as friendly. In one account a farmer's wife described how she had lost her way on the Berkshire Downs when a little man dressed in green with a round smiling face appeared and told her which path to take; a local of Hampshire suggested he was a derrick.

Devas

(Also known as the "Shining Ones.") Benevolent supernatural beings in Hindu belief. Some devas represent the forces of nature, while others represent moral values. In the *Rigveda*, the ancient Indian collection of sacred hymns, **Indra** is the leader of the devas.

See also ***Apsaras, Gandharvas.***

Diana

In Roman mythology she is the goddess of the hunt, the moon, and birth, and is associated with wild animals, the wilderness, and the forest. She was said to dwell in the Forest of Nemi with the **nymph Egeria**. In Greek mythology she became identified with the goddess Artemis.

Diana is also a key figure in witchcraft, particularly the Italian witchcraft tradition *Stregheria. Aradia: Gospel of the Witches* (1899) describes Diana as the great spirit of the stars who made all men,

giants, and **dwarves**, and relates how one night a poor orphan boy saw a thousand little white figures dancing under the full moon. When he asked them who they were, they replied:

"We are moon-rays, the children of
Diana.
We are children of the moon;
We are born of shining light;
When the moon shoots forth a ray,
Then it takes a fairy's form."

DINNY MARA

(Pronounced *dunya mara.)* Manx **merman**. The *dinny mara* has a gentler temperament than the English merman. In Dora Broome's story "The Baby Mermaid," he is described as an affectionate father who played with his baby and gave her presents. This contrasts with the Cornish legend "Lutey and the Mermaid," in which the **mermaid** of Cury herself was harmless enough, but feared that her husband would eat their children if she didn't get home to feed him.

See also **Ben Varrey**.

DIREACH, THE

(Pronounced *jeeryuch.*) The Direach Ghlinn Eitidh is a type of **fachan** described in **J. F. Campbell**'s *Popular Tales of the West Highlands* (1860–1862). Fachans were particularly ugly creatures that had one hand protruding from their chest and a tuft of hair sprouting from the top of their head. The Direach was described as a **giant** woodcutter with one leg and one eye in the middle of his forehead.

DIVS

(Or *Deevs.*) Demons of Persian mythology, who are in constant battle against the **peris**, the good spirits or fairies. According to the Koran, they are gigantic, ferocious spirits ruled over by the evil spirit Eblis. William Finch, in *Purchas' Pilgrims*, describes them thus:

At Lahore, in the Mogul's palace, are pictures of Dews and Dives with long horns, staring eyes, shaggy hair, great fangs, ugly paws, long tails, and such horrible deformity, that I wonder the poor women are not frightened.

See also **Berkhyas**.

Djinn

(Also *jinn*, *jinni*, **genie**.) Shapeshifting spirits of Arabian mythology. There are many regional variations on the spelling; here *djinn* is used to indicate both singular and plural. Female *djinn* are named with the honorific title ***lalla***.

Djinn are described in **Thomas Keightley**'s *The Fairy Mythology* (1828) as spirits formed from smokeless fire, or the hot, dusty Simoom wind that blows across the Sahara and the Arabian peninsula. This fire is their life force and will erupt from their veins if they are injured, reducing them to nothing but ashes.

They can appear as gigantic and terrifying beings, such as the evil spirit in the tale of "The Fisherman and the *Djinn*" in *The Thousand and One Nights*, who takes the form of an *Ifrit*, one of the classes of *djinn*, or in human forms of great beauty, although it is said that a *djinn* disguised in the form of a beautiful woman can be recognized by certain tell-tale signs: vertical pupils in the eyes, or the hooves of a goat or a camel instead of feet.

According to Islamic tradition, the *djinn* rebelled against the powers of good, like the Fallen Angels of Christian belief. Azazel grew up among the angels, but when he refused to bow to Adam, he was transformed into the fearsome Iblis, father of the *Sheytans*, or evil spirits, and led the *djinn* in battle against the angels.

Djin or Diju is the name the occultist Elephas Levi used to refer to the 'sovereign' of the elementals of fire, known as **salamanders**.

Beliefs about *djinn* vary from region to region. In Egypt, malignant *djinn* pelted travelers with stones and were wont to steal food and women. *Zoba'ah*, or "dust devils," tall whirlwinds of sand in the desert, were said to indicate the path of a malevolent *djinn.*

In Morocco, there were various types of *djinn*. Each person was believed to have their own personal *djinn*, sometimes known as a ***qarin***, who accompanied them throughout their life. Earth *djinn* inhabited dark and isolated places such as graveyards and ruins, and their permission had to be sought before digging into the earth to lay the foundations for buildings. The malevolent water *djinn* inhabited lakes, rivers, wells, and fountains, and lured humans into the water to drown them. The tree *djinn*, on the other hand, were generally benevolent, affording shade for humans to rest in.

In Serbia and Albania, *djinns* were nefarious nature spirits dwelling in forests, mountains, and lakes. Travelers who fell foul of these evil spirits were subjected to nightmarish visions and became disoriented, wandering lost in the forests or the mountains.

Poets and prophets have taken inspiration from the legends of the *djinn* for many centuries, and through Islamic texts knowledge of their supernatural presence and attributes has been disseminated across many parts of the world.

The most famous descriptions of *djinn* are to be found in *The Thousand and One Nights*, which incorporate tales from Arabic, Persian, Indian, and Egyptian folklore. The tales are framed by the story of Scheherazade and the Sultan Shahriyar. After executing his wife for adultery, the sultan vows to take a different wife each night and have her executed in the morning. When Scheherazade is called upon to go to him, she uses her talent for storytelling to captivate his imagination, so that each morning he longs to hear what will happen next and thus preserves her life for one more day.

"The Fisherman and the *Djinn*" is the second tale that Scheherazade narrates in Jonathan Scott's English translation of the *Arabian Nights Entertainments* (1883).

Once there was an old fisherman so poor that he could barely feed his family. Very early one day, as was his habit, he cast his nets and as he drew them in they felt very heavy.

"At last," he thought, "my fortune has changed for the better."

But as he hauled his nets onto the beach, he saw that all he had caught was the carcass of an ass. He was greatly disappointed, and had to spend time mending his damaged nets.

He waded into the sea and cast the nets once more, and again found them offering great resistance as he pulled them to the shore. But all he found was a basket of gravel and slime.

"Alas," said he, "fortune has deserted me!"

But he could not give up and tried again, only to haul in stones, shells, and mud.

As the day dawned, he said his prayers and added a plea, saying, "Good Lord, grant me a good catch on this my final cast of the day."

Yet again his nets were very heavy, but this time he found a vessel of yellow copper. He examined it closely and when he saw that it had been sealed with a lid of lead, he thought, "Maybe my prayers have been answered—this may contain something of great value."

He took his knife and carefully broke the seal. As he removed the lid a very thick black smoke poured out, causing him to stumble backward. The smoke filled the sky and covered the shore, finally forming into the gigantic terrifying form of a *djinn.*

Frozen with fear, the fisherman cowered before the apparition as these words boomed out: "Solomon, Solomon, great prophet, grant me pardon. I will never more oppose your will. I will obey all your commands!"

At this, the fisherman somewhat recovered and said, "Proud spirit, what is this? It is 1,800 years since Solomon died. Tell me your story and how you came to be imprisoned in this vessel."

The *djinn* looked down upon the man and said, "You must have more respect for me or I will take your life!"

"Why would you do that?" asked the fisherman. "Did I not set you free?"

"Yes, but that is not enough to save your life. The only favor I can grant you is to choose the manner of your death."

The *djinn* then explained his story. He had been a rebellious spirit and had not submitted to the will of Solomon, even when brought before the prophet himself. As a punishment he was shut up in the copper vessel and the prophet stamped the leaden seal with the great name of God . . . The vessel was thrown into the sea and there the *djinn* had remained.

Despite all the promises he had made of rewards for anyone who released him, no one had done so. Finally becoming quite deranged, he swore that he would kill anyone who released him, only granting him the choice in the manner of his death.

The fisherman begged the *djinn* to spare him, and spoke of his wife and his children, who must surely perish without his support. But the *djinn* was unmoved and said, "Make haste, all your pleas will not change my mind. Decide only what kind of death you will prefer."

"I ask you one more question, in the name of God, engraved by Solomon, the son of David, on the leaden seal, that you should answer me truly," said the fisherman.

"Very well," said the *djinn.* "But only one question."

"It is this," said the fisherman, "will you swear that you were in this copper vessel?"

"Yes!" bellowed the *djinn.* "I swear by the name of God that I was."

"This I cannot believe," said the fisherman. "One of your great size could not be in such a vessel."

"But I have sworn it to be true!" shouted the *djinn,* losing patience.

"I will not believe you until you demonstrate the truth of this matter," said the brave fisherman.

So the *djinn* dissolved once more into smoke and gradually slipped back into the copper urn until not a trace of him was left.

"Now do you believe me?" came a voice from within the vessel.

Instead of answering, the fisherman quickly re-sealed the leaden lid and hurled the copper vessel far into the sea. He could hear the pleading voice of the *djinn* promising him all the riches of the world if he would only release him once more, but he cried, "Thou art a traitor, and I would deserve to lose my life if I were to trust you. You would treat me in the same manner as a certain Grecian king treated the physician Douban. It is a story I will tell you."

And so Scheherazade ended one tale and began another in order to preserve her life.

Dobbs

(Or Master Dobbs.) A Sussex **brownie** who helps around the home. Like the Highland ***Bo-***

dachan Sabhaill, he is particularly kind and helpful to old men. The saying "Master Dobbs has been helping you" is used when someone has got through more work than was expected. In Yorkshire the same character is called **Dobby**.

Dobby

A friendly, playful **hob** in Yorkshire and Lancashire. Like a **brownie**, he can be helpful, but is prone to a bit of mischief-making as well. He is similar to **Robin Goodfellow**. More recently, this old folklore character has been given a new lease of life as Dobby the house elf in J. K. Rowling's Harry Potter stories.

Dobie

A type of **brownie**. According to William Henderson in *Notes on the Folklore of the Northern Counties of England and the Borders* (1866), he is less quick-witted than most brownies, which is confirmed by the colloquial usage "She's but a dobie" or "Ye stupid dobie!"

In times of unrest on the Anglo-Scottish border, it was the custom for people to hide their valuable items by burying them and entrusting them to a brownie for safekeeping. In the event that no brownies were available, people would resort to enlisting the help of a willing but often gullible dobie.

A different type of dobie was the Dobie of Morthan Tower, Rokeby, who was part-ghost, part-**hobgoblin**, similar to the **Cauld Lad of Hilton**. He was said to be the ghost of one of the Lord of Rokeby's ex-wives, who had been murdered by her jealous husband in the glen below the tower.

Domovoi

A domestic spirit of Slavic folklore. Traditionally, they made their home at threshold points of the house, such as the hearth, the cellar, or the loft, and were guardians of the household and its property, including its animals. Members of the household left offerings of milk or bread to thank the *domovoi* for completing household chores or to ensure their continued protection and guardianship.

Domovoi were believed to prefer livestock that matched their own coloring. Families chose cattle or horses on this basis to encourage a *domovoi's* help in tending the animals, for it was said that a *domovoi* lavished attention on beasts that he favored, grooming them and ensuring that they were well cared for. However, if a *domovoi* took a dislike to an animal, he tormented it by tangling its mane, riding it at night to the point of exhaustion, or hiding its food.

Domovoi were usually heard, but not seen. When they did show themselves, it was often as small, bearded old men, sometimes with hairy hands and feet, sometimes covered entirely in hair.

Don

Mother goddess of Welsh mythology, who features in the *Mabinogion* stories. There are parallels between her and the Irish goddess **Dana**. The Children of Don were in frequent conflict with the Children of **Llyr**. Some interpreted this as a battle between powers of light, represented by the Children of Don, and the powers of darkness, represented by the Children of Llyr, while others characterized it as struggle between the indigenous Welsh deities and the deities of an invading people.

Don's children included **Govannon** the silver-handed smith (similar to the Irish Gobniu), Ludd or Nudd of Nuada, and the many-skilled Gwydion, a warrior, magician, poet, and musician, similar to the Irish **Lug**.

Dormette, La

A sleep fairy in Franch folklore. She is a nursery spirit who, like the English **Sandman** and the Danish **Ole Luk Øj**, lulls children into a pleasant night's slumber.

Dracs

In the folklore of southern France, shapeshifting water spirits that dwell in caverns and rivers.

The medieval chronicler **Gervase of Tilbury** gave an account of *dracs* in his thirteenth-century work the *Otia Imperialia.* According to him, they could be seen on moonlit nights in the shape of men, bathing in great pools on the banks of the river Rhone by the north gate of the city of Arles. Taking human form, they were also known to visit the marketplace early in the morning. They could assume the shape of golden cups, or rings and would float down the river to entice women or children bathing to reach out for the glittering treasure. However, on attempting to catch their prize, the bathers would be dragged down to the bottom of the river. Suckling women were particularly sought after by the *dracs* to nurse their offspring.

In one tale a woman was washing clothes on the bank of the Rhone when a wooden bowl floated past. Attempting to catch it, she waded out into the deep water and a *drac* dragged her down. After seven years of living with him and his wife and rearing their son, she was returned unharmed. She related how the *dracs* lived off the people they carried away and of how one day when the *drac* had given her an eel pasty to eat she had wiped her eye with a greasy finger and experienced perfectly clear vision underwater.

After she had returned to her family on land, she visited the marketplace very early one morning and saw the *drac.* She greeted him and asked after the health of his wife and child. "With which eye do you see me?" he replied. When she pointed to the eye that she had rubbed with fat, he immediately poked it out, whereupon he was no longer visible to anyone.

See also **Eilian of Garth Dorwen**.

Draugen

A Norwegian sea spirit. Described as a headless fisherman dressed in oilskins who rides the seas in half a boat, he takes him name from *draugr*, the Old Norse for "ghost," and is the personification of all the souls the sea has claimed. His wailing is said to portend a shipwreck or death at sea.

DRYADS

Tree spirits, or **nymphs**, from Greek mythology. Deriving from the Greek *drus*, meaning "oak tree," "dryad" has come to refer to all tree spirits.

These female spirits were guardians and protectors of the forest. Hamadryads were spirits associated with one particular tree, who died when their tree died or was felled.

Eurydice, the wife of **Orpheus** the poet, was a dryad.

DUERGAR

Brewer's Dictionary of Phrase and Fable (1898) describes Duergar thus:

Dwarfs who dwell in rocks and hills; noted for their strength, magical powers and skill in metallurgy. They are the personification of the subterranean powers of nature. According to the Gotho-German myth, the Duergar were first maggots in Ymir's flesh, but afterwards assumed the likeness of men. The first Duergar was Modsogner, the next Dyrin.

A tale of the malicious Duergar of the Simonside Hills of Northumberland is related in F. Grice's *Folk-tales of the North Country* (1944).

A stranger on his way to Rothbury got lost in the hills. As night fell, with no familiar landmarks to guide him, he decided to find shelter and wait for morning. When he found a shepherd's hut with a fire smoldering inside he couldn't believe his luck. There were two gray stones on either side of the fire, to the right of which was a pile of kindling and to the left two great logs. The traveler settled himself on the stone on the right and stoked up the fire with some kindling.

He had been sitting there only for a moment when the door burst open and a strange figure came into the room. He was a dwarf, no taller than the traveler's knee, but very broad and strong. He was dressed in a lambskin coat, a green hat of moss decorated with a pheasant's feather, and moleskin shoes and trousers. He scowled at the traveler, but remained silent and perched himself on the other stone. Suspecting this was a Duergar, the traveler daren't speak.

As the fire began to die down it became bitterly cold. When the traveler could bear it no longer, he put some more kindling on the fire. The dwarf looked at him with anger and disdain, and picked up one of the large logs. Though the log was bigger than he was, he easily broke it across his knee and looked at the traveler as if challenging him to do the same.

The fire blazed up for a time, but soon it began to die down. The kindling was all gone. Still the dwarf scowled and looked at the traveler as if to challenge him to put on the last log. Suspecting a trap, the traveler did nothing, despite the cold that was gnawing into his body.

The fire died out and two sat on in cold darkness, until a faint light crept into the sky and a cock crowed in the distance. At the sound the dwarf vanished, and the hut and fire with him. The traveler was still sitting on his stone, but he now saw that he was perched high up on the peak of a steep crag. If he had moved to pick up the log in answer to the Duergar's silent challenge, he would have fallen down the sheer drop to certain death.

Dunnie

A shapeshifting spirit of Northumbria, the dunnie has been described variously as a donkey, a horse, and a man.

According to the *Denham Tracts* (1892–1895), the Hazelrigg dunnie was the ghost of a Border reiver. In the Middle Ages, when England and Scotland were often at war, reivers were raiders who lived along the Anglo-Scottish border, making their living by plundering communities on the opposing side, taking livestock and valuables. It was said that the Hazelrigg dunnie was a reiver who had hidden his ill-gotten gains in a cave on Belford Moor near Hazelrigg but had been put to death for robbing a local granary and died before he could reveal the hiding place. He had haunted the area ever since. He was a mischievous spirit and one of his favorite pranks was to take the form of the ploughman's old plodding horse, allowing himself to be yoked and walked out to the field, only to slip the harness, kick up his heels and gallop away across the fields, leaving a startled ploughman in his wake.

See also **Colt Pixy**.

DUNTERS

See **Powries**.

DWARVES

Diminutive, humanoid creatures found in the folklore of many cultures around the world, often described as wizened males, dwelling in underground caverns or subterranean palaces.

In Teutonic mythology white, brown, and black dwarves inhabited the Isle of Rügen. White dwarves were gentle creatures, skilled in the art of metalwork, brown dwarves were similar in nature to the **brownie** of British and Scottish folklore, and black dwarves were malicious, using their skill in metalwork to forge deadly weapons.

According to Scandinavian mythology, dwarves developed from maggots that crawled out of the flesh of the **giant** Ymir. Like their Teutonic counterparts, they were skilled smiths; in Norse legends retold in Bulfinch's *Mythology: The Age of Fable* (1913), they fabricated Gleipnir, a magical and unbreakable chain, to bind the wolf Fenris. As fine and soft as a ribbon, the binding was fashioned from "the noise made from the footfall of a cat, the beards of women, the roots of stones, the breath of fishes, the nerves [sensibilities] of bears, and the spittle of birds." In the *Prose Edda*, a major repository of Old Norse mythology, "Loki and the Dwarf" describes the magical items forged by the dwarf Brock, a master smith (*see "Fairies in Literature and Legend," p.407*).

Elsewhere, the ***biloko*** is a malevolent flesh-eating dwarf of the forests of Zaire. In northern England, the nefarious **duergar** lured travelers up dangerous mountain crags.

See also **Brown Man of the Muirs**, ***Gahongas***, **Galar**, **King Herla**, **Laurin**, ***Mmotia***, ***Nain Rouge***, **Nuno sa Punso**, **Thekk**, **Tom Thumb**, **Trows**, **Yellow Dwarf**.

Dzunukwa

See ***Tsonokwa***.

E

E Bukura e Dheut

The Albanian Queen of the Fairies. She dwells in a fairytale castle on top of a mountain guarded by fabulous creatures, including a three-headed dog. The epitome of beauty and happiness, she is sometimes invoked as the ideal woman. She rules over a host of beautiful, capricious, unpredictable spirits, who can be kind and generous or malevolent and destructive.

Originally she was the goddess of beauty and love of the Illyrians, an Indo-European people who were the ancestors of many Albanians. Tomor, her lover, was the supreme deity of the Illyrians.

Her name means "Beauty of the Earth." Her sisters are E Bukura e Detit and E Bukura e Qeillit, respectively "Beauty of the Sea" and "Beauty of Heaven."

Each Uisge

(Pronounced *ech-ooshkya.)* The **water horse** of the Scottish Highlands, a malevolent and treacherous shapeshifter dwelling in the sea and lochs. Appearing as a noble horse, it would wait beside a loch for an unwary rider, who would find themselves held firmly to its sticky skin, unable to dismount as the horse galloped full pelt into deep water in order to drown its victim. It would then voraciously consume the body, leaving only the liver, which would later appear on the shores of the loch, the only evidence of another victim claimed by the *each uisge.*

The *each uisge* could assume human form in the shape of a handsome man, a boy, a ring, or even a tuft of wool, according to accounts in **J. F. Campbell**'s *Superstitions of the Highlands and Islands of Scotland* (1900).

See also ***Aughisky***, ***Cabyll Ushtey***, **Noggle**.

Edimmu

See ***Ekimmu***.

Efnisien

See **Bran the Blessed**.

Egeria

A wise Roman **nymph**, Egeria dwells in the Forest of Nemi with the goddess **Diana** and acts as her servant and assistant midwife. She appears as a beautiful woman or mermaid. She was once the advisor to and lover of Numa Pomilius, second king of Rome after Romulus. Her spring was said to flow from a giant oak in the forest; its waters carried powers of prophecy, wisdom, and fertility.

Ehaema, Twilight Mother

In Estonian and many other folk legends, the hours at dusk and dawn are rife with the actions of the spirit world, the Twilight Mother being one whose intentions could be benign yet could also cause illness and nightmares in adults and children. Should the light of dawn fall across a baby as it lay asleep, it could cause a painful stomach upset that could only be cured by taking a spoonful of mother's milk, placing it on the windowsill where the light could reach it, and dosing the child with it as medicine.

In her benign aspect, the Twilight Mother encouraged the practice of work, especially spinning, but if the spinning wheel was left untidy, the ghostly sound of the Twilight Mother could be heard as she sat at the wheel.

Eidothea

A sea **nymph** in Greek mythology, daughter of the sea god Proteus. In Homer's *Odyssey* she rescues Menelaus from the island of Pharos by concealing him and three stalwarts beneath sealskins, the "hideous stench of the briny creatures" being mitigated by the ambrosia that she puts beneath their nostrils. They capture Proteus as he walks on the shore and force him to reveal the means of their escape.

Eilian of Garth Dorwen

The golden-haired Eilian was the servant of an elderly midwife and her husband who lived in Garth Dorwen in Wales. On moonlit winter evenings she would go into the meadow to spin while the ***Tylwyth Teg*** danced and sang around her. One spring evening, as the days grew longer, she went to the field—and was never seen again.

Some time later, a horseman knocked on the old woman's door to ask her to come to his wife. They arrived at a cave dwelling, which appeared to the old lady as sumptuously furnished. When the babe was born, the midwife took it to be dressed and the husband handed her some ointment to put upon the baby's eyes. He admonished her to be sure not to touch her own eyes, but absentmindedly she scratched an itch on her eyelid—immediately, with that one eye, the cave appeared as dark and meanly furnished, and she saw that the mother of the child, lying on a bed of rushes, was her own former servant Eilian.

Sometime later, the midwife was at market and saw the husband and asked him, "How is Eilian?"

He replied, "She is well, but with which eye do you see me?"

When she pointed to it, he took a bulrush and put it out.

Ekimmu

(Or *edimmu.*) Ancient Assyrian mythology describes an *ekimmu* as an undead spirit of the wind, possessed of vengeful powers and hostile to mortals. Forever denied entrance to the Underworld, these spirits were feared for their ability to attach themselves to the living.

See also **Utukku.**

Elabigathan

See **Elaby Gathen**.

Elaby Gathen

(Or Elabigathan.) A spell to call a fairy appears in a seventeenth-century manuscript, part of which reads: "I conjure thee Elaby Gathen . . . that thou appeare presently meekely and myldly in this glasse without doeinge hurt of daunger unto me or any other livinge creature . . . This call *ut supra* [as above] is to call Elabigathan A Fayrie."

Elder Tree, the Old Lady of the

In folklore the elder tree is a powerful symbol of healing and regeneration, owing to its vigorous growth, and there are many superstitions about not cutting down an elder for fear of causing offense to the Old Lady, the guardian spirit of the tree. In Danish folklore she is a **dryad** known as ***Hylde-moer***, Elder Tree Mother, who will haunt the houses of those who chop down the tree to make furniture. To make a baby's cradle from elderwood is considered very unlucky, for the Elder Tree Mother will take revenge by pinching the poor child mercilessly until it is black and blue.

Elf

See **Elves**.

Elf-Bull

The elf-bull is described in Robert Jamieson's *Northern Antiquities* (1814) as:

. . . small, compared with earthly bulls, of a mouse-colour; mosted [crop-eared], with short corky horns; short

in the legs; long, round and slamp [supple] in the body, like a wild animal; with short, sleek and glittering hair, like an otter; and supernaturally active and strong. They most frequently appear near the banks of rivers; eat much green corn in the night-time . . .

The story continues with an account of a farmer "who lived by the banks of a river, had a cow that was never known to admit an earthly bull; but every year . . . she regularly quitted her pasture, walked slowly along the banks of the river, till she came opposite to a small holm covered with bushes . . ." She swam the river and stayed on the little island for a time then returned to her pasture. Each year a calf was born, "all alike, mouse-coloured, mosted, with corky horns, round and long-bodied, grew to a good size, and were remarkably docile, strong, and useful . . ." After several years the farmer said to his wife that Hawkie should be slaughtered, being "fat and sleek . . . and now I think we may afford to pick her old bones." No sooner was this uttered than Hawkie "walked out through the side of the byre with as much ease as if it had been made of brown paper; . . . lowed once upon each of her calves; then set out, they following her in order . . . along the banks of the river." They were neither seen nor heard of again and the farmer and his sons "returned with heavy hearts to their house, and had little thought . . . or merriment for that year."

Elidor and the Golden Ball

The story of Elidor, his visits to fairyland, and his eventual disgrace was first recorded in the year 1188. In **Thomas Keightley**'s *The Fairy Mythology* (1828), the story runs as follows.

Elidor, a "youth of twelve years," was hiding from his tutor's harsh discipline by concealing himself by a river when "two little men of pygmy stature appeared to him, saying, 'If you will come with us, we will lead you into a country full of delights and sports.'" They arrived in a beautiful country that was but "obscure and not illuminated by the full light of the sun. All the days were cloudy and nights extremely dark, on account of the absence of the moon and stars." The denizens of this country were small, with long, golden hair, and lived on a diet of milk "made up into messes with saffron." They revered truth above all else and denounced mortals for their "ambition, infidelities, and inconstancies."

Elidor told his mother of his secret visits to the magical land rich in gold, whereupon his mother asked him to bring her a golden gift. On his next visit he fled with a golden ball belonging to the king's son. Hastening back to his mother, he tripped and fell on the threshold of the house, dropping the golden ball in his alarm. Following closely behind him, ". . . the two Pygmies seized the ball . . . and departed, spitting at and deriding the boy. On recovering from his fall, confounded with shame, and execrating the evil counsel of his mother, he returned by the usual track to the subterraneous road, but found no appearance of any passage though he searched for it on the banks of the river for nearly the space of a year."

After many years, and having been "restored to his right way of thinking," Elidor became Elidurus, a priest.

Ellylldan

A Welsh name for the **will o' the wisp**. In *British Goblins* by **Wirt Sikes** (1880), there is an account by Iolo the Bard of an encounter with this tricksy **elf**:

One night, when the moon had gone down, as I was sitting on a hill-top, the Ellylldan passed by. I followed it into the valley. We crossed plashes of water where the tops of bulrushes peeped above, and where the lizards lay silently on the surface, looking at us with an unmoved stare. The frogs sat croaking and swelling their sides, but ceased as they raised a melancholy eye at the Ellylldan . . . I felt the trail of the eels and leeches peering about, as I waded through the pools. On a slimy stone a toad sat sucking poison from the night air. The Ellylldan

glowed bravely in the slumbering vapours. It rose airily over the bushes that drooped in the ooze. When I lingered or stopped, it waited for me, but dwindled gradually away to a speck barely perceptible. But as soon as I moved on again, it would shoot up suddenly and glide before . . . Suddenly it shot away from me, and in the distance joined a ring of its fellows, who went dancing slowly round and round in a goblin dance, which sent me off to sleep.

ELOKO

See **Biloko**.

ELVES

In Norse mythology, elves were divided into dark elves and light elves, in a similar way to the Scottish **Unseelie** and **Seelie Court**. Some people equate the dark elves with **trolls**.

According to **Snorri Sturluson**'s "*Gylfaginning*" (The Tricking of Gylfi) in the *Prose Edda*:

*There is one place there that is called the Elf Home [*Álfheimr, *which is the elven city]. People live there that are named the light elves [*Ljósálfar*]. But the dark elves [*Dökkálfar*)] live below in earth, in caves and the dark forest and they are unlike them in appearance – and more unlike them in reality. The Light Elves are brighter than the sun in appearance, but the Dark Elves are blacker than pitch.*

The elves and the Norse Vanir spirits are closely affiliated. The Vanir god Freyr, spirit of vegetation, was said to have dominion over the elves and is sometimes referred to as the elven king.

Scandinavians continued to believe in the elves, or *huldre* folk, into Christian times. In gray dresses and white veils, *huldre* females were alluring and enticing, but had long cows' tails. Danish elves, or *ellewomen*, appeared as beautiful, but with a hollow space where their back should be. The males appeared as old men, wearing low-crowned hats, often to be seen basking in sunbeams on Elle-moors. Get too close to a male elf and he would open his mouth wide, breathing on you with breath that brought sickness and pestilence. The females were more often to be seen by moonlight, gracefully dancing and playing stringed instruments. Young men, beware, it is said that when you hear them playing their music, it will steal your heart away.

The name "elf" came to Britain from the Scandinavian tradition and in Anglo-Saxon *leechdoms*, or charm books, containing medicines and healing remedies, we find references to remedies for elf-shot and other elvish tricks and misdemeanors. To be elf-shot was to be struck by the elves' small flint arrowheads. Livestock or people who were elf-shot experienced illness or disability, including sudden cramps and seizures. Scottish witch Isobel Gowdie claimed to have visited elf-hills where she saw elf-boys fashioning the arrows under the direction of the Devil himself. Witches would sometimes venture on airborne flights with the Devil, taking the elves' arrows to flip at people or cattle passing below.

There every herd, by sad experience, knows
How, winged with fate, their elf-shot arrows fly,
When the sick ewe her summer food forgoes,
Or, stretched on earth, the heart-smit heifers lie.

William Collins, Ode on the Popular Superstitions of the Highlands of Scotland *(1750)*

The Old English for "nightmare" is *aelfadl*, and "hiccup" is *aelfsogoða*—both afflictions were apparently thought to be caused by elves. In German folklore, an *Alp*, a variation of the word "elf," is a creature, usually male, that sits on its victim's chest during the night, causing horrible nightmares. The German for nightmare is *Alptraum*, literally, "elf dream." An *Alp* attack is an *Alpdruck*, meaning "elf pressure." *Alpdruck* is caused by the *Alp* sitting on the sleeper's chest, its weight pressing down until the terrified, breathless dreamer is awoken by the crushing pressure. This may be an early explanation for conditions such as sleep paralysis or sleep apnea.

Less terrifying are unruly elf-locks—tangles and knots that appear in the morning after elves have spent the night playing in the hair of sleeping children or the manes of sleeping beasts.

She is the fairies' midwife, and she
comes
In shape no bigger than an agate
stone . . .
That plaits the manes of horses in the
night
And bakes the elflocks in foul sluttish
hairs,
Which once untangled, much
misfortune bodes.

Mercutio's speech about Queen Mab in Shakespeare's Romeo and Juliet.

In Elizabethan times, light elves came to be viewed as more homely, similar to the small **trooping fairies** in Shakespeare's *A Midsummer Night's Dream.* Like Scottish fairies in character, they were small, tricksy creatures who terrorized cattle, stole humans away, and avenged injuries done to them.

Elves played a central role in J. R. R. Tolkien's fictional universe Middle Earth, with the Elven folk featuring in *The Hobbit* and *The Lord of the Rings* as a beautiful, wise race of beings, skilled in archery with highly attuned senses and a love of song and nature, who dwell in Rivendell and other places.

Modern depictions of Christmas elves in the United States, United Kingdom, Canada, and Ireland are of Santa's busy helpers in green hats, with pointy ears and pointed shoes (as portrayed in the film *Elf* [2003]). In Greek folk tradition, the *Kallikantzaroi* are not so benign. Every year, they leave their underground dwellings and come to the surface of the Earth from the winter solstice until Epiphany on January 6th. For the rest of the year they live underground, sawing at the World Tree that supports the Earth. Just as they are about to finally saw through the tree, Christmas dawns and they are able to come to the surface for the 16 days following winter solstice, when the sun was said to cease its movement. The *Kallikantzoroi* forget about the tree and come to wreak havoc among the humans. Keeping a fire burning in the hearth or leaving a colander on the doorstep are traditional forms of protection against their evil doings. Seeing the colander, they are compelled to count the holes. Not being able to count above two, three being the holy number of the trinity, they have to remain on the doorstep counting all night, until the sun rises and they are forced to seek the cover of darkness and hide. When Epiphany comes around and the sun commences its course once more, the *Kallikantzoroi* are forced back underground to start their sawing again, only to discover that in their absence the World Tree has healed itself and they must start their task all over again. And so the cycle continues each year.

Erdhenne

According to German tradition the *Erdhenne*, or Earth Hen, is a guardian spirit of the farm, remaining hidden from sight but clucking loudly to warn of imminent danger.

Erdluitle

Literally, the "earth folk." In the folklore of the Alps of northern Italy and Switzerland, these **elf**-like beings dwell in mountain forests and caves. Between 1 and 3 feet (up to 1 meter) tall, they are described as having ruddy complexions, long beards, and webbed feet, which they are careful to keep hidden from the view of humans.

The animals of the mountain are under their stewardship, and they particularly prize chamois mountain goats for their milk, which they turn into *chamois* milk cheese.

They also hold sway over the weather and can command avalanches, floods, and storms.

Ergetz, Fairy Princess of

"Ergetz, the land of demons, of djinns and of fairies" is described in a Jewish fairy tale which relates the adventures—and misadventures—of Bar Shalmon in his quest to find his father's riches.

Bar Shalmon was obliged to marry the fairy king's daughter when, in captivity in a city, he opened a forbidden door and saw "a beautiful woman, the most beautiful he had ever seen . . . seated on a throne of gold, surrounded by fairy attendants, who vanished the moment he entered." Years passed, but Bar Shalmon had not forgotten his native land or his wife and children. He promised to return to the fairy princess if he could only return home for a year.

Once there, he resumed his former life and the year went by. The princess sent many messengers asking him to return to her, but he refused.

"'Nay, I will go,' said the princess; 'it will be impossible for my husband to resist me." She selected a large number of attendants, and the swift flight of the princess and her retinue through the air caused a violent storm to rage over the lands they crossed. Like a thick, black cloud they swooped down on the land where Bar Shalmon dwelt, and their weird cries seemed like the wild shrieking of a mighty hurricane. Down they swept in a tremendous storm such as the city had never known."

The fairy princess implored Bar Shalmon to return to her and showed him their son, "a dainty elfin boy whose face was the image of Bar Shalmon," as evidence that he was her husband, but he steadfastly denied her and replied, "I agree to anything that will rid me of the demon princess."

Flushing crimson with rage and shame at these cruel words, the princess asked for one last kiss and cried, "Take thy punishment for all thy sins, for thy broken vows and thy false promises—thy perjury to thy God, to thy father, to my father and to me."

As she spoke, Bar Shalmon fell dead at her feet.

At a sign from the princess, her retinue of fairies and demons flew out of the building and up into the air, with their royal mistress in their midst, and vanished.

Erlking

There is some debate about the origin and form of this omen of death. According to the original Danish myth, it is a female malicious spirit, the Alder King's daughter, but in translation it has been rendered as male, the Alder King—Erlking or Erlkönig—himself.

Goethe's poem *Der Erlkönig* describes a father's desperate ride to save his child from the attack of the Alder King, but to no avail:

My father, my father, he seizes me fast,
For sorely the Alder King has hurt
me at last.
The father now gallops, with terror
half wild,
He holds in his arms the shuddering
child;
He reaches his farmstead with toil
and dread –
The child in his arms lies motionless,
dead.

Erlkönig

See **Erlking**.

Eschenfrau

See ***Askafroa***.

Eshu

In the Yoruba belief system, which originated in Nigeria, West Africa, and has spread throughout the Caribbean and South America, Eshu is a venerated ***orisha*** who acts as the messenger between the gods and humankind. He is mostly benevolent and has knowledge of the future. As a trickster, however, he has the power to help or hinder, therefore requires many sacrifices if a beneficial outcome is to be assured.

Etain of the Tuatha de Danann

In Irish folklore, *The Destruction of Da Derga Hostel* describes her beauty:

A gentle, womanly dignity in her voice; a steady, stately step, the walk of a queen. She was the fairest and most perfect and most beautiful of all the women in the world; men thought she was of the Síde, and they said of her: "Lovely anyone until Étain. Beautiful anyone until Étain."

Her love story with **Midhir** has been the inspiration for many plays, books, and music in which the fairy folk are portrayed in the heroic tradition as powerful and fearless.

Lady Wilde, in *Ancient Legends, Mystic Charms, and Superstitions of Ireland* (1887), relates how Midhir, a fairy chief of the ***Tuatha de Danann*** became enraptured by Etain's great beauty and won her from her husband, Eochaid of Munster, High King of Ireland, in a game of chess. Midhir took Etain to live in the fairy hills, and fighting ensued between Eochaid and the *Tuatha de Danann.*

Lady Gregory gives a fuller account of Etain and Midhir's story in *Gods and Fighting Men* (1904) and it runs as follows.

Etain was the second wife of Midhir, fairy chief of the *Tuatha de Danann.* His jealous first wife, Fuamnach, cast a spell on her, turning her into a fly and sending a cold blast of wind to carry her away from the fairy hills to Ireland.

For seven years Etain was blown to and fro across Ireland in great misery, until she came to the hall of a king, where she fell into the queen's goblet of wine. The queen swallowed her, and after nine months in her belly, Etain was reborn, and again called Etain. She grew into a beautiful woman and married Eochaid of Munster.

Midhir, who had been searching for her, discovered her whereabouts and challenged Eochain to three games of chess. He lost the first two, but won the third and named Etain as his prize. Eochain was reluctant to give up his wife, but agreed to allow Midhir one kiss. When he came to claim his kiss, Midhir raised his sword in his left hand and put his right arm around Etain and the two rose up out of the roof of the palace and flew back to the fairy hills as two white swans joined by a golden chain.

Eochaid and his men came to find Etain and dug into Midhir's fairy hill. Eventually Etain returned to her mortal husband and the *Tuatha de Danann*'s power dwindled thereafter.

Ethna the Bride

The story of the abduction of the beautiful young bride, Ethna, by Finvarra, the fairy king, is told in

Ancient Legends, Mystic Charms, and Superstitions of Ireland by **Lady Wilde** (1887).

Ethna was loved by her young lord, but during festivities at her castle, she "was floating through the dance, shining like moonlight in her silver dress, [when] her hand slipped from her partner's and she fell to the ground in a swoon. Nothing would revive her, and they carried her to bed where she lay motionless. In the morning she seemed to revive, but would speak of nothing but a beautiful country that she had visited, and to which she longed to return."

Finvarra and his sprites held Ethna captive in his seemingly impregnable underground dwelling, but "the young lord had a brave heart" and tried to rescue her. After many a thwarted attempt, Ethna was restored to him, but "on the bed she lay . . . like a waxen image and nothing would rouse her." Her husband was aided by friendly voices in the air who said he "could win her back to mortal life if he undid the girdle round her waist and took out the fairy pin with which it was fastened. If he burned the girdle and sprinkled the ashes outside her door and buried the pin in the earth, then her human soul would come back to her."

This he did, and Ethna "sat up in bed and stretched out her arms to him. She knew and remembered everything, except that the year she had spent in Fairyland was like the dream of a single night."

See also **Fin Bheara**.

Evans-Wentz, Walter Yeeling *(1878–1965)*

An American anthropologist and folklorist, Evans-Wentz was born in Trenton, New Jersey, to a German father and Irish mother. As a teenager he read Madame Blavatsky's books and became interested in Theosophy. He graduated from Stanford University, where he met **W. B. Yeats**. He then went to Jesus College, Oxford, England, where he studied Celtic mythology. He traveled widely through Ireland (where he met Yeats again), the Highlands of Scotland, Wales, Cornwall, the Isle of Man, and Brittany, collecting and recording fairy stories, experiences, and beliefs from the people he met.

Evans-Wentz was especially interested in the Celtic doctrines of rebirth. He published the results of his research in *The Fairy-Faith in Celtic Countries* (1911). He later traveled through Mexico, the Far East, and Ceylon (now Sri Lanka) to India, where he mixed with the Theosophist community in the land that had inspired Madame Blavatsky and encountered the spiritual teachers about whom he wrote in his books. He is most noted for the book *The Tibetan Book of the Dead or the After Death Experiences on the Bardo Plane*, published in 1927 (although he is often credited with the translation, Evans-Wentz did not speak Tibetan and the text was probably translated by the Lama Kazi Dawa-Samdup).

Ezerinis

A Lithuanian water spirit taking its name from *ezeras*, meaning "lake."

F

FACHAN

(Also Fachin, Fachen, or Peg Leg Jack.) A most frightening creature from Scottish and Irish folklore with only half a body, one eye, and one leg, he is described by **J. F. Campbell** in *Popular Tales of the West Highlands* (1860–1862) thus: "Ugly was the make of the Fachin; there was one hand out of the ridge of his chest, and one tuft out of the top of his head, it were easier to take a mountain from the root than to bend that tuft."

See also **Direach**.

FACHEN

See **Fachan**.

FACHIN

See **Fachan**.

FAIRY BUTTER

Part of the culture surrounding fairy folk relates to their churning butter while the household sleeps. H. S. Cowper writes in his history of *Hawkshead* (1899) in the Lake District: "They were, however, rather thriftless little folk, for . . . it was common to find bits of butter scattered in the woods, dropped, it would seem, by the uncanny churners in their morning flight."

FAND

In Celtic mythology, a *Sidhe* fairy queen and sea goddess, married to Manannan mac Lir, a Manx sea god. A shapeshifter taking the form of a seabird and of exceptional beauty, she is described in *The Sickbed of Cuchulain* (*see* **Cuchullin**):

Fand's beauty stuns, like sound of
rushing waters;
Before her splendour kings and
queens seem small . . .

In her manifestation as a seabird she received a blow from a stone slung by Cuchulain and in retribution while he slept she and her sister **Liban** laughed and whipped him "and for a long time were they thus, each of them in turn coming to him and striking him until he was all but dead; and then they departed from him."

His subsequent year-long sickness was cured when she called for his aid in an Otherworld battle and they fell in love. However, his wife was jealous and fought for him, and Cuchulain bid farewell to Fand, who returned to Manannan. "And Manannan shook his cloak between Cuchulain and Fand, so that they might never meet together again throughout eternity."

FARISEES

See **Feriers**.

FARRALIS

The fire fairy associated with summer, a spirit of courage with the power to destroy or rejuvenate and without whom fire cannot be started.

FATES, THE

Classical Greek and Roman female deities said to be present at a baby's birth and to determine the future course of that life. Their name originates from the Latin root *fatum*, meaning "destiny" or "fate." In Spain they were known as the *Hadas*, in France as the *Feés*, and in Nordic mythology as the **Norns**. In Albania, the ***Fatit*** rode in on butterflies three days after a birth to determine the course of the child's life. In Serbia, the **oosood** performed a similar function.

There were three Fates, known as the *Cataclothes*, or Spinners. Their names were Clotho, Lachesis, and Atropos. Clotho spun the thread of each individual life. Lachesis shaped and twisted the thread. Atropos took her shears and cut it at the appointed time.

The belief in the Fates as guardian spirits who watch over us, especially at times of transformation such as birth and death, has endured over time and they have entered into popular fairy tales, such as the story of *Cinderella*, in the form of fairy godmothers.

Fatit

(Also *Miren.*) Birth fairies in Albanian folklore. Similar to the three **Fates** of classical Greek and Roman mythology, these female spirits foretold the destinies of newborn babies. They were said to arrive three days after a birth, flying in on the backs of butterflies, to visit the baby in its cradle and determine the future course of its life.

Fear Dearig

See **Fir Darrig**.

Fear Gorta

An Irish spirit of hunger in the guise of an emaciated human, roaming the land seeking sustenance and rewarding the generous. A portent of famine.

Feens

(Or Fians.) Thought to emanate from Lapland, Finland, and northern Europe and have spread to England, Scotland, Ireland, and Wales, these short-statured beings became, in Scottish and Irish tradition, the Fianna, conquerors of the **Firbolgs** of Ireland. They were in turn conquered and forced to live underground.

Feeorin

Merry little fairies clothed in green and wearing red caps, with a love of dancing and music. Also used as a collective noun for small fairies.

See also ***Ferrishyn***.

Fennel

(Or Finnen.) The sister of **Aine**, the fairy goddess, daughter of a king of the ***Tuatha de Danann***. She is commemorated in the place name of Knock Fennine on the shores of Lough Gur.

Fenodoree

(Or Phenodree and many other variants.) A handsome Manx **brownie** said to have been one of the ***ferrishyn***, a fairy tribe from the Isle of Man. He fell in love with a human girl, and his punishment was banishment from fairyland and the loss of his looks. Now large, uncouth, and hairy, he possesses great strength and is generally helpful to mortals, although likely to take offense at any gift of clothes offered as reward. More renowned for his brawn than his brain.

Feriers

(Or ferishers.) Also known as farisees, Pharisees, or **frairies**, these are Suffolk names for secretive little fairies who dance and sing out of human sight and, if witnessed, vanish immediately. As Rev. A. G. H. Hollingsworth wrote in his *History of Stowmarket* (1844), "In the houses after they had fled, on going upstairs sparks of fire as bright as stars used to appear under the feet of the persons who disturbed them."

Ferishers

See **Feriers**.

Ferrishyn

A Manx tribe of fairies. Also a Manx word used as a collective noun for small fairies.

The red campion flower is known in Manx dialect as *pinkyn ferrishyn*, fairies' pinks.

See also **Feeorin**, **Fenodoree**.

Fetch

This has two meanings: i) a doll made of grass and sticks glamored to represent a human child that has been kidnapped by fairies; ii) an apparition of foreboding, one's double or doppelgänger, which portends death. In Irish folklore a fetch seen in the morning can mean a long life, but seen in the evening is an ominous warning. In the north of England it is known as a **waff**.

See also **Changeling**, **Co-walker**, **Swarth**.

Fianna

See **Feens**.

Fians

See **Feens**.

Fideal, the

A water demon inhabiting the Loch n Fideil in Scotland, ensnaring mortals and drowning them.

Fin Bheara

(Or Finvarra.) King of the ***Daoine Sidh*** in Irish folklore, also known as King of the Dead in some legends, who dwelt at Knockmaa in Co. Galway with his wife, **Oona**. A lover of mortal women, he captured the beautiful **Ethna** and took her to live with him for a year in his underground abode. Respected and feared for his association with the company of the dead, he is nevertheless generally considered a benevolent being who ensured abundant harvests.

Finland Men

See **Finmen**.

Finmen

Seafaring Finmen, or Finland men, were reportedly seen around the scattered islands of Orkney in the seventeenth century. Fishermen were puzzled by their sightings of these unknown beings who could evade capture by rowing at great speed away from their inquisitive pursuers; whenever Finmen were seen, a dearth of fish followed. They were believed to have the magical ability to disappear beneath the waves in their small sealskin boats to avoid being capsized in dangerous seas.

Finn

See **Fionn mac Cumhaill.**

Finnen

See **Fennel**.

Finvarra

See **Ethna the Bride**, **Fin Bheara**.

Fionn mac Cumhaill

(Also Finn.) (Pronounced *Fin M'Coul.*) Born of a warrior father and Muirne, the mother of the ***Tuatha de Danann***, Fionn (the Fair) was a magical hero in the Fenian Cycle of Irish legends. He possessed both courage and visionary power, and was taught in childhood by a druidess and a warrior woman. He was the father of the poet, singer, and warrior **Oisin**, and leader of the Fianna warriors.

According to legend, Fionn gained his special abilities and knowledge as the result of an encounter with a magical fish, as related in the Irish tale "The Salmon of Knowledge."

Many centuries ago there was a salmon that regularly swam through the Tobar Segais, or Well of Wisdom, a deep pool near the river Boyne in Ireland. One year nine hazelnuts fell from the nine trees that surrounded the pool and the salmon ate them and gained all the world's knowledge. It became known as Bradan an Eólais, or Fintan, the Salmon of Knowledge.

Living in a small house on the banks of the Boyne was the poet and great master Fineagas, or Finn Eces. He spent many hours every day tutoring his pupil and servant Fionn, son of Cumhaill, and constantly watching for the legendary fish. He knew that whoever first tasted it would gain all the knowledge of the world.

One bright spring morning as the old man sat outside his house, tutoring his eager pupil, he suddenly leaped to his feet and grabbed the large fishing net that was always close at hand. Fionn looked to where his master was pointing and saw a great swirling, silvery shape swimming toward them.

Fineagas cast his net and skillfully trapped the huge salmon, but as he hauled in the net he looked into its eyes and was temporarily blinded by their brightness. Fionn realized what had happened and blindfolded Fineagas, and together they managed to land the fish. With a single blow, Fionn dispatched it with a heavy branch of wood.

Fineagas was quite exhausted, so he asked Fionn to light a fire and cook the salmon, warning him not to taste the fish. So, while his master rested, Fionn put the fish on a spit over the fire and slowly turned it to cook it evenly. As he did so, some of the hot fish oil ran down the spit onto his thumb and he instinctively put it in his mouth.

When he called Fineagas to come and taste the fish, the master took one look at his pupil and realized that a change had come over the youth.

"Did you eat any of the fish?" he asked.

"No," replied Fionn, "but I did lick my thumb when it was burned by the hot oil."

"Well," said Fineagas, "you had better eat the rest, as I can see that you have already gained knowledge from the fish. It was meant for you, not for me."

Fionn ate the fish and did indeed gain great knowledge. He became the legendary hero known forever as Fionn McCumhail, the ablest and most celebrated of the Fianna warriors.

Fir Chlis

(Or Merry Dancers.) The spectacular lights of the *aurora borealis* give rise to many tales of the *fir chlis*, or "lively/nimble ones" in Scots Gaelic: one version is of rival chieftains in combat to win the love of a fairy woman, the red lights in the sky being a pool of blood from their battle. Also known as the Mirrie Dancers in the north of Scotland, meaning "shimmering" rather than "merry."

Fir Darrig

(Or Fear Dearig, Fir Dhearga.) A solitary fairy of Irish tradition. The name means Red Man, as he said to wear a red cap and coat. Given to practical joking of a more than merely mischievous nature, such as substituting human babies with **changelings**, he is of a "sluttish, slouching, jeering" appearance, according to **W. B. Yeats**'

Fairy and Folk Tales of the Irish Peasantry (1888).

FIR DHEARGA

See **Fir Darrig**.

FIRBOLGS

Ancient inhabitants and rulers of Ireland who were vanquished by the ***Tuatha de Danann***, the Firbolgs showed such courage in battle that the conquerors gave them land on which to settle.

FIRE DRAKE

A **will o' the wisp** in the folklore of the English fens, described as a snake or dragon, seen flying over marshes.

In German mythology it is a dragon, deriving its name from the Old English *fyr-draca*, literally, "fire dragon."

FLIBBERTIGIBBET

The "foul fiend Flibbertigibbet . . . who squints the eye and makes the harelip . . . and hurts the poor creature of earth," appears in Shakespeare's *King Lear* and in *The Folklore of Warwickshire* (1976) by Roy Palmer. He is described as a night demon who "mopped and mowed" between the ringing of the curfew bell and the crowing of the first cock in order to terrify young women.

FOIDIN SEACHRAIN

(Or stray sod.) In Irish tradition, a piece of turf that has a spell put upon it by fairies which confuses and disorientates any human stepping on it so that they lose their way even in familiar territory. Eventually the spell is lifted and their direction becomes clear again.

Follets

House spirits in the north of France, described in **Thomas Keightley**'s *The Fairy Mythology* (1828) as demons who attacked householders with sticks, stones, pots, and pans, were impervious to all forms of exorcism, and could clearly be heard speaking although they themselves were invisible.

Fomorians

The origins of the Fomorions are obscure, but in Irish folklore they were the original inhabitants of Ireland, variously described as evil demons or sea gods. Balor of the Evil Eye was one of their kings.

Fossegrim

In Norwegian tradition the *fossegrim* is a mostly benign water spirit of outstanding musical ability who will teach others to play in exchange for a good meal. However, if the offering is less than sumptuous, the *fossegrim* will only show them how to tune the instrument.

Foul-Weather

Cornish version of **Tom Tit Tot**.

Four Winds, the

Nature spirits in Native American folklore. In the legends of the Algonquin, the Four Winds were brothers: Kabibonokka the north wind, Shawano the south wind, Kabun the west wind, and Wabun the east wind.

The Four Winds feature in American poet Henry Wadsworth Longfellow's epic poem "The Song of Hiawatha" (1855), based on Native American lore and legends. Kabibonokka is the fierce north wind who dwells in Wabasso. He paints the autumn leaves scarlet and yellow, sends the snow, binds the rivers in ice, and drives away the seagull, cormorant, and heron. Shawondasee is the name Longfellow gives to the lazy south wind, who dwells in the south, where it is never-ending summer. He smokes his pipe, filling the sky with dreamy softness and giving a twinkle to the water. He sends the bluebirds and swallows north, and brings forth the melons and tobacco and clusters of purple grapes.

See also **Norouas, the Northwest Wind**, and **Surouas, the Southwest Wind**.

Frairies

A local name for fairies in Norfolk and Suffolk.

See also **Brother Mike, Feriers**.

Frau Wachholder

The spirit of the juniper tree in German folklore. Victims of theft invoke her for help in securing the return of stolen items. The victim goes to the juniper tree, bends one of its branches until it touches the ground, and demands that the thief or thieves show themselves. The thief is then bound by the power of Frau Wachholder to present themself and return the stolen goods.

Friar's Lantern

See **Will o' the Wisp**.

Fuathan, the

A name encompassing all Scottish water spirits inhabiting sea and freshwater lochs and rivers. Most are of a spiteful and threatening nature.

See also ***Brollachan***.

Fyglia

(Pronounced *Fee-yee-a*). Native American sprite serving as a personal guide, often in animal form.

PART 3
Connecting with Fairies

CONNECTING WITH FAIRIES

Musicians, artists, and poets are traditionally thought of as those favored by fairies, and many wonderful tales describe their experiences in the fairy realm, such as "The Ballad of Thomas the Rhymer," in which a Scottish minstrel is whisked away to fairyland for seven years by the Elf Queen. However, as the Irish poet W. B. Yeats wrote, often it is the "ordinary" people, the farmers and woodsmen, who encounter the little people. In cultures around the world, folk traditions and customs describe how to win the favor of the fairies and increase the chances of seeing them—as well as how to avoid unwanted attention from tricksy or pernicious inhabitants of fairyland.

PROTECTION FROM MISCHIEVOUS OR PERNICIOUS FAIRIES

Fairies are well known for their capricious nature—sometimes helpful to humans, at other times mischievous, sometimes downright dangerous. Those wishing to connect with the denizens of fairyland would be wise to acquaint themselves with methods of protection against unwanted attentions from the little people.

Metal

In widespread traditions, the spirit world has a supposed aversion to metal. In *The Golden Bough* (1890), J. G. Frazer records that in the late 1800s, the Nicobar Islands in South East Asia experienced unusually heavy downpours of rain. The islanders put this down to the fact that the English had recently visited to carry out a survey of the islands; they believed that the strange metal instruments used by the English had incurred the wrath of the spirits, and attempted to placate the weather spirits through the sacrifice of a pig.

Taboos concerning iron, in particular, have a long history and stretch far across the globe. In some places, such as Java, locals still refuse to use iron tools to till the fields lest they should anger the spirits presiding over the growth of the crops.

The fairies' aversion to metal does, however, equip humans with a powerful form of protection against them. In Scotland, when entering a fairy dwelling, sticking a piece of metal such as a fish-hook, needle, or knife into the door ensures that the fairies aren't able to shut the door until you have left, while sticking a knife into the carcass of a deer prevents the fairies from weighing it down as you carry your quarry home. An iron placed under the bed and a hook in the window keep fairies away from sleeping women and their babes.

Similar practices are found around the world. In Morocco a dagger or knife placed under a sick man's pillow offers protection against demons. In Sri Lanka placing an iron nail on top of good food such as cakes or roast meats before transporting them from one place to another prevents a demon from possessing the food and making those who eat it ill. And a sick person always carries a bunch of keys or a knife in their hand when leaving the house to prevent bad spirits from taking advantage of their weakened state and slipping into their body.

In Africa food was used to lure demons out of a sick child's body, and while the demon was feeding, a metal chain was hung around the child's neck or bells were placed around their ankles to prevent the demon from returning.

In Britain, especially in rural areas, it is still common practice to hang a horseshoe above the door of a stable or a dwelling to safeguard the people or animals inside. The horseshoe must be hung the right way up, in a "U" shape, in order for the charm to be effective.

Bells

Bells are considered another effective method of warding off pernicious sprites. Church bells, bells worn around the neck of sheep or cattle, and Morris dancers' bells all stave off unwanted attention from the little people. Other loud sounds, such as clapping or whistling, serve the same purpose.

Turning Clothes

One of the fairies' favorite tricks is to lead lone walkers astray, luring them into bogs or marshes or thickets. Tales of this kind are particularly prevalent in the West Country of England. Turning clothes inside out is a popular way for such "pisky-led" travelers to break their enchantment and find their way home. Turning a coat or a pair of gloves inside out is thought to confuse the fairies by changing the wearer's identity, thus allowing the lost wanderer to find their way back onto the path.

Running Water

Running water acts as a threshold between the human and fairy worlds. Crossing running water is therefore one way to escape the pursuit of malicious fairies. Southward-flowing streams are thought to be particularly effective—although one should beware when crossing that the waters are free from evil, freshwater-dwelling spirits such as kelpies.

Crosses

Crosses have been used as a protective symbol since the earliest days of Christianity. Their potency in warding off evil may even predate Christian beliefs, as crossroads have long been held in special regard and used as places of sacrifice. Whatever the origin of its efficacy, the sign of the cross is considered to offer powerful protection against all manner of bad spirits, including ghosts, demons, and fairies. The cross can be formed in various ways, either by "saining" (making the sign of the cross on your own body, or someone else's), by wearing or carrying a cross-shaped charm or pendant, or by forming the shape of a cross out of metal, wood, or stone. Using a particular material, such as rowan wood or metal, both thought to have protective properties themselves, increases the potency of the charm.

CURRYING FAVOR WITH THE FAIRIES

If you want to enlist the help of the fairies, it's worth knowing what kind of behavior attracts their praise, and what they dislike. Traditionally, they have singled out certain qualities in humans for reward, such as hospitality, cleanliness, and discretion, and have tended to avoid or punish gossips and slovenly housekeepers.

Discretion is a must when dealing with matters of the *fae.* Fairies are fiercely protective of their secrets and in order to preserve their privacy and traditional way of life, they will confide only in humans whom they can trust to keep their dealings private. So people who are fond of solitude and contemplation are more likely to find favor than gossips.

Conversely, openness is also highly valued by the fairies. While on the one hand human confidents must be able to keep fairy secrets close, at the same time they must be ready to speak openly and truthfully about themselves, sharing their own dreams, plans, and quests.

Cleanliness is of utmost importance, especially to household spirits. If you want to make the fairies feel welcome in your home, be sure keep your hearth or fireplace freshly swept and set out a bowl of clean water for the fairies to drink or wash their babies with.

Hospitality and generosity are held in high esteem by the fairies. It is always advisable to treat an unexpected stranger seeking food or shelter kindly, as they may turn out to be a fairy in disguise.

A saucer of milk and a morsel of cheese or freshly baked bread or cake are also well received as offerings of goodwill.

Sincerity and the notion of fair play are upheld by the good-natured fairies of the Seelie Court. A promise kept may reap a reward, either straightaway, or when one is most in need.

SEEING FAIRIES

There are many tales of individuals who have seen the fae, and even visited their realm.

Anne Jefferies and the Fairies

A woman named Anne Jefferies was a particular favorite of the little people of Cornwall. Her fairy encounter included a visit to fairyland, after which it is said she gained miraculous powers of healing.

Back in the year of 1626, a daughter was born to a poor man and his wife. They lived a simple life in the parish of St. Teath, which lies on the rugged coast of north Cornwall, not far from the fishing village of Port Isaac. The Jefferies lived in a little cottage and ate mainly vegetables and occasionally a mackerel or two bought from the fishermen. Rarely did they taste any meat—just once in a while when old man Jefferies was given a scrap or two from the farmers for whom he labored.

Despite, or even because of, this simple living, Anne grew to be a very bright and lively young woman, forever vanishing into the countryside, clambering over rocks and cairns, chasing butterflies, and wading through streams. Even the boys were afraid to follow her into the wild country. Of course, she had her household chores to do, and very diligent she was too. Her parents loved her dearly and in the evenings they would often sit at the fireside and old Mrs. Jefferies had a seemingly endless collection of ballads and tales of fairies and sprites and knockers and spriggans to pass the time in the flickering light of the burning logs.

In the summer of 1645, when Anne was 19, her parents thought it was time that she went into service, as most of her friends had already long gone, as was the custom in those days. So it was that she went to live as a servant in the family of Mr. Moses Pitt.

Anne was a good worker, but once the day was done, she often set off into the countryside in search of the fairies, or little people, whose stories she knew so well. As she frolicked among the ferns and peered into the petals of the foxglove, she sang little rhymes:

"Fairy fair and fairy bright,
Come and be my chosen sprite."

On moonlit nights she strolled by the stream, singing:

"Moon shines bright, waters run
clear,
I am here, but where's my fairy
dear?"

The fairies, however, were not yet ready to show themselves.

Then came a hot, humid afternoon when time itself seemed to have languished in the soporific stillness. Anne sat in the shady arbor of her master's garden, knitting and daydreaming, her thoughts drifting aimlessly yet contentedly. Her reverie was disturbed when she heard a rustling in the bushes behind her. At first she thought it must be her mischievous sweetheart creeping up to surprise her, so she pretended not to have heard anything but continued with her knitting. Then came a little chuckling laugh and more rattling of the leaves, and Anne said, "You may stay there till the moss grows on the gate afore I'll come to 'ee."

There was the sound of tinkling bells, as sweet as the babbling of water from a sparkling spring, and a light musical laugh, nothing like the deep voice of her lover.

Anne grew wary and she thought she heard the quiet click of the garden gate. A long moment passed, then drifting into her vision came six little men, all dressed in green, bright-eyed and smiling. One, who appeared to be the leader, was wearing a bright red feather in his cap, and as he approached Anne put down her hand to greet him. The little man jumped into her palm and she lifted him into her lap. Boldly he climbed up to her bosom and her neck and began kissing her. She was taken aback by his intimacy, but also found his attention most pleasurable and did nothing to prevent his companions climbing up to join him. She felt quite overcome as they kissed her neck, her lips and her eyes. One of them stroked her eyelids and she felt a prickling sensation, then a darkness filled with whirling stars as she was whisked away to a faraway land.

Then she heard the fairies uttering words that sounded like, "Tear away! Tear away!" and at once she could see again, and what a sight she did see!

She had entered a most marvelous world, full of trees laden with fruit and lush green carpets of grass sweeping up to temples and palaces of gold and silver. Lakes teeming with fish shimmered under a dazzling blue sky, where brightly colored songbirds darted on the breeze. Countless flowers cast their colors and their fragrances all around, and among these were finely dressed ladies and gentlemen playing and dancing. Anne looked down at herself and saw that she, too, was dressed in the finest silks and pretty ruby-red shoes. She had become one of the happy throng, and her six friends were now as large as real gentlemen and continued to attend on her.

Her favorite remained the leader with a bright red feather in his cap. Gently he led Anne away from the crowd and they lay hidden among the delicate flowers towering over their heads. But all too soon the jealous fairies came looking for them and came rushing angrily upon them. Anne's lover drew his sword to defend her, but he was beaten down and as he lay at her feet, the fairy who had stroked her eyelids did so again.

Once more she was whirled into the darkness, spiraling through the stars until she landed with a bump and found herself lying on the grass by the arbor in the garden. Looking up, she saw the anxious faces of her worried friends peering down at her, fearing that she had been in a convulsive fit.

It is said that the little people continued to visit Anne and from them she learned special powers of healing. As word spread of her ability to cure all manner of illnesses, people came to visit her from far and wide.

In 1646 the authorities caught wind of Anne's activities as a fairy healer and she was arrested and imprisoned. It was said that she forsook eating human food, but subsisted on victuals fed to her by the little people. She was eventually released and went on to marry, but was reluctant to talk any more of her encounters with the fairy realm.

Robert Hunt's *Popular Romances of the West of England* (1865) contains an account of Anne Jefferies' dealings with the little people, and includes in the appendix a letter written by her employer, "Moses Pitts' Letter Regarding Anne Jefferies," with details of the "strange and wonderful cures she performed."

Second Sight

Some people are said to be born with "second sight"—the natural ability to see fairies and the fairy realm. These people are known variously as "seers," "sighted," or "gifted." Robert Kirk, a Scottish minister who believed in fairies, wrote about the burdens, as well as the joys, that the "gift" of second sight brought with it in *The Secret Commonwealth of Elves, Fauns and Fairies* (1691) and described a ceremony for those who wished to acquire second sight, which involved placing their foot under the foot of a "wizard," meaning one who was already a seer:

The usewell Method for a curios Person to get a transient Sight of this otherwise invisible Crew of Subterraneans, (if impotently and over rashly sought) is to put his (left Foot under the Wizard's right) Foot, and the Seer's Hand is put on the Inquirer's Head, who is to look over the Wizard's right Shoulder, (which hes ane ill Appearance, as if by this Ceremony one implicit Surrender were made of all betwixt the Wizard's Foot and his Hand, ere the Person can be admitted a privadoto the Airt;) then will he see a Multitude of Wight', like furious hardie Men, flocking to him hastily from all Quarters, as thick as Atoms in the Air; which are no Nonentities or Phantasms, Creatures proceiding from one affrighted Apprehensione, confused or crazed Sense, but Realities, appearing to a stable Man in his awakening Sense, and enduring a rational Tryall of their Being.

Fairies may also choose to show themselves to humans who have gained their favor or who are familiar with fairy lore when it comes to seeing the little folk. There are several means of doing so.

Four-leafed Clovers

Four-leafed clovers are supposed to have magical properties allowing anyone who carries or holds one to see fairies. Milkmaids were said to be especially prone to witnessing the little people after unwittingly picking a four-leafed clover while going about their work, as in the following tale.

There was once a cow called Daisy who had the creamiest milk but would not allow the milkmaid a drop more than two gallons. One evening, after collecting the allotted amount, the milkmaid set off across the meadows back to the farm. On the way she stopped to pick a handful of grass and placed it on her head to soften the weight of the pail.

As she crossed the stile, she paused and looked back at Daisy. To her astonishment, she saw that the cow was covered in cavorting fairies. Daisy was clearly enjoying the attentions of the little people and was allowing them to milk her, pat her, and stroke her.

At first the farmer's wife didn't believe the milkmaid's story, but when they discovered a four-leafed clover tangled in the grass that she had picked, she was convinced by the girl's tale.

Realizing that Daisy's reluctance to part with her milk was on account of her little friends, the farmer's wife ordered that she be washed all over with a mixture of saltwater, fish, and grease. The fairies were known to have a particular dislike for this and were driven away, but misfortune dogged the farm as a result.

Fairy Ointment

In many tales, humans are able to see fairies as a result of rubbing fairy ointment on their eyes. In some cases, the ointment is made of crushed four-leafed clovers.

In the Cornish tale "Cherry of Zennor," a girl is instructed to anoint a little boy's eyes every morning with a green ointment. Curiosity gets the better of her and she rubs her own eye with the strange ointment. Immediately, hundreds of little fairy men and women become visible to her, but later she is punished by her fairy master.

In the instance of the French *dracs*, it is not crushed four-leafed clovers but the grease from an eel pasty that grants fairy sight to a woman taken to live in the *dracs'* underwater realm. She, too, endures a punishment—a prod in the eye from her fairy master. In other stories, fairy ointment allows humans to see through fairy glamor.

In "Eilian of Garth Dorwen," a midwife attends a fairy birth in what at first appears to be a sumptuously furnished abode. On accidently rubbing her eye with ointment meant for the child, she sees that in fact mother and baby are lying in a dark, dank cave. The fairy master puts out her eye with a bullrush.

The blinding of the anointed eye is a common theme in these tales, offering a warning that fairy ointment should be approached with caution.

A Steady Gaze

It is said that should you glimpse a fairy, you mustn't let it out of your sight, for if you so much as blink it will vanish. There are many tales of leprechauns escaping from their captors in this way, using a box of snuff to make them sneeze or otherwise distracting them into looking away in order to make a hasty exit and slip away out of sight.

Fairy Stones

Stones with a hole through the middle are said to provide a window onto the fairy realm. The holes in these stones, also known as "self-bored stones," are formed naturally by the force of the rushing water of a stream or river. The stones were sometimes used as protection against fairies and were hung up on stable walls to keep the little people away from horses and livestock.

Spells to See a Fairy

Various spells were used to call upon the fairies by those wishing to make contact with the little people.

One such spell, in an old manuscript, suggests using a piece of crystal dipped in the blood of a hen, but a less extreme method is also put forward in the form of an ointment made of flower waters:

An excellent way to gett a fayrie. (For myself I call Margarett Barrance but this will obtaine any one that is not allready bound.)

First gett a broad square christall or venus glasse in length and breadth 3 inches [7.5 centimeters], then lay that glasse or christall in the blood of a white henne 3 Wednesdayes or 3 Fridayes: then take it out and wash it with holy aquae and fumigate it : then take 3 hazle sticks or wands of an yeare groth, pill them fayre and white, and make soe longe as you can write the spirits name, or fayries name, which you call 3 times, on every sticke being made flatt one side, then bury them under some stone hill whereas you suppose fayries haunt, the Wednesdaye before you call she, and the Fridaye followinge take them uppe and calle she at 8 or 3 or 10 of the clock which be goode plannetts howres for that turne: but when you call, be in cleane Life and turne thy face towards the East, and when you have she bind her to that stone or glasse.

An unguent to annoynt under the eylidds and upon the eylidds evninge and morninge, but especially when you call, or finde your sighte not perfect. Putt sallet oyle into a viall glasse but first wash it with rose water, and marygold flower water, the flowers be gathered to the east, wash it til the oyle come white, then putt it into the glasse, ut supra, and put there to the buds of hollyhocke, the flowers of marygold: the flowers or topps of wild time, the budds of younge hazle, and the time must be gatherred neare the side of a hille where fayries use to go oft, and the grasse of a fayrie throne, there, all these putte into the oyle, the glasse, and sett it to dissolve 3 dayes in the sonne, and thou keep it for thy use; ut supra.

Times of Day

Fairies dwell at thresholds and borders, and so favor liminal times of day. Twilight, the hour before sunrise, midday, and midnight are traditionally the hours when they are most active and most likely to be visible to human eyes.

THE FAIRY CALENDAR

Just as fairies favor particular times of day, there are times year, too, when they are at their most active. These fall at cross-over points, such as the midpoints of summer and winter, and at the turning of the seasons.

Before we developed precise instruments for measuring the movements of the sun and moon, our ancestors relied on the breeding patterns of animals and cycles of nature to make calculations about the seasons. The Celts divided their calendar into four parts, marked by the summer and winter solstices—the longest and shortest days—and the spring and autumn equinoxes—when day and night are of equal length. Important festivals, known as quarter days, marked the halfway points between solstices and equinoxes. All eight festivals were often represented as a wheel with eight spokes, known as the Celtic wheel of the year. The Celtic New Year began on November 1st, the first day of winter. Summer began on May 1st.

Each year, the precise dates and times of the equinoxes and solstices vary slightly; dates given here are approximate.

Paying attention to the shifting of the seasons and the phases of the Celtic calendar establishes a connection with the rhythms of the fairy realm, sharpening your senses to be alert to the times at which the fairies are at their most active, and therefore more likely to be seen.

Imbolc

February 1st in the northern hemisphere

July 31st in the southern hemisphere

Falling between the winter solstice, when the days at their shortest, and the spring equinox, when day and night are of equal length, the festival of Imbolc marks the halfway point to spring and the return of the light in the northern hemisphere.

Probably deriving from the Old Irish *I molg*, "in the belly," Imbolc is generally thought to be connected with the start of the lambing season. Cows' milk would not have been available until late spring, so sheep's milk provided people with important nutrients at a time of year when food supplies were often scarce. Therefore, the beginning of the season of the lactation of ewes was a cause for much celebration.

The festival has long been connected with the fire goddess Brigit, pagan goddess of poetry and smithcraft, possessed of the powers of divination and healing. She later became known as the Christian St. Brigid in Ireland and St.

Bride in Scotland. St. Brigit was the patroness of sheep and was associated with holy wells. In parts of Ireland and the British Isles, February 1st is still celebrated as St. Brigid's day.

In Scottish folklore, Imbolc is the time of year when *Cailleach*, the old woman of winter, drinks from the Well of Youth and metamorphoses into Bride, who, with her white wand, heralds the growth and regeneration of spring. A "bridie doll" of corn is left by the hearthside with offerings of bread and milk to ask for protection and abundance, and candles are lit to celebrate the return of the light and lengthening of the days.

The Spring Equinox

March 21st in the northern hemisphere

September 21st in the southern hemisphere

Halfway between the winter solstice and summer solstice, the spring equinox marks the point at which days and nights are of equal length. It is a time when light and dark are balanced. Nature comes back to life following the dark winter, flowers come into bloom, and the fields are prepared for the coming season of growth. This time of year is associated with fairies and spirits symbolizing the power of nature, such as the Green Man.

It is not just in Celtic regions that the spring equinox is recognized as a significant time of year. In Bulgaria, *Baba Marta*, Grandmother March, presides over the month of March. Red and white woolen bracelets known as *martenitsi* are exchanged as symbols of spring, fertility, and health. On March 21st, people take off their *martenitsi* and tie them to the branch of a tree for luck, or place them under a rock to bring happiness in marriage.

Beltane or May Eve

April 30th in the northern hemisphere

October 31st in the southern hemisphere

"The fair maid who, the first of May,
Goes to the fields at break of day,
And washes in dew from the
hawthorn tree,
Will ever after handsome be."

Old English rhyme

Beltane falls between the spring equinox, when day and night are of equal length, and the summer solstice, when the days are at their longest. The beginning of May is traditionally a time to celebrate the growth of new life.

The lighting of fires played an important part in Beltane celebrations and it is likely that the origins of the word come from *bel*, meaning "brilliant" or "shining," and *teine*, meaning "fire." In Ireland, Scotland, Wales, Cornwall, and Brittany, beacons were lit on hills and mountains at this time to celebrate the beginning of summer.

For the early Celts, this was the time of year when herdsmen began to prepare to move livestock such as cattle and sheep to summer pasture. Before setting off, they drove the animals between two bonfires for protection against disease. People also passed between the fires, or jumped over them, for luck or fertility. Large round flat cakes of oats or barley, known as Beltane cakes, or *bannocks*, were cooked on the fires. It was considered an auspicious time to begin a new project or embark on a journey.

Celtic Beltane celebrations merged with May Day traditions from other European countries, such as the Roman Florilia celebrations held in honor of Flora, the goddess of flowers. Villagers went into the surrounding woods, fields, hills, or mountains to gather flowers and greenery to deck the village with garlands of blossoms. The most prized of their foraged items was the maypole, which was decorated with flowers, herbs, and ribbons. Maypole dances were a celebration of the regeneration of nature.

Beltane was also the time of fairy rades. As Thomas Keightley explains in *The Fairy Mythology* (1828):

The Fairy Rade, or procession, was a matter of great importance. It took place on the coming in of summer, awl [all] the peasantry, by using the precaution of placing a branch of rowan over their door, might safely gaze on the cavalcade, as with music sounding, bridles ringing, and voices mingling, it pursued its way from place to place.

According to an account of a Scottish woman who saw a fairy rade:

A beam of light was dancing over them more beautiful than moonshine; they were wee folk with green scarves, riding on white horses with long tails and manes hung with bells that whistled in the wind. They left no hoofmarks in the ground and not even a blade of grass was broken where they had passed.

The Midsummer Solstice

June 22nd in the northern hemisphere

December 22nd in the southern hemisphere

The summer solstice marks the point of the year when daylight hours are at their longest. Traditionally the longest day is a time to celebrate the power of the sun at its zenith, before the year begins to wane and the days gradually get shorter, reaching equal length at the autumn equinox then dwindling to their shortest at the winter solstice.

The Celts lit fires on hills and mountains from sunset on Midsummer Eve to sunset on Midsummer Day. They represented the sun and symbolically enhanced its potency to ripen fruit and crops and protect humans and livestock from disease.

Midsummer, when plants and flowers are in full bloom, was traditionally the time when herbs were cut for use in healing, medicine, food, and drink. Herbs and plants, particularly St. John's Wort, were burned on the fires or hung over doors to guard against unwanted attention from the fairies, who were particularly active on Midsummer's Eve. According to fairy lore, this is the time when the veil between the mortal and fairy realms is thin, making it a favorable evening to see the fae and practice divination.

In *Popular Romances of the West of England* (1865), Robert Hunt describes popular midsummer divination rituals for revealing the identity of a future sweetheart or husband:

If a young lady will, on midsummer-eve, walk backwards into the garden and gather a rose, she has the means of knowing who is to be her husband. The rose must be cautiously sewn up in a paper bag, and put aside in a dark drawer, there to remain until Christmas-day.

On the morning of the Nativity the bag must be carefully opened in silence, and the rose placed by the lady in her bosom. Thus she must wear it to church. Some young man will either ask for the rose, or take it from her without asking. That young man is destined to become eventually the lady's husband.

A late-night foray into the fields to sow hemp was another means by which a maiden might discover her true love:

"At eve last midsummer no sleep I
sought,
But to the field a bag of hemp-seed
brought;
I scatter'd round the seed on every
side,
And three times in a trembling accent
cried,
'This hemp-seed with my virgin hand
I sow,
Who shall my true love be, the crop
shall mow.'
I straight look'd back, and, if my eyes
speak truth,
With his keen scythe behind me came
the youth."

Lughnasa

July 31st in the northern hemisphere

February 1st in the southern hemisphere

(Also Lughnasad.) Falling between Beltane at the beginning of May and Samhain at the beginning of November, Lughnasa marks the midpoint of the summer half of the year. Traditionally, it was a time for harvesting and sharing the bounty of the land.

According to Irish tradition, the hero Lug, the Shining One, founded the festival, overcoming a spirit of the Earth in order to win the harvest for his people. In Scotland and England the Christian festival of *Lammas*, or loaf mass, was celebrated on August 1st, when a loaf was made from flour using the first grain of corn from the harvest. It was a time for celebrating the ripening of the crops.

Fairies connected with agriculture, such as the pisky threshers, were said to become active at this time of year, lending a hand with the threshing of the grain and other tasks related to the harvest.

Traditions associated with this time of the year include the symbolic sacrifice of the corn spirit, known as "crying the neck." The last sheaf of wheat to be harvested represented the spirit of the corn. It was considered unlucky to cut it, and thus slay the corn spirit, so farm workers threw their sickles at it in order that no one person bore the burden of having done the slaying.

William Bottrell describes the tradition of crying the neck in *Traditions and Hearthside Stories of West Cornwall* (1873):

It was nearly dark when the last handful of wheat, called 'the neck,' was tied up and cut by the reapers throwing their reap-hooks at it. Then it took a good bit longer to cry the neck according to the old custom of the harvest-hands dividing themselves into three bands—one party calling, three times, as loud as they could cry, 'We have it, we have it, we have it!' The second demanding, 'What have ye? What have ye? What have ye?' And the third replying, 'A neck! a neck! a neck!' Then all join, hats in hand, in a 'Hip! hip! hip! Hurrah!'

A corn dolly was woven from the last sheaf of corn and kept indoors until the following spring, when it was added to the rest of the seed, ensuring the continuation of the cycle of growth, reaping, and sowing.

The Autumn Equinox

September 21st in the northern hemisphere

March 21st in the southern hemisphere

Halfway between the summer solstice and winter solstice, the autumn equinox marks the point at which days and nights are of equal length before the days gradually become shorter. As with the spring solstice, it is a time when light and dark are balanced.

Thanks are given now for the fruits of the harvest, and the full moon occurring closest to the autumn equinox is called the harvest moon. According to fairy lore, this equinox is a high festival not only for humans but also for the little people, who are fond of feasting on this night. "The Fairy Revels on The Gump," in Robert Hunt's *Popular Romances of the West of England* (1865), tells of a great fairy harvest moon feast held every year near the Cornish village of St. Just, when the fairies gathered on a hillside with "vessels of silver and vessels of gold . . . laden, almost to overflowing, with the richest meats, pastry, preserves, and fruits."

This was the time to gather blackberries from the hedgerows and make preserves for the winter ahead. It was important to pick the berries before month was out, for it was widely believed that the Devil or another evil spirit, such as the Irish *phouka,* spoiled them by spitting, defecating, or urinating on them in early October, so that they were no longer considered fit to eat.

Samhain

October 31st in the northern hemisphere

April 30th in the southern hemisphere

Falling between the autumn equinox and winter solstice, the festival of Samhain takes its name from *sam,* meaning "summer," and *fuin,* meaning "end." It marks the end of summer and the beginning of a new cycle of the Celtic year. Having the new year in the winter months followed the principle of dark coming before light in the measuring of time, as can be seen in certain sacred or religious events such as Passover beginning at sunset.

Today the ancient Celtic festival of Samhain is more widely known as Halloween. This name is derived from the Christian All Saints' Day on November 1st, hence October 31st being All Hallows' Eve, which was shortened to Halloween.

This is a time of completions and new beginnings. It marks the end of the season of reaping and the start of the season of resting. In Scottish folklore the *Cailleach,* old woman of winter, is reborn each Samhain, when she smites the earth with her staff to bring the snow and the winter. She rules the dark part of the year until Imbolc, when she drinks from the Well of Youth and metamorphoses into Bride, who heralds the regeneration and growth of spring. In other versions of the tradition, with the arrival of Beltane she throws her staff under a holly tree or gorse bush and turns into a stone.

In Ireland, Samhain was the main calendar festival of the year and was celebrated with the lighting of beacons to mark the end of the old year and the beginning of the new. It was traditionally a time when the boundary between the mortal world and the Otherworld was believed to be at its thinnest, when spirits could visit the human realm, and thus a time for remembering the ancestors and commemorating the departed. As the nights drew in and the storytelling season began, people exchanged stories of the dead. Yet it was also a time for divination, for looking ahead at what was to come.

In fairy lore, Samhain is also a time of fairy rades—dark counterparts to the bright processions at the beginning of summer. These rades often have associations with the Underworld, or land of the dead. In the Scottish "Ballad of Tam Lin," the Queen of Fairies holds a mortal man, Tam Lin, captive in fairyland, but he is rescued by his true love during the fairy rade at Halloween.

The Midwinter Solstice

December 22nd in the northern hemisphere

June 22nd in the southern hemisphere

The winter solstice marks the point of the year when daylight hours are at their shortest. After the solstice, the year begins to wax and the days gradually get longer, reaching equal length with the hours of darkness at the spring equinox, and their longest at the summer solstice. So the winter solstice is a time to celebrate the return of the light.

At this festival, greenery such as holly and mistletoe would be brought inside to decorate houses as a symbol of the enduring power of nature even at the year's darkest point. Vestiges of these ancient customs can still be seen at Christmas, when evergreen trees are brought into the home and decorated with tinsel and baubles.

The winter solstice appears to have been an important part of the calendar since ancient times. There are many examples of prehistoric monuments being built in precise alignment with the position of the sun on this day. For example, Newgrange in Ireland is a mound with a passageway running through the center. As the sun rises on the winter solstice, its rays flood the passageway with light. In England, the famous standing stones at Stonehenge are aligned with the setting sun on the midsummer solstice and the rising sun on the midwinter solstice. The purpose of these structures remains a mystery, yet people still gather in their hundreds at these monuments to mark the important turning points of the year, just as our ancestors would have done hundreds of years ago.

MUSICIANS, DANCERS, AND REVELERS

Many of the fairies' favorite times of year are connected with music, dancing, and revelry. In tales from around the world, fairies have a love of music, and are often to be found dancing in moonlit fields and meadows, forming light circles of grass known as fairy rings. It is said that anyone entering a fairy circle at midnight can see the fairies and may join in their dance—but exiting may not be so easy. One woman in Ireland was said to have returned after a seven-year sojourn with the fairies bereft of her toes—she had danced them all off.

Fairies are often skilled musicians and have a particular fondness for humans with an ear for a tune or a passion for dancing.

In Norway, elves are known as *huldra* and their music is *huldraslaat*, a melancholy, haunting refrain played in a minor key. According to Keightley in *The Fairy Mythology* (1828):

> *. . . there is also a tune called the Elf-king's tune, which several of the good fiddlers know right well, but never venture to play, for as soon as it begins both old and young, and even inanimate objects, are impelled to dance, and the player cannot stop unless he can play the air backwards, or . . . some one comes behind him and cuts the strings of his fiddle.*

All kinds of fairies have a love of music. In Scotland the *loireag* has a finely tuned ear and punishes those who sing out of tune or repeat the same verse twice. The Swedish *näcken* will give lessons on the violin—but his pupils should be mindful, for he is said to keep mortal souls trapped in upturned urns on the riverbed. In America, the drumming of the *Yunwitsandsdi* of Cherokee lore can be heard deep in the forests or high in the mountains. In Ireland, *sheoque* fairies inhabit the ancient fairy forts, and mortals who listen to their enchanting tunes become great musicians, poets, or fairy doctors, or else leave the mortal realm behind to abide in the fairy realm forever.

Thomas the Rhymer

The famous "Ballad of Thomas the Rhymer" tells of a Scottish musician who was spirited away for seven years by the Queen of Elfland.

Hundreds of years ago it was not uncommon for men blessed with the gift of music and flowing words to travel the countryside providing entertainment for their fellows. Thomas of Ercildoune was such a man. He lived in the border county of Berwickshire in the distant days of the thirteenth century, when people lived much more closely to the land than today and felt a kinship with the fairies and elves and spirits that seemed a natural part of the world around them.

One bright May morning Thomas awoke feeling all the joyous energy of the season flowing through him. He decided to take his lute and walk through the vibrant beauty of the hills and vales to visit a friend and his family some 20 miles (32 kilometers) distant. On such a day the journey itself was a delight and Thomas felt more akin with the sights and sounds and scents that surrounded him than he ever had before.

After 10 miles (16 kilometers) of lively walking he came upon the banks of the Huntly burn, where he sat down to rest a while under the white blossoms of a hawthorn tree. He was so filled with the beauty of the place that he fell into something of a trance listening to the chuckling and tinkling of the stream as it flowed below him. Gradually he realized that the tinkling sound was growing louder and he looked up to see an astonishing vision. The sound was coming from dozens of silver bells that were hanging from the mane of a fabulous white horse. Upon the horse was an even more beautiful sight: a woman of such loveliness that Thomas felt quite overcome with wonder. Her long, red-gold hair flowed down over her soft green cape of velvet, beneath which shone a silken dress of bright emerald. She carried a golden hunting horn and a quiver of arrows hung from her saddle.

Thomas thought he must have died and gone to heaven, so he kneeled before the vision and said, "Greetings to thee, my Queen of Heaven!"

The lady smiled and spoke with a voice as soft and gentle as the breeze, saying, "No, Thomas. I am indeed a queen, but not of heaven, of Elfland."

Her eyes were the sparkling blue of the sea on a summer's day and her lips the red of ripe strawberries in June. Thomas felt an irrepressible desire to kiss those sweet lips and the Elf Queen understood his thoughts.

"If you kiss me, Thomas," she said, "you will be in my power and you will have to come with me and serve me in Elfland for seven years."

Thomas was quite enchanted and gladly agreed to the bargain, so the queen slipped off her horse into his arms. The kiss was even sweeter than Thomas had imagined. He happily mounted the magnificent steed behind the queen and they rode away on the long journey to Elfland.

It seemed to Thomas that they rode deep into the hollow hills of Eildon and through great rivers until they came to a wondrous orchard where the trees hung heavy with ripe fruit.

Thomas was about to pluck the fruit when the queen stopped him. "No, Thomas, do not eat the fruit. It would spell your doom!"

Instead they dismounted and the queen produced a loaf of bread and a flask of red wine for their refreshment. As they rested, she said, "Close your eyes, Thomas, and you will see what you will see."

When he did so, Thomas saw three roads lying ahead of them.

One was flat and easy and pretty, the second was steep and rocky and difficult, and the third was a green slope that ran down through heather and ferns.

He told the queen what he saw and she said, "There is a meaning to what you see. The first road is of earthly pleasures and leads only to despair and despondency; the second is the hard, difficult road requiring courage and endurance and leading to righteousness and heaven. The third is the road to Elfland and that is the way we shall follow."

Then she gave an apple to Thomas and bade him eat it.

"This is the fruit of the Tree of Truth. Eat it and you will never lie again."

They rode on over the moors, through the heather and ferns, up hill and down dale, until they arrived at a magnificent castle. The queen blew her horn and the gates swung open.

"Now, Thomas," she said, "once inside you must speak to no one but me, nor must you eat or drink, or you will be trapped here forever, never to return to your home."

Thomas dismounted and found a quiet corner in the great hall where he could watch as the queen joined her husband the king on their thrones above their subjects, who were all seated at long tables overflowing with food and drink. There followed three days of celebrations with music and dancing and entertainments. But Thomas neither ate nor drank and spoke to no one.

Eventually, the queen came to him and said, "The time has come for me to take you home."

"But I have been here only three days and I have promised you seven years of my service!"

"Dear Thomas," said the queen, "time in Elfland is quite different from your worldly time. You will find that seven of your years have indeed passed by. I fear that if you stay you may be taken by the Lord of Darkness to languish forever in hell."

So they mounted the great white horse and with bells a-jingling they made the long ride back to the banks of the Huntly burn, beneath the hawthorn tree.

"My lady," said Thomas, "may I ask you one more favor? Could you give me something so I may remember my visit to Elfland?"

"You already have the gift of Truth," she replied, "but as I have enjoyed your company and you are a good man, I will also add the gifts of Prophecy and Poetry, and in place of your lute you will now have a harp to play the sweetest tunes, by which you will remember me."

With that, the beautiful Queen of Elfland rode once more into the Eildon Hills and the magical Land of the Fairies.

True Thomas became a legend, renowned for his skill on the harp, his prophecies, and his tongue that couldn't lie. He foretold many events that came to pass in Scotland. He sang of the death of King Alexander III, and the terrible Battle of Bannockburn, and the Union of Scotland and England under a king born of a French queen. These stories and ballads earned him the name of Thomas the Rhymer.

One night when he was old and gray, Thomas found a snow-white hart and hind waiting outside his door. He knew they had been sent by the Queen of Elfland and he followed them into the hills, never to be seen again.

Even today you can find a stone erected on the site of the hawthorn, now known as the Eildon Tree, where Thomas met the Queen of the Fairies. The inscription reads:

This stone marks the site of the Eildon Tree where legend says Thomas the Rhymer met the Queen of the Fairies and where he was inspired to utter the first notes of the Scottish Muse.

The Legend of Knockgrafton
A well-known Irish tale, collected by Thomas Crofton Croker, in *Fairy Legends and Traditions* (1825), relates how Lusmore the humpback was rewarded for his lyrical skill by a troop of music-loving fairies. The tale is also a warning to those who lack sensitivity against blundering in to a fairy's tune uninvited. Here, sensitivity and timing are key to successfully connecting with the fairies. Very similar tales

are found in Scotland, the Isle of Man, France, Germany, Italy, Japan ("How the Old Man Lost His Wen"), and China ("The Story of Hok Lee and the Dwarves"), indicating that these rules apply to dealings with fairy musicians the world over.

In the mists of time gone by, in the fertile glen of Aherlow in the shadow of the gray Galtee mountains of Ireland, there lived a poor man who was cursed with a great hump upon his back. Despite his ugly deformity, he was a gentle, harmless man and he always wore a sprig of the fairy cap, or *lusmore* (the foxglove) in his little straw hat. This gave rise to his name, Lusmore, by which he was known to all the people of the glen.

He made his living by weaving straw hats and baskets, and he was so skilled in his trade that his name was known for many miles around. However, perhaps because of jealousy, and his deformity, too, there were those who spread rumors about his knowledge of herbs and spells and other, darker, tales about him.

To obtain the work to keep himself, he often walked from farm to village to town, a particularly wearisome task owing to the burden of his hump. One evening he was walking slowly from the town of Cahir toward his home in Cappagh when he reached the moat, or ancient barrow, of Knockgrafton. He sat upon the stones, the weight of his hump forcing him to rest his chin on his knees. When darkness was complete, a silver glow appeared on the horizon and Lusmore watched as the moon:

Rising in clouded majesty, at length
Apparent Queen, unveil'd her peerless light,
And o'er the dark her silver mantle threw.

As he watched this wonderful sight, he became aware of a strange, unearthly music that gradually increased in volume until the choir of voices blended to form these words: "*Da Luan, Da Mort, Da Luan, Da Mort, Da Luan, Da Mort* . . ." then there was a pause, before the chorus was repeated. Of course, to Lusmore these words were of his own Gaelic language, meaning "Monday, Tuesday, Monday, Tuesday," and so on.

Lusmore realized that the mystical music was coming from within the moat, and for a time he was quite enchanted. However, after a while the repeated words became somewhat monotonous, so, waiting for the appropriate pause, he took up the song, adding, "*Augus Da Dardeen*," meaning "and Wednesday too." The choir of voices harmonized and blended the new words perfectly into their performance.

The fairies, for that is who they were, singing within the barrow were so delighted with this addition to their tune that they brought Lusmore into their company. He felt as if he were being swept into a whirlpool of sound and light. He was the center of attention and given a place of honor, with servants attending to his every need.

As the singing gradually faded, the fairies gathered together and for a moment Lusmore was uncertain as to their intentions. Then one of the little people stepped up to him and said:

"Lusmore! Lusmore!
Doubt not, nor deplore,
for the hump which you bore
on your back is no more;
the Trooping Fairies
look down on the floor,
and view it, Lusmore!"

As the words were said, Lusmore suddenly felt a great lightness and joy, such that he might have jumped over the moon, like the cow in the song of the cat and the fiddle. He looked down and there upon the ground lay his grotesque hump. Carefully, he raised his head and straightened his back until he stood as tall and proud as any man. The world now seemed a wonderful place and he was quite overcome with the beauty of it all and fell into a deep and happy sleep.

Lusmore slumbered right through the night and was woken by the songs of the birds and the bright light of the morning sun. He was lying on the grassy bank beside the barrow of Knockgrafton, and as he kneeled to say his prayers, he realized that not only had his hump vanished, but he was dressed in a fine new suit of clothes. He gave thanks to the fairies and then strode boldly along the road to Cappagh. No one he met recognized him, and it was with great difficulty that he made them believe he was indeed the Lusmore they had always known.

As the days turned into weeks and the weeks into months, the story of Lusmore losing his hump passed from farm to village to town and so throughout the county and beyond.

One morning, as Lusmore sat outside his door, warming himself in the sun, an old woman came to him and said, "Kind sir, could you direct me to the place called Cappagh?"

"But, my good woman, you are already here. Whom do you seek?" said Lusmore.

"I am from Decie's country, in the county of Waterford, and I have come to find a man called Lusmore, for I have heard that he had his hump removed by the fairies," said the woman.

"Look no more," said Lusmore, "I am that very man for whom you seek. Now, what can I do for you?"

"Well," said the woman from Waterford, "I have an old friend whose son is afflicted with a hump just as you were. We were hoping you might tell us how it was that you were so transformed by the little people of Knockgrafton."

So Lusmore told the story of his encounter with the fairies, how he had added to their tune and they had taken off his hump and even given him a new suit of clothes.

The old woman was very grateful to Lusmore and soon took her leave, returning once more to her friend's house in Waterford. Now, her friend's son, the humpbacked man, was not a good-natured soul like Lusmore, but a rather greedy, unpleasant character. Nevertheless, the mother and her friend took him on a cart all the way back to the moat at Knockgrafton and as night fell they left him beside the ancient barrow.

The man, named Jack Madden, soon heard the sweet song of the fairies, with the extra words from Lusmore: "*Da Luan, Da Mort, Da Luan, Da Mort, Da Luan, Da Mort, augus Da Dardeen . . .*"

Jack, being impatient to lose his hump, did not wait for a suitable pause in the melody but broke in with a coarse shout of "*Augus Da Dardeen, augus Da Hena!*" "And Thursday and Friday!"

Immediately the fairies whirled

him into the moat and crowded angrily around him, shouting, "Who spoiled our tune? Who has done this terrible thing?"

One fairy stood before him and said:

"Jack Madden! Jack Madden!
Your words came so bad in
the tune we felt glad in;
this castle you're had in
that your life we may sadden,
here's two humps for Jack Madden!"

With that, the fairies added Lusmore's hump to the one Jack already carried, fixing it so firmly he could hardly move. They threw him roughly out of the barrow, and there he was, lying despondent upon the ground, when the two women came to collect him in the morning. With some difficulty, they loaded their unfortunate cargo onto the cart and rattled and bumped all the way back to Waterford.

What with the long journey and the extra hump to carry, poor Jack Madden lived only a few more days, and on his death he left a curse on anyone who listened to the fairy tunes again.

FAIRY MUSIC

You don't necessarily need to be able to dance, sing, or play an instrument to connect with fairies through music. There are plenty of fairy-inspired pieces of music, from operas to folk songs, to transport you off to fairyland.

Foque's novella *Undine,* the sad love story of a water sprite who marries a man to gain a human soul, has inspired various musical interpretations, including Hoffman's opera *Ondine,* Hans Henze's ballet *Undine,* and enchanting piano pieces by Debussy and Ravel. Dvorak's opera *Rusalka* tells a similar love story, of the *Rusalka* water sprite from Slavic folklore, and includes the haunting "Song to the Moon."

Other fairy operas include Wagner's *Die Feen* (The Fairies) and Weber's *Overture to Oberon,* which whisks the listener from fairy courts to a mermaid's cave to the court of Charlemagne.

Fairy ballets include Tschaikovsky's classic fairytale ballets *Swan Lake, Sleeping Beauty,* and *The Nutcracker*—the last of which features the famous sugar-plum fairies. Schneitzhoeffer's ballet *La Sylphide* follows the story of a Scottish bridegroom who falls for a winged sylph.

From the stage, the world of Norwegian fairy tales is brought to life in Grieg's music for Ibsen's play *Peer Gynt*, including the "March of the Trolls" and "In the Hall of the Mountain King," while Mendelssohn's overture for *A Midsummer Night's Dream* magically transports listeners to the enchanted woods where Oberon, Tatiana, and Puck dwell.

Celtic ballads and tales have inspired numerous musical interpretations, from traditional reels to pop songs, including Fairport Convention's *Ballad of Tam Lin*, while tales of the Irish hero Cuchlainn were the inspiration for the Pogues' *The Sick Bed of Cuchulainn.*

THE ART OF FAYERIE

"Fayerie" is an old word meaning "the state, or art, of enchantment" (as cookery is the art of cooking, and witchery is the art of witching).

Fairy encounters are often connected with a sense of enchantment, as in "The Ballad of Thomas the Rhymer," when the Queen of Elfland appears while Thomas is daydreaming beneath a tree, enchanted by the beauty of nature.

In his novel *Sylvie and Bruno* (1889), Lewis Carroll explains that in order to see a fairy, it is important to be feeling "fairyish":

The first rule is, that it must be a very hot day—that we may consider as settled: and you must be just a little sleepy—but not too sleepy to keep your eyes open, mind. Well, and you ought to feel a little—what one may call "fairy-ish"—the Scotch call it "eerie," and perhaps that's a prettier word; if you don't know what it means, I'm afraid I can hardly explain it; you must wait till you meet a Fairy, and then you'll know.

And the last rule is, that the crickets should not be chirping. I can't stop to explain that: you must take it on trust for the present.

So, if all these things happen together, you have a good chance of seeing a Fairy—or at least a much better chance than if they didn't.

Losing yourself in fairy art is another way to induce a "fairyish" feeling. Becoming absorbed in the details of fairy paintings and illustrations, one drifts off into a state of fayerie.

Richard Dadd painted the intricately detailed "Fairy Feller's Master Stroke" over a period of nine years (1855–64) while a patient at Bethlem psychiatric hospital, known as Bedlam. This work of art has inspired many other artists. It has influenced the work of writers Angela Carter, Terry Pratchett, and Neil Gaiman, and singer Freddie Mercury, of Queen, wrote a song about it.

From fairy paintings by Henry Fuseli, William Blake, and Joseph Noel Paton to illustrations by Arthur Rackham, Edmund Dulac, Kay Nielson, Richard Doyle (uncle of Sir Arthur Conan Doyle), and Brian Froud (whose creations feature in Jim Henson's films *Dark Crystal* and *Labyrinth*), there is plenty of scope for delving into the art of fayerie as a means of connecting with the fairy realm.

G

Ga-Gaah

In Iroquois mythology Ga-Gaah the Crow is the bringer of corn and therefore ensures the continuing sustenance of the people.

Gabija

In Lithuanian folklore Gabija is a protective fire spirit, a mostly benevolent guardian of the hearth, but she must be treated with respect or the flames will go wandering and cause devastation in the home. Clean water to douse her flames, a neatly piled blanket of ash to cover the embers overnight, and offerings of salt and bread will keep this fiery spirit content.

Gabriel Ratchets

A pack of supernatural hounds in the folklore of Durham, Lancashire, and Yorkshire in the north of England. Similar to the Welsh ***Cwn Annwn***, they were believed to be portents of death. Sometimes described as hounds with human heads, they flew through the skies on stormy nights, with howls like the cries of geese.

See also **Seven Whistlers**, **Yeth Hound**.

Gahongas

One of the types of ***jogah*** nature spirits in Iroquois tradition, *gahongas* are the guardian spirits of rivers and streams, dwarvish people living in caves beside the water. Although small in stature, their strength is immense and they take great delight in rock-hurling contests, so have become known as the Stone Throwers.

A folk tale recounts the legend of a small boy who acquires the wisdom of the *gahongas* when he is taken to their rocky dwelling and taught their magic songs and incantations. After many years, he returns to his home to pass on this fruitful knowledge.

Gaki

The Japanese variant on the ***preta***, or "hungry ghosts," depicted as starving entities with human form but tiny mouths.

Galar

According to the thirteenth-century Icelandic *Prose Edda*, the **dwarf** Galar and his brother, Fjalar, are responsible for the death of the wise Kvasir, whose blood they mix with honey and transform into a magic elixir, the Mead of Poetry. Those who drink this potion gain wisdom and the gift of poetry.

Galatea

A **nereid**, or sea **nymph**, in Greek mythology, who was loved by the Cyclops Polyphemus. Galatea in turn loved the shepherd Acis, who was crushed to death by the jealous **giant**, and transformed his flowing blood into the river Acis.

Galgenmannlein

See ***Kobold.***

Galland, Antoine *(1646–1715)*

A French archeologist who, while in Constantinople (modern-day Istanbul) during the 1690s, came across a manuscript of "The Tale of Sinbad the Sailor." In 1701 his French translation of *One Thousand and One Nights* as *Les milles et une nuits* brought the tales to a

European audience. They proved immediately popular in the French *salons*, where the literary fairy tales of **Charles Perrault** had recently come into vogue.

Galland went on to publish 12 volumes of tales between 1704 and 1717. Early volumes were based on a fourteenth-century Syrian manuscript, while later volumes included tales that were recounted to him by a Syrian monk and scholar. These later tales include some that went on to be the best known in the English-speaking world, such as "Aladdin" and "Ali Baba and the Forty Thieves." There is some speculation as to what extent Galland fabricated or invented these later tales. Notwithstanding, his rendition of *One Thousand and One Nights* was extremely popular throughout Europe, painting a fantastical image in the European mind of magical flying carpets, wish-granting genies, and beautiful princesses inhabiting fragrant and exotic lands. The 1706 English translation, *Arabian Nights Entertainments*, captured the imagination of the English-speaking world and influenced many writers, including Samuel Taylor Coleridge, Thomas de Quincey, Lord Alfred Tennyson, Edgar Allen Poe, and Herman Melville. Later English editions include John Payne's *The Book of a Thousand Nights and a Night* (1882–1884) and Richard Burton's *The Book of a Thousand Nights and a Night* (1885–1886).

Gallas

See **Gallu**.

Gallu

(Also Gallas.) In ancient Babylonian mythology the Gallu demon spirit, sometimes in the form of a bull, conveyed his hapless prey to the Underworld unless a sacrificial lamb was forthcoming to propitiate him.

Gally-Beggar

A fearsome skeletal spirit clutching its head beneath one bony arm, the Gally-Beggar is an apparition of northern England with a piercing shriek and the unnerving ability to curdle blood. Its southern counterpart takes delight in a little snow tobogganing in the dead of night, hurtling downhill while screeching with mirth.

Gally-Trot

In the areas of northern England frequented by the **Gally-Beggar** there is also a shadowy, rough-haired white hound, a large phantom of frightening size but, it seems, of little harmful intent.

Gamayun

A large magical bird with the face of a woman in Russian mythology, the gamayun is a wise and prophetic creature.

Gancone

(Also Gean-Cannah or Love-talker.) Beware the handsome Irish Love-talker, a clay pipe-smoking fairy who seduces solitary maidens with his handsome looks and sweet whispers, although his lips are cold and he casts no shadow. His conquest accomplished, he vanishes into thin air, abandoning the lovelorn girl to her fate: to slowly fade away out of despair and a broken heart.

Gandarewa

(Or Genderuwo.) Mythical and mostly invisible spirits in legends from Java, inhabiting dark watery areas of forest. Shapeshifters in visible form, sometimes apelike and covered in red hair or in the guise of mortals, they are the spirits of those who have died a violent death. In the form of a man, the Gandarewa is a sexual predator with awesome powers of seduction.

Gandayah

Iroquois nature spirits with special powers over the harvests, ensuring crops, fruits, and berries are protected against disease and nurturing with particular attention their favorite strawberry plants. When the ground is dormant under winter snows the *gandayah* sleep, only appearing when the spring sun is in the sky.

GANDHARVAS

In ancient texts the *gandharvas* are Hindu male spirits of the air, tending and guarding the magical soma drink of the deities. They are lovers of women and, being skilled musicians, play in celestial courts where their consorts, the beautiful ***apsaras***, dance to entertain the gods.

GANS

Powerful and benevolent mountain spirits in Navajo and Apache folk tradition, bringing good luck, safeguarding travelers, ensuring rain for their crops, and providing protection from hostile forces. Special ceremonies and dances with specific costumes celebrate and solicit the *gans* and their beneficent guardianship.

GASHADOKURO

In traditional Japanese ghost stories, or *kaidan*, the Gashadokuro appears as a monstrous skeleton many times the size of a human and consisting of a collection of bones from the bodies of those who died of starvation. If a mortal is unlucky enough to be caught by the monster, their head is bitten off.

GEAN-CANNAH

See **Gancone**.

GENDERUWO

See **Gandarewa**.

Genie

The English popularized form of the Arabic ***djinn***, *jinn*, or *jinni*. When **Antoine Galland** translated the Arabian tales *The Thousand and One Nights* into French, he translated *djinn* or *jinni* as *génie*. The word derived from the Roman ***genius***, which originally referred to a personal guardian spirit. This form was adopted into English and is now most often associated with tales such as "Aladdin and his Wonderful Lamp," in which a wish-granting spirit is released by rubbing a magical lamp or bottle, while *djinn* is more often used to refer to the Middle Eastern beings of myth, religion, and folklore.

Genii

In the traditional beliefs of Sierra Leone, the *genii* are nature spirits to whom the tribes make simple offerings such as a few beads in a bottle, a torn piece of white cloth attached to a stick, or a gourd placed on a rag.

See also ***Genius***.

Genii Cucullati

Hooded spirits depicted in stone carvings across the Celtic regions. In Britain they occur as a trinity and are shown as cloaked, mysterious figures. They are sometimes depicted bearing egg-shaped objects, which has led to conjecture that they may represent a fertility spirit, although there are no contemporary written descriptions of their role or identity in the spirit world.

Genius

Guardian spirits in Roman mythology. *Genii* (plural of *genius*) protected individual human beings and natural phenomena.

At birth, each individual was assigned a *genius* that shaped their destiny and character, determining the course of their life. Each aspect of nature had its own *genius* too—animals, crops, water, mountains, volcanoes, and trees all had their own individual *genius* spirit, while the *genius loci*, "spirit of place," was the indwelling spirit and guardian of specific locations.

In Mesopotamian mythology a similar notion is found in the female ***lamassu*** and male ***shedu***, benevolent protective spirits who are pitted against the malevolent influences of the ***utukku***.

Gentle Anne

See **Gentle Annis**.

Gentle Annis

(Or Gentle Anne.) In the northeast of Scotland Gentle Annis is the duplicitous weather spirit who whips up the wind and water in sudden blustery storms.

Gentry, the

An Irish term referring to the fairies in a polite and deferential manner in the hope of avoiding the consequences of their more baleful powers.

German, the

A nature spirit in the folklore of Bulgaria and Serbia, his effigy is constructed from cloth and earth and buried on riverbanks in a ritual observed solely by females to ensure sufficient rain for the crops to flourish. Bread and wine are also offered to him at Christmas in the hope of securing his special protection from damaging rain and hail in the summer months.

Gervase of Tilbury *(c.1150– c.1228)*

Gervase was a lawyer, statesman, and chronicler. He was born in Tilbury, England, but brought up in Rome, Italy. He taught law in Bologna, Italy, and later worked as clerk to the Archbishop of Reims, France.

While still a young man he returned to England, where he formed a close friendship with King Henry II. When the king died, Gervase returned to the continent, where he traveled extensively in the employment of many dignitaries and most notably served the German ruler Otto IV as marshal of the kingdom of Arles, France.

He wrote his most famous work, *Otial Imperalia* (Recreation for an Emperor), finished in 1211, for Otto IV. *Otia Imperalia* is in three volumes, the last of which contains a wealth of folklore and popular beliefs, including accounts of the ***dracs*** of Brittany and the English **portunes**.

Geryon

In Greek mythology the warrior **giant** Geryon is variously described as a three-headed monster with human features or as three-bodied and six-legged, and is sometimes portrayed with wings. His demise was brought about when Hercules, performing the tenth of his great Labors, stole his herd of cattle, first killing Orthrus, his two-headed guard dog, and then shooting a poisoned arrow into the giant's head.

Ghillie Dhu

A solitary, shy fairy of the birchwoods near a Scottish loch, black-haired and clothed in leaves and moss, the Ghillie Dhu is a benevolent entity who sheltered a lost girl and returned her unharmed to her home.

See also **Hyter Sprites**.

Ghoul

The Anglicized "ghoul," from the Arabic ***ghul***, in the Western tradition describes a sinister, formless being haunting graveyards to prey on the flesh of corpses.

Ghul

In pre-Islamic Arab legends, the *ghul* was usually a spirit or demon in female form who abducted or killed lone travelers in desert areas after terrifying them with her ability to swivel her head completely around. The traveler's sole defense was to strike one, and only one, mighty blow with a sword to sever the *ghul*'s head.

See also **Ghoul**.

Giants

Giants feature in numerous folk tales from around the world, their characters ranging from malevolent and cannibalistic to stone-throwing and playful, if sometimes fatally forgetful of their own tremendous strength, as in the tale of the Cornish giant who playfully tapped his mortal friend on the head, killing him stone dead.

Responsible for earthquakes in Greek mythology, through the shaking of their buried bodies, and the building of huge megalithic structures in, for instance, Basque folk tales, the common attribute of giants is phenomenal strength. How this force is used depends upon the character of each giant, which determines the outcome as either disastrously evil or an explanation of otherwise unusual features in a landscape such as randomly scattered boulders.

See also **Biriir ina Baroqo**, **Bran the Blessed**, **Direach**, **Dwarves**, **Galatea**, **Geryon**, **Great Giant of Henllys**, ***Ispolini***, **Jack in Irons**, **Jimmy Squarefoot**, ***Otne-Yar-Heh***, **Peerie Fool**, **Raven**, **Sedna**, **Spriggans**, **Thardid Jimbo**, ***Tsonokwa***, ***Tündér***.

Girouette

An exceedingly careless and flighty fairy who is godmother to a prince in the story of Princess Minon-Minette in **Andrew Lang's** *The Pink Fairy Book* (1897). The story recounts the fabulous adventures of Girouette's awkward and ill-educated charge in his quest for a suitable princess to marry, while Girouette herself tends to many other things and forgets him completely. She spends most of the story in blissful ignorance of his vicissitudes and is only reunited with her prince at the end of the story to attend his marriage, which owes little thanks to her inept fairy-godmotherly abilities.

See also **Aveline**.

Gjenganger

The restless spirit of a suicide or one who suffered or perpetrated a violent death, appearing in the form of a mortal and bent on revenge. As described in early Icelandic sagas, the *Gjenganger* had the power to destroy his victims (see the tale of **Glam**) and occupied an amorphous area between man and apparition. In his present form his malicious intent is to spread infection, disease, and death by administering a fatal pinch of his fingers to a sleeping victim.

Glaistig

(Also Green Glaistig, Green Lady.) An enigmatic water spirit from Scotland, described variously as malign, helpful, sorrowful, dangerous to children, seductive, and sometimes appearing in the form of half-woman, half-goat. She is described in *Superstitions of the Highlands and Islands of Scotland* (1900) by **J. G. Campbell**:

> *The true Glaistig is a woman of human race, who has been put under enchantments, and to whom a Fairy nature has been given. She wears a green dress, like Fairy women, but her face is wan and grey, whence her name Glaistig, from* glas, *grey.*

In yet another form she is described as a "house and castle-haunting" presence, given to joyful utterances or resounding laments when good or bad fortune befell her domain. In this guise the Glaistig's activities presaged the arrival of guests with the sound of much loud rearranging of furniture in locked rooms. When treated disrespectfully, she was not averse to some mischievous chastisement, as she "disarranged the bedclothes, put dust in the meat, led the objects of her resentment a fool's chase about the house, or in the dark gave them a slap to be remembered on the side of the head."

A peripatetic green lady has become a modern legend in Hawaii, where a botanical garden plays host to a spectral figure haunting the trails in search of her lost child.

Glam

The evil ghost of Glam appears in an Icelandic saga recounting the life and adventures of Grettir the Strong, a hero-villain with a nasty temper who performs courageous deeds.

The shepherd Glam was hired by a wealthy farmer, but subsequently murdered, and the efforts of the villagers to bury him in the churchyard were thwarted. Eventually they were forced to leave the unconsecrated body beneath a cairn on the mountainside. Glam's uneasy and malevolent spirit soon began to haunt them, causing madness and death and destroying their houses through nighttime ghostly rides upon the rooftops. In the winter snows he rampaged along the valleys and mountains, killing men and animals in a frenzy of bloodlust until the terrified villagers fled his unholy presence.

When Grettir the Strong appeared at the door of the farm asking for shelter he was warned of the terrible ghost, whereupon he determined to fight the evil fiend and rid the area of it forever. He settled down in a house to wait. Eventually he heard the clatter of hooves and saw a huge and ugly head appearing through the door of the house. When the apparition entered the hall, it was as high as the roof beams.

A deathly struggle ensued until outside in the light of the moon Glam placed a curse upon Grettir, damning him to eternal exile and loneliness. With that, Grettir drew upon his last reserves of strength and slaughtered the monster with his sword.

His life was subsequently dogged by misfortune as Glam had ordained—he was condemned as an outlaw and suffered exile and loneliness.

Glashtin

See **Glastyn**.

Glashtyn

See **Glastyn**.

Glastyn

(Also *glashtin, glashtyn*). A **water horse** of the Isle of Man, dangerously manifesting as a handsome man who takes great care to hide his ears beneath his curly, dark hair, as they are those of a horse. Luring his female victims with his good looks and tempting presents, he aims to subject them to a watery death. He is believed by some also to manifest in the guise of the ***cabyll ushtey***.

Gnomes

Earth-dwellers, variously known as dwarves or **goblins** in traditional tales, but originally described as earth elementals by the fifteenth-century alchemist and physician Paracelsus. He divided fairies into four groups: the gnomes of the earth, the **sylphs** of the air, the **salamanders** of fire, and the **undines** or **nymphs** of water. Each elemental represented the pure form of that elemental energy. Elementals were said to be creatures partway between humans and pure spirits. They were made of flesh and blood, and ate, drank, slept, and procreated like human beings, but they were capable of superhuman speed and movement, lived longer than humans, and did not have immortal souls.

Other descriptions of gnomes are found in *Brewer's Dictionary of Phrase and Fable* (1898):

> *Gnomes according to the Rosicru'cian system, are the elemental spirits of earth, and the guardians of mines and quarries. (Greek,* gnoma, *knowledge, meaning the knowing ones, the wise ones) . . . The gnomes, or demons of the earth, delight in mischief.*

In *British Goblins* (1880), **Wirt Sikes** states, referring specifically to Welsh spirits: "Under the general title of *coblynau* I class the fairies which haunt the mines, quarries and underground regions of Wales, corresponding to the cabalistic Gnomes." He then conflates gnomes and goblins.

See also **Barbegazi**, **Haltija**, **Kabouter**, **Maanväki**, **Meister Hammerling**.

Goblins

In *British Goblins* (1880) **Wirt Sikes** refers to the "lowly goblins" thus:

The word coblyn has the double meaning of knocker or thumper and sprite or fiend; and may it not be the original of goblin? It is applied by Welsh miners to pigmy fairies which dwell in the mines, and point out, by a peculiar knocking or rapping, rich veins of ore.

The coblynau *are described as being about half a yard in height and very ugly to look upon, but extremely good-natured, and warm friends of the miner. Their dress is a grotesque imitation of the miner's garb, and they carry tiny hammers, picks and lamps. They work busily, loading ore in buckets, flitting about the shafts, turning tiny windlasses, and pounding away like madmen, but really accomplishing nothing whatever.*

The grim and devilish aspect of goblins is thoroughly explored with accounts of fearful appearances such as a death portent in the form of a corpse candle in which "the goblin is a light which issues from a person's mouth or nostrils . . . the size of the candle indicates the age of the person who is about to die, being large when it is a full-grown person whose death is foretold, small when it is a child, still smaller when an infant."

In one account, whirling Welsh goblins who spin around on hands and feet caused one narrator terror as he witnessed the "dreadful apparition . . . and felt his hair to move on his head; his heart panted and beat violently, his body trembled, and he felt not his clothes about him."

In general, goblins are synonymous with malevolent and dangerous spirits, although the addition of the prefix **Hob**, as in **hobgoblin**, implies a hearth-and-home, helpful entity, not without mischief but lacking the spiteful malice of a goblin.

See also **Baumesel**, **Bogles**,

Brag, **Bullbeggar**, **Mara**, ***Nain Rouge***, **Redcaps**, **Skriker**.

Goibniu

See **Govannon**.

Goolagaya

In Australian aboriginal folk tradition Goolagaya's spirit and that of her canine companion, a wild white dingo, live in a twisted tree trunk on the banks of a lonely lagoon. During her lifetime this spiteful woman's scheming caused a baby to drown in the lagoon and the tribe lost no time in taking their revenge, killing her and her dingo and burying them deep beneath the waters. Escaping from this watery grave, their spirits began to haunt the area after sunset and to search for children who left the safety of their fires to wander in the darkness.

Gooseberry Wife

A gigantic, hairy caterpillar who lurks in gooseberry bushes in gardens on the Isle of Wight, southern England. A bugbear or **bogie** invoked as a deterrent to would-be marauders of the fruit bushes.

Goryos

Japanese spirits of aristocrats during the Heian dynasty of the eighth to twelfth centuries, whose deaths were attributable to political plotting and chicanery and whose vengeful spirits returned to cause death and destruction. Efforts to propitiate them bestowed them with ever-increasing status.

In time it was thought that people whose death was violent could also become a *goryos*, and various incantations and rituals were devised and performed to guard against them.

Govannon

(Also Goibniu [Irish].) In the *Mabinogion*, the collection of stories derived from medieval Welsh texts, Govannon is a deity of metalsmithing possessed of the power to forge invincible weapons for his fairy tribe. His powers include giving eternal youth to those who drink his magical potions.

Grant, the

A fairy horse of England. In **Thomas Keightley**'s *The Fairy Mythology* (1828), he is described as a "friendly demon." The thirteenth-century chronicler **Gervase of Tilbury** wrote that he was an apparition in the form of a "yearling foal, erect on its hind legs, with sparkling eyes." Appearing in broad daylight or at sunset and thoroughly frightening the population by his sudden presence, the Grant serves as a warning of imminent danger.

Grave Watcher, the

See **Ankou**.

Gray Neighbors

In Shetland the **trows** are also known as gray neighbors, an indirect reference to the gray-clothed supernatural beings that is used as a mark of respect.

Gray Paw, the

John G. Campbell, in *Witchcraft and Second Sight in the Highlands and Islands of Scotland* (1902), relates the story of this malignant spirit whose unearthly presence terrified the local population, for those who ventured into the vicinity of the church or graveyard during the night heard all manner of strange sounds and were never seen again.

A brave tailor made a wager that he would sit in the church one night and stitch a pair of hose. As he sat sewing in the moonlight, all was quiet until . . .

. . . at the dead hour of midnight . . . a big ghastly head emerged from a tomb and said, "Look at the old grey cow that is without food, tailor."

The tailor said, "I see that and I sew this," and soon found while he spoke the ghost was stationary, but when he drew breath it rose higher.

The neck emerged and said, "A long grizzled weasand [gullet] *that is without food, tailor."*

The tailor went on with his work in fear, but answered, "I see it, my son, I see it my son, I see that and I sew this just now."

This he said drawling out his words to their utmost length. At last his voice failed and he inhaled a long breath.

At that moment, the last stitch was put in the hose and the tailor gave one spring of horror to the door. The claw struck at him and the point of the fingers caught him by the bottom against the door-post and took away the piece. The mark of the hand remains on the door to this day. The tailor's flesh shook and quivered with terror, and he could cut grass with his haunches as he flew home.

Each time the tailor was forced to draw breath, the spirit rose higher and higher. First his arm: "Without flesh or food, tailor." Next the thigh: "A long crooked shank that is without meat, tailor" and each time the trembling tailor would make his reply.

At length a bony arm was extended toward him and the apparition said, "A long gray paw without blood or flesh or muscles, or meat, tailor."

By now the tailor had nearly finished his sewing and answered one last time, "I see it, my son, I see it, my son; I see that and I sew this just now," until he had to draw breath, when the spirit, spreading out its long and bony fingers and clutching the air in front of him, said, "A big gray claw that is without meat, tailor."

Similar tales are found throughout Scotland, as in the cathedral on the island of Iona where there is a corner called "the tailor's hole."

Great Giant of Henllys

The British literary magazine the *Athenaeum* of 1847 recounts the Welsh tale of a vicious and despotic man known as the Great **Giant** of Henllys on account of his wicked ways.

The death of the Great Giant was greeted with great rejoicing and relief that his terrible power had come to an end—but the celebrations were short-lived. In the form of a hideous demon he reappeared to terrorize the people, who were soon too frightened to venture out after sunset for fear of his evildoing.

Three clergymen were determined to exorcise this malignant presence and they gathered at the dead of night by the altar of the village church. They drew a circle on the floor, stepped inside, and stood with lighted candles while they prayed.

With a ghastly commotion the demon appeared, rushing toward the men at prayer, and so terrifying was his proximity that one man quailed and his candle went out. However, the demon could not penetrate the circle and after many demonic manifestations he appeared in his mortal form, declaring that as a man he had been wicked but as a devil he was even worse. With this, he vanished in a fiery flash, and the candles burned brightly once more while the clergymen prayed steadfastly.

As the prayers continued, the Giant appeared again, gradually becoming smaller and smaller until he was only a fly, which the clergymen placed in a tobacco box and cast into a nearby lake, there to lie undisturbed for 99, or possibly 999, years.

GREEN CHILDREN

In the county of Suffolk, England, a folk tale from the twelfth century was told by **Ralph of Coggeshall**, recounting how two green children were found near the mouth of a pit: "[They] had the form of all their limbs like to those of other men but they differed in the colour of their skin from all the people of our habitable world; for the whole surface of their skin was tinged of a green colour."

The sickly boy and his sister, whose language could not be understood by the puzzled villagers and who, though ravenously hungry, would not touch the food offered to them, were taken to the house of a knight. **Keightley**'s *The Fairy Mythology* (1828) describes the food that eventually tempted them to eat:

At length, when some beans just cut, with their stalks, were brought into the house, they made signs, with great avidity, that they should be given to them. When they were brought, they opened the stalks instead of the pods, thinking the beans were in the hollow of them; but not finding them there, they began to weep anew. When those who were present saw this, they opened the pods, and showed them the naked beans. They fed on these with great delight, and for a long time tasted no other food.

But this sustenance came too late for the sickly boy, who died shortly afterward. The girl regained her health, lost the green tinge of her skin, and talked of the country she and her brother had come from: "She asserted that the inhabitants, and all they had in that country, were of a green colour; and that they saw no sun, but enjoyed a degree of light like what is after sunset."

The present-day village of Woolpit, the location of this tale, features on its sign the two figures of the green children.

Green Fairy, the

La Fée Verte, or the Green Fairy, is another name for absinthe, the intoxicating drink made from wormwood, green fennel, and other herbs. In France during the nineteenth century it became the drink of choice for writers and artists and known as their "Green **Muse**." It was so popular that the hour of 5 p.m. in the boulevard cafés and bars became known as the "green hour."

Green Glaistig

See **Glaistig**.

Green Lady

See **Glaistig**.

Green Man, the

A nature spirit, or wild man of the woods, in European folklore. He is a guardian spirit of woodlands and a symbol of the fertility of nature. He features prominently in May Day celebrations, when people dress in costumes made of greenery and flowers, representing the Green Man in the guise of Jack-of-the-Green, the King of the May, or the Garland, in celebration of the regeneration of springtime.

Carvings of the Green Man as a head with foliage emerging from the mouth, nose, and beard are found in Christian churches dating back to the sixth century.

Greencoaties

Another way of referring to the fairy folk indirectly, thereby avoiding offense to them. The fairies, or **tiddy men**, of the Lincolnshire fens in England were thus addressed, as their powers over the streams and rivers of the area were a potential threat if they were treated without due deference.

So-called because of the green coats they dressed in, on summer nights the greencoaties were said to dance on the moonlit flat stones of the fens.

Green-haired Fairy, the

The French legend of the fisherman Brincan and his love for the Green-haired Fairy is told in **Keightley**'s *The Fairy Mythology* (1828).

The ill-fated and handsome Brincan rows out to sea one night and is transported to the depths of the ocean, where a beautiful fairy captivates him with her slender waist and brilliant eyes, her soft voice and delicate hands. Her green hair notwithstanding, he is seduced and when they part she gives him two fishes and demands that he not speak of their love to anyone.

Time and again Brincan returns to her embraces and his hair, too takes on a greenish tinge, which causes many questions; he is, however, silent about his magical lover.

In time he meets a mortal girl with whom he falls in love and, summoning great resolve, he discards his watery mistress. His hair once more becomes flaxen and his memories of the fairy's power fade. She, however, wreaks revenge on her erstwhile lover: each time he draws near to his new love he is struck with invisible blows that mark his white skin with welts and in his head he is tormented by voices.

Finally he is compelled to return to the depths of the ocean to confront the angry fairy. Implacably, she condemns him to be eaten by sea monsters as retribution for his betrayal—although some say she keeps him with her for a time instead and then returns him to the land, prematurely grizzled and wrinkled, where he lives out his days as a fisherman.

Gregory, Lady Augusta

(1852–1932)

Born Isabella Augusta Persse in County Galway, Ireland, Lady Gregory was a writer and playwright with a special interest in Irish folklore and mythology. She translated Irish legends and her plays were mainly inspired by Irish folklore.

Lady Gregory was a considerable influence on the renaissance of nineteenth-century Irish literature known as the Irish Literary Revival. She was introduced to Irish mythology by her nanny, a native Irish speaker. In 1880 she married Sir William Henry Gregory, a landowner 35 years her senior. He was well educated, and interested in literature and the arts. Although Lady Gregory had a keen interest in literature herself, her literary career did not start until her husband's death in 1892. In 1896 she met the Irish poet **W. B. Yeats** and they remained lifelong friends. She was also involved in the foundation of the Irish Literary Theatre and became a director of the Abbey Theatre.

In 1893 Lady Gregory undertook a trip to the Aran Islands which rekindled her interest in the Irish language as well as the Irish folklore. She began collecting tales, which led to the publication of many books, including *Cuchulain of Muirthemne* (1902), *Gods and Fighting Men* (1904), *A Book of Saints and*

Wonders (1906), and the *Kiltartan Wonder Book* (1910).

Grim

In Jabez Allies' *On the Ignis Fatuus or Will-O'-the-Wisp and the Fairies* (1846), an account of hauntings and apparitions in the villages of Worcestershire, England, Grim appears as one of four fairies in the guise of black horses pulling a "mysterious black waggon . . . in the night's dread gloom." The fairies are described as shapeshifters: "Pinch and Patch, Gull and Grim/ Goe you together;/for you can change your shapes/Like to the weather."

Grim is also described as taking on the form of a black dog, similar to the Church Grim, the guardian spirit of a church and its graveyard.

Grimm, Jakob and Wilhelm
(1785–1863) (1786–1859)

The Grimm brothers were German academics, linguists, cultural researchers, and authors who collected and published folklore and fairy tales. They were born in Hanau, the second and third children of a family of nine. At the ages of 13 and 14, following the death of their father, they moved in with an aunt in the town of Kassel. They went on to study law at the University of Marburg, but had already established an interest in traditional tales. Their professor introduced them to Clemens Brentano, a German Romantic who wrote folk poetry. He urged the brothers to collect and write down all the stories they had heard.

Despite having to work as librarians to support their younger siblings (their mother died in 1808), the brothers continued with their task, and their first book, *Children and Household Tales,* also known as *Grimms' Fairy Tales,* was published in 1812. The book contained 86 tales and included some of **Charles Perrault**'s stories. The second volume was published two years later, with 70 additional tales. In its final version it would contain more than 200 tales.

The Grimms collected tales that they thought typically represented German culture and heritage, such as "Little Red Riding Hood," although stories with the same thread can be found throughout Europe and beyond. Over the years they rewrote some of the tales, adding details and often eliminating the violent and sexual content in order to make them suitable for children. There are too many tales to be listed here, but some of the best known include "Rapunzel," "Hansel and Gretel," "Sleeping Beauty," "Cinderella," and "Tom Thumb."

The Grimms' influence on the fairytale genre is undeniable, and their work inspired many similar collections of folklore and fairy tales in various countries. Their tales continue to be adapted and recounted around the world.

Grindylow

Haunting pools and bogs, this malicious water spirit of the northern counties of England lures children to their death by drowning. A similar spirit to **Jenny Greenteeth**, it serves as a warning to unwary children not to venture too close to water.

Groac'h of the Isle of Lok

The Breton tale of the Groac'h is recounted in *The Lilac Fairy Book* (1910) by **Andrew Lang**. The tale tells of Groac'h, a rich fairy possessing many treasures on her island stronghold in the middle of a lake, and of Houarn and Bellah, cousins who wish to marry each other but are too poor "to buy a cow and a pig to fatten."

Houarn sets off to seek his fortune, armed with two magical charms given to him by Bellah, who tells him, "This bell can be heard at any distance, however far, but it only rings to warn us that our friends are in great danger. The knife frees all it touches from the spells that have been laid on them, while the stick will carry you wherever you want to go. I will give you the knife to guard you against the enchantments of wizards, and the bell to tell me of your perils. The stick I shall keep for myself so that I can fly to you if ever you have need of me."

Houarn eventually arrives at the underwater palace of the beautiful Groac'h, where he sees "her long black hair . . . intertwined with strings of coral, and her dress of green silk seemed formed out of the sea. At the sight of her Houarn stopped, dazzled by her beauty."

He consents to marry her, forgetting his love for Bellah, but when the Groac'h brings him a meal he belatedly realizes that the fish on his plate are previous suitors under a wicked spell. He touches each fish with the enchanted knife and reveals four men. As they try to escape, the Groac'h captures them and changes Houarn into a little green frog. Quickly, he rings the bell.

Bellah, on hearing the tinkling of the fairy bell, flies to his rescue with the aid of the magic stick, which transforms into a swift steed, then a giant bird, and with much cunning she manages to trap the Groac'h in her own steel net. "Become in body what you are in soul," she cries. At once "the lovely fairy of the sea was a toad, horrible to look upon."

The evil fairy is thrown into a pit and sealed in with a gigantic stone, the four suitors are restored to human form and recompensed from the treasure hoard, and Houarn and Bellah buy herds of cows and plenty of pigs to fatten, get married, and live happily ever after on their bountiful farm.

Grogach

See **Gruagach**.

Grogan

See **Gruagach**.

Gruagach, the

In the *Carmina Gadelica*, a late-nineteenth-century collection of Gaelic folk tales and lore by **Alexander Carmichael**, the Gruagach is described as living on a remote Scottish island as a beautiful woman:

. . . moving about in the silvery light of the kindly moon . . . with her tall conical hat [and] her rich golden hair falling about her like a mantle of shimmering gold, while with a slight swish of her wand she gracefully turned on her heel to admonish an unseen cow. At intervals [the man witnessing this] seemed to hear her mellow voice in snatches of eerie song as she moved about among the grassy ruins of the old nunnery . . .

As a guardian of cattle, she received offerings of milk poured onto special stones, and if this ritual was neglected, the farmer could expect his cows to cause devastation to his crops. If no further offerings were made, his best cow would be struck dead.

Another account, from 1895 in the Arran area of Scotland, recounts the good husbandry of crops and cattle that "throve and fattened and multiplied right well" under the Gruagach's care. She would "come forth with the radiant sun, her golden hair streaming on the morning breeze, and her rich voice filling the air with melody. She would wait on a grassy hillock afar off till the people would bring out their . . . creatures, crooning a lullaby the while, and striding to and fro."

The grateful population wanted to make her a gift of clothes (always a mistake where fairy folk are concerned). They made her "a linen garment to clothe her body and down sandals to cover her feet" and waited with eagerness for her to wear them. But the Gruagach was so displeased that she made to leave and in a giant stride placed her feet on two mountaintops. As she did so, a tall ship sailed along the water separating the mountains, grazing her thigh and tipping her into the sea.

The Irish **brownie** called the Grogan, or Grogach, is similar to the Gruagach, although in this case is a strong, hairy little entity with a penchant for hard work which in one tale is literally the death of him. The story of the Grogach of Ballycastle describes what happens when a farmer forgets to put out the correct number of sheaves to be threshed. The Grogach arrives at the barn to find the threshing-tool atop the whole cornstack and sets to with a will, but is found in the morning, dead upon the pile of grain.

Gryla

Descended from **trolls** and mother of the equally hideous Yule Lads, Gryla is a cannibalistic ogre whose appearance is described in

Jon Arnason's nineteenth-century collection of Icelandic folk tales:

Grýla has three heads and three eyes in each head ... Horribly long, curved fingernails, icy blue eyes at the back of the head and horns like a goat, her ears dangle down to her shoulders and are attached to the nose in front. She has a beard on her chin that is like knotted yarn on a weave with tangles hanging from it, while her teeth are like burnt rocks in a grate.

With such a gruesome aspect she could hardly be more qualified to frighten misbehaving children, especially at Christmas, when she is partial to feasting on them.

Her 13 sons, the Yule Lads, accompany her but have undergone modification over the years and are now benign present-givers, leaving their gifts in children's shoes.

On a satirical news website, the blame for the eruption of Eyjafjallajökull, an Icelandic volcano, and the subsequent devastation of airline schedules caused by the dense cloud of ash, was laid at Gryla's door.

Gualichu

A malevolent spirit in folk tales from Chile and Argentina, malignant in the extreme, having no visible form, and believed to cause all manner of evil from sickness and death to possession of the body requiring exorcism. "*Gualicho*" has entered the language as a curse.

Gui

Gui, or ghosts, form an important part of Chinese culture, especially with regard to respect for the ancestors and the need to redress injustices suffered by them.

The story of Nu Gui tells of a beautiful young woman who is treated badly in life and commits suicide wearing a red dress. She reappears in spirit form to take her revenge dressed all in white.

The *shui gui* is a watery ghost, the spirit of a drowned person seeking revenge by attacking the living and taking possession of their body.

Among these restless and vengeful spirits there is, however, also the *gui po*, a helpful household presence.

A ghost festival is held each year on the fifteenth night of the seventh month in the Chinese calendar, during which offerings are made to the ancestors by burning incense and preparing food not only to be shared with the monks and poor of the neighborhood but as propitiation to the unseen presences at the table.

Gull

Along with **Grim**, this prankster of a fairy is associated with **Robin Goodfellow**. Among his dubious skills he lists the stealing of children and leaving **changelings** in their place, thieving cream, causing nightmares by lying on the stomachs of sleeping mortals, and "gulling" or bamboozling people by using a different voice.

Gunna

In the *Superstitions of the Highlands and Islands of Scotland* by **J. G. Campbell**, the Gunna is described as "an invisible herdsman" who guards the cattle and ensures they do not stray into the crops.

No one ever saw this presence until a man, gifted with second sight, observed a naked man looking after the cows. Feeling compassion for his nakedness, the seer made the Gunna a pair of trousers, or trews, and some shoes. As he watched the ghostly figure donning the clothes, he heard him say:

"Trews upon Gunna
because Gunna does the herding,
but may Gunna never enjoy his trews,
if he tends cattle any more."

With this he went away and was never seen again.

Gurumapa

A Nepalese demon with a penchant for abducting and devouring the children of Kathmandu, Gurumapa was eventually destroyed by the racing hooves of horses on the

Tundikhel meadow where he lived. Before he expired, a bargain was struck with him that a buffalo feast would be prepared each year and rice cooked near to the tree under which he had lived. To this day, a great horse race takes place at this place, the thunder of the horses' hooves keeping the evil spirit from returning.

In a slightly different version, two plaques commemorating the tale show the demon polishing off a child for his meal and partaking of the buffalo feast and keeping his part of the bargain. These plaques are sited next to a school.

GURUMUKAS

Aboriginal tales from the Northern Territory of Australia tell of the *gurumukas*, tall gaunt spirits of the night who sink their prominent teeth into the neck of an unsuspecting solitary traveler in the darkness. Without immediate assistance from a medicine man, the victim suffers a painful death.

See also **Nadubi**.

GUYTRASH

See **Gytrash**.

GWACH Y RHIBYN

A death portent, the *gwrach y rhibyn* is described in one folk tale as "a hideous being with dishevelled hair, long black teeth, long, lank, withered arms, leathern wings, and a cadaverous appearance" uttering piercing shrieks and howls as it flaps its wings against windows in the night. A **banshee**, it appears when death is imminent, as in the tale of the Cow and Snuffers Inn visitation, witnessed by "a respectable-looking man of the peasant-farmer class," in **Sikes**' *British Goblins* (1880), in which the narrator describes being woken by loud screeches and rattlings at his window. He sees "a horrible old woman with long red hair and a face like chalk, and great teeth like tusks, looking back over her shoulder at me as she went through the air with a long, black gown trailing along the ground below her arms, for body I could make out none." The awful apparition disappears through the door of the inn and is not seen to come out although the man watches long into the night. The next day the innkeeper is found dead.

Gwern

See **Bran the Blessed**.

Gwragedd Annwn

Numerous Welsh folk tales of the **Lady of the Lake** recount the union of the beautiful water fairy and a mortal man in marriage, after he overcomes her reluctance by agreeing to certain stipulations. **Sir John Rhys'** *Celtic Folklore: Welsh and Manx* (1901) tells the story.

A young man sent to look after his mother's cattle beside a small lake, the Llyn y Fan Fach, sees a beautiful maiden combing her long, flaxen hair while seated on the glassy water. He is mesmerized by her beauty and holds out to her a portion of the bread he has been eating. She quietly refuses, saying the bread is too hard, and promptly dives beneath the waters.

The youth is utterly forlorn and love-struck and hurries home to his mother, who gives him some unbaked dough the next day to take as an offering. After many hours of patient waiting, the man spies the cattle on the far side of the lake and is just hastening to herd them to safety when the beauteous maiden rises from the waters and he proffers her his heart, his fidelity, and his handful of dough. But again she smilingly refuses and again he returns home.

This time his mother makes a loaf of melting softness and the youth sets out yet again to woo the lake fairy. He spends the entire day watching the undisturbed surface of the water, and as the evening sun sinks, despondency starts to descend on him. Suddenly, he notices with amazement that his cattle are walking on the lake and his hopes rise as his beautiful maiden appears.

At last they meet, clasping hands as his offering is finally accepted, and his persuasive talk elicits her promise to become his wife on condition that he will never strike her three times without just cause.

At this, she disappears into the water and his joy turns to despair before being replaced by wonder as now three figures emerge and come towards him: a fine old man with two identical daughters, one of whom the ardent lover must correctly select as his bride. With a subtle and deft movement of her foot, one of them shows him the distinctive lacing of her sandal, thus solving his dilemma, and the young man and his fairy bride are given herds of goats, cattle, sheep, and horses, which rise from the lake as rapidly as the lake maiden can count them.

The man and the fairy live a happy life together and three fine sons are born, but the fairy wife's ways are sometimes strange and her husband reprimands her for this, touching her each time, though gently. On the third such occasion, she cries that he has broken his vow and the marriage must end. Gathering her cattle and sheep, she leads them away over the hills to the little lake, where they all disappear beneath the waters.

Her wisdom and knowledge of healing are not lost, however, for when her sons are grown men they meet her by the shores of the lake and she imparts her secrets to them. They become renowned throughout Wales for their medicinal skills and are remembered ever after as the Physicians of Mydffai.

See also **Van Pools**.

GWYLLION

Welsh mountain fairies of a gruesome and haglike appearance. Uttering cries of distress, they haunt travelers on lonely mountain roads "in the semblance of a poor old woman, with an oblong four-cornered hat, ash-coloured clothes, her apron thrown across her shoulder, with a pot or wooden can in her hand, such as poor people carry to fetch milk with, always going before the spectator," according to **Sikes**' description in *British Goblins* (1880). Unwary walkers will hurry toward the old woman, but, fast as they walk she is always further ahead, until eventually the hapless victim finds themselves floundering in a bog or completely lost while listening to the unearthly cackle of the *gwyllion.*

Gwyn ap Nudd

King of the Welsh Underworld, appearing in early Arthurian tales and later medieval poems as a warrior and knight possessed of enough strength to control the demons he rules over in the otherworld.

Gyhldeptis

A Native American guardian spirit of the northwest coast, responsible for the well-being of the forest and its inhabitants.

Gyre-Carling

In *St Baldred of the Bass: A Pictish Legend*, written in 1824 by J. Miller, the Gyre-Carling, the great hag or mother witch of the Scottish peasantry of East Lothian, appears in a poem as Queen of the Fairies.

This "monstrous lady," also known as Nicnevin, also appears in Alexander Montgomerie's sixteenth-century poem *Flyting with Polwart*, as a witchlike fairy queen riding through the night with the fairy king and a procession of dark fairies and *incubi* on Samhain (Halloween).

Gytrash

(Also guytrash.) A dialect word from the north of England to describe a sinister death portent appearing in the form of an animal.

In *Jane Eyre* by Charlotte Brontë, Jane remembers a gytrash ghost story in which the specter appears as a horse or dog, and is momentarily alarmed as she sits all alone and hears the sound of hooves.

H

Habetrot

Scottish patron fairy of spinning. An account in Henderson's *Notes on the Folklore of the Northern Counties of England and the Borders* (1866) relates a story that has similarities with **Rumpelstiltskin**, **Terrytop**, and **Whuppity Stoorie**. The main difference is that Habetrot is a kind and helpful fairy, unlike the devilish characters in the other tales.

There was once a lass who preferred wandering the countryside picking flowers to working and spinning. One day, her mother, despairing of her daughter's idle ways, set her the task of spinning seven heads of lint into yarn in three days. The girl set to work in earnest, but at the end of the first day all she had to show for her labors was a short piece of lumpy thread. That night she cried herself to sleep.

The next morning was no better and she took a walk by a river to get some air. Sitting down to rest on a stone with a hole through the middle of it, she burst into tears. As if out of nowhere, an old lady with a very long bottom lip appeared next to her, busily spinning. Being a friendly soul, the girl struck up a conversation and asked the woman how her lip came to be so long. Looking pleased at the question, the woman told her, "With drawing the thread for spinning my honey."

"That's what I should be doing," said the girl, and told the woman her story, whereupon the old lady offered to help with the spinning. The girl brought her the lint and was about to enquire as to her helper's name, but the old woman disappeared before she had a chance to ask.

The afternoon sun was warm and the girl soon fell asleep on the stone. When she woke up, it was sunset and she heard a whirring noise and the sound of voices coming from under her head. Putting her eye to the hole in the stone, she saw a great cavern where a group of old women were spinning, sitting on white marble stones worn smooth by the river. They all had long, long lips too. The old lady was there, overseeing the spinning. "Little does the wee lassie know that Habetrot is my name," she said and went to a spinner sitting apart from the others, "Bundle up the yarn, Scantile Mab, it's time the lassie gave it to her mother."

Realizing the three days were up, the girl ran home to her mother's cottage. Habetrot was waiting there with seven beautiful hanks of yarn. The girl was very grateful and asked what she could do in return. "Nothing," replied Habetrot, "but don't tell your mother who spun that yarn." And with that she was gone.

The girl went into the cottage and found her mother sound asleep. She left the beautiful yarn on the table and was overcome by hunger, for she hadn't eaten for three days. Her mother had been hard at work making black puddings and they looked too delicious to resist. The girl took down the frying pan, cooked the first black pudding and ate it. Then she cooked a second, and a third, and a fourth, until all seven were gone and, full up, she climbed into bed and fell asleep.

When her mother woke up, she saw the seven beautiful skeins of yarn and was overjoyed. Then she saw there was no trace of her seven black puddings, save for a blackened frying pan, and she was furious. See-sawing between joy and rage, she rushed out of the house singing:

"Ma daughter's spun seven, seven,
seven,
Ma daughter's eaten seven, seven,
seven,
And all before daylight!"

The young local laird happened to be riding past and stopped to ask her what all the fuss was about. Again she sang:

"Ma daughter's spun seven, seven,
seven,
Ma daughter's eaten seven, seven,
seven!"

"If you don't believe me, come and see for yourself," she added.

When the laird saw how perfect and even the yarn was, he asked to meet the person who had spun it. When he was introduced to the bonny lass, he asked her to be his bride. He was a handsome and kind fellow and she was only too pleased to accept, but one thing troubled her—he kept talking about all the fine yarn she would spin for him after their wedding. So she went back to the stone with a hole through the middle to find Habetrot, who told her to bring her husband-to-be the following evening.

At sunset the next day, the

couple arrived at the stone and Habetrot opened a hidden door and led them into a room where her long-lipped helpers sat spinning. The laird was astonished to see their stretched lips and asked how they had come to be so distorted.

"With sp-sp-spinning," came the barely distinguishable replies.

"Aye! They were once bonnie, but this is a spinner's lot," said Habetrot. "Your own lass will be the same, bonnie though she is now, for she's fair mad about spinning."

The laird vowed that his wife-to-be would not touch another spindle from that day forward.

"Just as you say, laird," she replied, away they rode, and from that day on every head of lint on their land to be spun went to old Habetrot.

Habetrot really was believed to be the patron of spinners. Garments made by her were highly valued and believed to be a remedy for all manner of diseases.

It's interesting to note that many of the spinning fairies have names ending in "trot," "tot," or "top," such as Terrytop and **Tom Tit Tot**, although Habetrot is friendly and helpful while the others are sinister and associated with a curse.

Hag

Probably derived from the Old English term for "witch," *haegtesse*, in folklore a hag is usually an old woman who practices witchcraft. Similar to a crone, a hag is associated with magical or supernatural powers and often portrayed as malevolent, ugly, and wizened, although hags can also be helpful and offer protection, advice, or gifts. In certain tales, if the hero treats a hag with love and respect despite her outwardly ugly appearance, he is rewarded by her revealing herself to be a beautiful young woman.

Supernatural or **giant** hags such as the ***Cailleach Bheur***, who is a personification of winter, have their roots in belief in nature goddesses.

The Old Hag, or Hagge, is a name for a nightmare that dates back to the sixteenth century. The Old Hag was a repulsive succubus who sat on a man's stomach in his sleep, causing bad dreams.

Hairy Meg

See **Meg Mullach**.

Haltia

See ***Haltija***.

Haltija

(Also *haltia.*) **Gnome** or **elf**-like creatures in Finnish folklore. *Haltijat* (plural of *haltija*) are guardian spirits and the name probably derives from the Finnish for "to own" or "to guard."

Each aspect of nature is associated with its own *haltija.* The *veden haltija,* presided over by Ahti and his wife, Vellamo, are guardians of water. The *metsan haljita,* ruled over by Tapio and his wife, Mielikki, are protectors of the forest. *Mann haltija,* or *tonttu,* are guardians of the household, similar to **brownies**. Even saunas have their own *haltija,* the *saunatonttu,* who acts as a caretaker and makes sure that any inappropriate behavior in the sauna is punished.

Haltija and *haltia* are also both used to refer to elves in Finland, although following Kersti Juva's use of *haltia* in the Finnish translation of J. R. R. Tolkien's *The Lord of the Rings,* this form is more commonly associated with the type of elves found in fantasy fiction, while *haltija* is more commonly associated with the elves and supernatural beings of traditional Finnish folklore.

Hamadryad

See ***Akakasoh***, **Dryads**.

Hantu

Malay spirits, demons, or ghosts. There are many varieties, including the *hantu air,* evil water-dwelling spirits, *hantu gunung,* mountain spirits, and *hantu hutan,* tall, hairy, fish-eating spirits dwelling in the Malaysian rainforest.

Harpies

Winged spirits from Greek mythology, the daughters of the sea god Thaumas (Wonder) and Electra, daughter of Oceanus. The name literally means "That which snatches." Usually depicted as birds with women's faces, according to Hesiod and Homer they were the personification of violent winds that were strong enough to carry people away.

Hathor

Ancient Egyptian goddess of women. Also known as "the Great One with Many Names," she took on many different forms, including that of the Seven Hathors. Similar to the Three Fates of Greek mythology, the Seven Hathors attended births and were believed to know the length of every child's life and to be able to read—and determine—their fortune. They may be one of the earliest examples of birth fairies associated with fate and fortune-telling—fairies who later went on to be represented as fairy godmothers.

Havmands

See **Merman**.

Hebu

One of numerous bush spirits named in legends from tribes in northeastern South America. The *hebu* is distinctive in both appearance and habits, as it is without buttocks, displaying from the rear a glowing fire, and in order to look at the sky it must stand on its head, as its eyebrows are so protuberant they prevent any upward sight. Sometimes manifesting as skulls or skeletons and shunning daylight hours, these hairy beings live in forest trees, which they smite all night, causing much hullabaloo.

One tale recounts that a *hebu* whose name was Kau-nassa enticed children to a creek, and while they were playing, always in front of her, she plaited a basket and asked them to get inside for a game. When they did, she quickly placed a lid on top and dropped the basket into the water, where the children drowned.

Next she sought out two more children, a girl and her brother, and asked them to play where she could see them, in front of her. At this, the boy became curious and inched his way around behind her, where he saw the tell-tale sign of a glowing posterior. Yelling her name, "Kau-nassa, Kau-nassa!" he carried his sister away with great haste.

The *hebu*, incensed at hearing her name called aloud, burst into flame and vanished.

HEINZELMANNCHEN

See **Kobold**.

HENKIES

See **Trows**.

HERNE THE HUNTER

A woodland spirit with stags' horns on his head. He appears in Shakespeare's *Merry Wives of Windsor* as the ghost of a hunter who hanged himself on Herne's oak, but older beliefs place him as a spirit of the woods or a demon of the oak. He has reportedly been sighted standing beneath his oak at Windsor castle on moonlit nights.

HEROK'A

Native American earth spirits found in the northern forests. Their name means "Those without horns."

HESPERIDES, THE

Nymphs of Greek mythology who tended the goddess Hera's garden. Three apple trees, a gift from the goddess Gaea or Gaia, grew in the garden. The golden light of their fruit was said to give the sunset its glow. Thus the hesperides were also known as the nymphs of the evening and the golden light of the sunset.

Their number varies from three to seven in various accounts. Aegel, Erythia, and Hesperesthusa are the three most commonly named. Different traditions name their parents as Hesperus (Evening) and Atlantis , Nyx (Night) and Erebus (Darkness), or Prokris, a shepherd, and Kephalos, a nymph.

Hidarugami

In Japanese legends these hungry ghosts are the spirits of those who have died of starvation. Without a burial place, these restless spirits possess the bodies of those walking in the mountains, causing them to feel the pangs of starvation so acutely they are themselves in danger of death. Travelers must therefore always carry food with them, as the only defense against the *hidarugami* is to eat at once. Even a few grains of rice will suffice to rid the body of these evil spirits.

Hillmen

See **Hobmen**.

Hinky Punk

A form of **will o' the wisp** on the Devon–Somerset border. There are many local names for these "ghost lights" that appear at night to travelers, like a flickering lantern, leading them to stray from their path, often into bogs, marshes, or swamps. Members of the Dulverton Women's Institute described the Hinky Punk as having one leg and a light.

Hinzelmann

German household elf or ***Kobold***. According to an account in **Thomas Keightley**'s *The Fairy Mythology* (1828), Hinzelmann was a household spirit who arrived at the castle at Hudemühlen in northern Germany in 1584, when he caused much fear among the household, who could hear him banging and knocking but not see him. Gradually, however, both master and servants became used to his presence and he spent hours conversing with them. He also enjoyed singing verses, one of his favorites being:

"If thou here wilt let me stay,
Good luck shalt thou have alway;
But if hence thou wilt me chase,
Luck will ne'er come near the place."

Hinzelmann was, however, a spirit of an ambivalent nature. Sometimes he made himself very helpful, spending all night cleaning and tidying the kitchen and asking only for a dish of sweet milk and some breadcrumbs in return for his labors. But at other times he delighted in making mischief. In the evenings, when the servants were tipsy with liquor, if one should drop anything under the table he would give them a good box on the ear from behind when they bent to pick it up, while at the same time pinching their neighbor's leg. Then he would take great delight in watching a scuffle ensue. The next day, when black eyes and swollen faces bore testament to the fray, he would gleefully relate how he had started the fight on purpose. But he always took care that the matter didn't get out of hand and no one risked their life.

Though he generally remained invisible to the inhabitants of the castle, occasionally he was seen playing with the children, appearing as a beautiful child with curly, blonde hair, dressed in a red silk coat. However, when the cook once begged to see him in bodily form, he appeared as a young child who had been stabbed to death.

Various noblemen and exorcists tried to rid the castle of Hinzelmann, but none were successful. After staying there for four years, he departed of his own accord in 1588, saying that he would return when the family were in need and that they would flourish once more as a consequence of his return.

Before leaving, he presented the family with a plaited cross, a straw hat, and a leather glove, with the words: "As long as you keep these things together and in good condition, your entire race will flourish and enjoy good fortune, but if they are divided, lost, or wasted, your race will decline and sink." It is thought that the hat was later given as a gift to Emperor Ferdinand II, who thought it quite wonderful. The glove remained in the family's possession, but it is not known what became of the cross. Today, nothing but the walls remain of Hudemühlen castle.

Neil Gaiman's novel *American Gods* (2001) features a modern adaptation of Hinzelmann.

See also **Cauld Lad of Hilton**.

Hob

(Or Hobthrust.) Hob is the general term for friendly household spirits who help around the home but sometimes have a mischievous streak. The **brownie** is a type of hob. Stories of individual hobs tell of their specific areas of expertise, such as the Hobhole Hob who lived in a cave in Runswick Bay near Hartlepool in the north of England, whose speciality was curing whooping cough.

In *Rustic Speech and Folklore* (1913), Elizabeth Mary Wright warns of the consequences of annoying these usually helpful creatures:

This benevolent and humble sprite, though very useful when properly treated, would disappear, or become openly mischievous, if annoyed. Chief among the things whereat he would take offence is the offering of recompense for his labours. A hobthrust, who used to wear an old tattered hat when at work, found a new one put for him in his accustomed haunt, whereupon he straightway departed, crying: "New hat, new hood, hobthrush'll do no more good." If the farmer or any of his servants had spoken disrespectfully of the hobthrush, they would presently find cream-pans smashed to atoms, horses and cattle turned loose and driven into the woods, and the housewife's churning would produce no butter.

See also **Killmoulis**.

Hobgoblin

The term "hobgoblin" is sometimes used to refer to wicked goblin-type creatures, after the famous line in John Bunyan's hymn *To Be a*

Pilgrim: "Hobgoblin nor foul fiend/ shall daunt his spirit." However, in its original sense, "hobgoblin" refers to good-humored spirits akin to **brownies**, who enjoy playing pranks, but are helpful on the whole.

Hobgoblins appear in folklore traditions around the world. The Rev. John Batchelor, who spent many years living with the Ainu people in Japan, relates the following tale of a Japanese hobgoblin in *The Ainu and their Folklore* (1901), although the cannibal hobgoblin in this story has more in common with the fearsome, one-eyed **fachan** than the kindly, mischievous household hobgoblins of British folklore.

A great hobgoblin made his home in the midst of the mountains of Ainu-land. He was the size of an exceedingly large man and was covered with hair; "in fact, his skin was like that of a bear, so hairy was he." He had only one eye, as "large as a common pot lid," in the middle of his forehead.

This creature was a great nuisance to the Ainu. So huge was his appetite that he was in the habit of catching, killing, and eating everything and everybody that came in his way. The people were afraid to go far into the mountains to hunt, for, although the one-eyed monster had been shot at many times, no arrow had had any effect upon him.

One day a brave hunter, who was an expert with the bow, was hunting game when he strayed near to the cannibal's lair and was startled to see something bright glaring at him through the forest undergrowth. As he drew near he discovered it to be "the big-bodied, hairy, fierce-looking hobgoblin."

Despite his fear, the hunter drew an arrow from his quiver, fitted it in his bow, and stood on the defensive. As the creature came closer, he took aim at his solitary eye. Being a good shot, he hit it fair in the center and the hobgoblin immediately fell down dead, for the eye was the only vulnerable part of his body.

The brave hunter made a bonfire over the hobgoblin's body to make sure that so foul a creature and so deadly an enemy was quite killed, and wouldn't come to life again to trouble the people. He burned him up, bones and all, then he took the ashes in his hands and scattered them in the air, so as to make doubly sure that the monster was destroyed . . . "But lo, the ashes became gnats, mosquitoes, and gad-flies as they were tossed upward. However, we must not grumble at these things, for the lesser evil of flies is not so bad as the greater evil of having the one-eyed man-eating monster among us."

See also ***Bauchan***, **Blue Burches**, **Booman**, **Dobie**, **Puck**, **Robin Goodfellow**.

HOBMEN

(Or Hillmen.) Manx fairies of a menacing nature. On Hollantide (November 11th) it was considered advisable to stay inside, for this was the eve when the hobmen moved from one dwelling to another. People made offerings of fruit to appease them.

HOBTHRUST

See **Hob**.

HODEKIN

See ***Kobold***.

HONGA

Earth spirits of Native American folklore. The Osage people of the Great Plains give this name to the earth people who live below the ground.

HONOCHENOKEH

Iroquois name for the Invisible Helpers, spirits of goodwill found in the eastern woodlands of America.

HULDEN

German hill fairies.

HULDRA

In Scandinavian folklore the *huldra* is a beautiful creature of the forest. Her back is hollow like an old tree trunk and she has a cow's tail (sometimes it is a fox's tail). To see her from behind is to break the spell, and she will appear as ugly.

Huldra desire to be human and, in order to achieve this, must marry a man. They are kind to charcoal burners and will watch over their kiln while they rest. In exchange the charcoal burners leave provisions for them. Despite this kindness *huldra* can also be malevolent, luring men into the forest to seduce them; should the man not satisfy her, she might kill him, or else he is likely to die of exhaustion.

Like fairies, *huldra* abduct human children and replace them with **changelings**. In certain cultures they are said to be related to **trolls**. They are part of the **Rå** (wardens of the Earth) as keepers of the forest.

HULDRE

See **Elves**.

HULI JING

Chinese "fox spirit." In Chinese mythology, fox spirits are supernatural beings. Like their European fairy counterparts, they have a capricious nature and can be benevolent or malign, helpful or obstructive, good or bad. In many Chinese tales a *huli jing* appears as a beautiful young woman who is a dangerous seductress. In modern usage, *huli jing* is also a derogatory term for a woman who seduces married men.

Daji is one of the most famous fox spirits. A beautiful but cruel concubine, she appears in the epic sixteenth-century Chinese novel *Fengshen Yanyi*. A king of the Shang Dynasty falls in love with her, she bewitches him, and the dynasty is subsequently overthrown. On her death, it is revealed that she has been possessed by a nine-tailed fox spirit.

In the same way that fairies are often referred to as "the Good People," or "Fair Folk," or by other euphemistic names in English-speaking countries, either out of deference or fear of causing offense, *huli jing* are often referred to as *Xian*, meaning "transcendent" or "immortal."

See also **Kitsune, Kumiho**.

Hunt, Robert (1807–1887)

Robert Hunt was one of the first people to publish a collection of Cornish folk tales. He was born in Devonport, near Plymouth, England. His father was a naval officer who drowned when Hunt was a boy. He started studying medicine in London, but had to abandon his studies due to ill-health. He settled in Cornwall where, in 1845, he became keeper of mining records at the Museum of Economic Geology and, from 1851, lectured at the newly founded School of Mines.

He was a keen photographer and developed the actinograph, an instrument for measuring the amount of light available to expose photographic film. He also wrote the *Manual of Photography* (1841), the first English book on the subject.

In 1849 he started collecting the myths and legends of old Cornwall. Some he collected from traveling droll-tellers (wandering storytellers), some he garnered from fellow Cornish folklorist and collector **William Bottrell**. He wrote *Popular Romances of the West of England*, published in 1865, which includes, among many others, the tales of the **knockers** and "Cherry of Zennor."

Hylde-Moer

(Also *Hyldemoder*.) Literally, "the elder tree mother," the guardian spirit of the elder tree in Scandinavian folklore. **Thomas Keightley**, in *The Fairy Mythology* (1828), relates that in Denmark it was customary to ask the *Hylde-moer* before cutting any wood from an elder, repeating three times: "O *Hylde-moer*, O *Hylde-moer*! Let me take some of thy elder, and I will let thee take something of mine in return." Anyone who took wood without asking permission could expect to face a punishment from the *Hylde-moer*.

Hans Christian Andersen based his literary fairy tale "The Elder Tree Mother" on Scandinavian folklore concerning the *Hylde-moer*.

See also **Elder Tree, the Old Lady of the**; ***Hylde-Vinde***, ***Waldgeister***.

Hylde-Vinde

Literally, "the elder queen," the guardian spirit of the elder tree in

German folklore. It was customary for anyone wishing to cut down an elder tree or take wood from it to seek permission from the elder queen first. Failing to properly consult the tree spirit was said to result in misfortune.

See also **Elder Tree, the Old Lady of the**; ***Hylde-Moer***, ***Waldgeister***.

Hyldemoder

See ***Hylde-Moer***.

Hyter Sprites

Green-eyed, sandy-colored fairies of East Anglia and Lincolnshire, hyter sprites are shapeshifters and can take on the form of sandmartins. Little is known about these supernatural creatures. It is said that they appreciate human kindness but can't abide bad manners. Like the **Ghillie Dhu** of Scotland, they have been known to help return lost children to their homes.

1

Iansan

An Afro-Brazilian ***orisha***, a spiritual entity with control over the elements of nature. She has power over the wind and command of hurricanes, cyclones, and tempests. Dwelling at the graveyard gate, she also presides over the realm of the dead. Associated with the color red, she is often portrayed as a warrior dressed in red robes.

Belief in *orishas* originated with the Yoruba people and spread from their homeland in Nigeria to other parts of Africa and to South America. Today belief in Iansan is particularly prevalent in Brazil.

Ignis Fatuus

See **Will o' the Wisp**.

Ijirait

Invisible mountain spirits from the Inuit tradition. They dwell inside hills in stone houses that resemble the houses of white men. Their appearance is unusual in that their eyes and mouths are set lengthways in their face, so that they blink sideways. Invisible to normal mortals, they make their presence known with a whistling sound.

They are also shapeshifters, often taking the form of caribou. They are visible to the *angakkuit*, the Inuit shaman, and can be helpful as well as frightening. It is wise for humans not to show fear in the presence of *ijirait*, as they are said to attack the weak and cowardly. However, there are many accounts of them abducting humans, so it is only natural to become afraid on hearing their whistling.

Illes

Earth elementals in Icelandic and Scandinavian folklore. These dark, hairy **trolls** are nocturnal creatures that dwell underground. They are shapeshifters, transforming themselves into attractive human forms to entice members of the opposite sex into their underground caverns.

Ilona

See ***Tündér***.

Imp

A mischievous **sprite**. Imps are creatures of small stature that are usually, though not always, male. The name may derive from *ympe*, meaning an "offshoot, graft, or cutting." A *ympe* tree is one grown from a cutting and not from seed. Imps are sometimes described as being small demons, or "offshoots of the Devil," and are often attendants to wizards, witches, or warlocks. However, they are generally mischief-makers rather than evil or seriously dangerous.

In Robert Louis Stevenson's story "The Bottle Imp" (1891), the protagonist buys a bottle with an imp inside it that grants wishes. However, the owner of the bottle must sell it on before his death, otherwise his soul will go to the Devil.

The theme of a bottle imp is also found in the German legend *Spiritus Familiaris*, collected by the Brothers **Grimm**. There are parallels between the bottle imp and the stories found in Arab traditions of wish-granting **genies** or ***djinns*** in a bottle.

The medieval Lincoln cathedral contains a sculpture of an imp, known as the Lincoln Imp. According to legend, the Devil sent two imps to wreak havoc on Earth. They caused mayhem across the north of England, then went to Lincoln cathedral, where they got up to all sorts of mischief, smashing furniture and terrorizing the bishop. An angel appeared out of a book of hymns and told them to stop. One of them was bold and threw things at the angel, while the other hid and cowered. The angel turned the first imp to stone, allowing the other time to escape. It is said that now, even on calm days, there is always a wind blowing around Lincoln cathedral, which is the second imp searching for his friend. The imp has become an emblem of the city, its mischievous mascot.

Ina, the Fairy Voyager

A legend from the Cook Islands, related in *Myths and Songs from the South Pacific* by Rev. William Wyatt Gill (1876), tells the story of Ina, daughter of Ngaetua and Vaitoor-inga, the wealthiest islanders in Nakutere, in the South Pacific. Her magical journey to the Sacred Isle on the back of a shark begins with the theft of all the family's worldly treasures by the thief Ngana.

Ina, left in charge of laying out the beautiful adornments that she has been bidden to place in the sun but, without fail, to take indoors the moment a cloud appears, fails to notice that Ngana has crept out of hiding and uttered a spell to cover the sun. He attempts to snatch away all the treasures, but Ina is too quick for him. He begs and wheedles to be allowed to try them on and reluctantly she agrees, although holding on to the most beautiful and costly headdress of scarlet and black feathers.

Once inside the house, she locks the doors to prevent him running off and Ngana is soon arrayed in all the finery, including the precious headdress, dancing wildly around the rooms secretly looking for a way to escape. He spies a tiny hole in the roof, through which he disappears in a trice.

Ina's parents are distraught when they return home, and begin to punish her. While her father is belaboring her with a branch, Ina's body is possessed by a spirit, or *manu*, which utters in a strange voice:

"Most sacred is my person;
Untouched has been my person;
I will go to the Sacred Isle,
That Tinirau alone may strike it."

Ina rushes from the house and runs to the shore to find a means of traveling to the Sacred Isle where Tinirau, royal lord of all the fishes, awaits her.

She rides on the back of a small fish toward the open sea, but the little fish cannot support her and she falls into the lagoon. She angrily berates the fish and beats it, resulting in the stripes called "Ina's tattooing." Different fish carry her ever further and each one she leaves with distinctive markings when they fail to take her where she desires, the sole suffering an angry stamp on its head so that its eye is displaced.

At last a shark appears, providing a broad back for her journey and a sharp fin on which to pierce the shell of one of the coconuts she carries for its sweet juice.

When she asks the shark for help again, the creature raises its head and Ina cracks the shell onto its forehead with a forceful blow. The shark dives, Ina is left afloat upon the ocean, and the shark gains a large lump on its forehead known as "Ina's bump."

Ina is rescued from her plight by the King of Sharks, Tekea, who delivers her safely to the Sacred Isle where she plays upon a magical drum that summons the noble lord Tinirau to her side and he takes her as his cherished bride.

Ina Pic Winna

According to **Ruth Tongue**'s *Somerset Folklore* (1965), as the fishermen of Somerset walked over a particular hill on their way to work at sea it was customary for them to place a white stone on top of a cairn, or fairy mound, there and saying: "Ina pic winna, send me a good dinner."

In one version the mound is called Peak Winnard and the saying goes: "Peek weena, send me a deesh of feesh for my deener." In this way, the fishermen would be rewarded with a good catch of fish.

Incubus

An evil spirit or devil that assumed the form of a man and lay with a woman, similar to a succubus, which took on the form of a woman or **hag** and lay with a man.

According to legend, Merlin was the offspring of an incubus. The child of an incubus and a human is sometimes called a "cambion."

Indra

In Buddhist and Hindu mythology, Indra is ruler of the **Devas** and lord of the heavenly realm of Svargaloka.

Indrásan People

In Indian folklore, the Indrásan people are the fairy (*parí*) inhabitants of the underground country. According to Dunkní, an Indian storyteller whose tales were collected in *Indian Fairy Tales* (1880) by M. Stokes, they are beautiful, winged creatures who play musical instruments exquisitely and delight in dancing and singing. They sometimes impart their knowledge to mortals. There are many similarities between these Indian fairies and the Good People of Ireland, who live in the clefts of rocks, hills, mounds, caves, and the Land of Youth.

Dunkní tells the story of the beautiful Phúlmati Rání , the Pink-Rose Queen whose beauty lit up even the darkest of rooms.

"On her head was the sun; on her hands, moons; and her face was covered with stars. She had hair that reached to the ground, and it was made of pure gold." She was very slight and weighed the same as one flower. And so it was decided that her husband, too, must weigh the same as one flower.

Underground lived the fairy people and the Indrásan Rájá ruled over them all. He, too, was very beautiful. On his head was the sun; on his hands, moons; and on his face stars. And he weighed the same as one flower.

It was decided that the two should be married, on the condition that after one year they returned to the Indrásan Rájá's fairy kingdom beneath the ground and that on the journey the Indrásan Rájá wore flowers behind his ears so that the fairies could recognize him as their great raja and keep the couple safe as they traveled to the fairy land.

The two lived very happily for a year and when the time came to return to the fairy kingdom, they set out together, but the Indrásan Rájá forgot to wear flowers behind his ears and so the couple traveled without the protection of the fairies. A wicked one-eyed shoemaker's wife was therefore able to cause them grave troubles along the way. First she drowned Phúlmati Rání. Then, when she came back to life as a flower, she burned her. Phúlmati Rání came back to life a third time when they all arrived in the fairy kingdom, but then the wicked shoemaker's wife tricked the Indrásan Rájá into cutting her into pieces.

Realizing what he had done, he was full of sorrow. But, unbeknownst to him, "the Phúlmati Rání's arms and legs grew into four houses; her chest became a tank, and her head a house in the middle of the tank; her eyes turned into two little doves; and these five houses, the tank and the doves, were transported to the jungle."

One day when the Indrásan Rájá was hunting in the jungle he heard two doves talking. "This is the man who cut his wife to pieces," said the husband dove. And he told of how the Indrásan Rájá had married the beautiful Phúlmati Rání, who weighed only one flower, and how the shoemaker's wife had drowned her; how God had brought her to life again, how the shoemaker's wife had burned her, and last of all, how the Rájá himself had cut her to pieces.

"And can't the Rájá find her again?" said the little wife dove.

"Oh, yes, he can," said her husband, "but he doesn't know how to do so."

"But do tell me how he can find her," said the little wife dove.

"Well," said her husband, "every night, at 12 o'clock, the Rání and her servants come to bathe in the tank. Her servants wear yellow dresses, but she wears a red one. Now, if the Rájá could get all their dresses, every one, when they laid them down, and throw away all the yellow dresses one by one, keeping only the red one, he would recover his wife."

On hearing all this, the Rájá at once determined to be reunited with his wife. At midnight when the Rání and her fairy servants came to bathe at the water tank, he waited until they were in the water then picked up all the dresses and ran.

The servants came running after him, demanding he give back their dresses. One by one he dropped the yellow dresses, which the servants picked up, and then ran away. When only the red dress was left, he took it to the beautiful Phúlmati Rání.

"Please give me my dress back," she said. "If you don't, I will die. I have been brought back to life three times, but will be brought back again no more."

The Rájá fell at her feet and begged her forgiveness.

The couple were reconciled, he gave her the red dress, and the two lived happily together. The Indrásan Rájá ordered the wicked one-eyed shoemaker's wife to be cut into pieces and buried in the jungle.

See also **Seal Maidens**, **Swan Maidens**, **Valkyries**.

IRATXOAK

Impish creatures of Basque mythology. Similar to other **agricultural spirits**, the *iratxoak* help with farmers' work—milking cattle, carrying out repairs, and so on—in return for offerings of food.

One story tells of a farmer who bought a box of *galtzagorriak*, a type of *iratxoak* whose name means "red pants," to help him in his labors.

"What shall we do?" the *galtzagorriak* asked him.

He set them a long list of tasks, which were finished in next to no time. When eventually he ran out of jobs for them, however, they became frustrated and undid all the good work that they had done.

Eventually, he managed to coax them back inside their box and from then on did all the work himself.

ISPOLINI

Giants described in ancient Slavic myths as inhabiting caves in the mountains of present-day Bulgaria. Of enormous stature and strength, they are nevertheless at the mercy of the humble blackberry bush, becoming trapped by the dense thorny foliage if they inadvertently stumble into one.

It

An amorphous creature in Shetland folklore. No two people looking at it ever saw the same thing and no one was ever able to describe it satisfactorily. To some it appeared as a "slub," or jellyfish, to others like a bag of white wool, a beast without legs, or a headless human, and it never appeared in the same form twice. Jessie Saxby, in *Shetland Traditional Lore* (1932), described the creature as a master of the art of fairy glamor:

Without legs or wings, It could run faster than a dog, and fly faster than an eagle. It made no sound of any sort, yet folk could understand what It meant to say, and repeated what It told one without a word being uttered.

J

Jack in Irons

Yorkshire **bogie**. Travelers, beware when walking lonely Yorkshire roads at night, for this **giant** figure clad in clanking chains is said to lie in wait to pounce on unsuspecting victims. Some say he wears the heads of his victims and wields a big spiked club.

Jack of the Bowl

See **Napf-Hans**.

Jack O'Lantern

One of the names for the **will o' the wisp** lights that appear at night, particularly over marshes and bogs, and lead travelers from the path. Today the Jack O'Lantern gives its name to the carved Halloween pumpkins in the USA.

See also **Joan the Wad**.

Jacobs, Joseph *(1854–1916)*

A folklorist, literary critic, and historian, Jacobs wrote for journals and books on folklore as well as editing collections of fairy tales. He was born in Australia, his parents having emigrated from London *c.*1837, but at the age of 18 he left to study in Cambridge. From 1890 to 1916 he collected and edited a series of collections of fairy tales: *English Fairy Tales* (1890), *Celtic Fairy Tales* (1892 anthology), *More Celtic Fairy Tales* (1894), *More English Fairy Tales* (1894), *Indian Fairy Tales* (1912), and *European Folk and Fairy Tales* (1916). He was inspired by the **Grimm** Brothers and **Charles Perrault**.

Janaína

Brazilian queen of the ocean, patron of fishermen. Often depicted as a **mermaid**. Her origins lie in the African Yoruba people's belief in ***orishas***—spiritual entities that have control over the elements of nature—which spread from their homeland in Nigeria to other parts of Africa and to South America. On

New Year's Eve in Rio de Janeiro, thousands of *cariocas*—citizens of Rio—gather on the beach at Copacabana to welcome in the new year and make offerings of flowers and candles to Janaína to bring good fortune in the coming year.

Jean de la Bodiéta

See **Napf-Hans**.

Jeannie of Biggersdale

A malevolent spirit dwelling in an old mill in Mulgrave Woods near Biggersdale, Yorkshire. She was well known in the area and the locals were afraid of her.

One evening a young farmer, grown bold with wine or local ale, accepted a challenge to visit her. He rode to Mulgrave Woods and asked Jeannie to show herself.

"I'm coming!" came her angry reply.

The young farmer rode toward the stream with her following close behind. Just as he got to the water, she swiped at his horse and split it clean in two. Its hindquarters fell on her side of the stream, but the farmer had a lucky escape, as he shot to safety over the horse's head and onto the other side of the stream.

Jengu

An African water spirit in southern Cameroon beliefs, the *jengu*, dwelling in rivers, streams, and the sea, is a benevolent and healing force who also acts as an intermediary between the people and their spirit world. Sometimes described as having the appearance of a **mermaid**, it also possesses healing powers and can bring good luck and prosperity to those who believe in it.

Jenny Greenteeth

Pond-dwelling Lancashire **bogie**. Mothers and nannies frightened children with stories of her to stop them from playing in ponds and streams. She was often described as having green skin and long, green, fanglike teeth, which she used to seize children and drag them down under the water.

See also **Grindylow**, **Peg Powler**, **Rawhead and Bloody Bones**.

Jikininki

The ancient Japanese tale of the *jikininki*, a flesh-eating spirit, is told in *Kwaidan: Stories and Studies of Strange Things* by Lafcadio Hearn (1904).

Muso, a priest on his way through the mountains, begged a night's accommodation and some food from an old holy man in a tiny hermitage, or *anjitsu*, who roughly refused him but directed him to a nearby village, where he found a bed for the night.

He was woken in the night by the sounds of lamenting and was told by the young head of the household that his father had died and all the people of his village had to leave, as was the custom when there was a death in the house. He urged the priest to come with them, but surmised that as he was a holy man he might not have qualms about staying with the body, to which the priest announced he had no fear of demons or evil spirits, so he would be glad to perform the funeral rituals over the dead body:

All then left the house, except the priest, who went to the room where the dead body was lying. The usual offerings had been set before the corpse; and a small Buddhist lamp was burning. The priest recited the service, and performed the funeral ceremonies, after which he entered into meditation. So meditating he remained through several silent hours; and there was no sound in the deserted village. But, when the hush of the night was at its deepest, there noiselessly entered a Shape, vague and vast; and in the same moment Muso found himself without power to move or speak. He saw that Shape lift the corpse, as with hands, devour it, more quickly than a cat devours a rat—beginning at the head, and eating everything: the hair and the bones and even the shroud. And the monstrous Thing, having thus consumed the body, turned to the offerings, and ate them also. Then it went away, as mysteriously as it had come.

On their return to the house the next morning the villagers were unsurprised by the disappearance of the body and offerings, explaining that in order to avoid misfortune it was tradition to leave overnight for this mysterious process to take place.

Muso enquired, "Doesn't the priest on the hill sometimes perform the funeral service for your dead?"

"What priest?" the young man asked.

"The priest who yesterday evening directed me to this village," answered Muso. "I called at his anjitsu *on the hill yonder. He refused me lodging, but told me the way here."*

The listeners looked at each other in astonishment and, after a moment of silence, the master of the house said: "Reverend Sir, there is no priest and there is no anjitsu *on the hill. For the time of many generations there has not been any resident priest in this neighborhood."*

When Muso left the village he sought the old priest in his ancient hermitage and when he found him was bidden to enter, whereupon the hermit was abject with apology, repeating how ashamed he was by his behavior. Muso demurred, saying he had found comfortable lodgings, but the hermit sought his forgiveness:

". . . it is not for the refusal that I am ashamed. I am ashamed only that you should have seen me in my real shape—for it was I who devoured the corpse and the offerings last night before your eyes . . . Know, reverend Sir, that I am a jikininki, *an eater of human flesh. Have pity upon me, and suffer me to confess the secret fault by which I became reduced to this condition.*

"A long, long time ago, I was a priest in this desolate region. There was no other priest for many leagues around. So, in that time, the bodies of the mountain folk who died used to be brought here, sometimes from great distances, in order that I might repeat over them the holy service. But I repeated the service and performed the rites only as a matter of business; I thought only of the food and the clothes that my sacred profession enabled me to gain. And because of this selfish impiety I was reborn,

immediately after my death, into the state of a jikininki. *Since then I have been obliged to feed upon the corpses of the people who die in this district: every one of them I must devour in the way that you saw last night . . ."*

Begging Muso to pray for his escape from his terrible existence, the hermit and his small dwelling instantly disappeared, and Muso was left on his knees on the hillside, his eyes beholding nothing but a moss-covered tomb.

Jimmy Squarefoot

Manx pig spirit. Manx folklore makes many references to fairy pigs. According to Walter Gill's *A Manx Scrapbook* (1929), Jimmy Squarefoot was a huge pig who belonged to a **giant** who rode him over the land and across the sea. The giant, who lived on Cronk yn Irree Lhaa, "Hill of the Rising Dawn," had a tempestuous relationship with his wife, the supernatural **hag** and weather spirit ***Caillagh ny Groamagh***. When they argued, he threw rocks at her, some of which became prominent geographical features of the Manx landscape, such as the rocky outcrop Creg ny Arran.

After one argument the couple disappeared, leaving their porcine pet behind. After that Jimmy Squarefoot was more often seen in the form of a man with a pig's head with two large tusks, like those of a wild boar. Despite his startling appearance, he doesn't appear to have done much harm to humans. His hunting ground was an area in the south of the Isle of Man around Grenaby.

In some versions of the story, Jimmy Squarefoot was a mortal who was transformed into a pig-headed beast when his wife left him for throwing stones at her.

See also **Arkan Sonney**.

Jinn

See ***Djinn***.

Jinni

See ***Djinn***.

Joan the Wad

Queen of the Cornish piskies. According to Jonathan Couch's *History of Polperro* (1871), the **pisky** folk are about a hand span long, clad in green, and wear straw hats or little green caps on their heads. However, Joan the Wad is often depicted naked. Today, she is popular as a good luck charm. Brass Joan the Wad figurines are carried or worn to bring good fortune and luck in love.

"Wad" comes from an old colloquial Cornish word for a torch or bundle of straw, and Joan the Wad also takes the form of a **will o' the wisp** light. Traditionally, this type of spirit led travelers astray at night. However, as suggested by an old Cornish rhyme quoted by Couch, Joan the Wad is believed to guide people to safety:

"Jack o' the lantern! Joan the wad,
Who tickled the maid and made her
mad;
Light me home, the weather's bad."

See also **Jack O'Lantern**, **Pixy**.

Jogah

(Or *jo-ga-oh.*) The collective name for the small, invisible nature spirits of Iroquois legend, which comprises three divisions, each of which is responsible for an aspect of nature: the ***gahongas*** of river and rock, ***gandayah***, who nurture crops, and ***ohdowas***, underground dwellers guarding animals and creatures of the night. With these three guardians, the natural environment and its seasonal cycles are protected.

Jo-Ga-Oh

See **Jogah**.

Joint-eater

See **Alp Luachra**.

Jones, Davy

According to the folklore of seafarers, Davy Jones presided over the spirits of the deep. He appeared in various forms as a warning that death was at hand.

There are various explanations

for the origins of this belief and the sailors' idiom "He's gone to Davy Jones's locker," meaning, "He's drowned or shipwrecked." One, given in *Brewer's Dictionary of Phrase and Fable* (1898), is that "Jones" is a corruption of Jonah, the prophet, who was thrown into the sea. In seaman's terms, a locker was any receptacle for private stores, and Duffy was a ghost or spirit among the West Indians. So the whole phrase is: "He's gone to the place of safe-keeping, where Duffy Jonah was sent."

JUST-HALVER

See **Alp Luachra**.

K

Kabibonokka

See **Four Winds, the**.

Kabouter

Friendly **gnomes** in Dutch folklore, similar to the Irish **leprechauns** or German ***Kobolds***. They offer help around the home, cooking, cleaning, and tending the fire, and lend farmers a hand threshing grain and attending to livestock. In the Dutch tale "The Legend of the Wooden Shoe" it is a *kabouter* who teaches a carpenter how to make the famous Dutch *klompen*, or clogs.

Kabouter are usually depicted as little old men with long white beards wearing red pointy hats. This image was popularized by Dutch illustrator Rien Poortvliet in *Leven en werken van de Kabouter* (1976), published in English as *Gnomes* (1977).

See also ***Kaboutermannekin***.

Kaboutermannekin

A household fairy of the lowlands of Holland, similar to the **brownie**. *Kaboutermannekin* help around the home, on the farm, or at the mill. Like other brownies, they appreciate payment for their labors in the form of bread, milk, or beer. However, leaving a new suit of clothes as a tribute is a sure way to lose the help of a *kaboutermannekin*. Either he will take offense at the gift, or, once dressed in his new garb, think himself too refined to continue with menial chores and depart in search of a better occupation.

In *Notes on the Folklore of the Northern Counties of England* (1866), Henderson likens the Dutch *kaboutermannekin* to the English **redcap**. Other brownie-type beings who depart after being gifted new clothes include the **Cauld Lad of Hilton, pisky threshers**, and the ***phouka***.

See also ***Kabouter, Killmoulis***.

Kabun

See **Four Winds, the**.

Kachinas

(Also *katsinas.*) Spirit beings in the mythology of the Pueblo peoples of North America. There are hundreds of *kachinas*, male and female, taking the form of aspects of the natural world such as rain, corn, birds, or animals. Each Pueblo culture has its own distinct forms and variations.

The Hopi people believe that the *kachinas* live in the San Francisco Peaks. Every year they are said to come down from the mountains and reside with the tribe from the winter solstice until July. During this time the Hopi men perform many rituals and ceremonies to appeal to the *kachinas* to bring the rains needed to prepare the land for the growing season and ensure a good harvest. Special masks and costumes representing the *kachinas* are worn during the ceremonies. When wearing a mask, a performer is temporarily transformed, as the spirit being depicted by the mask is thought to be actually present with or within them. In July, the *kachinas* return to their homes in the mountains.

Carved *kachina* dolls are traditionally made by the men of the tribe and presented to the children to teach them about the life forces of nature.

See also **Cloud People, the**.

Kakamora

Halflings of the Solomon Islands. In "Beliefs and Tales of San Cristoval" anthropologists note the local description of the *kakamora* as small, not quite human creatures varying in height from about six inches to 3 or 4 feet (15 centimeters to around a meter). Their appearance varies from dark to pale skinned, with long, straight hair down to their knees, and tiny teeth. They dwell in holes, caves, and banyan trees, subsist on a diet of fruits and nuts, and are particularly fond of eating opossums. Although generally not aggressive, they are extremely strong and have been known to lash out with their long, sharp nails. They love dancing, especially on moonlit nights in heavy rain. They sing as they dance, although their language is not like any Melanesian tongue.

They are said to fear the color white.

Kakua Kambuzi

A protective nature spirit in the folk beliefs of the Basoga people of Uganda. Kakaua Kambuzi dwelt in the tall, spreading incense tree. It was said that if a man seduced a virgin, the couple's punishment was to be tied to the incense tree overnight. In the morning, when they were released, they were allowed to settle near the tree where the protective spirit resided.

Kaluk

Tree spirits in the Burmese and Thai folk beliefs. Each tree is believed to have its own indwelling spirit known as a *kaluk*. Before a tree is felled, the *kaluk* must be respectfully consulted. It is said that failing to do so can lead to misfortune or even death.

Kanaima

An evil spirit, the scourge of humankind, cause of all fatal maladies, violent deaths, and vengeful acts of reprisal in the ancient legends of tribes in Guyana. The name applies not only to the murderous spirit but encompasses the whole process of possession of the victim in many forms, using insects, worms, or even inanimate objects to effect their death. It is also the name of a tree with hallucinogenic properties.

A person charged with avenging the murder of a relative is also known as a Kanaima and will disappear from his community in order to search for, and kill, the perpetrator; this may take many years during which he must live as an outcast on whatever food he can find. In some tales the Kanaima takes on the identity of an animal such as a jaguar, painting his body with startling red spots and wearing animal skins. Should the avenger come upon his victim as he sleeps, a poisonous powder is brushed onto his lips and nostrils, which causes an agonizing death over many weeks; as further assurance that the victim cannot betray the identity of his killer, his tongue is mutilated. In the days before the death, the Kanaima must perform certain purification rituals, such as licking a sharp stabbing stick covered in the blood and juices of his victim, in order to free himself from his obligations and return to his home.

KATE CRACKERNUTS

This unusual folk tale from the Orkneys illustrates how fairy magic can both harm and heal. It was collected by D. J. Robertson and published in *Folk-Lore* (September 1890), then edited by **Joseph Jacobs**, who republished it in *English Fairy Tales* (1890).

A king and queen each had a daughter by a previous marriage, and both were named Kate. The king's Kate was more beautiful than the queen's Kate, and the queen was very jealous. The queen's henwife, who looked after the poultry, had a reputation as an enchantress, so the queen asked her to spoil the beauty of the king's Kate.

After three visits to the henwife, supposedly to collect eggs, the king's Kate lifted the lid of a boiling pot and a sheep's head rose out of it and fastened itself over her pretty head.

The queen was delighted, but her daughter was horrified, as she loved her stepsister. She wrapped her sister's head in a linen cloth and the two Kates ran away from the king and queen.

When they came to the next kingdom, the queen's Kate went to the palace and got work as a kitchen maid, and was allowed to keep her sister in the attic.

The eldest son of the king of this kingdom was very ill and no one knew what was wrong, particularly as all those who had watched over him at night had disappeared. So the queen's Kate offered to stay with him overnight for a peck of silver.

At midnight the prince rose and dressed and mounted his horse. Kate jumped on behind him. As they rode through a thicket of hazels, she picked handfuls of nuts.

Soon they came to a fairy mound.

"Let the prince in with his horse and hound," said the prince.

"And his fair lady behind him," said Kate.

At this, a door in the hillside opened and Kate slipped off the horse and hid behind it. The prince danced with the fairies inside the hill until he collapsed with weariness. At the break of day he mounted his horse and rode back to the palace, and Kate again rode behind him.

The next night Kate watched over the prince again, this time for a peck of gold. Again they rode to the fairy dancers. This time a fairy boy was playing among them waving a silver wand and Kate overheard one of the dancers say, "Take care of that wand, for one stroke of it will restore Kate's beauty."

As soon as Kate heard that, she started to roll the hazelnuts across the dance floor. The fairy boy dropped the silver wand to gather them and Kate snatched it up and carried it back to the palace.

When day came and she could leave the prince, she ran up to the attic and touched her sister with the wand. The king's Kate had her looks restored and was even more beautiful than before.

The third night the queen's Kate again went to the fairy dance with the prince, and this time the fairy child was playing with a dead bird. "Don't lose that bird," said one of the dancers, "for three tastes of it and the prince will be as well as he ever was."

On hearing that, Kate rolled out more hazelnuts, and when the child dropped the bird to pick them up, she took it, and back at the palace she plucked it and roasted it.

At the first smell of it, the prince sat up and said, "I could eat that bird!"

As soon as he had eaten it he was as well as he had ever been, and he married Kate Crackernuts, and his brother married the king's Kate, and they all lived happily ever after.

Katsinas

See **Kachinas**.

Keightley, Thomas (1789–1872)

Author of *The Fairy Mythology* (1828), a collection of fairy lore whose ambitious aim was to "collect, arrange, classify and give under one point of view the various ideas and legends respecting the Fairies and similar beings of the popular creed, which lie scattered in a variety of books and a variety of languages," Keightley studied at Trinity College, Dublin, with the ambition of becoming a barrister, but after a breakdown in health he moved to London, where he earned his living by writing educational textbooks. There he made friends with the antiquarians **Thomas Crofton Croker** and Douce, and worked with Crofton Croker on his book *Fairy Legends of South Ireland* (1825).

The Fairy Mythology was followed in 1834 by *Tales and Popular Fictions.* Two further and enlarged editions of *The Fairy Mythology* were brought out in 1860 and 1878. Keightley wrote many other books, but those are his great contributions to folklore.

Kelpies

These shapeshifting water spirits dwell in rivers and are the best known of the Scottish **water horses**. Most often the kelpie appears in the form of a horse or pony and lures unsuspecting wanderers into jumping onto his back. Once the victim has mounted, the kelpie rushes headlong into the water, striking it with his tail with a sound like thunder and disappearing beneath the surface in a flash of light to devour his hapless rider.

Although the kelpie is generally a dangerous beast, it is possible to tame one. In *Popular Superstitions and Festive Amusements of the Highlanders of Scotland* (1823), Grant Stewart tells how a bold member of the MacGregor clan named Wellox divested a kelpie of its power by removing its magic bridle.

Another popular tale related how Graham of Morphie used a human bridle to harness a kelpie to do his will, putting him to work dragging stones to build his new castle. When the castle was built, he took off the bridle and the kelpie galloped into the river, pausing only to say that as long as he lived, Morphie would not thrive. And so it was that henceforth that misfortune dogged the Grahams of Morphie.

Being a shapeshifter, the kelpie could also assume human form, in this case as a rough, shaggy man. In this shape he sometimes leaped up behind a solitary rider, gripping and crushing him, and frightening him almost to death. Before storms he was heard howling and wailing.

A kelpie appears as both hungry river spirit and harbinger of death in a Scottish version of the story "The Time is Come But Not the Man."

A group of Highlanders were gathering in the harvest by the river Conan in Sutherland when a kelpie appeared out of the ford.

"The hour but not the man is come," he proclaimed, before darting off through the water as fast as a drake.

As the workers were trying to figure out what the message meant, a rider came cantering toward the ford. Understanding that this must be the man to whom the kelpie had referred, they stopped him from entering the water and told him to wait in the safety of the church until the "kelpie's hour"—the fatal hour in which the kelpie preyed upon its victims—had passed.

When the time was up, they went to check on him, only to discover that he was face-down in a trough, drowned. Despite their best efforts to avert tragedy, the kelpie had succeeded in claiming his victim.

Keremets

Spirits in the folklore of the Mari people of Russia. In different traditions, *keremets* are either considered malevolent or perceived as guardians or helpers.

Various different origins are attributed to the *keremets*; according to some, they are the spirits of wicked humans continuing to do evil after death, while in other traditions they are the envoys of the gods, sent to mediate between mortals and the Otherworld, and yet others associate them with the primordial forces of nature. In their guise as nature spirits, they dwelled in the ravines, bogs, canyons, and other wild places feared by humans, each *keremet* controlling an aspect of the natural world.

In order to avoid unwanted attention from the *keremets*, the Mari people referred to them using euphemistic names such as *kuguza*, "old man," or *kugerak*, "prince."

Keshalyi

Benevolent fairies in Romany gypsy folklore. They live in a mountain castle with their beautiful queen, **Ana**. As a result of a bargain struck between the king of the ***loçolico***, evil earth-dwelling spirits, and the fairy queen, when a *keshalyi* reaches 999 years of age, she must be sacrificed to the *loçolico* spirits.

In some traditions, the *keshalyi* are fairies with powers over human destiny, similar to the **Fates** of Greek mythology.

In the autumn, the *keshalyi* are said to tear out their hair in mourning for their mortal husbands. Hungarian gypsy women would gather floating threads of cobwebs from the fields, believing them to be strands of fairy hair. The women and their husbands ate the strands during a waxing moon, murmuring an incantation to the *keshalyi* to bless them with a child and inviting the *keshalyi* to the birth to bring good fortune.

The name probably derives from *kachli*, meaning "spindle." *Keshalyi lispersen*, "Fairies spin," is a Romany charm against sterility.

KIJIMUNA

In Okinawa, the southernmost island of Japan, these mischievous little spirits live in the banyan trees and many tales are told of their pranks when they descend from their lofty perches as evening falls. About the size of small children, they have reddish hair that sometimes grows all over their bodies and they are associated with spectral fires that burn beside them as they walk. Excellent fishermen, they use their skill to ensure bountiful catches for those who befriend them, requiring in return only the eyes of the fish as their food. Generally more playful than unpleasant, they bring good fortune to those they favor, but if they are neglected or taken for granted, they have no qualms about returning those they have made rich to a state of poverty. There is only one creature that can deter their attentions, and that is an octopus, which is repugnant to these little tree-dwelling spirits.

KILLMOULIS

Once every mill was believed have its own *killmoulis*, or mill servant, a gnarled sort of **hob** or **brownie**. In *Notes on the Folklore of the Northern Counties and England and the Borders* (1866), Henderson described this servant as a little old man with an enormous nose but no mouth.

According to an old rhyme, the *killmoulis* was fond of eating pork, which presumably he must have snuffled up through his nose. He made his home in the *kilogee*, or kiln, in front of the fireplace. He was a dedicated servant. Like a **banshee**, he wailed if illness or misfortune was destined to come to the mill or the miller's family. However, he was a practical joker too. One of his favorite tricks was to blow ashes over the shelled oats spread out to dry. But when the miller called to him, he would dutifully appear to be given his orders. Although he was loathe to leave his favorite corner, he could be relied on in an emergency to thresh the corn or fetch the midwife.

In Roxburghshire, he was also used at Halloween in the spell of the "blue clue," when he was employed to snort out the name of future spouses. He seems to have been a spirit of the Scottish Lowlands, for the Highland mills were haunted by brownies, **urisks**, and ***brollachans***, most of them more sinister than *killmoulis.*

In Holland, the helpful ***kaboutermannekin*** was sometimes found in mills.

KING GOLDEMAR

(Also King Vollmar.) A household spirit, or ***Kobold*** in German folklore.

According to **Thomas Keightley** in *The Fairy Mythology* (1828), King Goldemar inhabited Hardenstein castle in North Rhine-Westphalia, Germany. The *Kobold* brought good luck to the household and forewarned the nobleman of impending danger, and King Goldemar was on good terms with the master of the house, Neveling von Hardenberg, whom he referred to as "brother-in-law."

Like other *Kobolds*, such as Hinzelmann, King Goldemar could generally be heard but not seen. When he allowed members of the household to touch him, his hands were said to be thin, like a frog's, and cold and soft to the touch. He was an accomplished harp player and also a keen gambler who was in the habit of staking large sums of money at games of dice.

King Goldemar lived amicably within the household for three years, until one day a man put ashes and tares in his path, hoping to see his footprints. This enraged him. He chopped the man into pieces, boiled the head and legs, roasted the body, and ate it. After that he vanished, leaving a message stating that the house would be as unlucky as it had been lucky while he had been living there.

That was the last that was heard of King Goldemar.

King Herla

Legendary king of the Britons who became leader of the **wild hunt** after a visit to the Otherworld. Herla is associated with the Germanic and French wild hunts in the guises of Woden and Herlequin. He was portrayed by the twelfth-century writer Walter Map in *De Nugis Curialium.*

King Herla of the ancient Britons was approached by another king, a short hairy man with a large head, a red beard, and hooves instead of feet. He said to Herla, "I am lord over many kings and princes. Yet I rejoice in the fame that has raised you above other kings, for you are of all men the best, and connected to me by position and blood. You are to be married to the daughter of the King of France, and the embassy will arrive today. Let there be an everlasting treaty between us, as I will be present at your marriage and you will be at mine on the same day a year hence."

With that, the pygmy king departed.

King Herla received the embassy from France and was married to the king's daughter. At the wedding feast the pygmy king arrived, accompanied by countless dwarves, who proceeded to set up wonderful furniture and to serve marvelous food and wine.

The little king then addressed Herla, saying, "Most excellent King, God be my witness that I am here in accordance with our agreement, at your marriage. If there is anything more that you desire, I will supply it gladly, on the condition that when I demand a return you will not deny it."

Without waiting for an answer,

he retired to his tent, and left at dawn with his entire retinue.

After a year he suddenly came again to Herla and demanded the observance of the treaty. Herla consented and followed him at his bidding.

They entered a cave in a very high cliff, and after journeying through the darkness, which appeared to be lighted not by the sun or moon but by numerous torches, they arrived at the dwarf's splendid palace.

The marriage was celebrated and gifts exchanged. The pygmy king gave Herla and his men a final gift of a small bloodhound and strictly forbade anyone to dismount until the dog had leapt from his carrier. He then left them and returned home.

King Herla came into the light of day, where he met an old shepherd and asked for news of his queen.

The shepherd was astonished and said, "Lord, I scarcely understand your language, for I am a Saxon and you a Briton. I have never heard the name of that queen, except in the case of one who they say was Herla's wife, queen of the earliest Britons. Herla himself is fabled to have disappeared with a dwarf at this cliff and never to have been seen again. The Saxons have now held this realm for 200 years, having driven out the original inhabitants."

The king was amazed, for he had thought he had been away only three days.

Forgetting the dwarf's commands, some of the king's companions then dismounted, and instantly crumbled to dust. The king forbade anyone else to dismount before the dog had leaped down.

The dog has not leaped down yet. According to which version of the legend you believe, Herla and his entourage were either overwhelmed by the river Wye and are at rest or still they continue to wander on mad journeys, without home or rest.

Kinnara/Kinnari

Throughout South East Asia and in Buddhist and Hindu beliefs, the male Kinnaras and female Kinnaris are the celestial lovers, symbols of pleasure, gracefulness, and skill in dance, music, and poetry. In Indian mythology they take the form of half-human, half-horse, and in Indonesia they are depicted guarding the Tree of Life in the form of birds with human faces.

Although the name is spelled in varying ways, the Kinnaras occur in the popular culture of many countries, on ancient carvings, statues, trophies, in ballets, and films, and on the national flag of Myanmar.

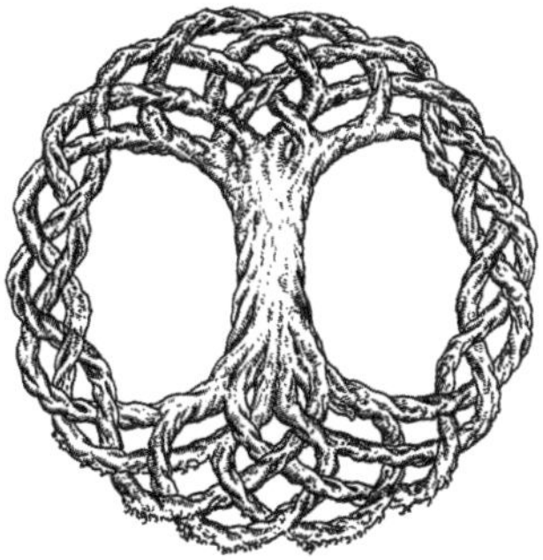

Kirk, Robert (1644–1692)

A Gaelic minister, scholar, and folklorist. Kirk was born in Aberfoyle, Scotland, and, like his father before him, became a minister. He was called to serve at his place of birth on his father's death. During his lifetime he was well known for translating the Psalms into Gaelic (published in 1684).

Kirk had an intimate knowledge of the traditions and myths of the area, and was a believer in fairies—to him they were proof of a supernatural world. He collected many stories about **elves**, fairies, and other creatures. The manuscript was first published in 1815 by **Sir Walter Scott** under the title *The Secret Commonwealth or an Essay on the Nature and Actions of the Subterranean (and for the most part) Invisible People heretofore going under the names of Fauns and Fairies, or the like, among the Low Country Scots as described by those with second sight.* It was re-edited in 1893 by **Andrew Lang**, who gave it the title *The Secret Commonwealth of Elves, Fauns and Fairies.* The book is a mix of religion, folklore, and science. In it Kirk theorizes on the possible origins of fairies and writes about fairy food, fairy craft, and the appearance of fairies.

After his death Robert Kirk himself became part of a fairy legend: his parishioners believed that he had been taken away to fairyland for delving into matters of the fae.

Kirkegrim

Church spirit of Scandinavian folklore, also known as a church **grim**. Once every church was believed to have its own *kirkegrim*, or **nisse**, dwelling either in the tower or wherever he could find a place of concealment. He kept the church in order and punished the perpetrators of any scandals.

In Soero church there was a large, round hole in the roof in which that church's *nisse* dwelled. It was said that in former times the Evil One was accustomed to fly out through this hole when the priest, in baptizing, said; "Go out, thou unclean spirit!"

See also **Strand Varsels**.

Kirnis

The guardian spirit of cherry trees in the folklore of Lithuania.

Kisar Bonga

See **Bongas**.

Kit with the Canstick, or Candlestick

A type of **will o' the wisp**. In *Rustic Speech and Folklore* (1913), Elizabeth Wright includes Kit with the Canstick with will o' the wisp, along with other variations like Kit-in-the-candlestick (Hampshire), Kitty-candlestick (Wiltshire), and Kitty-in-the-wisp (Northumberland).

Kit with the Canstick is included in Scott's "List of Hobgoblins and Night Fears" as reproduced in the *Denham Tracts* (1892–1895), and he is also mentioned in *Egregious Papist Impostures* by Samuel Harsnet.

Kitsune

Japanese fox spirits—shapeshifting beings that transform from humans into foxes. Believed to possess longevity, great intelligence, and magical powers. these spirits are broadly classified as *zenko*, "good foxes," or *yako*, "field foxes." Field foxes are often said to be tricksters, while good foxes are generally benign.

One of the earliest known Japanese fox tales, "Come and Sleep," was written down by the monk Kyoukai in the late eighth or early ninth century. It tells the story of a man and a fox bride.

During the reign of Emperor Kinmei (A.D. 510–571), a certain man from the Ouno district of Mino province rode out looking for a good wife. He soon came by a pretty girl working in a field and she agreed to be his wife.

Before long she became pregnant and gave birth to a boy. It so happened that their dog gave birth to a puppy on the same day, which was the fifteenth day of the twelfth month. The puppy barked fiercely at the mistress and she became fearful that it would attack her. She asked her husband to kill it, but he did not have the heart to do so.

A couple of months later, the mistress was taking refreshments to the servants as they ground the rice. The puppy saw her and immediately started to chase her. The mistress was terrified. Suddenly she transformed into a wild fox and jumped up onto a high hedge to escape the fierce dog.

On seeing this, her husband proclaimed that he still loved her and asked her to come always and sleep with him. She abided by his wishes and every night came and slept in his arms, arriving each evening as a woman dressed in a red skirt and departing each morning as a fox. For this reason she was named "Kitsune," which means "come and sleep." In Classical Japanese, *kitsu-ne* means "come and sleep" while *ki-tsune* means "comes always."

This tale is unusual in that the wife returns to her husband. In most stories, the fox wives disappear and the husbands can meet them only if they track them down in the wild. Secondly, the fox wife is credited with the founding of a family, whose descendants are chronicled. More often, such families are quietly forgotten once their role in the story has been fulfilled. One of these descendants, Mino no kitsune, appears in another story by Kyoukai entitled "On a Contest between Women of Extraordinary Strength."

In other tales, *kitsune* are wedded to one another. When rain falls from a cloudless, clear sky it is known as *kitsune no yomeiri*, or a "foxes' wedding." In some regions rainbows are associated with fox weddings. These are considered to be good omens.

Generally, tales and beliefs associated with Japanese *kitsune* are of a more romantic nature than tales of their Chinese and Korean counterparts, the ***huli jing*** and the ***kumiho***.

Klabautermann

See **Kobold**.

Knackers

See **Knockers**.

Knockers

(Also knackers.) Cornish spirits of the mines, seldom seen but often heard. So-called for the sound their picks made as they worked their own lodes of tin out of sight of the human miners. Described as little men about 3 feet (1 meter) in height, they dressed like human miners, carried picks and shovels, and wore helmets with candles fixed to them with wax.

Tin mining was one of the oldest industries in Cornwall, dating back to the Bronze Age (bronze being an alloy of copper and tin). From about 2000 B.C., the mining and trading of tin drew merchants from far and wide to the area, including a Jewish community—still evident in place names such as Marazion and Market Jew Street. Some early Cornish miners believed knockers were the ghosts of Jewish miners who had been sent to work the mines as a punishment for the crucifixion of Christ. This may account for the superstition, recorded by **Robert Hunt** in *Popular Romances of the West of England* (1865), that mine spirits cannot endure the sign of the cross, and therefore the miners avoided marking anything with a cross for fear of aggravating them.

Sometimes blamed for causing mining accidents such as rockslides, at other times the knockers were credited with warning miners with the knocking of their picks when danger was close at hand. At the end of a shift, miners left coins or food—typically the end of a pasty—as an offering to the knockers in return for their protection and in the hope that the little miners would guide them to rich lodes of tin. When the offering was not forthcoming, the knockers could turn spiteful, as described in the tale of "Tom and the Knackers" in **William Bottrell**'s *Traditions and Hearthside Stories of West Cornwall* (1873).

Tom had been working alone in the mine nearly all day and all night for a week. He had heard the knockers working away at a distance all the time he had been there and had taken no notice of their noise, but they had come nearer and nearer every day, till he could hardly hear the sound of his own tools above the din and clatter of theirs. As far as he could judge by the sound, they were only 2 or 3 yards (3 meters) off, close behind him.

One night Tom got quite annoyed listening to their confounded clattering, and every time he made a clumsy blow with his pick he heard them squeaking and tee-heeing in a mocking way. Being a devil-may-care sort of fellow, without thinking, he threw a handful of small stones back toward the spot where they seemed to be working and called out at them to be quiet and go away.

The words were no sooner out of his mouth than a shower of stones fell upon and around him, frightening him out of his senses. Still, Tom resolved to work on till morning, and in about an hour, when his candle was burned down and he stopped to light another, he sat down to eat the rest of his fuggan [flour and raisin cake often eaten by miners] and touch pipe [smoke a tobacco pipe] for a few minutes.

He had nearly finished his supper, and was still hungry, when he heard ever so many squeaking voices sing out:

"Tom Trevorrow! Tom Trevorrow!
Leave some of thy fuggan for Bucca,
Or bad luck to thee, to-morrow!"

At first he couldn't make out the words very well. He knew that sounds heard underground could often seem like voices, but the more closely he listened, the more plainly he could hear them.

When he had finished eating, there was a change to the words and he heard:

"Tommy Trevorrow, Tommy Trevorrow!
We'll send thee bad luck to-morrow,
Thou old curmudgeon, to eat all thy fuggan,
And not leave a didjan for Bucca!"

They kept on singing, squeaking, and tee-hee-ing, until they were out of hearing.

Tom was somewhat scared, yet he felt so tired and drowsy that when he had smoked out his pipe he leaned back, thinking to take a doze for a few minutes. But when he woke up all was quiet. He rubbed his eyes, and, looking down the tunnel, where it was nearly dark, he saw scores of knockers resting on their tools. They were miserable, little, old, withered, dried-up creatures, the tallest of them no more than 3 foot 6 inches (1.5 meters) or thereabouts, with shanks like drumsticks, and their arms as long or longer than their legs. They had big, ugly heads, with gray or red locks, squinting eyes, hook noses, and mouths from ear to ear. The faces of many were very much like the grim visages on old cloman jugs.

One older and uglier than the rest—if possible—seemed to take the lead in making wry faces and doing all sorts of mocking tricks. When he put his thumb to his nose and squinted at Tom, all those behind him did the same. Then all turned their backs, stooped down, lolled out their tongues, and grinned at him from between their spindle shanks.

Tom was now very scared. He noticed that his candle was burned down to the clay and knew that he must have slept for nearly two hours.

"Good Lord, deliver me," said he, rising to light another candle; and all the knockers vanished by the time he was on his legs. They seemed to melt away, one into another, changing shapes like curling smoke.

Feeling very stiff, tired, and cold from having slept so long, Tom dressed and mounted the ladders. He was hardly able to crawl to grass [out of the mine shaft].

In the blacksmith's shop, where he stopped for a few minutes to change and warm himself, he told other men who were there, putting on their underground clothes, what he had seen and heard. The old tinners told him that they weren't at all surprised, because the levels he had been working in were more infested with knockers than any other part of the bal [mine]. One and all, they blamed Tom for having anything to do or say with the knockers in an unfriendly way, and told him that as it was an old custom he might as well have left a bit of bread on the ground for good luck.

After that Tom was indeed dogged by bad luck, "for go wherever he might, about that old bal [mine], the knackers were forever tormenting him, till they fairly drove 'n away." Eventually, his luck did change, but only after his wife, Betty, enlisted the help of a local "pellar"—a conjuror or wise man—and his sons were able to save enough money to go to America, doing so well over there in the gold mines that they sent money home to keep the old couple in comfort, "and to bring the younger boys out to them, where they, with hundreds more from here about, are making another Cornwall for 'one and all.'"

Bucca is a Cornish word for a spirit, similar to the Irish ***phouka***, or Welsh ***bwca***.

For examples of other mining spirits, see the English **blue-cap**, Welsh ***coblynau***, German ***Kobold***.

KOBOLD

Fairy creature of German folklore. Belief in *Kobolds* is widespread, occurring in many northern European cultures and traditions. There are three main types of *Kobold*: household spirits, mining spirits, and seafaring spirits.

Most common are the house spirits. Similar to the Scottish **brownie**, the Dutch ***kabouter***, and the Scandinavian ***nisse*** or ***tomte***, these are typically attached to a specific household and are of a capricious nature. They can be hardworking and helpful in performing domestic chores, but they are quick to anger and will take offense should they feel insulted, neglected, or otherwise maligned. They take revenge on those who have disrespected them by playing tricks, which vary in degrees of jest and spite. Famous household *Kobolds* include **King Goldemar**, **Heinzelmann**, and Hodekin. In some regions, *Kobolds* are known by local names, such as the *Galgenmannlein* of southern Germany and the *Heinzelmannchen* of Cologne.

The *Kobolds* of the mines have their counterparts in the Norse **dwarves,** the English **blue-caps**, the Welsh ***coblynau***, and the Cornish **knockers**. The element cobalt is said to have been named after the *Kobold*. Medieval miners accused the *Kobolds* of taking precious copper and silver ores and replacing them with "false ores" in the form of cobalt, which released noxious fumes when smelted and polluted other mined elements. Miners often associated *Kobolds* with accidents, such as rockslides and cave-ins. However, the knocking sound the *Kobolds* made as they worked underground could also serve as a warning of impending disaster. Miners left offerings of coins as a mark of respect in the hope that the *Kobolds* would show them where the rich veins of metal were situated.

The *Klabautermann* was a seafaring *Kobold* that lived aboard ships. If shown due respect by the crew, he helped by attending to the upkeep and the maintenance of the vessel, performing the duties of a ship's carpenter. However, if he felt slighted, he caused mischief by tangling ropes and beleaguering those who attempted to shirk their duties. He generally remained invisible and it was considered a bad omen among sailors and fishermen to see a *Klaboutermann*, for it was believed to be a portent of death, or of the imminent sinking of the ship.

Kodinhaltia

A domestic spirit or household fairy, in Finnish and Estonian folklore. Performing a similar role to the Scottish **brownie**, the *kodinhaltia* helps around the home, lending a hand with the household chores.

Korrigan

(Also corrigan.) Supernatural beings in the folklore of Brittany, described variously as water spirits or a type of creature similar to a **brownie**.

In *The Fairy Mythology* (1828), **Thomas Keightley** describes korrigans as water spirits, often to be found at springs combing their long, flowing hair, dressed in long, white veils. They appeared radiantly beautiful at night, but if spotted in daylight had red eyes, wrinkled faces, and white hair. Their breath was believed to be deadly. They were believed to have been princesses who were cursed for refusing to embrace Christianity.

Like other fairies, korrigans spirited away human children, leaving **changelings** in their place. A human child could be protected from them by wearing a scapula or a string of rosary beads.

In order to perpetuate their race, korrigans were said to seek out attractive young men to father their offspring.

In other descriptions, Breton beliefs about korrigans and *lutins*—a French counterpart to brownies—appear to have become intermingled. The term "korrigan" is applied to various spirits and elves, such as *follets* or *esprit follets* (playful elves), which bear similarities to other mischievous spirits such as **pixies** in Cornwall, **Robin Goodfellow** in England, **goblins** in Wales, and brownies in Scotland. In an article in the *Revue des Traditions Populaires* (v.101), M. Sebillot classified more than 50 names given to korrigans and *lutins* in Lower Brittany, according to the form in which they appeared, their peculiar traits, dwelling places, and the country they inhabited.

In *Baraz Breiz* (Ballads of Brittany) (1839), collected by Villemarqué, korrigans are described as small beings, no more than 2 feet (approx. 0.5 meters) in height, with transparent bodies. They have powers of prophecy, are accomplished warriors, can shapeshift into any animal form, and are able to travel from one end of the world to the other in the twinkling of an eye.

Like their British cousins, korrigans are fond of feasting, music, and dancing, and gather on moonlit nights near menhirs, dolmens, and tumuli, at crossroads, or in the open countryside for their revels.

In the early twentieth century the tradition of dancing korrigans was still very much alive. **W. Y. Evans-Wentz** collected various accounts of korrigans in *The Fairy-Faith in Celtic Countries* (1911), including one given by Madame Marie Ezanno of Carnac in January 1909:

The korrigans are little dwarfs who, formerly, by moonlight, used to dance in a circle on the prairies. They sang a song the couplet of which was not understood, but only the refrain, translated in Breton: 'Di Lun, Di Merh, Di Merhier' (Monday, Tuesday, Wednesday). They whistled in order to assemble. Where they danced mushrooms grew; and it was necessary to maintain silence so as not to interrupt them in their dance. They were often very brutal towards a man who fell under their power, and if they had a grudge against him they would make him submit to the greatest tortures. The peasants believed strongly in the korrigans, because they thus saw them and heard them. The korrigans dressed in coarse, white linen cloth. They were mischievous spirits who lived under dolmens.

Another story collected and related by W. Y. Evans-Wentz was told by Madame Louise Le Rouzic in her home at Kerallan, a hamlet about a mile from Carnac. Apparently, Madame Le Rouzic was sitting on a wooden bench by the window knitting and her daughter was watching the savory-smelling dinner as it boiled in great iron pots hanging from chains over a brilliant fire on the hearth. Large, gleaming brass basins were ranged on a shelf above the broad, open chimney-place wherein the fire burned and massive bedsteads carved after the Breton style stood on the stone floor. This is the story the good woman told:

In former times, a young girl, having taken the keys of the church and having entered it, found the korrigans about to dance; and the korrigans were singing 'Lundi, Mardi' (Monday, Tuesday). On seeing the young girl they stopped, surrounded her, and invited her to dance with them. She accepted and, in singing, added to their song 'Mercredi' (Wednesday). In amazement, the korrigans cried joyfully, 'She has added something to our song; what shall we give her as recompense?' And they gave her a bracelet. A friend of hers meeting her asked where the fine bracelet came from; and the young girl told her what had happened. The second girl hurried to the church and found the korrigans still dancing the rond. She joined their dance, and in singing, added 'Jeudi' (Thursday) to their song; but that broke the cadence; and the korrigans, in fury, instead of recompensing her, wished to punish her. 'What shall we do to her?' one of them cried. 'Let the day be as night to her!' The others replied. And by day, wherever she went, she saw only the night.

(*See also "Connecting with Fairies," p.159.*)

Kratt

In Estonian mythology Kratt is a demon whose power lies in bringing great treasure to his owner, but at the cost of his soul. The tale is told in J. Jannsen's "The Treasure-Bringer" in W. F. Kirby's *The Hero of Esthonia* (1895), a collection of Finnish-Estonian folk tales.

The demon is fashioned and brought to life by a poor and idle farmer; he gathers a broomstick for the body, along with broken pottery and glass, and with great trepidation places the ugly effigy on a lonely crossroad for three consecutive Thursdays.

The evil figure of the Kratt springs into life on the third night and the terrified farmer takes to his heels when he hears the rasping voice asking him what service his master wishes him to perform.

The demon pursues the fleeing figure, taunting him that he has sold his soul to the Devil, and screams that through abandoning him, the farmer has set him free and he will torment him for the rest of his days.

Thereupon the farm falls into ruins, the terrified servants leave, the cattle die, and the farmer himself is shunned by all except his dreadful demon, who is invisible to all but him. At his wits' end, he leaves the farmhouse, locks all the doors, and sets fire to it, with the Kratt still inside.

As he rejoices that this will put an end to his tormentor, he sees the grinning evil spirit appearing out of the flames and falls to the ground in terror, quite dead.

The tale of Kratt has been put to music in a ballet by the Estonian composer Eduard Tubin.

Kumiho

Korean fox spirit. In Korean tradition fox spirits are shapeshifting beings similar to the ***kitsune*** of Japan and the ***huli jing*** of China.

According to Korean lore, if a fox lived to 1,000 years old, it became a *kumiho.* These supernatural creatures could transform from a fox into a human at will, although they generally retained some foxlike features such as a tail or pointed ears. Most often they took the form of a seductive young woman.

The *kumiho* features in a number

of legendary tales, some of which appear in the *Compendium of Korean Oral Literature* (*Hanguk Kubimunhak taegye*). In "Transformation of the *Kumiho*," a *kumiho* transforms into the likeness of a bride at a wedding. Her true identity is revealed only when her clothes are removed.

The story of "The Emperor's *Kumiho* Daughter-in-law" tells of the son of a Chinese emperor who married a *kumiho*. Soon after the marriage the country's leaders start to fall ill and die. The hero of the story discovers the *kumiho* and is given permission by the Emperor to kill it, thereby saving the country from ruin.

In another story, "The *Kumiho* and the *Samjokku*," the *kumiho* shows vampiric tendencies in wanting to suck the blood of her intended victim, but is ultimately thwarted by a three-legged dog (*samjokku*), who kills her.

As mythology around the *kumiho* has developed, it has come to be seen as a wholly malevolent spirit. In some tales it is said that the *kumiho* devours the hearts or livers of its victims, making it an altogether darker creature than its Japanese and Chinese counterparts.

L

Lady of the Lake, the

Fairy lady of Arthurian legend. Best known for bestowing the gift of the magical sword Excalibur upon Arthur at the start of his reign. It is she who receives the sword again when Arthur is mortally wounded in battle before he is ferried to the otherwordly Isle of Avalon. A mysterious figure, in early versions of the legend she is a lake maiden resembling the **Gwragedd Annwn**, who rules over an enchanted isle of women where it is always summer. In some later versions she is portrayed as a sorceress, her title sometimes given to the shadowy **Morgan le Fay**. However, she is more usually portrayed as the benign counterpart to the malevolent Morgan le Fay. She is given many names, including **Nimuë** and **Vivian**, and variations of these, but her true identity remains enigmatic.

Dozemary Pool on Bodmin Moor in Cornwall is one of the supposed sites of the Lady of the Lake's domain.

Lalla

A Berber term meaning "lady" and used as a term of respect when referring to female ***djinn***.

Among the female *djinn* are: Lalla Mira, a powerful spirit both venerated and feared, associated with healing, love, and fertility, who is sometimes said to aggressively pursue mortal male lovers; Lalla Mkouna Bent Mkoun, a benevolent guardian spirit, protector of the home; and Lalla Rekya Bint El Khamar, a protective spirit associated with *hammams*, or bathhouses, and springs, who is petitioned for healing and fertility and acts as a guardian of women.

Lalla Mira

See ***Lalla***.

Lalla Mkouna Bent Mkoun

See **Lalla**.

Lalla Rekya Bint El Khamar

See **Lalla**.

Lamashtu

Demonic goddess in Mesopotamian mythology. She killed or kidnapped unborn and newborn babies, and victimized pregnant mothers and those who had recently given birth. She was often depicted with the head of a lion, the ears and teeth of a donkey, breasts, long fingernails, a hairy body, and birdlike feet with talons, suckling a pig and a dog, and riding on the back of a donkey through the Underworld. Said to bring evil for her own edification, she was much feared by the Assyrians and Sumerians. She is believed to be a precursor to other child-stealing fairy creatures such as **Lamia**.

Lamassu

Benevolent guardian spirits of Mesopotamian mythology. Their male counterparts were the ***shedu***. These protective spirits, similar in nature to the Roman *genii* (see ***genius***), were generally depicted as winged lions or bulls with human heads. They were assigned to a particular human, whom they safeguarded throughout the course of that individual's lifetime, protecting them against the malevolent influence of the ***utukku***.

Lamassu were also the protectors of important buildings such as temples and palaces, where their effigies can still sometimes be seen guarding the entrance, similar to the Chinese **zhong kui**, "door gods."

Lamia

A child-stealing or child-devouring spirit in Greek mythology. There are many versions of the myths connected with Lamia. She is generally described as a Libyan woman who transformed into a child-stealing spirit as a result of her affair with the Greek god Zeus. She had at least two children by Zeus, and when his wife, Hera, discovered his infidelity, she flew into a jealous rage and had Lamia's children either stolen or killed. Distraught, Lamia retreated to a cave, where she became a vengeful spirit, stealing or devouring other people's children out of grief over the loss of her own.

A story concerning Lamia appears in Robert Burton's *The Anatomie of Melancholy* (1621). It was this account that inspired Keats to write his famous poem *Lamia* (1819), in which she is depicted as having the upper body of a woman with a serpent's tail—an image that has endured in many modern depictions of her.

A young man, Menippus Lycius, was traveling from Cenchreas to Corinth in Greece when he met a fair lady dressed in fine clothes. She took him to her impressive home in the suburbs of Corinth and told him that if he stayed with her a while he could hear her sing and play and drink the finest wine he had ever tasted.

Lycius was a philosopher, and usually of a staid, moderate nature, but he was unable to resist the charms of the beautiful lady. He stayed with her a long while and eventually asked her to be his wife.

Among their wedding guests was Apollonius the philosopher. He saw through the fairy glamor of Lycius' bride-to-be. She wept and begged him not to give her secret away, but he would not be shaken and revealed her as Lamia, whereupon she vanished, along with her fine clothes and house, and everything in it, down to the last plate.

See also **Lamashtu**, **Melusine**.

Lang, Andrew (1844–1912)

A fairytale collector, critic, journalist and translator, and a prolific writer of poetry, fiction, anthropology, history, religion, myths, legends, and folklore, Lang was born in Selkirk, Scotland, and was educated first at Selkirk Grammar School and thereafter at Edinburgh Academy and St. Andrews University, Scotland, and Balliol College, Oxford, England. It is thought that he read the **Grimm** brothers' fairy tales, and **Madame d'Aulnoy**'s work, as well as that of **Sir Walter Scott**, when still a young man. This gave him a lasting taste for what was to become one of his passions: folklore.

In 1875 Lang married a woman called Leonore Alleyne and they moved to London the same year. He became literary editor of *Longman's Magazine* but also contributed articles to many other publications. His wife was to become a close assistant in the production of the "rainbow" series of fairytale books for which he is well remembered today. In these books he collected, translated, and retold fairy tales from various nations. These had, in one form or another, been recounted for centuries, but in many instances this was the first time they had appeared in the English language. The first of the series was published in 1897 (*The Pink Fairy Book*) and the last (*The Lilac Fairy Book*) in 1910. In all, there are 12 books in the collection: the *Pink, Blue, Red, Green, Yellow, Grey, Violet, Crimson, Brown, Orange, Olive,* and *Lilac Fairy Books.*

After suffering ill-health, Andrew Lang died in Scotland.

Laurin

A **dwarf** king in German mythology. In the *Heldenbuch* (Book of Heroes), a collection of medieval epic German poems, he possessed a magic ring and girdle that endowed him with strength of 24 men, and a *Hel Keplein,* or *Tarnkappe,* a magical cape or hat that made him invisible. However, his tale as related by **Thomas Keightley** in *The Fairy Mythology* (1828) goes to show that sometimes even magic rings and capes are not enough to win the day.

When Laurin stole a mortal woman away to his mountain kingdom, Prince Dietrich of Bern was sent to win her back.

A furious combat ensued. Despite the dwarf's array of magical items, Dietrich succeeded in striking off his finger, breaking his girdle, and removing his *Hel Keplein.*

The defeated Laurin befriended the victorious Dietrich and invited him to a banquet in his mountain palace. When he and his men entered Laurin's domain, though, the devious dwarf made them his prisoners.

However, Dietrich once again succeeded in overcoming Laurin. He plundered his treasures and led him to the city of Bern, where the dwarf king was reduced to earning his bread as a buffoon, or court jester.

Lazy Lawrence

Hampshire and Somerset guardian of the orchard. According to an account in **Ruth Tongue**'s *Forgotten Folk-tales of the English Counties* (1970), he took the form of a wild colt who galloped so swiftly he could almost fly. Anyone bold or foolhardy enough to attempt to steal apples from his orchard could expect to incur the nip of his teeth and the kick of his hooves, or else become rooted to the spot like a scarecrow, transfixed by his hypnotic green eyes.

See also **Colepexy**, **Colt Pixy**.

Leanan Sidhe

(Pronounced *lan-awn-shee.*) The Irish "fairy mistress" or "fairy sweetheart," the **muse** of Irish artists, poets, and singers. According to Irish poet **W. B. Yeats**, most of the Gaelic poets, down to quite recent times, had a *leanan sidhe.* He describes her as a spirit who bestows inspiration, but at a price: she seeks the love of men. If they refuse her love, she becomes their slave. However, if they succumb to her charms, they become hers and can escape only by finding another man to take their place. Her lovers waste away, for although she provides artistic inspiration, she lives on their life, burning them up. Therefore, the Gaelic poets died young. When she grew restless, she carried them away to other worlds, for death did not destroy her power.

Lady Wilde, in *Ancient Legends, Mystic Charms, and Superstitions of Ireland* (1887), placed the emphasis on the *leanan sidhe*'s positive aspects, describing her as a life-giving spirit in contrast to the **banshee**, the Irish spirit of death.

See also ***Lhiannan Shee***, **Muse**.

Leprechaun

The Irish fairy shoemaker. His name is commonly thought to derive from *leith bhrogan,* meaning the "one shoemaker," as he was most often seen working on a single shoe, rather than on a pair of shoes. Alternatively, the name may have an older origin—it has been suggested that the leprechaun first appeared in Irish literature in the seventh or eighth century as the *luchoirp* or *luchorpain*, literally, "small water sprite," in "The Adventure of Fergus mac Leti."

Fergus, King of Ulster, encountered three tiny water sprites and asked them to grant him the power to swim underwater in lakes, pools, and seas. The sprites furnished him with magical herbs to place in his ears and a magical helmet, granting his wish on the condition that he must not swim in a particular loch, Loch Rudraige.

However, Fergus broke the pact and swam in the loch, where he was attacked by the water monster *muirdris*, who swapped his mouth from the front of his head to the back.

Fergus eventually vanquished the sea monster, but at the cost of his own life.

If these miniature water **sprites** are the first "leprechauns," they bear little resemblance to the popular image of the leprechaun today.

In *Fairy and Folk Tales of the Irish Peasantry* (1888), **W. B. Yeats** describes the leprechaun as belonging to the **solitary fairies** and speculates as to whether the leprechaun, **cluricaune**, and **fir darrig** are three aspects of the same fairy in different moods. Whether or not they are three separate fairies or three aspects of the same being, Yeats says that they all resemble one another, appearing as small, withered, old men. The leprechaun is the hardworking shoemaker, who has amassed great riches in the form of crocks of gold, which he keeps buried in secret hiding places. The cluricaune is the reveler, most often found drunk in wine cellars. The fir darrig is the practical joker who spends his time playing pranks.

Many of the leprechaun's typical characteristics are described in

William Allingham's poem "The Lepracaun." He is described as a wrinkled, wizened, bespectacled elf, a span (handspan) and a quarter in height, dressed in a leather apron, and wearing shoes with silver buckles. He is a fairy miser with 99 crocks of treasure, full to the brim with gold, hidden in mountains, woods, caves, rocks, and ruins. In the poem, a human finds a leprechaun and is determined to make the little fellow lead him to his crock of gold. For it was said that if you found a leprechaun and didn't let him out of your sight, he was obliged to take you to his treasure. However, the leprechaun takes out a box of snuff, causing the man to sneeze and in doing so close his eyes. When he opens them again, the leprechaun has vanished, taking all hopes of fairy treasures with him.

There are many tales of leprechauns outsmarting humans in their attempts to win the fairy's gold. One of the best known is "The Field of Boliauns," which appears in **Crofton Croker**'s *Fairy Legends of the South of Ireland* (1925) and **Joseph Jacobs**' collection *Celtic Fairy Tales* (1892). The boliauns in this tale are a type of plant, also known as ragwort or ragweed. The red garter that Tom ties to the boliaun is a piece of material worn by men at that time around their shirt sleeves to prevent their cuffs from getting dirty when they were working in the fields.

One fine day at harvest time, a farmer's son named Tom Fitzpatrick was strolling through the fields when he discovered a tiny old man dressed in a cocked hat and leather apron in the hedgerow drinking ale. Realizing that he had stumbled across a leprachaun, Tom approached the little man, never taking his eyes off him for a moment, and struck up a conversation. When the leprechaun tried to distract him into looking in the other direction, Tom grabbed the little fellow up in his hand and demanded to be taken to his fairy gold.

Looking frightened, the leprechaun said it was a couple of fields away and directed Tom where to go. They went through bogs and over hedges, and all the while Tom held tight to the leprechaun and fixed him with a stare.

When they came to a field of full of boliauns, the leprechaun pointed to a big one, saying, "Dig under there and you'll find a big crock of gold, filled with guineas."

In his hurry, Tom hadn't thought to bring a spade and decided he must run home to fetch one. In order to make sure he knew which spot to return to, he took off one of his red garters and tied it to the boliaun.

Then he turned to the leprechaun. "Swear you'll not take the garter away from that boliaun."

The leprechaun gave his word not to touch it. "I suppose," he said most civilly, "you'll be having no farther occasion of me?"

Intent on claiming the gold, Tom told the leprechaun he had no further need of him and bid him goodbye. Then he ran as fast as could all the way home, got his spade, and ran back to the field.

He arrived back, out of breath and red in the face, only to discover that lo and behold, every single boliaun in the field had a red garter tied to it, identical to his own. Save for digging up the entire field—which was a good 40 acres (16 hectares) in size—Tom had no choice but to return home with his spade slung over his shoulder, cursing the cunning leprechaun for getting the better of him.

LESHII

Forest spirits of Slavic folklore. *Leshii* can refer to an individual male or a group of *leshii*; their female counterparts are *leshovikha.* Listed as demons in the *Dictionnaire Infernal* (1818), these shapeshifting spirits are protectors of the forest and its creatures. In human form, the males are often depicted as bearded men with horns, a blueish tinge to their skin, and either backward-facing feet or their shoes on the wrong feet. The females are variously depicted as old women with pendulous breasts or beautiful young women dressed in sarafans, traditional Russian folk garb. Mischievous tricksters, they are accomplished mimics, imitating familiar voices or the sounds of birds or animals to lure visitors to the forest and deeper into the woods, away from the path.

According to traditional Russian folk beliefs, herdsmen and hunters entered into pacts with *leshii*, removing the crucifixes from their necks and swearing fidelity to the forest spirits in return for protection from the predatory beasts of the forest. In some accounts, *leshii* provided a spirit assistant as a helper to aid the hunter or herdsman.

Leshii were known to steal away children and nursing mothers, or carry off young women to be their brides. Offerings of bread, salt, and blini, wrapped in a clean cloth tied with a red string and left at a forest crossroads, were made to petition the *leshii* for the return of those they held captive in the forest. Those who did return were often described as wild-looking, covered in moss, in a state of distraction, and struck dumb by their sojourn in the forest. As is often the case in tales of those who have visited the fairy realm, many never recovered from their experiences, while others put to use what they had learned during their time with the *leshii* and became sorcerers.

LHIANNAN SHEE

(Pronounced *lannan-shee.*) The Manx "fairy mistress" or "fairy sweetheart," the **muse** of poets and artists, similar to the Irish ***leanan sidhe***. Like her Irish counterpart, she was regarded by some

as a life-giving spirit, while others believed that the inspiration she bestowed on poets, writers, musicians, and other artists came at a cost. She was said to attach herself to a particular man, to whom she appeared irresistibly beautiful, but to remain invisible to all others. Should the artist succumb to her charms, he would enjoy artistic brilliance, but his success would invariably be short-lived, for the *lhiannan shee* sapped the life from her lovers and they were destined to die young.

In a different account, in A. W Moore's *The Folk Lore of the Isle of Man* (1891), the *lhiannan shee* appears in the guise of a "spirit friend" or guardian household spirit. The Cup of the *Lhiannan*

Shee or the Ballafletcher Drinking Glass was a crystal goblet in the possession of the Fletcher family of the Ballafletcher estate on the Isle of Man. It was kept in a strong oak box, mounted with silver. Once a year, at Christmas, the head of the house drank from it as a libation to the *lhiannan shee* for her protection of the household.

Li Ban

See **Liban**.

Liban

(Also Li Ban.) In Celtic mythology, the strikingly beautiful sister of the *Sidhe* fairy queen and sea goddess **Fand**, and wife to Libraid Luathlam ar Claideb, "Swift Hand on the Sword," ruler of the otherworldy realm of Mag Mell.

The legend of the "Sickbed of Cuchulain" tells of how Liban and Fand, in the form of seabirds, received a blow from a stone slung by the hero **Cuchulainn**. In retribution, while he slept, the sisters laughed and whipped him, and he took to his bed with a strange illness that no doctor could cure. But Liban later sought his help in repelling her husband's enemies in return for curing him of his sickness.

Liban the Mermaid

One of the daughters of **Etain** in Irish mythology.

When a sacred spring overflowed, Liban's family were drowned except for Liban, her pet dog, and two of her brothers, Conang and Curman.

Liban and her dog were swept away by the flood, but found shelter in an underwater cave. Seeing fish swimming past their bower, Liban prayed that she might be turned into a salmon. Her prayer was granted when she was transformed into a mermaid. She had the tail of salmon, but from the navel up remained a beautiful woman. Her dog was transformed into an otter.

The two traveled the seas for 300 years until a holy man caught Liban in his net. Given the choice of living on Earth for another 300 years or ascending straight to heaven, she chose the latter.

It is said that many wonders were done in her name and she may be the reason why mermaids appear so frequently in church carvings.

Li'l Fellas, the

Manx euphemistic name for the fairies. Others include ***Ad-hene***, the ***ferrishyn***, the mob, and the good neighbors.

Euphemistic names were widely used when talking about the fairies in order to avoid incurring their anger or attracting unwanted attention from them.

Limos

In Greek mythology Limos is the spirit of hunger or famine (the Roman name being Fames). Bulfinch's *Mythology, the Age of Fable* (1913) relates the tale of Erisichthon, who was punished for his desecration of a sacred grove of trees by Famine "taking possession of his bowels."

The **oread**—mountain nymph—messenger sent to find her to avenge this act found Famine "in a stony field, pulling up with teeth and claws the scanty herbage. Her hair was rough, her eyes sunk, her face pale, her lips blanched, her jaws covered with dust and her skin drawn tight, so as to show all her bones."

The spirit sped through the air to Erisichthon. Finding him asleep, she folded her wings around him and "breathed herself into him, infusing her poison into his veins." Even in his dreams he craved food, and when he woke, his hunger was insatiable: "The more he ate, the more he craved. His hunger was like the sea, which receives all the rivers yet is never filled; or like fire that burns all the fuel that is heaped upon it, yet is still voracious for more." The cursed victim in his interminable quest to satisfy his appetite began to eat his own limbs and thus died.

Llamhigyn y Dwr

(Pronouced *thlamheegin er doorr.*) Welsh water spirit, also known as "the Water Leaper" and described as a legless, winged toad, prone to breaking fishermen's lines and emitting a high-pitched shriek.

According to **Sir John Rhys**' *Celtic Folklore: Welsh and Manx* (1901), an old fisherman by the name of Ifan Owens loved to tell stories about the *Llamhigyn y Dwr*, and when he started on this theme, "his eloquence was apt to become highly polysyllabic in its adjectives."

Owens had not himself seen the Llamhigyn, his father had seen it "hundreds of times". Many an evening it had prevented him from catching a single fish in Llyn Gwynan. Once in particular, when he had been angling for hours towards the close of the day without catching anything, he found that something took the fly clean off the hook each time he cast it. After moving from one spot to another on the lake, he fished opposite the cliff at Benlan Wen, when something gave his line a frightful pull, "and, by the gallows, I gave another pull," the fisherman used to say, "with all the force of my arm: out it came, and up it went off the hook, whilst I turned round to see, as it dashed so against the cliff of Benlan that it blazed like a lightning." He used to add, "If that was not the Llamhigyn, it must have been the very devil himself." That cliff must be two hundred yards at least from the shore. As to his father, he had seen the Water Spirit many times, and he had also been fishing in the Llyn Glâs, or Ffynnon Lâs, once upon a time, when he hooked a wonderful and fearful monster: it was not like a fish, but rather resembled a toad, except that it had a tail and wings instead of legs. He pulled it easily enough towards the shore, but, as its head was coming out of the water, it gave a terrible shriek that was enough to split the fisherman's bones to the marrow, and, had there not been a friend standing by, he would have fallen headlong into the lake, and been possibly dragged like a sheep into the depth; for there is a tradition that if a sheep got into the Llyn Glâs, it could not be got out again, as something would at once drag it to the bottom. This used to be the belief of the shepherds of Cwm Dyli within my memory, and they acted on it in never letting their dogs go after the sheep in the neighbourhood of this lake.

Lleu Llaw Gyffes

"Lleu the Fair of the Steady Hand," a magical hero in Welsh mythology. Son of **Arianhod** and husband of the adulterous **Blodeuedd**, featured in the fourth branch of the *Mabinogion*, the ancient epic stories of Wales.

Llyr

Welsh sea god. Father of the Children of Llyr: Manawydan, **Branwen**, and **Bran the Blessed**, featured in the ancient epic Welsh stories of the *Mabinogion.*

Lob

See **Hob**.

Loçolico

Malevolent earth-dwelling spirits in Romany gypsy folklore. It is said that these demonic creatures were once human, but the Devil transformed them into evil spirits.

The king of the *loçolico* fell in love with the beautiful fairy queen, **Ana**, who presided over the ***keshalyi***, the benevolent Romany fairies. When she spurned his advances, the king sent his horde of minions to devour the *keshalyi.* In order to save the *keshalyi*, Ana agreed to marry him. After fathering a succession of monstrous offspring, the king consented to grant Ana her freedom on the condition that whenever a *keshalyi* reached 999 years of age she must be offered up to the *loçolico* spirits.

Löfjerskor

The generic term for wood spirits in Swedish folklore, generally described as forest **elves** who were usually invisible to humans. ***Rå*** are a type of *löfjerskor.*

LOIREAG, THE

(Pronounced *lorryack.*) Water fairy and patroness of spinning of the Hebrides. According to **Alexander Carmichael**'s *Carmina Gadelica* (1900), she presided over the warping, weaving, waulking (making denser by soaking and beating), and washing of the web. This process involved the rhythmic beating of a newly woven piece of cloth in order to soften it and was traditionally accompanied by waulking songs. It was believed to be bad luck to repeat a song during a waulking session. If a song was repeated, or one of the singers had a harsh voice, the *loireag* would undo all of the women's work, so they would have to start the process again.

Libations of milk were left for the *loireag*, for if they were not, she sucked the goats, sheep, and cows of the town, placing a spell upon them so that they could not move. She was described as a plaintive little thing, stubborn and cunning, a small mite of womanhood, not belonging to this world, but to the world thither.

LONE SOD, THE

See **Stray Sod**.

LORELEI

Water spirit of the river Rhine in German folklore. Usually depicted as a **siren**-like creature sitting on a rock combing her long hair, luring fishermen and sailors toward her with her sweet singing, causing their boats to be dashed on the rocks. She shares her name with the large rock that juts 393 feet (120 meters) above the water on the eastern bank of the Rhine, marking one the narrowest and most treacherous stretches of the river. According to some, she is a water **nymph**, the daughter of the Rhine. More popularly she is associated with the tale of a young woman who jumped from the rock to her death following the loss or betrayal of her sweetheart. Clemen Brentano's ballad *Zu Bacharach am Rheine* (1801) and Heinrich Heine's poem *Die Lorelei* (1827) cemented her image in the popular folklore of Germany.

Love-talker, the

See **Gancone**.

Lug

(Also Lugh.) One of the sons of **Dagda** in Irish mythology. Often referred to as Lug Lamfhota, "Lug of the Long Arm," or Samildanach, the "Many-Skilled."

"The Battle of of Magh Tuiredh" tells of how Lug went to the court of Tara to gain access to the house of Nuada, leader of the ***Tuatha de Danann***, during a great feast.

Lug was told he could gain entry to the house only if he could claim a special skill. He claimed his skills as a wright, a smith, a harper, a historian, a poet, a warrior, and a sorcerer, but each time he was told that the role was filled within the *Tuatha de Danann.*

Finally he asked, "Do you have a man here who possesses all of these skills at once?"

They did not, and on those grounds, Lug gained entry to the house of Nuada and was admitted to the *Tuatha de Danann.* He later went on to kill Balor of the Evil Eye, King of the **Fomorians**, thus ending the long battle between the *Tuatha de Danann* and the Fomorians. The ancient harvest festival, Lughnasad, is named after him.

Lugh

See **Lug**.

Luideag

(Pronounced *lootchak.*) Water demon of the Isle of Skye, dwelling in the Loch of the Black Trout. Said to be of squalid appearance. Her name means "The Rag."

J. G. Campbell, in *Witchcraft and Second Sight in the Highlands and Islands of Scotland,* (1902), gives an account of the figure of a young woman often seen at night in the vicinity of the loch, described as a lonely place far from any houses. She went by the name Luideag and was said to have a coat wrapped about her head. She did not answer when spoken to and disappeared as silently and mysteriously as she made her appearance. An excise man passing along the way once spoke to her, first in

English and then in Gaelic, but she answered not a word. After a man was found lying dead on the road nearby, she was never seen again.

Lunantishee

According to an account in **W. Y. Evans-Wentz**'s *The Fairy-Faith in Celtic Countries* (1911), the *lunantishee* were a tribe of fairies who protected blackthorn bushes. Should anyone attempt to cut the bushes on the original All Hallow's Day, November 11th, and the original May Day, May 11th, the *lunatishee* would ensure that they met with misfortune.

Lutins

See **Korrigans**, ***Nain Rouge***.

PART 4
Elementals and Flower Fairies

WHAT ARE ELEMENTALS?

The ancient Greeks believed that everything in the world was made up of four elements: earth, air, fire, and water. They regarded these as the building blocks of the universe. In the sixteenth century, a Swiss-German alchemist, Theophrastus von Hohenheim, better known as Paracelsus, divided fairies into four groups based on the elements: the gnomes of the earth, the sylphs of the air, the salamanders of fire, and the undines or nymphs of water. These were known as the elementals.

Paracelsus's writings influenced the thinking of various individuals and groups, including Rosicrucians, Spiritualists and Theosophists, occultists, and psychologists (including Carl Jung and his theory of the collective unconscious). The occultist Elphas Levi named the "sovereigns" of each group of elementals: Gob of the gnomes, Paralda of the sylphs, Diju of the salamanders, and Nicksa of the undines. He ascribed the kingdom of each to a cardinal point: the kingdom of the gnomes in the north, the salamanders in the south, the sylphs in the east, and the undines in the west.

FAIRY ANATOMY: BEINGS OF A MIDDLE NATURE

In his work *Liber de Nymphis, sylphis, pygmaeis et salamandris et de caeteris spiritibus* (1566), Paracelsus described elementals as beings partway between humans and spirits. They were made of flesh and blood, and ate, drank, slept, and procreated like human beings, but they could move much more quickly than humans, lived longer, and did not have immortal souls.

In the seventeenth century, Scottish minister Robert Kirk, a believer in fairies, expressed a similar idea. In *The Secret Commonwealth of Elves, Fauns and Fairies* (1691), he wrote:

These siths or fairies . . . are said to be of a middle nature betwixt man and angel [with] light changeable bodies, like those called astral, somewhat of the nature of a condensed cloud, and best seen at twilight. These bodies be so pliable through the subtlety of the spirits that agitate them that they can make them appear or disappear at pleasure.

After Kirk's death legends arose that he had been taken away to fairyland for revealing the good people's secrets in his writings.

In *German Legends* (1812), the Grimm Brothers gave a similar description of the "quiet folk" living in the cliffs near Plesse castle, central Germany: as mortal creatures of flesh and blood, like humans, but with the ability to make themselves invisible and to walk through cliffs and walls as easily as humans pass through air.

These ideas were quite different from other theories that were current in the Victorian era. Interest in fairies was at its height at that time and there was lively debate between scholars from various disciplines over the origins of fairies. A popular theory was that they were actually ancient, dwarflike humans who were conquered by invading tribes and driven out to live in remote areas in hills, marshes, and mountains. (*To read more on the origins of fairies, see p.3.*)

FAIRY EVOLUTION — SPIRITUALISTS AND THEOSOPHISTS

The Victorian era saw the rise of the Spiritualist and Theosophist movements. Drawing on Paracelsus's notion of elementals and influenced by Eastern philosophy, these spurred a growing interest in fairies as connected to the elements of nature and in the spiritual aspect of fairies.

The Spiritualist movement captured public imagination in America and Europe in the mid-1800s, attracting some eight million followers at its peak. The Fox sisters started the movement in America in 1848. They claimed to have the ability to communicate with the spirit world through mysterious knocks and rapping noises on a table. Spiritualists believed that it was possible to contact both the spirits of the dead and supernatural beings that resided on a "higher plane" of existence than the human world.

At the end of the nineteenth century, Madame Blavatsky founded the Society for Theosophy. Like the Spiritualists, Theosophists believed in the existence of spiritual and supernatural beings that inhabited other planes of existence. Many prominent Theosophists believed in fairies.

In her book *Isis Unveiled* (1877) Madame Blavatsky wrote that elementals appeared in the traditions of all cultures around the world, from the *peris* of Persia and the *djinns* of Arabia to the elves and dwarves of Scandinavian and Teutonic belief. She said they had been "seen, feared, blessed, banned, and invoked in every quarter of the globe in every age."

One of Blavatsky's followers, Charles W. Leadbeater, developed a system of classification for the elementals. He believed they inhabited the astral plane between thought and flesh, which was divided into seven levels. Taking Darwin's theory of evolution as a model, he suggested that fairies were beings that had developed on a separate branch of evolution from humans and that their bodies were made of an aetheric substance, like gas, similar to the "condensed cloud" described by Robert Kirk.

Leadbeater put forward his theories of fairy evolution in *The Hidden Side of Things* (1913), claiming, "These beautiful little creatures will never become human because they are not in the same line of evolution as us." He drew charts showing the evolutionary chains of humans and of fairies. At the root of the diagram was mineral life. Humans then ascended the evolutionary ladder via the earth, plants, and mammals. The various fairy tribes ascended the evolutionary ladder via various routes. Some evolved via water and sea creatures into water spirits, while others evolved from the earth via grasses, cereals, and insects into fire spirits. Near the top of the ladder were nature spirits connected to the elements of earth, water, air, and fire. Beyond that, on the top rungs, nature spirits evolved into sylphs, then devas or angels, finally reaching the pinnacle of the evolutionary journey as "solar spirits." Spiritually enlightened humans, too, could ascend to the status of solar spirits.

FLOWER FAIRIES

Edward Gardner, secretary of the Theosophical Society, put forward the idea that fairies were part of the evolutionary line of the butterfly genus. Like Robert Kirk, he believed they were made of a hazy substance lighter than gas that made them generally invisible to humans, except for clairvoyants, or those with "second sight." According to Gardner, the function of these nature spirits was to make flowers and plants grow by providing a link between them and the sun's life-giving energy. He wrote that the "growth of a plant which we regard as the customary and inevitable result of associating three factors of sun, seed and soil would never take place if the fairy builder were absent." Groups of fairies were responsible for tending different parts of the flowers—some working at the cellular levels, some at the roots, and others on shape and color. Gardner, and the well-known author and Spiritualist Sir Arthur Conan Doyle, put forward the idea of fairies as forces of nature that were generally invisible to humans in Doyle's book *The Coming of the Fairies* (1922).

In this climate, it is easy to see where the artist Cicely Mary Barker drew the inspiration from for her hugely popular *Flower Fairies* books. Barker's illustrations, depicting pretty little winged fairies, enjoyed huge popularity at the beginning of the twentieth century and beyond.

In Australia, Mary Gibbs' Gumnut Babies, Snugglepot and Cutie Pie, were modeled on the fauna of the Australian bush, just as Barker's flower fairies took on the character of English gardens and hedgerows.

Like Leadbeater's elaborate diagrams detailing the different strands of fairy evolution, beliefs about fairies have evolved along many crisscrossing paths. It is possible to trace a path from Paracelsus's elementals via the Spiritualists and Theosophists to Cicely Mary Barker's flower fairies. While pretty winged flower fairies and talk of the astral plane and etheric bodies may have seemed odd concepts to the country people of Cornwall, Scotland, Wales, and Ireland, whose main concern was to avoid the unwanted attention of tricksy, troublesome fairies, the idea of fairies being connected to the natural world is both an ancient one and one that continues to have currency today.

In a famous case in Findhorn, Scotland, in the 1960s, a group of friends cultivated a thriving garden out of barren land by tapping into the power of elemental nature spirits. An ecocommunity still flourishes there today.

As the Irish poet and fairylore collector W. B. Yeats wrote in *Fairy and Folk Tales of the Irish Peasantry* (1888):

Many poets, and all mystic and occult writers, in all ages and countries, have declared that behind the visible are chains on chains of conscious beings, who are not of heaven but of the earth, who have no inherent form, but change according to their whim, or the mind that sees them. You cannot lift your hand without influencing and being influenced by hordes. The visible world is merely their skin. In dreams we go amongst them, and play with them, and combat with them.

FAIRIES OF THE EARTH, WATER, FIRE, AND AIR

While fairies characteristically defy strict classification, the human mind seeks order. Folklorists have made various attempts to categorize fairies, either according to disposition—as in the benevolent Seelie Court and malevolent Unseelie Court—or lifestyle—the solitary and trooping fairies. Many other attempts at categorization have been made, to greater or lesser degrees of success. While no system will ever adequately fit the amorphous beings of the fairy world, drawing on Paracelsus and considering the element that a fairy is aligned with provides a useful starting-point in approaching the myriad denizens of the fairy realm.

Earth Fairies

Folk tales, legends, and myths from around the world tell of fairies and spirits that inhabit the Earth, dwelling in underground caves, mountains, burial mounds, hills, and mines. In Ireland the noble *Sidhe* were said to live beneath the hollow hills and in ancient fairy forts. The Fair Folk of Wales, the *Tylwyth Teg*, reside in a subterranean realm beneath the land. The benevolent *nunnehi* of the Cherokee make their homes under the ground in the Appalachian mountains. In Norway the *underjordiske* live in ancient burial mounds. The *erdluitle* of the Swiss and Italian Alps have the animals of the mountain under their stewardship; they are skilled cheesemakers who particularly prize the milk of chamois mountain goats. Ugly shapeshifting spriggans live in old ruins on the Cornish moors, where they guard the treasure of the giants. In Northumberland the

wild-haired Brown Man of the Muirs lives on the lonely moorlands, fiercely protecting the wild creatures from hunters. Dark, hairy *illes* lure unwary humans into their underground caves in Iceland, while the trows of Scotland entice mortals into their earthen mounds with sweet fiddle music to join in their revels. The benevolent *gans* dwell in the mountains of North America, safeguarding travelers and bringing rain for the crops of the Navajo and Apache. The Hungarian *tündér* enlist magical helpers to construct their castles on remote mountain crags. In northern Europe dwarves—skilled smiths and miners—are famed for constructing glittering palaces and halls deep inside mountains. Mines across Europe abound with a host of tricksy spirits, including the German *Kobold*, the Welsh *coblynau*, the Cornish knockers, and the British blue-caps and Cutty Soams. Their knocking sometimes leads miners to precious veins of metals, but at other times signals imminent danger or disaster.

The earth element is also home to fairies and supernatural creatures of the forest, such as the oddly proportioned *Aitahqa-a-nukumaitore* of New Zealand and the mischievous *kijimuna* of Japan. Guardians of the forest appear in cultures around the globe, from the dryads of ancient Greece to the *Waldgeister* of Germany, the *löfjerskor* of Sweden and *tapio* of Finland. The gentle wood wives of Scandinavia and Germany have a deep connection with the forest; it is said that every time a tree is felled a wood wife dies. The *apuku* of Suriname and Curupira of Brazil are forest-dwellers with backward-facing feet, while the South American bush fairy *hebu* is notable for its glowing posterior and enormous eyebrows—so bushy that it must stand on its head if it wants to look at the sky. Goblinlike denizens of the woods include the German *Baumsel* and the Yorkshire *skriker*. The flesh-eating *biloko* of Zaire is a particularly unpleasant creature that dwells in hollow trees, while the benevolent, ground-dwelling *jogah* spirits of the Iroquois people nurture crops and assist in the smooth-running of the seasonal cycles of nature.

Water Fairies

Water fairies are found in folklore and fairy lore across the planet, dwelling in seas and oceans, ponds, fountains, springs, wells, waterfalls, rivers, lakes, and streams.

Sea fairies are often capricious creatures, sometimes helping fishermen, at other times luring them to a watery grave. To hear the song of the sirens meant certain death for the seafarers of ancient Greece. In Scandinavia fishermen give gifts of mittens to the *sjora* in return for a safe passage at sea. Candles and flowers are given as offerings to the mermaid Janaína in Brazil. The Scottish *ceasg* has been known to devour humans; the only way to destroy her is to find her soul, which she keeps hidden in an egg or a box, and destroy it. The Cornish mermaid Morvenna grants wishes—for the price of a soul. Her husband has the voracious appetite of a shark and will eat his own offspring if no other snacks are available. In contrast, the Manx merman, the *dinny mara*, is a loving father.

While mermaids are usually exquisitely beautiful, mermen are often ugly creatures, such as the Irish merrow with his green hair, green teeth, red nose, and piggy eyes. However, the bearded Havmand of Scandinavia is said to be devilishly handsome.

In Orkney and Shetland the seal folk, known as selkies, come ashore on moonlit nights and shed their sealskins, revealing themselves to be more beautiful than any mortals. Seven tears shed into the ocean are said to call a male selkie to a mortal woman's bed. A fisherman who desires a selkie for his bride must steal her magical sealskin.

Mortal men have often fallen for the beautiful Welsh lake maidens, the Gwaragedd Annwn, but, as is usually the case with marriages between humans and fairies, the union seldom goes smoothly.

Many water spirits are talented musicians. The river-dwelling nix of Germany and Scandinavia will pass on his musical skills to humans, but aspiring musicians should be wary—it is said the nix keeps the souls of mortals in upturned urns on the riverbed. The Scandinavian *näcken* plays enchanting but deadly tunes on his violin. The only way to break the spell and avoid being drowned is to cut the strings of his instrument. In Norway the fish-tailed musician Strömkarl dwells beneath a waterfall; ten of his tunes are safe to dance to, the eleventh must be avoided at all cost.

Some freshwater fairies are mischievous and playful, such as Shellycoat of the Scottish Lowlands, who delights in playing pranks on unwitting travelers. The beautiful Greek naiads of springs, fountains, streams, and lakes are usually benign, but have been known to kidnap mortal men to whom they take a particular liking. Dangerous freshwater fairies include Peg Powler, Peg O'Nell, and Jenny Greenteeth, a foul pond-dwelling water bogey of Lancashire with long, green fangs who drags her victims down into the water to their deaths.

Water fairies come in many guises. The shapeshifting *taniwha* of New Zealand can assume the form of a dragon, a shark, or an enchanted log. In Australia, the *bunyip* lurks in waterholes, with a head like an emu on an alligator's body. The malignant Slavic *vodyanoy* can take the shape of a frog or an old man and is blamed for floods. Uncegila, the fearsome Native American water serpent, wrecks crops and causes devastation to the land; she can be vanquished only with a shot to the heart.

In Celtic lands the Manx *cabyll ushtey* and Scottish kelpie and *each uisge* are treacherous shapeshifting water horses. They appear on the shores of lochs as noble horses or ponies, but do not be fooled—once they have tricked an unsuspecting rider into mounting them, they charge full pelt into the water to drown their victim. The *bäckahäst* and *nikur* are water horses of Scandinavia—look out for the telltale sign of the *nikur*'s backward-facing hooves. The Nuckelavee of the Orkney Islands is a particularly fearsome water horse, appearing as an ugly, skinless beast, a fusion of horse and rider; luckily this saltwater monster has an aversion to fresh water, so the best way to escape its clutches is to cross a freshwater stream.

Fire Fairies

Fire plays an important role in the mythologies of many cultures. It has the power to create or to destroy. According to Paracelsus, the salamander is the embodiment of the element of fire; other fire elementals include fire drakes and drachen. In Norse mythology the trickster Loki brings fire to mortals, which he steals from the gods.

The Aziza bring the secrets of fire to the kingdom of Dahomey in African myth. In Native American myths, the trickster coyote steals a flame from the Fire People to bring to humankind. The spiny *nadubi* of Australia lack knowledge of how to make fire and so steal food whenever they can find it. Fire is the life force of the *djinn* of Arabia; they are made of smokeless fire, which erupts from their veins if they are injured, reducing them to ashes. In Yoruba belief, Shango is the ruler of fire, thunder, and lightning, and loves drumming and dancing.

Traditionally, the hearth fire is a focal point in the home. In Lithuania, Gabija, the household fire fairy and guardian of the hearth, must be given clean water to douse her flames and a neatly piled blanket of ash, otherwise she is likely to go wandering into the house, leaving a trail of destruction in her fiery wake. Other fairies who make the hearth their home are the Russian *domovoi* and the Scottish wag-at-the-wa', whose favorite seat is the swinging pot hook in the kitchen. The *killmoulis* makes his home in the kiln in front of the fireplace in Scottish mills. One of his favorite tricks is to blow ashes over the shelled oats laid out to dry. The Lithuanian *aitvaras* takes the shape of a dragon with a meteorlike tail when outside; inside the home it assumes the form of a cockerel and brings prosperity to the household, providing it is fed on omelets.

Fire is traditionally used in ceremonies to mark the turning points of the year. In Ireland the ancient Celts drove livestock between two bonfires in a ritual of cleansing before moving the animals to summer pasture. In some parts of the British Isles beacons, or baal fires, are still lit at key times of the Celtic calendar, such as midsummer's eve and the winter solstice. On February 1st people light candles to celebrate St. Brigid's Day, connected with the fire goddess Brigit, to mark the coming of the spring and return of the light as the days lengthen.

Fire spirits often appear as flickering lights over marshes, bogs, or graveyards—will o' the wisps that lead travelers to stray from the path and lose their way. In Scotland they are spunkies; in East Anglia, the Lantern Man or Hobby Lantern; in Shropshire, Will the Smith; in Somerset, Hinky Punk; and in Wales Ellylldan. Follow them at your peril, for more often than not they will lead you a merry dance through bramble thickets and ditches. The Welsh *pwca* is fond of especially treacherous routes, leading his poor bewitched victims up a steep gorge where a wild torrent rages below. In Cornwall Jack O'Lantern and Joan the Wad might choose to be helpful and lead weary travelers to safety on stormy nights, but in Wales, seeing lights in the sky like slow-moving shooting stars, known as the *tan-wedd*, is an omen of death.

Air Fairies

Sylphs embody the element of air according to Paracelsus. They are strong, powerful beings, the essence of air and wind.

Cultures in every corner of the Earth have tales of fairies and spirits of the winds. The winged harpies of ancient Greece—bird-like creatures with women's faces—created violent winds strong enough to carry people away. In northern Spain the *ventolines'* gentle breezes steer fishing boats safely to harbor, while the fierce Galician Cloud Master El Nuberu wreaks havoc by sending wild storms. In Brittany farmers berate Norouas the Northwest Wind for destroying their crops. Veja Mahte is the benevolent Mother of the Wind in Latvia, who also rules over the birds and the woods. In Lithuania, the Master of the Wind, Vejo Patis, is a fearsome character who banishes undeserving souls from the heavenly realm with a blast of his mighty breath. In America many Native American legends tell of the Cloud People and the Wind People. In the tales of the Algonquin the Four Winds are brothers—Kabibonokka the fierce north wind sends the snow and binds the rivers in ice; Shawondese, the lazy south wind, smokes his pipe and fills the sky with dreamy softness. The Slavic *vila* command the wind and delight in stirring up storms. Their delicate sylphlike appearance belies the fact that they are powerful warriors, with voices that form gusts of wind strong enough to lift a house. In Scotland the Blue Hag, *Cailleach Bheur*, is reborn every Samhain when she smites the earth with her staff, calling down the storms and snow and bringing winter to the land.

Fairies of the air often take the form of birds. In the Dreamtime Aboriginal myths of Australia an evil sorcerer unleashed a dust storm to transform the graceful dancing girl Brolga into a bird. The birdlike alan hangs like a bat from the trees in the forests of the Philippines. In Irish legends the triple war goddess Morrigan manifests on the battlefield in the shape of a crow or a raven, possessing magical powers to create confusion, stir fury, and bestow courage and aid to her chosen victors in battle. In the myths of many countries the raven is a magical winged messenger between the human and spiritual realms. In Siberian tales *kutkh* the raven brings the sun, moon, stars, fresh water, and fire to the Earth. In Norse mythology the Valkyries are Odin's messengers who ride across the clouds on horseback, the flickering light of their armor painting the skies with the *aurora borealis*, or northern lights. When they venture to the earthly realm, they disguise themselves as white swans and bathe in secluded lakes. Like numerous other swan maidens, such as Peri Banu, if their feather cloaks are stolen, they lose their magical powers and are unable to return to the airy realm of the otherworld.

FAIRY FLOWERS AND TREES

One of the most commonly held beliefs about fairies that is still widespread today is that they are nature spirits, identified with flowers, trees, lakes, rivers, mountains, and other features of the natural landscape. They are as old as the hills, manifestations of the life force, or living spirit, present in all the aspects of the natural world.

The connection between fairies and the natural world is evident in the rich fairy lore and traditions associated with fairies and nature. Flowers, plants, and trees have long been venerated both as the homes of fairies and nature spirits and as the personification of those spirits. In the same way, some rivers or lakes are the homes of water fairies while others have a distinct personality of their own—the lake or river itself being synonymous with the spirit.

In the Dartmoor tale of the "Tulip Fairies" a troop of flower-loving piskies use tulip petals as cradles for their babies to sleep in while they dance beneath the moon, while in the Derbyshire tale of the "Crooker", collected by Ruth Tongue in *Forgotten Folk-tales of the English Counties* (1970), fairy women present magical posies of flowers to a traveler to guard against the evil Crooker, the malevolent ash tree spirit.

Late one evening a man was on his way to Cromford to visit his sick mother when an old woman dressed in green appeared from the hillside. She asked where he was going and warned that the road was not safe after dark.

The traveler remained silent, knowing that it was dangerous to converse with strangers on lonely roads at night, especially strangers clad in green, the color of the fairies.

"I see that you are wise enough not to speak and put yourself in danger, but I doubt if you'll be safe from Crooker without the right kind of help," said the woman, and she held out a posy of St. John's Wort flowers. "You are a good man and I wish you well, for you once freed a bird from a net. I know that bird. Take this posy, and when you travel to Cromford Road, show it to Crooker."

"Who is Crooker?" asked the traveler. But the woman had gone and he was alone on the road with the posy of St. John's Wort in his hand.

He continued along the road as darkness fell. Presently, he met another old woman. She, too, was dressed in green, and held a posy of primroses.

"Where are you going so late in

the evening?" she asked. "It isn't safe on Cromford Road after sunset."

"I am going to visit my old mother who is sick and needs me to care for her," the traveler replied.

"Then show these to Crooker," said the old woman, handing him the posy of primroses. "You are a good man and I wish you well, for you once freed a rabbit from a snare. I know that rabbit."

"Who is Crooker?" asked the traveler.

But this old woman, too, was gone.

The man hastened along the road as night closed in. When he reached a bend in the road, a third old woman was waiting for him, a posy of daisies in her hand.

"It is a dark and dangerous time to be traveling along Cromford Road," she said. "You need the right kind of help. Take this posy and show it Crooker."

"Who is Crooker?" asked the traveler.

She did not answer him, but said, "You are a good man—you once freed a vixen and her cub from a trap. I know that vixen and that cub. So I will give you a second piece of advice."

She warned him to keep as far from Darrent river as he could and to reach the shrine on Cromford Bridge before moonrise. Then she, too, was gone, and the man was alone on the road holding his three magic posies.

The man felt sure that he would need the magical protection of the flowers; he was so tired and weary he doubted he would arrive at the bridge before moonrise.

When at last he arrived at Cromford Road the moon had already risen and hung high and bright in the sky. The Darrent river ran fast and deep beside the road. The huge trees that grew on the riverbank cast strange shadows across the road in the moonlight. One tree stood alone, apart from the others. As it swayed in the wind, the moving shadows of its branches looked like skinny, clutching hands. The man was frightened of the tree and decided that, despite his weariness, he must run past it in order to avoid its shadowy clutches.

The Darrent river swirled and gurgled loudly, as though it was crying out "Hungry!", while the shadows of long, crooked branches like hands reached out from the moonlit road ahead. Running as fast as he could toward the bridge, the traveler threw the posy of daisies over his left shoulder. The river rippled and seemed to cry out, "Give!" There was a splash as the posy of daisies landed in the water and the clutching shadows disappeared.

Terrified, the traveler hobbled on, desperate to reach the safety of the bridge. But once more, the crooked hands of the Crooker tree rose up on the road ahead. Spurred on by fear, he broke into a run and cast the posy of primroses over his left shoulder. The Darrent river cried, "Give!" There was a splash as the posy of primroses landed in the water, and the Crooker relented.

The traveler continued fearfully on toward the bridge. When at last it was almost within reach, once more the Crooker laid his grasping hands across the path. Mustering the last of his strength, the traveler turned and hurled the posy of St. John's Wort directly at the malevolent tree. It uttered a terrible cry as the traveler leaped onto Cromford Bridge and collapsed at the foot of the shrine there.

The Darrent river swirled and gurgled, and in the village, the people of Cromford looked at one another with ashen faces.

"Darrent and Crooker," they said in hushed whispers. "At sunrise we must fetch the priest, for there is sure to be another poor victim to bury."

The next morning, when the villagers arrived at the bridge in bright sunlight, they discovered the traveler saying his prayers at the shrine. He was scared and footsore, but alive, thanks to the magical posies the fairy women had given him.

As he hobbled his way to his mother's house, the Darrent river chattered happily as it flowed shallow and sunny beneath the bank where a mighty ash tree stood.

FAIRY FLOWERS

Folklore is rich with connections between fairies and flowers. The relationship between the little people and flowers of the fields, meadows, hedgerows, and gardens has long captured the imagination of people from unlettered folk of the countryside to poets and playwrights. The following is a small selection of fairy flowers and trees and the lore associated with them. There are many more to discover.

Cowslip

"Where the bee sucks there suck I,
In a Cowslip's bell I lie."

The sprite Ariel in Shakespeare's The Tempest

The golden cowslip, harbinger of spring, has long been associated with the little people. It is a flower much admired by writers and poets. The seventeenth-century poet Michael Drayton described it as the special flower of the fairies in his poem *Nymphidia* (1627):

"For the queene a fitting bower,
(Quoth he) is that tall Cowslip
flower."

In the West Country of England cowslips were picked in spring and made into balls known as "titsy-tosties." Children threw a titsy-tosty to one another, chanting:

"Titsy-tosty, tell me true,
Who shall I be married to?"

Various names of boys and girls were called out until the tisty-tosty was dropped. The name being called out at that moment was the name of the future bride or groom.

In Wales the chant was:

"Pitey, Postey, four and twenty,
How many years shall I live?
One, two, three, four . . ."

Sometimes known as palseywort, the cowslip was believed to be a cure for palsey, a condition characterized by paralysis or shaking. An ointment of cowslip and linseed oil was recommended for a youthful complexion, while to dream of a cowslip in bloom was said to be an omen of a sudden change in fortune, for better or for worse.

Another name for cowslips is Culvers' Key. In fairy lore, carrying a posy of cowslips was said to unlock the way to fairy treasure.

Bluebell

Bluebell woods are traditionally places of fairy enchantment. In Scotland bluebells are known as Deadmen's Bells and to hear the tolling of a bluebell is said to be an omen of death. The traditional Scottish game "the dusky bluebells" has a fairylike quality, ending when all of the players have "vanished." The players stand in a circle and sing, "In and out the dusky bluebells/Who will be my master?/Tipper-ipper-apper on your shoulder/You will be my master," while one person dances, weaving in and out of the circle. When the song is finished, the dancer taps the shoulder of the player nearest to them, they link hands, and the game continues until no players are left in the circle.

In Somerset it was considered unlucky to walk alone in bluebell woods. It was particularly dangerous for children, who, it was said, were liable to be spirited away to fairyland, while pisky-led adults were unable to find their way out of the enchanted bluebell woods unaided.

Elsewhere the ringing of these tiny flowers is said to call the fairies to their midnight dances and revels.

Daisy

The "day's eye" opens its petals during the day and closes them at night. According to Greek legend, the origins of this flower are connected to the nymph Belides. One day she was dancing with her sweetheart when she attracted the attention of Vertumnus, deity of fruit trees. In order to escape his attentions, she transformed herself into a beautiful flower, known as *Bellis perennis*—the scientific name for the daisy.

Celtic legend gives a different account, in which the spirits of infants who died at birth scattered daisies on the earth to comfort their grieving parents.

A woman named Malvina was mourning the death of her infant son. The maidens of the court of King Morven consoled her, saying that they had seen her beautiful boy coming toward them in the misty sky looking radiantly happy and scattering the fields with flowers. These new flowers had a golden disk surrounded with silver leaves like the rays of the sun. As the blossoms moved gently in the breeze, they resembled children playing in a green meadow. The maidens called it a "day's eye" because it closed its petals at night and opened them with the first sunbeam of day.

There is much lore concerning the magical properties of the daisy. In France, where it is known as *marguerite,* or pearl, a posy of daisies picked before sunrise on St. John's Day (which falls close to midsummer) is said to protect against lightning when placed on the roof of a home. In Germany daisies are associated with the tooth fairy, for it is said that eating three daisies after a tooth is extracted will free the patient of toothache. Daisy roots placed under a pillow are said to bring dreams of absent loved ones or visions of the future. In England young girls used daisies in love divination, plucking the petals as they recited: "He loves me, he loves me not." Daisy-chains were considered to offer the wearer protection against fairy enchantment.

Daisies were believed to have medicinal properties, too, and were used in potions and remedies for a number of ailments and conditions, from dispelling madness to curing warts.

Dandelion

The dandelion takes its name from the French *dent de lion,* "lion's tooth," due to the jagged shape of its leaves. It is also known as the shepherd's clock; blowing on its head of seed-balls was used to guess the time of day.

Like other fairy flowers, dandelions were employed in games of love divination. If a girl wished to know whether she was in her lover's thoughts, she took a dandelion that had gone to seed and blew on the feathery down. If after three puffs a feather still remained, she could rest assured that her lover was indeed thinking about her.

A variation on this theme was recorded by Sir Walter Scott, who noted the plant's use as an oracle to determine whether a lover was on his way and in which direction—north, south, east, or west—he lived.

In Katharine M. Beals' *Flower Lore and Legend* (1917), one version of the fairy origins of the dandelion runs as follows:

Once upon a time the world was inhabited by fairies. Brownies and elves were skipping about in the grass. The trees were the homes of the wood-gnomes. The cheerful little flower-

sprites, in their gay colored gowns, were flitting about in the sunshine.

Suddenly human giants appeared, and the heavy foot of man wrought havoc and destruction in fairyland. The frightened little gnomes hid themselves deep in the earth. The elves sought shelter in crevices of the rocks. The brownies ran for the hollow trunks of trees. But the fairies loved the sunshine, and could not live in the dark ground nor hollow trees. The poor little things did not know where to hide themselves; and in their terror they clung to the stems of plants—each to the plant that was nearest—while the Queen changed them all into flowers of the color of the gowns they were wearing, and wherever there had been a fairy, there was then a flower.

That very morning a number of the fairies had appeared in new frocks, made of bright yellow sunbeams, and after all the excitement was over, these little people found themselves huddled close together on one stem, staring straight up at the sun.

Botanists who do not know very much about fairies call this flower a composite; but every child knows that it is a real fairy family, and they are so kind and helpful to each other that all the little ones are put in the center, and the older and stronger ones form a circle around them for protection. By some very old authorities, this is said to have been the origin of the dandelion.

Flax

It is not surprising that flax has fairy associations given its role in spinning and the large number of tales about spinning fairies, including "Rumpelstiltskin" and its many variations. Flax fiber extracted from the stem of the plant is used to spin yarn and make linen or twine and rope.

Flax cultivation was encouraged in Ireland, where spinning wheels were awarded based on the number of acres planted. Those who planted 1 acre (roughly 0.5 hectares) were awarded four spinning wheels and those growing 5 acres (2 hectares) were awarded a loom. Flax is the emblem of Northern Ireland.

Bundles of flax fiber have the appearance of soft, lustrous blonde hair, giving rise to the description "flaxen," which is reminiscent of descriptions of beautiful fairy maidens with flowing flaxen locks.

In *The Fairy-Faith in Celtic Countries* (1911), W. Y. Evans-Wentz notes that in Scotland this flower is sometimes called *lion na mna sithe*, the "flax of the fairy woman," and is said to be beneficial in curing certain illnesses.

In early versions of the tale of "Sleeping Beauty," such as Italian fairytale collector Giambattista Basile's *Sole, Luna e Talia* (Sun, Moon and Talia), it is not a spindle that Sleeping Beauty pricks her finger on but a sliver of flax.

Foxglove

The foxglove may derive its name from "folk's glove," meaning "good folk's glove" or "fairy's glove." In *The Fairy-Faith in Celtic Countries* (1911), Evans-Wentz notes that in Scotland it is sometimes called *miaran na mna sithe*, the "thimble of the fairy woman." In Ireland it is known as a fairy's cap, and it was said that if fairies were disturbed in their revels when dancing beneath the foxgloves, they took refuge among the plant's crimson blooms, where their red caps were camouflaged from human eyes. There are numerous folk names for foxgloves, including fairy bells, fairy petticoats, fairy dresses, and fairy fingers. The mottled patches on the petals are said to be where little fairy fingers have been placed.

Also known as goblin's gloves, foxgloves contain poisonous sap, called digitalis, which is a highly toxic heart stimulant. If parents suspected their child had been snatched away by the fairies and replaced with a fairy changeling, a remedy was to bathe the possible changeling in the sap of foxgloves or force it to drink a liquor drawn from the plant's leaves. Seeing one of their own kind subjected to the burning sensations of the foxglove's poisonous juice, the fairies were compelled to take back the changeling and return the human child.

Pansy

The pansy derives its name from the French *pensées*, or "thoughts." In Elizabethan times the wild pansy, or *Viola tricolor*, with its bright purple and yellow coloring, was much loved by country folk, as shown by the numerous names it inspired: heart's ease, heart's delight, tickle my fancy, Jack jump up and kiss me, three faces in a hood, or kiss me at the garden gate.

This colorful little flower with its unusual markings had many associations with the fairies. In *Plant Lore and Legend* (1927), Katharine M. Beals relates the story of how the fairies gave the pansy its colors:

Originally, as the story goes, it was of a milk-white color. One night, just before Midsummer Eve, the fairies had gathered to make preparations for their annual revel, and were discussing what they could do to make the world brighter for their being here. One little one timidly made a suggestion that they make a new flower. The rest were greatly pleased, and the very next night they went to work.

Getting out their paint boxes, they took blue from the sky, different shades of red from the sunset clouds, yellow from the sunbeams, and a warm brown color from mother earth. These colors they mixed in a cup with their brushes made of dandelion down. All night they worked and when morning came there were the flowers gorgeously colored. Some of the fairies had sketched in portraits of their fellows, so that the bed of pansies looked like a bed of cheerful little faces. The earth has been brighter and better, ever since, for that night's work.

Another story gives an explanation of why the pansy was called heart's ease.

When some foolish little sprites visited the human realm they fell in love with some handsome young men. They did not know that unions between fairies and mortals were forbidden, but the fairy queen was furious when she found out and forbade the sprites ever to leave fairyland again.

The love-struck sprites pined away and died. Taking pity on the love-lorn creatures, Cupid persuaded the fairy queen to transform them into flowers, which became known as heart's ease.

The sap or juice of heart's ease was thought to be a potent love potion, of which it was said:

On sleeping eyelids laid
Will cause a man or woman to madly dote
Upon the next live creature that it sees.

Shakespeare drew on country folklore and fairy lore in *A Midsummer Night's Dream*, in which the pansy is the "little western flower" or "love in idleness" used by Oberon, King of the Fairies, to concoct a love potion.

Primrose

These delicately scented flowers are heralds of springtime. In Ireland they were used as protection against fairies—primrose petals were scattered in doorways to keep fairies out, for it was said that they could not pass them.

In Somerset the pale yellow and pink flowers were prized by the fair folk. In a Somerset tale collected by Ruth Tongue, touching a fairy rock with the correct number of primroses opens the entrance to fairyland and brings fairy gifts, but the wrong number brings trouble.

A group of children were picking primroses in a valley called Goblin Combe, when one little girl wandered off and got lost. She began to cry and threw herself down upon a rock, and in doing so touched it with the bunch of primroses she had gathered. The rock opened, for it was a fairy rock. Out came a troop of little fairies and comforted the girl. They gave her a gold ball and led her safely home.

Hearing of this, the local conjuror or wise man decided he wanted some fairy treasures for himself. He picked a bunch of primroses and ventured to the fairy rock. But when he touched the flowers against the rock, the fairies did not reward him with gifts or treasures, for he was carrying the wrong number of primroses. Instead, he was taken by them, never to be seen again.

Some say that eating primroses is a way to see fairies. The flowers are said to have the power to make the invisible visible. On the other hand, in the folklore of Ireland and Wales, they confer the power of invisibility.

Primrose flowers and leaves are edible—tea can be brewed from the leaves and wine made from the young flowers.

Ragwort

Also known as fairies' horses, these wild flowers with gold petals appear in many tales as a means of fairy transport. In Evans-Wentz's *The Fairy-Faith in Celtic Countries* (1911), a Scottish crofter related how fairies sat astride stems of ragwort to fly through the air, in a similar way to witches on broomsticks.

A man on the Isle of Arran lived by a fairy knoll. He was fascinated by the ways of the fairies and often visited them to join in with their sports.

One night, the fairies decided to journey to Ireland and the man wanted to accompany them. Each of the fairies picked a stem of ragwort and sat astride it, and he did the same.

A tiny wee fairy shouted and asked were they all ready, and the others replied that they were. The little fairy called out:

"My king at my head,
Going across in my haste,
On the crests of the waves,
To Ireland."

"Follow me," said the King of the Fairies, and away they went across the Irish Ocean, mounted on their ragwort stems.

In an instant they had crossed the ocean, and behind them came the man, sitting astride his ragwort steed.

When it was time to return home to Arran, he did not know how on earth he would do so, but he leaped upon the ragwort as he saw the fairies do, and he called as he heard them call, and in an instant he was back home. But he had had his fill of fairy magic on that trip and never went traveling with the fairies again.

The seventeenth-century antiquarian John Aubrey gives the magic password to imbue ragwort with the power of flight as "Horse and Hattock."

In Ireland ragwort is also known as *boliaun.* In the Irish tale "The Field of Boliauns" ragwort marks the hiding-place of buried fairy treasure (*see* **Leprechaun**).

In the Isle of Man, the flower is known as *cushag* and it is the Manx national flower. In her poem "The Cushag" (1907), Manx poet Josephine Kermode wrote that ragwort's golden flowers might have fairy powers.

FAIRY TREES

"Touch wood" is the traditional saying to bring luck and banish malevolent forces. Trees feature in the fairy lore and mythology of many cultures around the world. They often symbolize the various planes of existence, with their roots in the earth, or Underworld, their trunks in the human world, and their branches in the heavenly or spiritual realm. Like fairies, trees span multiple realms, and they are powerful symbols of the mysteries of life. The following are just a few of the many trees that feature in a rich tradition of fairy lore.

Apple

Apple trees are sacred in Celtic mythology, connected with the Otherworld. The Isle of Avalon of Arthurian legend is thought to have derived from the Welsh word for "apple," *afal*, pronounced *aval*. In Irish legend, fairy people bring branches of silver or golden apples to invite mortals to join them in the Land of Eternal Youth, as in the legend of Bran Mac Febail and the Isle of Emhain. While in the Scottish legend "Thomas the Rhymer," the Queen of Elfland forbids Thomas to eat the fruits of fairyland, except for an apple that bestows upon him the gifts of prophecy, poetry, and truth.

In Cornwall Allantide was traditionally celebrated on October 31st as the first day of winter, known as *Kalan Gwav*. Part of the festival involved the giving of Allan apples—large red apples supposed to bring good luck.

Also in the West Country, wassailing is the name given to festivals in the cider orchards to bless the trees and bring a good crop of apples in the forthcoming season. The word *wassail* comes from the Anglo Saxon *wæs hæl*, meaning "be healthy," and was a common greeting or salutation. Originally the celebrations involved both house visiting and field visiting, but they have become more specifically associated with cider orchards. Traditionally, wassailing festivals involved splashing the trees with cider, or placing cider-soaked toast around the trunks and in the branches, and singing to the trees:

"Here stands a good old apple tree,
stand fast root,
Every little twig bear an apple big,

Hats full, caps full, and three score
sacks full.
Hip! Hip! Hurrah!"

Edward Swanton,
Bygone Haslemere *(1914)*

In Norse mythology Iduna was the keeper of the "apples of youth" for the gods. She was abducted by a giant, aided by the mischievous god Loki. As the gods began to age, they persuaded Loki to rescue Iduna, which he did, disguised as a falcon. Once the apples were returned, the gods regained their lost youth.

In a famous Greek myth, Hercules, or Heracles, traveled to the Garden of Hesperides to pluck the golden apples of the Tree of Life. In other myths, Atalanta outran all of her suitors to avoid marriage, until Hippomenes distracted her with three golden apples given to him by Aphrodite.

Another tale tells of Eris, the goddess of discord, who tossed a golden apple into a wedding party. The goddesses Hera, Athena, and Aphrodite all claimed the apple and Paris of Troy had to choose between them. Aphrodite offered the beautiful Helen of Sparta to Paris as a bribe, but he chose Aphrodite, indirectly starting the Trojan War.

The Roman goddess Pomona, known as the "apple mother," was the keeper of the Apples of Eternal Life. Roman banquets often ended with apples and a blessing in the name of Pomona.

Ash, Oak, Thorn

These were considered to be the magical trinity of fairy trees. A twig taken from each tree and bound with a red piece of thread was thought to be a powerful talisman to ward off spirits of the night.

Fairy folks
are in old oaks.

Old English rhyme

Oaks were sacred trees revered by the druids. The sinister Oakmen were said to be stewards of the forest, fiercely protective of their own kind and hostile to the incursions of humans into the woodlands. An oak coppice that sprang from the roots of a felled oakwood was thought to be particularly dangerous to humans, and walking in these coppices at night was to be avoided, especially if they happened to be in a bluebell wood.

Ash, too, was noted for its powers of protection and its seedpods were used in rituals of divination. Druids' staffs were often made of ash and it was believed to have healing properties. Children with weak limbs were passed through the middle of a split ash, the tree was then bound back together—if it thrived, it was said the child would be cured and they would grow strong.

Thorn trees were a favorite fairy dwelling place, especially solitary thorns growing in the vicinity of fairy hills. Rings of three or more hawthorns were typical fairy abodes and places to be treated warily by humans. The Irish *sheoque* fairies lived in thorn bushes, enticing mortals to listen to their enchanting fairy music, while the *lunantishee* fairy tribe were guardians of blackthorn bushes. They prevented humans from cutting blackthorn on the original May Day and original All Hallows Day—May 11th and November 11th. It was believed those who attempted to take wood from the blackthorn on these days would meet with misfortune.

Elder

"'Owd Girl, give me of thy wood, an 'Oi will give some of moine, when I grows inter a tree."

Old Lincolnshire saying

The elder tree is credited with a unique personality in many places, from the countryside of England to Scandinavia. Usually personified as a female spirit, sometimes she was considered to be of a kind and benevolent disposition, offering shelter to good fairies against witches and providing fruit and flowers prized for wine-making. Elsewhere, she was suspected to be a witch, or a form taken by a witch.

In one tale a man attempted to cut a branch from a sacred elder growing over a holy well. Twice he cut into the tree with his ax, and twice he stopped, for it seemed as though his house was on fire. Each time finding it to be a false alarm, the third time he persevered and chopped off the branch, only to find when he returned home that his house was burned to the ground.

In various cultures in order to avoid bad luck it is necessary to ask the Old Lady of the Elder Tree for permission before cutting any wood from her branches. In Scandinavia she is *Hylde-moer*, the Elder Mother, in Germany she is *Hylde-vinde*, Elder Queen. In the Cotswolds it was believed that an elder would bleed if it was cut. Furniture made of elder wood was considered unlucky, and babies should never be put to bed in a cradle made of elder because the fairies will pinch them black and blue.

Hazel

Traditionally, hazel is the tree of knowledge and wisdom. In the Celtic legend "The Salmon of Knowledge" when a salmon ate the hazelnuts that fell into the water of the Well of Wisdom, it gained all the world's knowledge. This was passed on to the Irish hero Fionn mac Cumhaill when he caught and cooked the magical fish.

As a tree associated with knowledge and wisdom, hazel is popular for use as a wand or divining rod. Hazelnuts are also connected with fertility, as attested in the old English saying: "So many cratchets [baskets], so many cradles." In the north of England the nut thickets were considered so important that they had two fairy guardians assigned to watch over them: Melsh Dick and the pipe-smoking Churnmilk Peg protected the nuts from pilfering human hands.

Rowan

Rowan tree, red thraid,
Pits witches to their speed.

Old English saying

As the saying suggests, rowan is traditionally associated with protection. In British folklore a piece of rowan tied with red thread is a safeguard against enchantment. Rowan crosses twined around with red thread were carried as good luck charms in the Celtic regions of Scotland and Cornwall. Rowan was the badge of various Scottish clans.

On the Isle of Man rowan crosses made without using a knife were placed over the door on May Eve to ward off the unwanted attentions of the little people, who were particularly active at that time of year. Wood from "flying rowans"—trees growing in a cleft of the rock or crevasses in other trees' trunks or boughs—was considered particularly powerful.

M

Maahiset

See **Maanväki**.

Maanalaiset

See **Maanväki**.

Maanväki

(Also *Maahiset, Maanalaiset.*) Literally, "Earth-dwellers." These **gnome**-like creatures from the folklore of Finland are guardian spirits of the Earth. They are generally benevolent, but will punish any humans who do not show respect for the territory under their stewardship.

Mab

A name for the fairy queen in English folklore, especially popular in sixteenth and seventeenth-century literature. She famously appears in Shakespeare's *Romeo and Juliet* as the fairy midwife, delivering men of their desires in the form of dreams. Described as being no bigger than an agate stone, she rides around in a hazelnut chariot drawn by insects. She also appears in Michael Drayton's *Nymphidia* (1627), and Ben Jonson's *Entertainment at Althorpe* (1603), and is generally characterized as being mischievous, delighting in fairy tricks such as tangling horses' manes into elflocks, swapping human children with **changelings**, or leading people on wild goose chases through ponds and ditches as a **will o' the**

wisp-type figure. In Joshua Poole's *Parnasus* she was first described as consort to the fairy king, **Oberon**, a role more often given to **Titania**. Her origins are not clear, but it is possible that her roots may be traced to the warlike Celtic queen **Medb** or Maeve of Ireland or Mabb of Wales.

Macha

One of the three aspects of the Irish war goddess of the ***Tuatha de Danann***. Manifesting as "Royston," hooded crows, or **ravens**, Macha, **Nemen**, and **Morrigu**, collectively known the ***badb***, possessed magical powers to create confusion, stir fury, and bestow courage to aid their chosen victors in battle. In the folklore of Ireland, a crow perching on a house was often taken as a sign of impending death or misfortune.

Maeve

See **Medb**.

Magnus, Olaus (1490–1557)

A Swedish patriot and man of the cloth, as well as a writer and geographer, Olaus Magnus was employed by Gustav I of Sweden for various diplomatic assignments and was sent to Rome in 1524 to obtain the appointment of his brother Johannes as archbishop. After the Reformation in Sweden he and his brother were exiled, as Sweden was no longer Catholic, and he remained abroad, finally settling in Rome in 1537.

He is best remembered for his work *History of the Northern People*, printed in Rome in 1555. It provided Europeans with a fascinating insight into the history, customs, and folklore of Scandinavia, such as accounts of fishermen's encounters with the water spirit ***sjora***. It was translated into many languages but, strangely enough, not into Swedish until 1909.

Malekin

Haunting Dagworthy Castle in Suffolk, according to the thirteenth-century chronicler **Ralph**

of Coggeshall, Malekin was a human child who had been stolen by the fairies while her mother was working in the fields. Consequently, she was trapped between the human and fairy realms for a period of 14 years. She could be heard but not seen. She talked to the servants in a broad Suffolk accent, but conversed with the chaplain in Latin. The servants left out food for her, which was always eaten. Presumably, it was important that she ate human food, for to eat fairy food would have meant remaining a permanent captive in fairyland. Although generally invisible, she appeared to a servant with whom she was on particularly friendly terms in the form of a small child wearing a white tunic. What became of her when her allotted time in fairyland reached an end remains a mystery.

Mama Padura

The Forest Mother in Slavic folklore. She dwells in woods and forests. Charles Godfrey Leland describes her, in *Gypsy Sorcery and Fortune Telling* (1891), as a benevolent spirit, especially protective of children who have strayed from the path and lost their way in the woods.

Manannan, Son of Lir

Irish sea god and protector of the Isle of Man. Husband of **Fand**. The "Son of the Sea," he traveled the seas in his chariot.

Manannan appears in the legend of "The Voyage of Bran," in which the Irish ruler Bran mac Febail ventured out in search of the enchanted Isle of Emhain, the Land of Women. As he and his men sailed across the sea, Manannan appeared to them and spoke to them in verse or song:

"It is what Bran thinks, he is going in his curragh over the wonderful, beautiful, clear sea; but to me, from far off in my chariot, it is a flowery plain he is riding on.

What is a clear sea to the good boat Bran is in is a happy plain with many flowers to me in my two-wheeled chariot.

It is what Bran sees, many waves beating across the clear sea; it is what I myself see, red flowers without any fault.

The sea-horses are bright in summertime, as far as Bran's eyes can reach; there is a wood of beautiful acorns under the head of your little boat.

A wood with blossom and with fruit, that has the smell of wine; a wood without fault, without withering, with leaves of the color of gold.

Let Bran row on steadily, it is not far to the Land of Women; before the setting of the sun you will reach Emhain, of many-colored hospitality."

Manannan's description reveals the topsy-turvy nature of the fairy realm, in which the mortal world is distorted; his boat becomes a chariot, the blue sea becomes a red, flowery plain, and the waves become woodlands.

Similar to the Scandinavian tales of Valhalla, where a wild boar was hunted every day and feasted on every night, Manannan's magical swine provided food for the ***Tuatha de Danann***. Every night the swine were slaughtered and eaten, and every morning they lived again.

Manitou

In the folk beliefs of the Native American Algonquian people of northeast America, *manitou* is a term used to describe the spirits of nature and universal life force. There are thousands of different *manitou*. Every aspect of the natural world possesses its own *manitou*, including animals, plants, stones, and features of the natural landscape such as mountains, lakes, and rivers, as well as clouds.

Shamans employed *manitous* to bring about a desired outcome: plant *manitous* were used in healing; buffalo *manitous* were used to ensure a good hunt.

The same concept exists under

different names in other tribes. To the Sioux it is ***wakanda***, and to the Iroquois ***orenda***.

Mara

(Or Mera.) Mara appears in various guises in different cultures as either a demonic or nurturing figure. An Old English word for "demon," its usage survives in terms such as "nightmare." Similar terms are found in Old Norse, German, Dutch, Swedish, Danish, and Icelandic, all identified with a malicious **goblin** or **incubus**-like creature that pressed down on sleepers' chest, inducing nightmares. (See also **Elves**.)

In Buddhism, Mara was the demon sent to tempt the Buddha into straying from his spiritual path through visions of beautiful women, said to be her daughters.

In some accounts, Mara's daughters are named as Tanha, "Craving," Arati, "Boredom," and Raga, "Passion."

In Latvian mythology, Mara is a positive being in the form of the wise and giving Earth Mother.

Mariora Floriora

See **Zina**.

Marrol, the

A savage sea spirit of Shetland. Described as a many-eyed fish with a crest of flickering flame, it delighted in storms and appeared when the sea foamed with phosphorescence. Its shout and exultant song could be heard when a ship was wrecked.

Matabiri

Malevolent nature spirits dwelling in swamps and mangroves in the folklore of the Wagawaga people of Papua New Guinea. Both male and female, old and young, are described as having large, protuberant bellies and huge, swollen cheeks. These malignant spirits put "medicine" on humans while they are sleeping, causing their stomachs and faces to swell up, a condition that often proves fatal.

Matagaigai

Nature spirits in the folklore of the Wagawaga people of Papua New Guinea. They make their homes in the branches of trees. The male appears as an ordinary human male while the female is distinguished by having one large breast and one small breast. The *matagaigai* push their fingers into the flesh of humans suffering from sickness or disease to determine whether they will live or die. If their fingers sink in deep, the patient is doomed to die.

Despite their association with illness and death, the *matagaigai* are benevolent beings and are not responsible for inflicting disease.

Matholwch

See **Bran the Blessed**.

Matshishkapeu

Literally, "the Fart Man." A powerful spirit in the folklore of the Innu people of Canada and also the source of much amusement.

When the Caribou Man, or Kanipinikassikueu, deprived the starving Innu people of caribou, Matshishkapeu inflicted him with an uncomfortable bout of constipation until he relented and provided caribou to the people once more.

According to the Innu, when someone farts, it is Matshishkapeu communicating, though his utterances are often cryptic and the Innu must interpret them. This is a great source of amusement, and so Matshishkapeu often manifests at public events and meetings if things start to get tense. The outburst of flatulence and its interpretation are the cause of much hilarity that dissipates the tension.

While being a humorous, amusing character, Matshishkapeu is also considered to wield great power and serves a serious function in having dominance over animal masters as well as human behavior.

Mazikeen

(Also *shedeem* or *shehireem.*) In Jewish belief, a being similar to the ***djinn*** of Arab tradition. Believed to have been created during the 130 years during which Adam and Eve were excommunicated from the Garden of Eden, they have been described as the offspring of unions between spirits and Adam and Eve. Like the ***jinn***, they are shapeshifters and can assume any form they please.

In *The Fairy Mythology* (1828), **Thomas Keightley** describes the *mazikeen* as creatures partway between humans and supernatural beings or angels. Like humans, they eat and drink, marry and have children, and are subject to death. Like supernatural creatures, they can see what happens in the mortal realm without being seen, they have wings and can fly, and they can foretell the future.

MEDB

(Or Maeve. Also Medhb.) Warrior queen of Coonacht in western Ireland.

In the legend of *Tain Bo Cuailnge*, or "The Cattle Raid of Cooley," Medb was foiled by a teenage **Cuchulainn**. She raised legions of magicians to fight the hero and laid a *geis*, or curse, upon him and eventually brought about his downfall.

MEDHB

See **Medb**.

MEISTER HAMMERLING

A wine-making **gnome** in the folklore of Germany. In the tale of "Nonnenworth and Rolandseck," related in *Nymphs, Nixies and Naiads: Legends of the Rhine* (1895), Meister Hammerling is described as a gnome (or alternatively a monk), residing in a mine on the banks of the Rhine, whose wine "strange fortunes brought to those who drank."

MEKUMWASUCK

Wood-dwelling fairies of the Passamaquoddy people in Native

American folklore, said to be 2.5 to 3 feet (1 meter) in height, fantastically dressed, and grotesquely ugly with hairy faces. Some said they were made of stone. They were much feared by the people of the Passamaquoddy for it was said that the gaze of the mekumwasuck caused illness or even death.

The Passamaquoddy people were converted to Catholicism in the seventeenth century and after that the mekumwasuck were said to be guardians of the Catholic Church, performing a similar function to gargoyles in driving away wrong-doers with their stern glare. One account tells of how a group of drunken men broke into a church to steal holy wine when the priest was away, but were driven out by the mekumwasuck.

See also **Nagumwasuck**.

Melsh Dick

Guardian of nut thickets in Yorkshire. "Melsh Dick'll catch thee, lad" was recorded in the 1800s as a common threat to prevent children from pilfering nuts from the bushes. Melsh Dick's pipe-smoking female companion, **Churnmilk Peg**, also performs the task of guarding the nuts in the north of England.

The old saying "So many cratches [baskets], so many cradles" hints at the value that was placed on nuts as a food associated with fertility, which may explain why they were considered important enough to have two spirits to protect them from thieving human hands.

Melusine

A half-woman, half-serpent in the folklore of France. The tale of Melusine has been described as the French romance version of the story of **Lamia**. Sometimes she is depicted as half-woman, half-fish.

Melusine was the daughter of the fay Pressina and the Scottish King of Albany. Her parents became estranged when the king broke a promise he had made to Pressina. As a result, Melusine and her two sisters, Melior and Palatina, grew up with their mother on the Hidden Island of Cephalonia. From the heights of the island, the land of Albany could be seen. Every day Pressina told her children that if it hadn't been for their father's broken promise they would be living there in happiness.

The girls grew bitter toward their father and plotted to take revenge on him for their exile. They confined him and all of his wealth in Mount Brandelois, then returned home and told their mother what they had done, expecting her to be pleased. Instead she flew into a rage at the disrespect they had shown to their father. As a punishment, she placed a curse on Melusine. Periodically, she would be turned from the waist down into a serpent unless she could find a man to marry her who would promise never to see on her Saturdays and stay true to his promise forever.

Melusine searched through France for such a man until she came to the fairy forest of Colombriers in Poitou, where the fays of the forest made her their queen. There, at the Fountain of Thirst, she met Raymond of Poitou. They fell deeply in love and were married, Raymond promising that he would never see his wife on Saturdays. Melusine built the fairy Castle of Lusignan for them to live in and they would have been completely happy but for the fact that every one of their children was born with a deformity. Raymond still loved his wife deeply, but a cousin planted the idea in his mind that the reason for their children's malformations was that they had been fathered by another man, and that Saturdays were kept sacred for his visits.

Eventually Raymond's curiosity got the better of him and he followed his wife in secret one Saturday and saw her emerge from her bath with the tail of a serpent. But he still loved her dearly and resolved never to speak of it or to tell her that he knew her secret.

However, one of their children, Geoffroi of the Tusk, was monstrous in character as well as in appearance. When he burned down an abbey and with it took the lives of his brother and many of the monks, Raymond in his grief blurted out at Melusine: "Get out of my sight you pernicious snake! You have contaminated my children!"

Melusine fainted on hearing his words. When she came round, she leaped onto the windowsill, transformed into a dragon, and flew away. It is said that she become a **banshee**-like spirit, destined to lament the death of each Lord of Lusignan as long as the castle remained standing.

There are many versions of the story of Melusine and her legend has inspired numerous works of literature and art. Goethe retells her tale in a short story entitled "The New Medusa," Marcel Proust mentions her in *Within a Budding Grove* (1919), and A. S. Byatt includes a poem about her in her novel *Possession* (1990).

MERA

See **Mara**.

MERMAID

Half-woman, half-fish, the mermaid is a familiar figure in the folklore of cultures around the world. Usually described as having the upper body of a beautiful woman, with long, flowing locks, and a shiny fish's tail from the waist down, she is most often depicted sitting on a rock combing her tresses. Her name derives from *mere*, Old English meaning "sea," and *maid*, "a girl or woman."

Sometimes the mermaid is portrayed as a gentle, romantic figure with the ability to grant wishes, heal, and foretell the future, warning sailors and fishermen of imminent danger. At other times she appears as a dangerous, lustful temptress, luring ships to crash onto the rocks or using her charms to entice men to a watery death. She is an ambiguous creature, by turns inspiring pity, love, lust, and fear. Different aspects of her character are emphasized in different cultures and tales. She is often shown holding a mirror and comb. Sometimes these are interpreted as symbols of power, the mirror being associated with the moon, and the comb having connections with female sexuality—the Greek and Latin words for "comb" can also signify "vulva." Alternatively these items are construed as symbols of vanity.

Though usually human-sized, there are instances of mermaids of huge proportions. One was supposed to have been 160 feet (nearly 50 meters) in height, with hair 18 feet (5 meters) long, her fingers and nose both measuring 7 feet (2 meters) in length. The precise dimensions were recorded in the Irish chronicles *The Annals of the Four Masters* after the mermaid was said to have washed ashore in about A.D. 887.

Mermaid brides appear in tales around the world, although as is often the case with a union between a mortal and a fairy creature, more often than not it does not end well. In *The Fairy Mythology* (1828), **Thomas Keightley** recounts the tale of an Italian mermaid bride.

A young man bathing in the sea late one evening noticed that something was following him. Thinking it was one of his companions, he caught it by the hair and dragged it to shore. Finding it to be a maiden of great beauty and of most perfect form, he threw his cloak about her and took her home, where she stayed with him till they had a son.

One thing, however, greatly grieved him, which was that so beautiful a form should not speak, for he had never heard a word pass her lips.

One day he was reproached by one of his companions, who said that it was a specter, not a real woman, that he had at home. Being both angry and terrified, the man laid his hand on the hilt of his sword, and urged the woman with vehemence to tell him who or what she was, threatening, if she did not do so, to kill the child before her eyes.

The spirit broke her silence to say that he had lost a good wife by forcing her to speak, then vanished, leaving her son behind.

A few years later, as the boy was playing on the seashore, his mother dragged him into the sea, where he drowned.

In other tales, mermaids are actively malicious, using their sweet singing voices or ravishing looks to lure men into their underwater domain in order to drown them or take them captive.

In the Scottish tale of "The Laird of Lorntie," a laird riding home one evening heard the calls of a beautiful golden-haired woman who appeared to be drowning in a lake. He was plunging into the water to rescue her when his manservant pulled him back and declared it to be the trick of a mermaid.

Realizing his servant was right, Lorntie made to ride off, leaving the mermaid calling fiercely:

"Lorntie, Lortnie,
Were it na your man,
I had gart your heart's bluid
Skirl in my pan."

Here, the mermaid made her malevolent intentions clear: if it had not been for the quick thinking of his manservant, she would have had the blood of Lorntie's heart singing as it cooked in her pan.

A Cornish tale collected by **William Bottrell** in *Traditions and Hearthside Stories of West Cornwall* (1873), recounts the story of "Lutey and the Mermaid," in which the mermaid displays elements of the temptress yet is also true to her word in granting Lutey's wishes.

In days of old, as is well known, the men of Cornwall would often comb the shoreline of their rocky coast in the hope of finding goods or even simple firewood washed ashore from the many ships that fell foul of the dangerous seaway.

One of these men, Lutey, lived near the Lizard Point at a place called Cury. Like so many, he was part farmer, part fisherman, part smuggler, and part wrecker in order to provide for his wife and children.

One day, when the tide was low, he was scrambling among the rocks seeking something that might be of value when he heard a sorrowful voice, sad but sweet. He followed the sound and came upon a beautiful young woman who seemed to be trapped in a pool of water left by the receding tide. Her hair shone like threads of gold in the sunlight as it floated on the water and her skin gleamed like mother of pearl. As he drew closer, Lutey realized that the reason she was trapped was because the lower half of her body was that of a silvery fish—for she was a mermaid.

She grew very fearful as he approached, but he said, "Don't be afraid, my dear, I am a sober and staid married man. Now what can I do to help thee?"

"You are a kind man," she said,

"Could you carry me to the waves, as I cannot get there myself?"

"Well, why not wait for the tide to return and carry you away?" asked Lutey.

"It is my fear that if I tarry here much longer, my husband will devour our children. I must always be at hand to feed him lobsters and crabs when he wakes, and that time will soon come. If you will only carry me to the sea, then I will grant you three wishes. Here, as a token of my faith, take this golden comb."

Lutey put the comb in his pocket.

The mermaid added, "Whenever you need help at sea, just pass the comb through the brine three times and call my name, which is Morvenna."

Lutey lifted her in his arms and started toward the tumbling waves.

"You must tell me your three wishes," she said. "Will you have gold and silver and a great palace to live in?"

Lutey thought for a long moment, remembering tales of old when such wishes had brought only sorrow and despair. "No," he said, "I wish only for the power to do good to my neighbors, to break the spells of witchcraft, and to compel familiar spirits for the good of others, and that these powers will pass on down my family forever."

Morvenna promised to grant these wishes, but as they grew closer to the waves, she described the beauty of her life beneath the sea and clung ever more tightly to Lutey, hoping to take him with her. He was sorely tempted to go, but just as the water lapped around their bodies, he heard his dog barking, and looking back at the shoreline he saw smoke coming from the chimney of his humble home. He knew he must return, but the mermaid had her arms firmly about his neck.

In desperation, Lutey pulled his knife from his belt and threatened to kill her if she would not release him. The shiny steel was enough to force Morvenna to drop from his arms into the welcoming depths of the sea, now surging about them. As she swam, she cried, "Farewell my sweet, for nine long years, then I'll come for thee, my love!"

The mermaid kept her promises and for generations the Luteys of Cury were renowned as healers and defenders against witchcraft. However, Lutey himself never forgot the beautiful Morvenna. Nine years later, he was out one clear night fishing with a friend when out of the sparkling sea burst the fabulous form of the mermaid, her golden hair streaming around her.

"My hour is come!" cried Lutey, and without hesitation he plunged over the side of the boat, disappearing forever into the briny depths.

His body was never found and they say that one of his descendants is lost at sea every nine years.

In "The Mermaid of Zennor," another Cornish tale, the mermaid appears as a romantic figure who falls in love with a local fisherman and assumes human form to join him singing in the church choir before the two disappear together, presumably to live happily beneath the waves. The church in the village of Zennor in west Cornwall is still famous for its mermaid seat today—a wooden pew bearing the carving of a mermaid, one of many examples of mermaid carvings and sculptures to be found in churches throughout Europe and beyond.

Mermaids have long captured the imagination of artists, inspiring numerous works of art and literature, one of the most famous being **Hans Christian Andersen**'s popular tale of *The Little Mermaid* (1837). This tale was adapted into a film by Disney in 1989, bringing the mermaid to a new generation of audiences. This beguiling creature, in all of her guises, continues to fascinate people around the world.

See also **Asrai**, Manx ***Ben Varrey***, Scottish ***Ceasg***, Brazilian **Janaína**, Irish **Liban the Mermaid**, French **Melusine**, Irish **Merrow**, Welsh **Morgan**, Breton ***Morgen***, Orcadian **Selkies**, and Scottish **Roane**.

Merman

The male counterpart of the **mermaid** appears in the folklore of cultures around the world. While mermaids are generally described as beautiful, desirable creatures, mermen are often—although not always—portrayed as ugly and tend to have less contact with humans than the female of species. The male **merrows** of Ireland and Scotland are described as extremely ugly creatures with green hair, green teeth, red noses, and piggy eyes. The Scandinavian Havmands, however, are handsome creatures that sport green or black beards.

In Greek mythology Triton, the messenger of the sea, is generally depicted as a merman with a barnacled male torso and a fish's tail. The son of Poseidon and Amphitrite, god and goddess of the sea, he could summon furious storms or calm the waves by trumpeting on his twisted conch shell.

The Cornish merman in "The Old Wandering Droll-Teller of the Lizard, and his Story of the Mermaid and the Man of Cury" in **William Bottrell**'s *Traditions and Hearthside Stories of West Cornwall* (1870) has the voracious appetite of a shark. When a mortal man discovers a mermaid stranded in a rockpool at low tide she explains why she is desperate to return home before her husband awakes:

"I want to get back before the turn of the tide; because, then, my husband and all the rest of the mermen are sure to wake up hungry and look for their suppers; an, can 'e believe it of my monster (he looks a monster indeed compared with you), that if I am not then at hand with half-a-dozen fine mullets, a few scores of mackerel, or something else equally nice to suit his dainty stomach, when he awakes with the appetite of a shark, he's sure to eat some of our pretty children. Mermen and maidens would be as plenty in the sea as herrings if their gluttons of fathers didn't gobble up the tender babes. Scores of my dear ones have gone through his ugly jaws, never to come out alive."

In contrast, the Manx ***dinny mara*** is described as an altogether gentler creature, a loving father who dotes on his child.

Merrows

(Or Morduadh.) (Pronounced *muroo-cha.*) **Mermaids** of Ireland and Scotland. Their name probably derives from the Irish, *muir*, meaning "sea," and *oigh*, "a maid." Said to appear before storms, they were dreaded by fishermen for this reason. The females were similar in appearance to mermaids, with the upper part of their body that of a beautiful woman, while the lower part was a fish's tail, and they had small webs between their fingers. In contrast, the males were described as extremely ugly creatures with green hair, green teeth, red noses, and piggy eyes.

W. B. Yeats, in *Fairy and Folk Tales of the Irish Peasantry* (1888), relates how the merrows had a red cap, known as a *cohullen druith*. Similar to the **seal maidens** and their sealskins and **swan maidens** and their feathered cloaks, if merrows had their cap taken away, they were prevented from returning to the water, and there were tales of fishermen stealing the caps in order to win the merrows as their brides. The offspring of these unions were said to have scaly, fishlike skin.

Male merrows were said to keep the souls of drowned sailors caged up in their homes at the bottom of the sea, although whether this was out of compassion for the poor drowned souls or out of malice is unclear.

Crofton Croker's tale "Soul Cages" tells of a friendship between a human and a merrow.

Jack Dogherty longed to see a merrow. He lived with his wife, Biddy, in a snug little cabin on the seashore where his grandfather had lived before them. His grandfather had been fast friends with a merrow and would have asked him to be godfather to his children had it not been for fear of offending the priest. But Jack had never glimpsed so much as a merrow's fin.

At last one day he made out the shape of a creature on a rock about half a mile along the coast. It appeared to be wearing a red hat, but was standing so still that Jack couldn't be sure whether it was a merrow or a piece of rock with the sunset glinting off it. Then suddenly it plunged into the water and Jack knew he had seen a merrow at last.

After that he went to the rock every day, hoping to strike up a friendship, but it wasn't until the winter storms blew up that the merrow came to shore again. One blustery day Jack found him sitting on the rock. He was an ugly old fellow with green hair, a red nose, piggy eyes, scaly legs ending in a bit of a tail, finlike arms, and long, strong, green teeth. But he smiled at Jack and greeted him by name.

"How did you know my name?" asked Jack, surprised.

"Why wouldn't I?" said the merrow. "Your grandfather was like a brother to me. He was a great man."

Jack was pleased to have found his grandfather's old friend and arranged to visit his home the following Monday.

When Monday came round, the merrow was there with a second red hat, which he told Jack to put on. "Take hold of my tail and follow me down into the water," he said.

Jack did as he was told. They swam out to a rock, then went down, down, down, with the water rushing past Jack's head so that he couldn't see and could scarcely breathe.

At last they landed on the sandy seabed. Jack could see fish swimming in the sea above them, but to his surprise found that they were on dry land and he could breathe again. They went inside the merrow's house, which was slated with oyster shells, where they ate a fine fish supper and drank all manner of spirits. The merrow became very merry, while Jack kept a cool head and wasn't drunk at all. He put this down to all the cold water above him.

The merrow told Jack his name was Coomara and showed him around his house, which was full of curiosities that had come from the sea.

A row of wicker baskets that looked like lobster pots caught Jack's eye. "What might you keep in them, Coomara?" he asked.

"Oh, these are the soul cages," said Coomara.

"Surely fish don't have any souls," said Jack.

"No, they don't," replied Coomara. "These are the souls of drowned sailors."

He told Jack that when he saw a good storm brewing, he put out his baskets and the souls of the drowned sailors crept into them in search of warmth and shelter.

"Aren't they lucky to have such a warm, dry place to stay?" he remarked.

Jack was so shocked, he didn't know what to say. Although he couldn't see anything inside the cages, he thought he had heard a sobbing when Coomara had talked of how lucky the poor souls were.

He made his excuses to leave and Coomara placed the red hat on his head back to front, lifted him up onto his shoulders and launched him up into the water. Jack shot up like a bubble to the surface and tossed the hat back down into the sea as Coomara had asked. He made his way home, all the while thinking about the poor trapped souls and how he could go about setting them free.

He decided to invite Coomara to his home and ply him with fine spirits in order to sneak down and free the souls without him noticing. However, he hadn't counted on Coomara remaining as cool-headed above water as he had below. He woke up the next morning with a headache and Coomara was nowhere to be seen.

He resolved to try one last time. This time he watered down his own spirits and gave the strongest to Coomara. As soon as the merrow slipped off to sleep, he took his red hat and plunged down to the bottom of the sea. At Coomara's house he gathered up the soul cages. As he opened each one, he saw a tiny flicker of light and heard the faintest whistling as the souls were released. When he had emptied all of the cages, he put them back where he had found them.

Without Coomara to launch him up into the sea, he wasn't sure how he was going to make it home, but just then a cod swam by above him and he was able to grab hold of its tail. It pulled him up into the sea and the red hat carried him back to the surface in a flash.

Jack hurried home to find Coomara still asleep. He returned the red hat to the table beside him. When Coomara awoke, he was so ashamed at having been out-drunk, he returned home without a word.

However, the two remained firm friends. Jack continued to visit the merrow's home, and whenever he did, he made sure to secretly free all of the new souls that had been caught. Coomara never noticed that they were gone.

The two remained friends for many years, until one day Jack threw a stone into the water as usual to call for the merrow, but Coomara never came up. He threw another and another, but there was no reply. As merrows were known to live for hundreds of years, Jack thought it most likely that his old friend had moved on to another part of the sea. But as Coomara had the second red hat, he could never venture down to find out for sure.

Merry Dancers

See ***Fir Chlis.***

Midhir

Fairy chief of the ***Tuatha de Danann*** in Irish mythology. Husband of the beautiful **Etain**. Lady Gregory describes Midhir in *Gods and Fighting Men* (1904):

A long green cloak he had on him, and a shirt woven with threads of red gold, and a brooch of gold that reached across to his shoulders on each side. And he had on his back a shield of silver with a rim of gold and a boss of gold, and in his hand a sharp-pointed spear covered with rings of gold from heel to socket. Fair yellow hair he had, coming over his forehead, and it bound with a golden band to keep it from loosening.

The love story of Etain and Midhir has been the inspiration for many plays, books, and music in which the fairy folk are portrayed in the heroic tradition as powerful and fearless.

Etain was Midhir's second wife. His jealous first wife, Fuamnach, cast a spell on her, turning her into a fly and sending a cold blast of wind to carry her away from the fairy hills to Ireland.

For seven years Etain was blown to and fro across Ireland in great misery, until she came to the hall of a king, where she fell into the queen's goblet of wine. The queen swallowed her, and after nine months in her belly, Etain was reborn and again called Etain. She grew into a beautiful woman and married Eochaid of Munster.

Midhir, who had been searching for her, discovered her whereabouts and challenged Eochain to three games of chess. He lost the first two, but won the third and named Etain as his prize.

Eochain was reluctant to give up his wife, but agreed to allow Midhir one kiss. When he came to claim his kiss, Midhir raised his sword in his left hand and put his right arm around Etain and the two rose up out of the roof of the palace and flew away as two white swans joined by a golden chain. They returned to the fairy hills, but Eochaid and his men came to find Etain and dug into Midhir's fairy hill.

Eventually Etain returned to her mortal husband and the *Tuatha de Danann*'s power dwindled thereafter.

MIREN

See ***Fatit***.

Miru

A ***patupaiarehe***, or fairylike being, in Maori mythology, credited with imparting sacred knowledge and wisdom to the Maori people.

The traditional Maori tale "The Story of Miru and Hine-rangi" relates how Miru became the fairy lover of a mortal woman and passed on his people's knowledge of magical arts, love charms, and games to her tribe. It is one of a number of tales from the Maori-Polynesian tradition that explains how skills and wisdom were supposed to have been handed from *patupaiarehe* to mortals.

Long, long ago there lived a man in a village at Marewa in Hawaiki, the mythological homeland of the Maori. He had two daughters, the older called Hine-rangi (Heavenly Maid) and the younger named Hine-mai-te-uru (Girl from the West).

It was not uncommon in those days for the older daughter to be set apart from the rest of the tribe and live alone in her own dwelling, not indulging in relationships with her peers.

Sometimes the tribe was visited by men from the *patupaiarehe* people, who lived far away in the forests. They were regarded as fairy people, for their appearance and customs were very different from those of the Marewa tribe.

One day a *patupaiarehe* called Miru was passing through the village when he saw Hine-rangi and was greatly attracted to her. But, as she lived alone as a *puhi* or virgin, he could not approach her by day. Instead he crept back at night and Hine-rangi took him as her fairy lover. He left at dawn so as not to be seen.

After a time it became obvious that Hine-rangi was with child, and the rest of the tribe was most excited and curious to know who the father might be. Hine-rangi would only say that he was not of this world.

The rest of the tribe devised a cunning plan to discover the identity of this mysterious lover. One night, after Miru had crept unseen into Hine-rangi's house, the people covered all the openings of the house so Miru would not know when day had come. The deception worked and in the middle of the day the people unplugged all the holes and rushed in to discover the identity of Hine-rangi's mysterious lover.

Miru decided to stay with his beloved Hine-rangi and for many years they lived happily in the village and had two fine sons called Tonga-te-uru and Uru-makawe. However, one day Miru felt a powerful need to return to his own people and he said to his father-in-law, "Come with me, you and your tribe and visit my people." His father-in-law agreed to go, along with his younger daughter, Hine-mai-te-uru, and several members of the tribe, but he insisted that Hine-rangi should remain behind with her sons.

Upon arrival at Miru's village, the visitors were shown into a very large house, where the *patupaiarehe* people greeted them in friendship. It turned out that Miru was one of the leaders of his people and expert in many fields such as the rites of *makutu* wizardry, the spells of *atahu* or love charms, and other aspects of sacred knowledge. The visitors were shown many games and skills, such as *whai*, or cat's cradle, and other string games, the *tititorea* or throwing sticks, the working of wooden marionettes to imitate *haka* dances, and the art of woodcarving.

Miru's father-in-law was most impressed and asked Miru to instruct him so that he might take back this knowledge and these skills to his own tribe. In return he offered his younger daughter to Miru as his wife. Miru was happy with this arrangement and over time his father-in-law learned the priestly arts and games, and became quite skilled at woodcarving. Eventually, however, he had to return to his own village. He was sad to leave his daughter, but by now she had become accustomed to her new way of life.

When her father arrived back, Hine-rangi was sorrowful to hear that Miru was not coming back as well, but now her sons had grown into fine young men and they looked after her well. Her father and his grandsons set about building a large house like the one that housed Miru's tribe. Tonga-te-uru learned all the wisdom and rites of the *patupaiarehe* from his grandfather, and they called the great house

Hui-te-rangiora, the assembly place of all beautiful things, the home of peace and happiness.

Tonga-te-uru became the chief teacher and *tohunga,* or shaman, among his people and Hui-te-rangiora was the first great lodge of instruction of the Maori people.

Even today there is a house named Hui-te-rangiora on the banks of the Puniu river near Kihikihi township on the North Island of New Zealand. It was the council house of Maori chief Rewi Maniapoto and served as an important meeting place where political policies and other matters of importance were discussed.

MMOTIA

Forest spirits in the folk beliefs of Ghana, West Africa. These dwarf-like creatures dwell deep in the forest. They are mischievous spirits with knowledge of the forest's plants and herbs.

MONACIELLO

"The Little Monk" in the folklore of Naples, Italy. Described as a short, thick little man dressed in the long garments of a monk with a broad-brimmed hat, he appeared to people in the dead of the night, beckoning them to follow him and leading those who had the courage to go with him to hidden treasure. There are tales in which people are supposed to have made sudden fortunes through encounters with the *monaciello.*

The seventeenth-century collection of Italian folk tales *Il Pentamerone* includes a different account of the *monaciello* as a mischievous household spirit, fond of whipping off bedsheets during the night. In one tale, when an ogre and ogress awoke in the night to find the quilt pulled off them, the ogre immediately blamed the *monaciello* and began to shout: "The *monaciello,* the *monaciello, hola*! Candles! *Un,* run!"

In *The Fairy Mythology* (1828), **Thomas Keightley** notes that belief in the *monaciello* is specific to Naples and does not appear in other parts of Italy. Naples being the place where the Normans settled, he speculates that the *monaciello* may have his roots in the Scandinavian ***nisse*** or German ***Kobold***.

Morduadh

See **Merrows**.

Morgan

A Welsh water spirit dwelling in Lake Glasfryn Uchaf. Said to carry away children who ventured too close to the water. **Sir John Rhys**, in *Celtic Folklore: Welsh and Manx* (1901), speculates that the Welsh Morgan may have its roots in the Breton ***morgens***.

Morgan le Fay

A complex figure best known for her role in Arthurian legend. Portrayed as a fairy healer in early versions of the Arthurian tales, in later versions she is more often ascribed the role of evil enchantress, Arthur's half-sister bent on his demise, the malicious counterpart to the benign **Lady of the Lake**.

The epithet "le fay" derives from the French *la fée*, so Morgan le Fay literally means "Morgan the fairy." "Morgan" itself has associations with sea fairies, such as the Welsh **Morgan**, the Breton ***morgens***, and the Irish **merrows**, and her roots most likely predate Arthurian legend.

In Italian folklore, Fata Morgana is the name given to an apparition or mirage appearing in the Straits of Messina and said to lure sailors to their deaths.

Morgens

Water spirits of Brittany. These Breton **mermaids** are described as seductive females who use their beauty to lure men to their deaths at the bottom of the sea. They are also blamed for flooding.

In the legend of the Breton city of **Ys**, it is said that the king's daughter, Dahut, transformed into a morgen, or **merrow**, after she caused the city to flood it and the city was lost beneath the waves.

Morrigan

See **Morrigu**.

Morrigu

(Also Morrigan.) One of the three aspects of the Irish war goddess ***Badb***, of the ***Tuatha de Danann***.

Manifesting as "Royston," or hooded crows, or **ravens**, **Macha**, **Nemen**, and Morrigu possessed magical powers to create confusion, stir fury, and bestow courage to aid their chosen victors in battle. In the battle between the *Tuatha de Danann* and the **Fomorians**, it was Morrigu who bestowed supernatural strength on the Irish hero **Cuchculainn**.

Moura Lavaderia

See **Mouras Encantadas.**

Moura Velha

See **Mouras Encantadas.**

Mouras Encantadas

Shapeshifting female fairies of Galician and Portuguese folklore. Generally described as beautiful females, singing and combing their long locks, they sometimes appeared in the guise of a serpent, dog, horse, or goat. Dwelling by wells, springs, fountains, caves, lakes, and ancient monuments, they guarded the entrances to the Otherworld. Some believed they were the souls of young maidens left to protect the treasures of the *mouros*, a race of beings who inhabited the land before withdrawing underground to the fairy realm or Otherworld known as Mourama.

Portuguese archeologist, ethnographer, and writer José Leite de Vasconcelos described the *mouras encantadas* as spellbound beings, condemned to live in a state of numbness or sleep unless the enchantment could be broken. Offerings of bread or milk were sometimes said to break the spell and allow a *moura* to become human. Should a mortal succeed in "disenchanting" a *moura*, she might take him as a husband. Or she might simply vanish.

Variations of the *mouras encantadas* included the *mouras fiandeiras*, spinning maidens, who were said to have constructed the ancient hillforts and monuments of Galicia and Portugal, carrying stones on their heads as they spun yarn with a distaff carried at their waist. The *moura velha* appeared in the form of an old woman, while the *moura lavaderia* was a washerwoman. Tales of these magical beings are spread throughout Galicia and Portugal, with almost every town having its own variant of fairy local lore concerning the *mouras encantadas.*

Mouras Fiandeiras

See **Mouras Encantadas**.

Muilearteach, the

(Pronounced *moolyarstuch.*) In Irish tradition, the *muilearteach* is said to be the ***Cailleach Bheur***, or Blue Hag of Winter, in the form of a water spirit. In **J. F. Campbell**'s *Popular Tales of the West Highlands* (1860–1862), she is described as a bald, russet-yellow wraith who comes across the top of the waves to do battle with **Fionn mac Cumhaill**. She sportively slays 100 warriors before going hand to hand with Fionn, who eventually succeeds in slaying her, piercing her side with his sword.

In a poem recited by Angus MacDonald in Ireland in 1860 she is described thus:

Her face was blue-black of the lustre of coal,
And her bone-tufted tooth was like rusted bone.
In her head was one deep pool-like eye,
Swifter than a star in a winter sky;
Upon her head gnarled brushwood,
Like the clawed old wood of the aspen root.

Meg Mullach

(Or Maggie Mulloch.) One of a pair of **brownies** who haunted the Scottish castle of Tullochgorm, home of the Grants of Strathspey. She appeared as a young lass, and her companion, **Brownie-Clod**, as a young lad. In *Popular Superstitions and Festive Amusements of the*

Highlanders of Scotland (1923), Grant Stewart gives an account describing her as an excellent housekeeper who kept the castle meticulously spick and span and served meals as if by magic, with dishes floating through the air and landing perfectly on the table. She was said to be able to foretell the future, a power she put to use in aiding the master of the house in games of chess—she stood invisibly behind his chair, advising him on his next move.

Tales of Meg Mullach persisted from the seventeenth century into the twentieth. In later tales, her character takes on a darker aspect. Also known as "Hairy Meg," in some accounts she is said to have hairy hands with which she snatches away children. One tale, set in a mill in Perthshire, tells of the death of Brownie-Clod when a servant girl, scared by his pranks, threw boiling water over him. Maggie took revenge and threw a three-legged stool at the girl, killing her. She then moved on to a farm, where she worked so efficiently that the farmer set about paying off his other servants. Maggie demanded her wages, too, and caused no end of trouble, spilling the milk, breaking the crockery, and making a nuisance of herself until the farmer agreed to reinstate his other workers and all went well again.

Maggie Mulloch

See **Meg Mullach**.

Mumpoker

Nursery bogie of the Isle of Wight who was listed by Elizabeth Mary Wright in *Rustic Speech and Folklore* (1913) as a figure used to frighten children into good behavior. "I'll send the mumpoker after ye!" was a threat used by parents to quiet noisy children. "Mum" referred to the silent, stealthy approach of this nursery fairy.

Muryan

Cornish name for "ant." There was a belief in Cornwall that fairies, or Small People as the locals called them, were shapeshifters who could take the form of beasts or birds. Every time they returned to their proper shape they were a little bit smaller than they were before, until eventually they became ants before disappearing altogether. Therefore, it was considered unlucky to harm an ant, for it might be a fairy.

There was also a Cornish belief that a piece of tin placed on an anthill at a certain phase of the moon would be turned into silver.

Muse

The personification of knowledge and the arts in Greek mythology. Generally said to be the nine daughters of the god Zeus and Mnmosyne, goddess of Memory, and named Calliope, Clio, Erato, Euterpe, Melpomene, Polyhymnia, Terpsichore, Thalia, and Urania. Each embodied an aspect of the arts, such as poetry or dance.

The temple of the muses was on Mount Helicon, but they were said to frequent the waters of the Castalian spring at the temple of the oracle of Delphi and were often depicted as **nymphs**. The "Musaeum," or Institute of the Muses, was an ancient Greek institution that brought together scholars of music and poetry, similar to a modern university.

In India, the ***apsaras*** have been compared to the muses, while in Celtic tradition the Irish ***leanan sidhe*** and Manx ***lhiannan shee*** bestow the gift of artistic genius, but often at the cost of the artist's sanity, or even life.

N

Nab

A fairy who offered food to **Orpheus** in the Underworld in the legend of Orpheus and Eurydice. Orpheus the great musician attempted to rescue his wife, the **nymph** Eurydice, from the Underworld and while he was there, Nab offered him a roasted ant, a flea's thigh, butterflies' brains, sucking mites, a rainbow tart, and other delicacies, washed down with dewdrops, beer made from seven barleycorns, and the *supernaculum* of earth-born topers. The last of these refers to a drop of fine wine, the *supernaculum*, meaning "on the nail," being the drop of wine left after the drinker has drained their cup, a bead of liquid small enough to sit upon a fingernail.

Näcken

Water spirit of Scandinavian folklore. The *näcken*, meaning "naked," generally took the form of an attractive, scantily clad male. He played the violin beautifully and enticed women and children to enter the water, where they drowned. The only way to break his spell was to cut the strings of his violin.

See also **Nix**.

Naddaha, El

'The Caller," an Egyptian water spirit dwelling in the Nile and said to appear as a beautiful woman dressed in white, with long, flowing hair. Like a **siren**, she tempted men into the watery depths with her irresistible singing and left them to drown.

Nadubi

Night-dwelling spirits in the mythology of the aboriginal people of Arnhem Land, northern Australia. Ever-ravenous spirits lacking the knowledge of how to make fire, they steal food whenever they can find it. With sharp spines protruding from their elbows and knees, they seek lone travelers to attack and then inject the spines into their bodies. Without the intervention of a medicine man whose magic can remove the spine, the victim is doomed to die.

See also **Gurumukas**.

Naga

In Hinduism and Buddhism, a *naga*, meaning "serpent" in Sanskrit, is a semi-divine being, half-man, half-serpent. Described as a strong, handsome race of creatures, *nagas* are believed to bring protection, prosperity, and fertility to those who venerate them, but can be dangerous if maltreated. They dwell in an underground kingdom called Naga Ioka or Patala Ioka, where they live in beautiful palaces decorated with gems. In some guises they are nature spirits associated with rivers, streams, lakes, seas, and wells, and are said to be guardians of treasure. They are said to bite only humans who are evil or those destined to die prematurely.

They are found in many different Asian cultures, including India, Thailand, Cambodia, Laos, Bali, and the Philippines, where they take slightly different forms and are invested with varying powers.

Nagumwasuck

Small fairies of the Passamaquoddy people in Native American folklore.

The Passamaquoddy of northeastern North America, close to the Canadian border, migrated to the ocean in summer and moved inland for the winter. The nagumwasuck were said to accompany them on the migration. Described as being 2.5 to 3 feet (just under 1 meter) in height and grotesquely ugly, they took an active part in the life of the tribe. They mourned the death of a tribe member, singing laments, and joined in the celebrations and dancing at weddings. Small cylinders of clay found on the shore at the Passamaquoddy ocean reservation were said to be the pipes of the nagumwasuck. Similarly, in Ireland, small clay pipes dug up were said to have belonged to the fairies.

According to one report, the nagumwasuck were seen leaving the reservation early one morning and traveling across the lake in a stone canoe, saying that they might return one day when more people believed in them.

See also **Mekumwasuck**.

Naiads

Freshwater spirits of Greek mythology. The naiads are a type of

nymph associated with fountains, streams, springs, and lakes. Taking their name from the Greek for "to flow," they were believed to move freely from one body of water to another and were not attached to one specific water source. Generally represented as beautiful and benevolent, occasionally they displayed a reckless side, such as in the tale of Hylas, friend of Hercules, who vanished after the naiads became transfixed by his beauty.

Nain Rouge (Red Dwarf)

Goblin, or *lutin*, of Normandy, France. Sometimes known as *le petit homme rouge* (the small, red man), he is friendly to fishermen, but is also fond of playing tricks. In *The Fairy Mythology* (1828), **Keightley** related accounts of the *nain rouge* who haunted the coast of Normandy:

He is kind in his way to the fishermen, and often gives them valuable aid; but he punishes those who do not treat him with proper respect. Two fishermen who lived near Dieppe were going one day to Pollet. On their way they found a little boy sitting on the road-side; they asked him what he was doing there. "I am resting," he said, "for I am going to Berneville" (a village within a league of Pollet). They invited him to accompany [them]; he agreed, and amused them greatly with his tricks as they went along. When they came to a pond near Berneville, the malicious urchin caught up one of them, and flung him, like a shuttlecock, up into the air over it; but, to his great disappointment, he saw him land safe and sound at the other side. The nain rouge *said, "Thank your patron saint for putting it into your mind to take some holy water when you were getting up this morning, but for that you'd have got a nice dip."*

In another account, a group of children were playing on the strand at Pollet when *le petit homme rouge* came by. When they made fun of him, he began to pelt stones at them at such a rate that they took refuge in a fishing boat. They crouched there for an hour, listening to the shower of stones falling and convinced that the boat must be buried under them. When at last the noise stopped, they peeped out, but there was not a stone was to be seen.

Belief in the *nain rouge* traveled from France to Detroit, Michigan, where it is said that his appearance is a sign of imminent disaster. He originally appeared, in 1701, to one of the first French settlers, Antoine de la Mothe Cadillac, who soon lost his entire fortune.

In order to banish the *nain rouge* and his bad luck from the city, the inhabitants of Detroit gather each year at the spring equinox for a procession known as the *Marche du Nain Rouge*. People taking part often disguise themselves lest the *nain rouge* makes an appearance and takes revenge on them the following year for driving him out of the town.

Näkki

Shapeshifting water spirit of Finnish mythology. It is said to take various human forms, including a fisherman and a three-breasted woman, but is sometimes depicted as half-man, half-horse, or as a silvery fish or a hound. In other accounts, it has iron teeth, or appears beautiful from the front, but is ugly and very hairy from behind.

Dwelling in pools or docks or in rivers, where it hides under bridges, the *näkki* is said to pull children into the water when they lean over to look at their reflection. On Midsummer's Eve it is said to rise from the water and come ashore to dance among the revelers.

Nancy Fairy

A collection of stories from the early twentieth century, *Popular Tales from the Norse* (1904) by G. W. Dasent includes "Nancy Fairy," originating from the folklore of West Africa, about a witch with a taste for eating children. The collector notes similarities between this tale and the Norse story "The Lassie and her Godmother."

One day, the witch captured a girl child so beautiful she couldn't bear to destroy her, so she decided to bring her up as her own. She named her Nancy Fairy and the girl knew her as Granny. The old woman kept up her evil ways, but concealed them from the girl, appeasing her wicked appetites behind closed and locked doors.

One day, however, the young woman spied upon her granny through a crack in the door and her shadow fell across the floor, giving away her presence. The old woman questioned the fearful girl about what she'd seen, but however vehemently Nancy Fairy denied any knowledge of what was going on, the witch was afraid her secret had been discovered and banished her to a hut in the woods.

Time passed and one day a servant of the prince saw the young woman near the hut and immediately informed him of her incomparable beauty. On hearing this, the prince dispatched a troop of soldiers to escort Nancy Fairy to the palace, where she became his bride.

In due course a baby was born. Soldiers guarded the gates to the palace and nurses tended the child around the clock, but in the dead of night the old woman arrived in a whirlwind and cast a spell on them to put them into a deep sleep. She snatched the baby and struck Nancy Fairy dumb with a blow to her mouth.

When the disappearance of the baby was discovered, Nancy Fairy was accused of having eaten her own child and promptly put on trial.

However, she was exonerated and a year later another infant was born. The old woman abducted it in the same way, striking Nancy Fairy such a blow that it made her mouth bleed. A jealous servant girl accused Nancy again of devouring her own child, pointing to the blood on her mouth as evidence. This time there was no reprieve for her and she was condemned to be hanged.

On the fateful day many fine carriages full of eminent nobles arrived, until the final coach appeared, a magnificent gold carriage in which sat an old woman and two resplendently dressed children. Nancy Fairy, magically regaining her speech on seeing this, begged for her life to be spared. The witch, turning to the gathered crowd, asked if they could discern a likeness in the children to anyone, to which they replied, "The prince," and then began to accuse her of stealing his children. The old woman bartered with them, replying that the king had stolen her daughter without her permission, so she had taken his in reprisal but had come to return them. Everyone was happy with this bargain, except for the jealous servant girl, who was hanged.

Nanny Button-Cap

Small, benevolent Yorkshire fairy. Nanny Button-Cap features in rhymes and stories which suggest that she watches over young children and ensures their safety while they sleep. She shares her name with a type of lily.

Napaeae

In Greek mythology, *napaeae* are **nymph**s of the valleys, woods, and caves. They are said to be beautiful, long-haired maidens who help make the flowers bloom, watch over cattle, and heal illnesses. The most famous of them is Eurydice, the nymph with whom **Orpheus** fell in love.

Napf-Hans

Also known as Jean de la Bodiéta, Napf-Hans is one of the ***Kobolds*** of Switzerland. His name means "Jack of the Bowl," and he was so called because, in order to gain his help, one had to leave a bowl of cream every evening near the cowshed. He would then look after the cattle. He would lead them to pastures along treacherous paths, yet they would always return safe and sound.

Narbrooi

A spirit in the beliefs of the people of Geel-vink Bay, Papua New Guinea. Narbrooi dwells in the mists that shroud the tops of tall, ancient trees. He draws out the souls of humans he is fond of and carries them away to the treetops. When a person falls ill, one of their friends goes to the tree where Narbrooi resides to recover their soul. According to custom, the friend lights a cigar and Narbrooi manifests in the cigar smoke and answers enquiries as to whether he has the friend's soul in his possession. If he does, he will return the sufferer's soul in a straw bag in return for an offering. However, he is not always to be trusted and may take away the soul again, in which case the person may die.

Nats

Burmese spirits. The term *nat* encompasses a wide variety of beings, including ancestor spirits and nature spirits. Types of *nat* associated with nature represent natural forces and features of the landscape such as wind, trees, and water, and include the forest guardians *taw saung nats* and mountain guardians *taung saung nats.*

Belief in *nats* predated Buddhism in Burma and they were incorporated into Buddhism by King Anawratha in the eleventh century, becoming the helpers and guardians of monks, the state, and the royal family. The Burmese people would ask them for protection and good fortune.

The home of the *nats* was considered to be Mount Popa (Flower Mountain), on which a shrine to the 37 Great Nats, or ancestor spirits, was erected.

Ceremonies and festivals for the *nats* are still performed today. These usually include a shaman, or spirit-wife, who is believed to channel a *nat* during her trance. Dancing and music are important parts of these ceremonies, and offerings are made to the *nats*, including alcohol, money, and other worldly goods.

Neck

See **Nix**.

Nemen

One of the three manifestations of the war goddess ***Badb*** in Irish mythology. These manifestations Nemen, **Morrigu**, and **Macha**, all took the form of crows, but each had a specific function. Nemen was "the confounder of armies." It was she who caused them to fight among themselves and mistake their kinsmen for foes.

Nereids

In Greek mythology, the 50 daughters of the sea god Nereus and sea **nymph** Doris, whose kingdom was the Aegean Sea. Usually depicted as beautiful young ladies, sometimes riding on the back of dolphins or sea horses, they took care of the sea's riches and protected fishermen. Each one represented a different aspect of the sea, such as sand, rocks, waves, and currents. They formed part of the sea god Poseidon's entourage and lived at the bottom of the sea.

See also **Galatea**, **Xantho**.

Niagriusar

An **elf**-like creature in the folklore of the Faroe Islands. Diminutive in stature, the *niagriusar* wears a red cap and brings good fortune to those he favors and those who treat him with respect.

Like the Swedish ***tomte***, the Scandinavian ***nisse***, or Scottish **brownie**, *niagriusar* are generally good-natured and helpful, unless maligned or disrespected by humans. They often reside in trees planted around human dwellings. It is considered very unlucky to fell these trees, especially the more ancient among them. Anyone attempting to chop down a tree inhabited by a *niagriusar* may be struck down by illness or subject to misfortune.

Nicnevin

See **Gyre-Carling**.

Night Wailer

See **Nututaja**.

Nikkommo

Forest spirits of the Wampanoag and Narragansett people in Native

American mythology. If treated with respect, the little people can be called upon for supernatural assistance. Feasts are held in their honor to bring luck to hunters and fishermen.

Nikur

(Or nennir.) **Water horse** of Scandinavian folklore. **Jakob Grimm**, in *Teutonic Mythology* (1883), relates how it appeared as a dappled, grey horse on the seashore. The telltale sign that it is a fairy beast is that its hooves point backward. Like the **kelpie** and other Celtic water horses, should someone mount it, it will plunge into the water, taking the rider to a watery grave. However, it was said to be possible to tame the creature by putting a bridle on it. One man succeeded in doing this and put the beast to work plowing his fields, but when the bridle came loose, the animal darted like fire back into the water, dragging the plow in with him.

Nimerigar

Malevolent fairies in the lore of the Native American Shoshone and Paiute people of the Rocky mountains. Taking their name from the local words for "people eaters," the *nimerigar* were regarded as aggressive, dangerous little creatures said to attack humans with poisoned arrows that they shot from tiny bows.

Nimuë

One of the names given to the **Lady of the Lake** of Arthurian legend.

Nisse

Small fairies in Scandinavian folklore, usually associated with a particular household or farm. Similar to the German ***Kobold***, Scottish **brownie**, and Swedish ***tomte***.

Nix

(Also nixie, nixy, neck.) Shape-shifting water spirits of German mythology. Nix are the males of the species, nixies the females.

Nixies are often depicted sitting in the sun, combing their long hair. Although sometimes described as resembling **mermaids**, with the upper body of a beautiful woman and a fish's tail, they are able to come ashore and walk among humans, with only their wet skirts hinting at their true identity.

The males were skilled musicians and it was said they could be persuaded to pass on their skills to mortals. However, they had a dark side, too, and were said to suck humans down into the water, drowning them and keeping their souls in upturned urns. Once a year, people made offerings of bread and fruit to the nix of the Diemel river in Germany in order to placate him and dissuade him from claiming his yearly victim.

A jet of blood shooting up from the water was a sign that a nix was angry. This expression of displeasure might be seen if the nixies had stayed too long dancing or if the nix's child was disobedient. A jet of milk or a plate with an apple, on the other hand, seen above the water, was a good sign, indicating that the nix was in a favorable mood.

In *Teutonic Mythology* (1883), **Jakob Grimm** examines various related water-dwelling spirits across northern and western Europe, such as the Scandinavian *näkken*, the Finnish ***näkki***, the Danish *nökki*, and the Scandinavian *neck*. These spirits also give their names to various water plants and seaweeds, such as the Danish *nökkeskäg*, or "nix beard," and the Swedish *näcköra*, or "nix ear."

Noggle

(Also nuggle or nygel.) Shetland **kelpie**, or **water horse**. It took the form of a pretty, small, grey horse, about the size of a Sheltand pony, wearing a bridle and saddle, and was generally thought to be less dangerous than the ***each uisge***, though anyone who was tempted to ride on its back would be treated to a severe dunking as the little horse darted into the water with its rider. A ride on a noggle did not usually prove fatal, though. Unlike the *each uisge*, which was known to rip its victim to pieces, the noggle would rise from the water with the rider on its back and vanish in a blue flame.

Noggles could be identified by their tails, which curled over their backs like a half-wheel. They were often found in the vicinity of water mills and were fond of causing mischief by seizing the wheel at night and preventing it from spinning. They could be driven away by the sight of a long, steel knife or a burning brand.

Nornir

See **Norns**.

Norns

(Also Nornir.) Birth fairies in Nordic mythology. Similar to the three **Fates** of classical Greek and Roman mythology, these female spirits foretold the destinies of newborn babies.

Urdr, Verdandi, and Skuld are the three Norns most commonly named, although there are many more, encompassing both benevolent guardians and malevolent harbingers of tragedy. In some interpretations, Urdr, Verdandi, and Skuld represent the past, present, and future respectively. They dwelled in the Well of Urdr, or Well of Fate, at the base of the sacred ash tree Yggdrasil, the world tree.

The *Poetic Edda*, a collection Old Norse poems and an important source of Norse mythology, contains a poem that tells of the birth of the hero Helgi Hundingbane and the arrival of the Norns to shape his destiny:

'Twas night in the dwelling, and
Norns there came,
Who shaped the life of the lofty one;
They bade him most famed of
fighters all
And best of princes ever to be.

Mightily wove they the web of fate,
While Bralund's towns were
trembling all;
And there the golden threads they
wove,

And in the moon's hall fast they made them.

NOROUAS, THE NORTHWEST WIND

Ruler of the northwest wind in Breton folklore. The southwest wind was known as **Surouas**.

The wind played an important part in Breton folklore. Fishing and farming communities, whose livelihoods depended on the fickle-natured winds, addressed the winds as if they were living beings, berating and cursing them for destroying crops, or forcing them to remain landbound. Lewis Spence's *Legends and Romances of Brittany* (1917) relates the traditional Breton tale "Norouas the Northwest Wind," which tells of a Breton farmer's quest for compensation when his flax crop is destroyed.

Long ago, there lived in Brittany a farmer and his wife. They made a simple living growing crops, mainly flax. Late one summer they had gathered a very good crop, the best they had seen for many a long year. As was their custom, they laid it out on the open ground to dry. They went into their house to eat and quite suddenly they heard the great, sweeping roar of the wings of the Northwest Wind, known as Norouas. They ran out of the house, but it was too late—their entire crop had been swept across the fields, over the cliff, and far out to sea.

"Curse you, Norouas!" cried the goodman in a rage. "I'll seek you out wherever you may go!"

And so saying, he took a stick and ran toward the mountains, which he knew were the home of all the winds.

In his haste he forgot to take any food or drink or money with him. As darkness fell, he came upon a wayside inn and explained to the landlady what had happened. She gave him a little refreshment and allowed him to sleep in the stable. In the morning she showed him the path that would lead him to the home of the winds.

The first wind the goodman met was Surouas the Southwest Wind.

"I have come to find that devil Norouas," said the goodman. "He stole my crop of flax from me!"

"Hush, hush," soothed the gentle Surouas, "Do not anger him, for he is strong and could easily toss you into the air like a piece of straw."

At that moment Norouas himself came along, whistling happily, and said to the goodman, "Why, what ails you, sir? On such a day we should all be content."

"I wish that I could be," said the goodman, "but you have blown away the best crop of flax that I have ever had, and I am here to demand some compensation."

"Calm yourself," said Norouas. "Here, take this napkin as a gift."

"One miserable napkin!" cried the goodman. "I could have made one hundred napkins with my flax."

"Ah, but not like this napkin. All you have to do is say 'Napkin, unfold thyself' and you will have the finest spread table in the world!"

The goodman took the napkin, and when he got to the bottom of the path, he thought he would put it to the test. So he said, "Napkin, unfold thyself," and to his amazement a table appeared before him laden with bread and meat and fruit and wines and many more good things. He sampled some of the feast then told the napkin to fold itself again and proceeded to the inn, where he spent the night once more, as it was quickly growing dark. He demonstrated the magic napkin to the landlady and they enjoyed a wonderful meal. She showed the goodman to the best room in the house and he soon fell into a deep slumber.

Now, the landlady was a greedy woman and wanted the magic napkin for herself. While the goodman slept, she substituted one of her ordinary napkins for it.

When the goodman awoke, he made his way home, anticipating his wife's joy when she saw the gift he had brought from Norouas. But when he said, "Napkin, unfold thyself," nothing happened.

"Husband, you have been deceived. Norouas has made a fool of you!" said his wife.

The goodman immediately hurried back to the mountain and berated Norouas, saying, "The napkin you gave me no longer responds to my command. What can you give me instead?"

"I am sure you must be mistaken," said Norouas, "But I will give you this ass. If you tell it to produce gold, a stream of golden coins will appear from its tail."

The goodman led the ass down the mountain and stopped again at the inn. He told the landlady how the napkin had failed him, and how Norouas had given him the ass as compensation.

"Produce some gold for your master," he commanded, and sure enough a stream of golden coins fell to the ground.

The landlady gave the goodman a splendid meal and plenty of wine and showed him again to the best room in the house. While he slept, she hid the ass in the stable and brought out another, which the goodman took home with him in the morning.

Once more his wife was disappointed when she saw that the ass had no magical qualities. "Husband," she said, "why do you keep bringing these gifts that have so little worth?"

Wearily, the goodman made his way back to Norouas. When he told the Northwest Wind his story, Norouas said, "I have one last gift for you. But before I show you, I want you to think on whom you have seen on your journey home, and who might have stolen your other gifts."

The goodman had only seen the landlady at the inn, so there could be little doubt as to the culprit.

"Here then is your final gift," said Norouas. "It is this cudgel and if you give it the command 'Strike, cudgel!', it will smite your enemies. When you want it to stop, say '*Ora pro nobis.*'"

He handed the cudgel to the goodman, who hurried down the mountain to the inn.

At first the landlady denied any knowledge of the napkin or the ass, but when the goodman commanded the cudgel, it beat her so hard that she confessed and the goodman had to call off the cudgel saying, "*Ora pro nobis.*"

Happily, the goodman took the napkin and the ass and the cudgel home with him, and his wife was delighted with the gifts. They lived like a lord and lady for some time, until the neighbors became suspicious of their wealth, and the goodman was arrested by the gendarmes and accused of theft and murder. He was brought before the magistrates, who found him guilty, and the judge sentenced him to be hanged.

As he was led to the scaffold, he asked if he might be granted one last request: "Could I have my old cudgel with me in my final minutes?"

The judge granted his request and the goodman shouted, "Strike, cudgel!"

The cudgel beat the judge and

the magistrates and the gendarmes until they submitted and pardoned the goodman of all the crimes of which he had been accused.

And so the goodman and his wife spent the rest of their days enjoying the gifts that Norouas the Northwest Wind had given them as compensation for the loss of their crop of flax.

Nuberu, El

The Cloud Master of Galician, Asturian, and Cantabrian mythology in the northwest of Spain. Described as having a long, thick beard and being clad in goatskins and a large hat, the Cloud Master resides on a mountain in Egypt, whence he rides out on great clouds bringing storms that wreak havoc, destroying the harvest, injuring livestock, and forcing fishermen to return to port.

On stormy nights when El Nuberu is believed to be active, the people of northwestern Spain light candles and ring bells to drive him away.

Nuckelavee, the

An ugly, skinless sea monster in the folklore of the Orkney Islands, depicted as half-horse, half-man, the rider being fused to the horse, whose sinews and veins are clearly visible. A harbinger of death and disease, the Nuckelavee is a much-feared being. Despite living in the sea, he is averse to fresh water and the only way to escape him is to cross a stream. He is blamed for many of the disasters that occur on the islands, from failed crops to famines.

Orkney folklorist **Walter Traill Dennison** collected an account from a man named Tammas who claimed to have encountered the Nuckelavee:

Tammas, like his namesake Tam o' Shanter, was out late one night. It was, though moonless, a fine starlit night. Tammas's road lay close by the seashore, and as he entered a part of the road that was hemmed in on one side by the sea, and on the other by a deep freshwater loch, he saw some huge object in front of, and moving towards him. What was he to do? He was sure it was no earthly thing that was steadily coming towards him. He could not go to either side, and to turn his back to an evil thing, he had heard, was the most dangerous position of all; so Tammie said to himself, "The Lord be aboot me, an tak care o me, as I am oot on no evil intent this night!" Tammie was always regarded as rough and foolhardy.

Anyway, he determined, as the best of two evils, to face the foe, and so walked resolutely yet slowly forward. He soon discovered to his horror that the gruesome creature approaching him was no other than the dreaded Nuckelavee – the most cruel and malignant of all uncanny beings that trouble mankind.

The lower part of this terrible monster, as seen by Tammie, was like a great horse, with flappers like fins about his legs, with a mouth as wide as a whale's, from which came breath like steam from a brewing-kettle. He had but one eye, and that as red as fire.

On him sat, or rather seemed to grow from his back, a huge man with no legs, and arms that reached nearly to the ground. His head was as big as a clue of simmons [about 3 feet/ 1 meter in diameter], and this huge head kept rolling from one shoulder to the other as if it meant to tumble off.

But what to Tammie appeared most horrible of all was that the monster was skinless; this utter want of skin adding much to the terrific appearance of the creature's naked body, the whole surface of it showing only red, raw flesh, in which Tammie saw blood, black as tar, running through yellow veins, and great white sinews, thick as horse tethers, twisting, stretching, and contracting, as the monster moved.

Tammie went slowly on in mortal terror, his hair on end, a cold sensation like a film of ice between his scalp and his skull, and a cold sweat bursting from every pore.

But he knew it was useless to flee, and he said, if he had to die, he would rather see who killed him than die with his back to the foe.

In all his terror Tammie remembered what he had heard of the Nuckelavee's dislike of fresh water, and, therefore, took that side of the road nearest to the loch. The awful moment came when the lower head of the mon-

ster got abreast of Tammie. The mouth of the monster yawned like a bottomless pit. Tammie found its hot breath like fire on his face; the long arms were stretched out to seize the unhappy man. To avoid, if possible, the monster's clutch Tammie swerved as near as he could to the loch; in doing so one of his feet went into the loch, splashing up some water on the foreleg of the monster, whereat the horse gave a snort like thunder and shied over to the other side of the road, and Tammie felt the wind of the Nuckelavee's clutches as he narrowly escaped the monster's grip.

Tammie saw his opportunity, and ran with all his might; and sore need had he to run, for the Nuckelavee had turned and was galloping after him, and bellowing with a sound like the roaring of the sea.

In front of Tammie lay a rivulet, through which the surplus water of the loch found its way to the sea, and Tammie knew, if he could only cross the running water, he was safe; so he strained every nerve. As he reached the near bank another clutch was made at him by the long arms. Tammie made a desperate spring and reached the other side, leaving his bonnet in the monster's clutches. The Nuckelavee gave a wild unearthly yell of disappointed rage as Tammie fell senseless on the safe side of the water.

Nuggle

See **Noggle**.

Nunnehi

Benevolent supernatural beings of the Cherokee people in Native American folklore. Usually invisible, their presence is sometimes indicated by the sound of drumming, for they are fond of music and dancing. They sometimes reveal themselves to humans to whom they take a liking, showing themselves in the form of noble Cherokee warriors. They are said to dwell in houses beneath the ground in the Appalachian mountains.

It is said that there is a waterhole in Nottley Lake that always emits warm vapors and warms the air around it. Hunters stop there to warm themselves in cold weather, but are wary not to stay for too long, for it is believed that the *nunnehi* have a house under the ground there and the heat from its fire causes the warm vapors to rise from the hole.

Nuno sa Punso

A **dwarf**-like creature that dwells in anthills in the folklore of the Philippines, literally, the "grandfather of the mound." Anyone walking near an anthill would be well advised to repeat, "*Tabi-tabo po, makikiraan land po,*" meaning, "Excuse me, just passing through." Failing to utter these words may result in retribution from the ill-tempered Nuno. He is described as an old man with a long beard and is easily angered. Children are warned not to play near his home, as should he be within striking distance of a human being and not hear the magic words, he may spit at them and curse them with illness. Great care must also be taken to avoid damage to the anthills.

It is believed that modern medicine is unable to cure any illness caused by the curse of Nuno sa Punso, but a patient can seek the help of a traditional medicine practitioner to find a cure. The practitioner will perform a ceremony during which he will place melted candle wax into a bowl of water which, when set, is said to show a map of where the anthill that was disturbed is located. The patient will be instructed to go back to the spot and ask forgiveness by leaving offerings of food. Many Filipino myths and legends are based on the premise that human beings must respect nature.

Nursery Bogies

Spirits that perform the function of warning children away from dangerous places or cautioning them not to misbehave. **Awd Goggie**, **Churnmilk Peg**, and **Melsh Dick** protected orchards and nut thickets, warding off would-be fruit thieves, while fearsome water spirits such as **Jenny Greenteeth** and **Peg Powler** served to warn children away from dangerous rivers, lakes, and ponds.

Nututaja, Night Wailer

Old Estonian folk tales recount the distress of a child under the influence of the Nututaja, an evil spirit who causes children to weep and wail excessively during the night and refuse to be comforted. Various cures describe somewhat brutal methods of restoring peace, such as setting fire to an item of clothing from an ill-wisher and holding the smoking cloth over the child, reciting incantations, placing herbs on the navel, and lightly striking the child with a wetted rope, coiling it and passing the child's body through the loops. This had to be performed on a Thursday evening.

Nygel

See **Noggle**.

Nymphs

Nature spirits of Greek mythology, usually depicted as beautiful young women and typically associated with a specific natural feature of the landscape such as a lake, stream, tree, mountain, meadow, or spring. There are many types of nymph, including **nereids**, the nymphs of the sea, **naiads**, the freshwater nymphs, and **dryads**, the tree nymphs.

Shrines to nymphs existed across ancient Greece, located at sites such as healing springs and wells. It was thought that nymphs had powers of prophecy, and some consulted them to divine their future, in a similar way to the Delphic Oracle.

Nymphs were also often associated with a particular god or goddess, such as the wild, intoxicated *maenads*, who formed part of the entourage of Dionysus, spirit of grapes and merrymaking, or the huntress nymphs who attended the hunting goddess Artemis.

O

Oakmen

Guardians of the woods and woodland creatures in the folklore of the north of England. According to **Wirt Sikes** in *British Goblins* (1880), fairies favored oak trees, as attested to in the old rhyme "Fairy folk are in old oaks."

"The Vixen and the Oakmen" in **Ruth Tongue**'s *Forgotten Folktales of the English Counties* (1970), relates the tale of a vixen who sought out the oakmen for help in protecting the woods:

The vixen made her way through the woods, pursued by the hounds of the hunt, to warn the oakmen that men with axes were coming to cut down a mistletoe bough. The oakmen rewarded her bravery and friendship by allowing her to bathe her sore paws in the oaktree rainpool, whereupon the pads of her paws were healed and her coat grew thicker. The oakmen thanked her and sent her home with a warning to avoid the wicked barren holly tree, and she returned to the safety of her den.

Oberon

A name frequently given to the King of the Fairies in English folklore and literature. Oberon makes an early appearance in the medieval French romance *Huon de Bourdeaux*, translated into English in 1548. This provided inspiration for Shakespeare's *A Midsummer Night's Dream*, in which Oberon was popularized as King of the Fairies alongside his queen, **Titania**. A similar character is found in the German story of Otnit in the medieval *Heldenbuch* (Book of Heroes), in the form of the **dwarf** king Elberich. The name "Oberon" may have derived from the German Elberich or Alberich, which changed into Auberich, then Auberon, in French and finally became Oberon. Oberon appears in many works of English literature, including **Edmund Spenser**'s epic poem *The Faerie Queene* (1590), Ben Jonson's *Oberon, the Faery Prince* (1616), and Michael Drayton's *Nymphidia* (1627).

Oceanid

Sea **nymphs** in Greek mythology, the oceanids were the 3,000 daughters of Oceanus and Thethys. Oceanus was ruler of the rivers and the seas, the oldest of the Titans, whose mother was Gaea,

Mother Earth, and father was Uranus, ruler of the heavens. Thethys was Titaness of the Oceans.

Each of the 3,000 oceanids had guardianship of a particular element of nature, such as a sea, lake, pasture, flower, or cloud. The oceanid **Xanthe** was patron of the golden clouds of sunsets and sunrise.

According to the ancient Greek poet Hesiod, Oceanus had 6,000 children in total, 3,000 daughters and 3,000 sons. The sons were known as the ***potamoi*** and were spirits of the rivers.

See also **Xantho**.

Odin

Ruler of the Aesir spirits of Asgard in Norse mythology, the all-father. Known as Woden in Old English, as well as being associated with war, victory, magic, death, wisdom, poetry, and prophecy, in folklore he was known as the leader of the **wild hunt**, in which his quarry was **wood wives** of the forest rather than souls of the dead. In his guise as a wanderer, he appears as a one-eyed old man with a long, white beard and wide-brimmed hat. J. R. R. Tolkien wrote that he thought of the wizard Gandalf as an "Odinic wanderer." It is common for magical beings to disguise themselves with glamor as old men or women, **hags** or vagabonds to test the kindness, compassion, or hospitality of the mortals they encounter.

See also **Raven**.

Ogme

One of the sons of **Dagda** of the ***Tuatha de Dannan*** in Irish mythology. He was a warrior and orator, regarded as one of the three principal champions of the *Tuatha de Danann* alongside Dagda and **Lug**.

Ohdowas

One of the three divisions of the ***jogah*** nature spirits in Iroquois legend, responsible for the wide plains and deep forests of the dimly lit Underworld where the captive creatures forever strive toward the sunlight. The ever-watchful Ohdowas must guard against the predations of these vengeful monsters, who would poison the springs and spread disease to the trees if they ever escaped into the human world above ground. These vigilant earth-dwellers, whose eyes would be blinded by the fierce rays of the sun, emerge only on moonlit nights to join with their kin in the deep shelter beneath great trees, where they dance and feast together.

Oisin

Son of **Fionn mac Cumhaill** and a fairy woman of the *Sidhe* in Irish legend. He was a great singer, poet, and warrior, and lived through many great battles. The tale "Oisin in the Land of Youth" tells of his voyage to the Irish Otherworld of *Tir Nan Og* (*see p.15*).

Old Cutty Soams

See **Cutty Soams**.

Old Lady of the Elder Tree, the

See **Elder Tree, Old Lady of the**.

Old Roger

In British folklore, Old Roger is the ruddy-cheeked guardian of apple trees and spirit of apples. In Celtic mythology apples were the fruit of life, granting passage to the land of the gods. In some versions of Arthurian legend the mystical land of Avalon is known as the Land of Apples.

See also **Appletree Man**.

Old Woman of the Mountain, the

A Welsh mountain fairy, belonging to the ***Gwyllion***, whose favorite trick was to lead travelers astray from mountain paths.

Ole Luk Øj

The sleep fairy in Danish folklore. Similar to the English **Sandman**,

Scottish Wee Willie Winkie, and French **La Dormette**, Ole Luk Øj is a nursery spirit who lulls children to sleep at night.

The Danish folk belief was popularized in **Hans Christian Andersen**'s literary fairy tale of the same name, in which Ole Luk is portrayed as a small fairy clad in a silk jacket, carrying an umbrella under each arm. One umbrella is decorated with beautiful pictures on the inside, and this he opens above the head of good children while they sleep so that they may dream rich and fabulous dreams. The other umbrella is blank inside; and this he reserves for the naughty children, who sleep heavily and do not remember their dreams.

Ombwiri

Guardian spirits in the beliefs of Central and West Africa. In some traditions they are regarded as ancestor spirits, while in others they are *genii loci*, or spirits of place (see ***genius***). As spirits of place, *ombwiri* reside in prominent features of the landscape such as large or unusual trees or rocks where humans leave token offerings of stones, wood, or grass as they pass by. In their guise as ancestor spirits, they take an interest in human affairs, choosing either to bring good fortune and health to those they watch over or to inflict ill-health and misfortune, depending on their whim. They manifest to humans in dreams and visions.

Ondine

See **Undine**.

Peg O'Nell

A pernicious Lancashire water spirit dwelling in the Ribble river. She may once have been a river **nymph**, but later became associated with the spirit of a servant girl from Waddow Hall, which is situated on the bank of the river. Henderson relates the tale in *Notes on the Folklore of the Northern Counties of England and the Borders* (1866).

One morning Peg O'Nell, a maid at Waddow Hall, argued with her mistress as she was on her way to the well to fetch water. In anger, her mistress called after her that she hoped she would fall and break her neck.

It was an icy morning and as Peg stomped to the well, her mistress's wish came true when she slipped on the ice.

From that day on a curse was upon the hall. The animals and children fell sick and every seven years Peg was said to take a life. If a cat or dog had not been drowned within the seven years, then, on what came to be known as "Peg O'Nell's Night," the Ribble would claim a human victim.

Oni-Bi

Spectral fires in Japanese folklore. Along a haunted shore in Japan, legends tell of the Heike crabs, who bear the faces of long-dead warriors on their shells, and *Oni-Bi*, spectral fires of the vanquished Heike, which flicker and flame on the sand and above the sea. In an effort to appease the restless, unhappy spirits of these drowned warriors, the priests built a temple and cemetery in remembrance of their heroic deeds and this had a calming effect on their ghostly activities. However, one tale recounts the unfortunate experiences of a blind man, Hoichi, who lived at the temple.

Hoichi was a musician and poet of great talent, famed for his recitations about the Heike and their great battles. As he sat one hot night practising his lute on the terrace of the temple, he heard a voice calling his name and asking him to come to the house of his lord and master, where he would perform his recitation.

Hoichi demurred; he was blind, he said, and did not know the way. But the voice of the stranger was not to be denied, and Hoichi felt his arm grasped in an iron grip and heard the sound of clanking armor as he and the stranger swiftly sped over the paths, through a gate, and into what seemed to the blind man a large house with many rooms full of the voices and sounds of an illustrious gathering.

He was bidden to play and sing

of a tragic battle, and this he did, being so skillful that his lute and voice became the sea on which the boats sailed, the clash of weapons and the hiss of arrows in flight, and finally the dying cries of women and children. His unseen audience responded with ever-increasing lamentations and he was quite frightened by the dreadful grief his music had evoked, until at last a silence slowly descended, and out of the utter hush a woman's voice requested that he come again the next night to continue the tale. Hoichi agreed and was guided back to the temple.

On the third night, his absence from the temple was noticed and servants were dispatched to find him, but, carrying their lanterns high through the black and rainy streets, they searched in vain.

As they were returning along the sand to the temple, however, they were alarmed by the sound of wild music coming from the cemetery, and there, alone in the graveyard, kneeling before the tomb of the infant Emperor who had perished in the ancient Heike battle, was Hoichi, singing and playing to a ghostly audience of *Oni-Bi*, the flickering, flitting flames of the dead everywhere about him.

When he was persuaded to return, the priest of the temple set about ensuring that the power of the spirits over him would be broken, for he knew that otherwise they would destroy him. With fine calligraphy brushes he and his helpers painted every part of Hoichi's body with holy words and advised him to stay silent and motionless when the stranger came for him and on no account raise his voice in a cry for help.

As Hoichi sat on the verandah in the night, he heard the footsteps approaching and the voice calling to him to come. He sat as still as a stone and presently the voice came nearer, complaining that he was nowhere to be found—except that the ghostly presence could see two ears, which he grasped and tore from Hoichi's head. With great self-command Hoichi remained silent, although he was in immense pain, and the footsteps retreated.

When the priest found him the next morning he was horrified that Hoichi had suffered so much due to the temple priests' lack of care, but assured him that he was now free from the malign attentions of the spirits. His fame spread and he became a wealthy man, and from that time on was known as Hoichi-the-Earless.

Oona

(Also Oonagh.) Queen of the ***Daoine Sidh*** in Irish folklore, who dwelled at Knockmaa in Co. Galway with her husband, **Fin Bheara**. In *Ancient Legends, Mystic Charms, and Superstitions of Ireland* (1887), **Lady Wilde** describes her as dressed in silver robes, glittering as if covered in diamonds, with golden hair so long that it swept the ground. Despite her unearthly beauty, her husband sought the love of mortal women, wooing them with his fairy music to enter his fairy chambers.

Oonagh

See **Oona**.

Oosood

A birth fairy in Serbian folklore, she visits mothers and their newborn babies on the seventh night after the birth to foretell the child's destiny. In this respect, she performs a similar function to the three **Fates** of classical Greek and Roman mythology, who determined the course of individual lives.

Oosood can be seen only by the mother and child to whom she is paying a visit. She is considered to be similar to a ***vila***, a forest-dwelling Serbian **nymph**.

Oread

A mountain **nymph** in Greek mythology. Taking their name from *oros*, the Greek for "mountain," the oreads dwelled in the rocky ravines and conifer forests of the mountains. They are sometimes associated with the hunting goddess known as Artemis in Greek mythology or **Diana** in Roman mythology, who favored mountainous terrain as her hunting ground.

Orehu

See **Oriyu**.

Orenda

In the beliefs of the Native American Iroquois, every aspect of the natural world possesses its own spirit, known as *orenda.* Clouds, mountains, lakes, and rivers, animals, plants, and rocks all have their individual *orenda.* As well as being the indwelling essence of a thing, this spirit has the ability to influence human experience, communicating with individuals and tribes via dreams.

Variations of this concept exist in other tribes under various names. To the Sioux it is ***wakanda***, and to the Algonquian ***manitou***.

Orisa

*See **Orisha**.*

Orisha

(Also *Orisa, Orixa.*) Spiritual entities of Yorubaland with control over the elements of nature. Belief in *orishas* originated with the Yoruba people and spread from their homeland in Nigeria, West Africa, to other parts of Africa and to parts of South America and the Caribbean, including Brazil, Argentina, and Jamaica.

According to Yoruba belief, Olodumare created the world and sent the *orishas* to be intermediary spirits between the mortal and spiritual realms, each performing a specific function and associated with a particular aspect of nature.

There are hundreds of *orishas,* including **Yemaja**, mother of the *orishas* and spirit of the sea, also known as **Janaína** in Brazil; **Eshu**, messenger between the human and spirit worlds; **Iansan**, ruler of the winds, and **Shango**, lord of thunder, lightning, and fire.

Orixa

*See **Orisha**.*

Oriyu

(Or Orehu.) A water spirit in the Arawak, Guiana, tradition who lives in the rivers and streams, accompanying fishermen in their dug-out canoes and sometimes appearing in female form, combing her long hair on the riverbank with a silver comb that is often forgotten and left behind in her haste to escape inquisitive human eyes.

Orpheus

A poet and musician in Greek mythology, whose enchanting music was said to charm all that heard it. His wife, Eurydice, was a **nymph**. Many stories and legends tell of Orpheus' attempt to rescue her from the Underworld using the magic of his music. The legend of Orpheus and Eurydice was reshaped in a Middle English verse romance, reproduced in Halliwell's *Illustrations of the Fairy Mythology of Shakespeare* (1853), and reprinted by W. C. Hazlitt in *Fairy Tales, Legends and Romances Illustrating Shakespeare* (1875).

Orfeo was king of the Thracians and his queen was Dame Meroudys. One May Day the queen had been dancing in an orchard when she fell asleep under a ymp tree—a grafted apple tree supposed to have magical powers. She awoke in the twilight, crying and wailing. She was carried to her room and Orfeo begged her to tell him what was the matter. Eventually she told him that the King of the Fairies had carried her away to a great palace in a fair country. He had eventually taken her back to the apple tree, but told her she must return the next day at twilight and be ready to go with him.

Orfeo said he would go and protect her with his army. He did so, but the host of the fairy king appeared, too, and as they fought, Meroudys was drawn away, invisible, from the center of the ring.

Orfeo was greatly distressed. He gave up his robes and his crown, handed over the care of his kingdom to his trusty steward and went out into the wilderness to find his beloved queen. The only possession he kept with him was his lyre, for he was the best lyre player in the world.

For ten years he roamed, living off the land. Then one day he heard the sound of hunting horns and a troop of fairy knights passed by. Then came a bevy of ladies, and among them was Dame Meroudys.

Orfeo followed them through a long, winding cave until he came into full daylight and saw before him a fair country with a great palace in the distance. He knocked at the gate and claimed the minstrel's right of entry.

Inside he found many mutilated bodies, but further on he came upon men and women sleeping in the twilight. Among them was Meroudys under a ymp tree. Beyond them again sat the fairy king and queen in a royal throne room.

Orfeo fell on his knees. "Lord," he said, "is it thy will to hear my minstrelsy?"

The king questioned who it was that presented himself. Orfeo replied without fear that he was a lyre player and that it was the duty of all minstrels to offer music to kings and nobles if they desired to hear it.

The king gave him permission to play, so he tuned his lyre and began. So sweet was his music that fairies came from every corner of the palace to listen.

When Orfeo had finished playing, the king promised him anything he asked, and, of course, he asked for the lady asleep under the ymp tree.

At first, the king resisted, stating that Orfeo was too wild and rough for the fair, gentle maiden and that it would be a foul thing for her depart in his company. However, Orfeo countered that it would be fouler still for a king to go back on his word. In admiration, the king declared that Orfeo was a true man and bid him to take the lady by the hand and go.

So Orfeo and his queen left the Underworld joyfully. When they got back to Thrace, the steward had been true to his trust; they were welcomed back with joy and lived out their lives in great happiness.

Elements of Celtic folklore appear in this version of the tale, such as the dangerous liminal time of twilight, the magic apple tree, and the connection between the fairies and the dead.

See also **Nab**.

Otne-Yar-Heh, The

In Native American legends there are several variations on the tale of the *Otne-Yar-Heh*, the Stone **Giants**.

One version tells of a great battle leaving an entire band of marauding strangers lying dead or wounded on the shores of a lake. Over time their bodies became covered with shells and rocky shards, and the waters of the lake washed over them and deposited silt, which hardened and turned them into strange humanoid shapes.

Ravenous grizzly bears discovered the encased bodies and began to devour them, beginning at the feet, where the stone casing was weakest. As they worked their way along the bodies, they found the stony carapace became flexible. Finally the Stone Giants woke and arose. When they stood at their full height, they were a fearsome sight.

They strode across mountains, forests, and rivers toward the tribes who had brought about their destruction, impervious to the arrows and weapons striking uselessly at their stony bodies until, so the story ends, the Master of Life took pity on the tribes and banished the *Otne-yar-Heh* back to their resting place, where their giant stone forms still lie, slowly eroding and drawing a circle of thunderbolts down to them that no living thing can pass.

Otteermaaner

See ***Alven***.

Owl Woman Monster

See ***Tah-Tah-Kle-Ah***.

P

PADFOOT

Shapeshifting **bogie** beast that haunts the roads of the north of England, described variously as an animal the size of a sheep with smooth, long hair, a bale of wool that burst through hedges and rolled down the road, a shadowy apparition, and a large white dog with big, saucerlike eyes.

Henderson, in *Notes on the Folklore of the Northern Counties of England and the Borders* (1866), provides examples of encounters with Padfoot. Some reported that the beast stealthily padded up behind them before drawing alongside and emitting a fearsome roar or rattling a chain. In one case, it was said to have appeared to a man in the form of a white dog. When he went to strike it with his stick, the stick went straight through the beast and the man subsequently died of fright.

See also **Skriker**.

PAKEPAKEHA

See ***Patupaiarehe***.

PAN

Nature spirit of fields, woods, shepherds, flocks, and fertility in Greek mythology, who is usually depicted with the lower half of his body as that of a goat, representing the asperity, or roughness, of the Earth, and the upper part as that of a man, representing his dominance over the natural world. His name may derive either from the Greek *pan*, meaning "everything," or *paein*, meaning "to pasture." Many sources favor the latter, as it is generally agreed that he was the god of shepherds and flocks. However, it could be argued that, as flocks and herds were the chief property of the pastoral age, he was the personification of a spirit pervading all things. According to *Brewer's Dictionary of Phrase and Fable* (1898), Pan is also the god of *hyle*, a Greek word that originally meant "wood," but which Aristotle adapted to mean "matter in general."

Pan's parentage is unclear. In Homer, he is described as the son of Hermes the messenger of the Olympian gods. In other tales, however, he is the son of Zeus or Odysseus. He dwelled in Arcadia, where he sported with **nymphs**, and on one occasion he pursued Syrinx, who was a favorite of Apollo (who is sometimes also described as the father of Pan). Apollo transformed her into a reed, but Pan cut down the reed and made it into the instrument known as panpipes, which he is often depicted playing.

As well as being a musician, Pan was a dancer. He joined the entourage of Dionysus, spirit of merry-making and the grape harvest, dancing alongside the *maenads*, Dionysus' wild, intoxicated female followers, and the bearded goat-like satyrs.

Pan was supposed to be the source of the sudden, inexplicable fear, or panic, which sometimes overcame travelers in wild and remote places, yet he was also linked with peace, wisdom, and happiness.

"Universal Pan
Knit with the Graces and the Hours
in dance,
Led on the eternal spring."
Milton, Paradise Lost, iv.265

Over the years he has inspired many works of art and literature. Kenneth Grahame's children's classic *The Wind in the Willows* (1908) includes a chapter entitled "The Piper at the Gates of Dawn" in which the principal characters, Rat and Mole, experience an awe-inspiring encounter with a horned, shaggy-legged, hooved piper. Rather than inspiring panic or terror, the being engenders a great sense of love, peace, and happiness. Although not mentioned by name, the description is clearly that of Pan. In 1967, psychedelic rock band Pink Floyd named their first album *The Piper at the Gates of Dawn* after the chapter. Pan also appears as a character in Tom Robbins' novel *Jitterbug Perfume* (1984).

PARIBANOU

See **Peri Banu**.

PATUPAIAREHE

(Also *pakepakeha, turehu.*) Fairylike creatures in Maori mythology. Dwelling in the forests or on misty mountaintops, they were described as pale-skinned beings with reddish or golden hair. The Tuhoe tribe described them as small in stature, while they assumed **giant**-like proportions in Whanganui stories. In other accounts they were a similar size to humans. One reason for the varying descriptions of height may be that *patupaiarehe* could generally be heard but not seen by ordinary Maoris. Usually only *tohunga*, or shamans, could see and communicate with them.

Like the Maori people, *patupaiarehe* lived in close-knit communities. In some accounts they built their homes or settlements, known as *pa*, out of mist. In others they built them from vines, or *kareao*. Although they engaged in some of the same activities as humans—hunting, fishing, making love—they were considered to be *iwi atua*, supernatural beings belonging to the spirit world, set apart from the world of mortals. As such they were regarded as *tapu*, taboo or sacred. Therefore, certain restrictions were associated with them. Unlike mortal Maori, they were never tattooed and they consumed only raw food. It was said that cooked food was offensive to them, and cooking fires and ash were used to ward them away. Another method of repelling *patupaiarehe* was to smear *kōkōwai*, a mixture of iron oxide and shark oil, on the walls of a home.

Patupaiarehe were most active at night or on misty days and were afraid of sunlight and fire. They were skilled musicians; when a male *patupaiarehe* played his flute to woo a mortal Maori woman, it was said she was powerless to resist. Albino and *urukehu* or red-haired offspring were believed to be the result of such unions.

Patupaiarehe were also skilled in the arts of magic and fishing and credited with imparting this sacred knowledge to the Maori people. A *patupaiarehe* named **Miru** shared his knowledge of games, love charms, and magic with the Maori people when he became the fairy lover of Hine-rangi, a mortal woman, while the story of how a mortal named Kahukara learned the secrets of net-making and fishing from *patupaiarehe* is related in "*Ko Te Korero Mo Nga Patupaiarehe*" (Kahukara and the Fairies) in *Polynesian Mythology and Ancient History of the New Zealand Race* by Sir George Grey (1855).

A man by the name of Kahukara set out to visit a place called Rangiaowhia to the north where the Te Rarawa people lived.

As he reached Rangiaowhia, he passed a place on the beach where people had been cleaning mackerel and the sand and seashore were strewn with fish guts. At first he thought the fish must have been left by the local fishermen, but when he looked more closely at the footprints in the sand he realized that the people who had been fishing had been going about their work at night.

"If these were the prints of men, some of the reeds and grass they sat on in their canoe would have been lying about," he thought to himself. "These are no mortals who have been fishing here—spirits must have done this."

Curious to learn more, he resolved to return that night.

At nightfall, just as he arrived back at the same place on the shore, he caught sight of the fairies. They were shouting out to one another: "The net here! The net here!" Some paddled out in canoes and dropped the net into the water. They sang joyfully as they worked: "Drop the net in the sea at Rangiaowhia and haul it at Mamaku."

As the fairies began to pull the net onto the shore, Kahukara managed to get among them and hauled on the rope. He had a very pale complexion and his skin was almost as white as that of the fairies, so he went unnoticed among them.

As the net was drawn closer to the shore, the fairies began to cheer and shout. Some waded into the water to ensure that the net did not become entangled on Tawatawauia a Teweteweuia, a rugged rock not far out from the sandy shore. Kahukara kept hauling away with the rest of them.

Dawn was just beginning to break as the fish reached the shore, rippling in the net. The fairies ran about on the sand picking up the fish, running a stick through their gills, and stringing them together. They worked hastily so as to be finished by sunrise.

Kahukara had only a short string and tied a slipknot in the end of it so every time his string was full the fish fell to the ground. Each time, one of the good-natured fairies helped him to re-string them, and by using this trick, he detained the fairies on the shore until the sun broke over the horizon.

In daylight, the fairies recognized him as a human and dispersed in confusion, making for their homes and abandoning their canoes, fish, and net on the beach.

Kahukara carefully examined the net the fairies had left behind and remembered their instructions on how to fish with it. And so it was that he discovered the fairies' art of weaving fishing nets. It was an art he passed on to his own children and as a result to all Maori people.

Another tale, "Te Kanawa's Adventure with a Troop of Fairies," relates a Maori chief's encounter with a group of curious *patupaiarehe.*

One day Te Kanawa, chief of the Waikato people in the North Island of Aotearoa (New Zealand), was out with a company of men hunting kiwis. When night fell they found themselves at the top of a high hill, known as Puke-more. They found a large tree with immense roots sticking up above the ground to shelter under for the night. They built a large fire and were settling down to sleep among the great roots of the tree when they heard the sound of voices coming toward them. There were the voices of men, women, and children, as if a large party of people were approaching, yet they could see no one. Te Kanawa realized it must be fairies.

The voices grew louder and more distinct as the fairies drew closer to the fire. Te Kanawa's people were very frightened and wanted to run away, but they were on top of a lonely mountain in a forest in the dark, and there was nowhere to run to.

Te Kanawa was a very handsome fellow and the fairies drew closer still to take a look at him, peeping over the large roots of the tree where the hunters were lying. When the fire blazed brightly they retreated, but when it burned low, they moved in, merrily singing:

"Here you come climbing over Mount
Tirangi,
To visit the handsome chief of
Ngapuhi."

It occurred to Te Kanawa that offering them a gift might encourage them to be on their way. He removed a carved greenstone figure from around his neck, a green pendant from one ear, and a tiger shark's tooth from the other. Thinking it best to avoid direct contact with the fairies, he hung these pieces of jewelry on a stick, which he stuck in the ground as an offering.

When the fairies had finished their song they came forward to examine the gifts. Rather than picking up the pieces of jewelry, they took their shadows, which they passed around the whole party. Then, satisfied with their gifts, they vanished.

Te Kanawa and his people were troubled no more by the fairies that night and, seeing that they were content with the shadows, he took back his necklace and earrings.

The next morning, as soon as it was light, the party went down the mountain as quickly as they could, without stopping to hunt kiwis.

Peallaidh, the Shaggy One

Malevolent Scottish water spirit, a type of **urisk** belonging to the ***fuathan***, the name given to the fearsome water spirits inhabiting Scotland's lochs, rivers, and seashores.

Shellycoat is said to be a less aggressive Lowland form of the Shaggy One.

Peat Fairy

See ***Ballybog***.

Peerie Fool

(Also Peerifool.) "The Princess and the Peerie Fool" is an Orcadian tale in which a girl must learn the secret name of her helper. It bears similarities to the well-known European tale of **Rumpelstiltskin**.

When the youngest of three princesses is captured by a giant, she must spin cloth for him in order to avoid the grisly fate that befell her two sisters before her.

When the giant leaves her on her own, hordes of fair-haired little folk appear and ask her to share her porridge with them. She does so and after they have eaten one of the little folk offers to help her in her spinning, asking only in return that she correctly guess his name.

The princess agrees and the little fellow sets to work. The princess learns his name from an old woman who comes to the giant's hall seeking lodgings and overhears him saying:

"Tease, teasers, tease,
Card, carders, card,
Spin, spinners, spin,
For Perrie Fool, Perrie Fool is my name."

Having impressed the giant with her masterful spinning, the princess escapes, rescuing her sisters on the way, and the three return safely home.

The term "peerie" is a variation of the Orkney dialect *peedie*, meaning "little."

See also **Habetrot**, **Terrytop**, **Tom Tit Tot**, **Whuppity Stoorie**.

Peerifool

See **Peerie Fool**.

Peg Leg Jack

See **Fachan**.

People of Peace, the

The name given to the **trooping fairies** of the Scottish Highlands by **Robert Kirk** in *The Secret Commonwealth of Elves, Fauns, and Fairies* (1691). They are similar to the ***Doaine Sidhe*** of Irish mythology.

People of the Hills, the

A euphemistic name for the fairies dwelling in the fairy mounds of England. One of many terms used to refer to the fairies without mentioning them directly, in order to avoid angering or offending them.

Peri Banu

(Also Paribanou.) A beautiful fairy in the tales of the *Arabian Nights.* She appears in **Andrew Lang**'s *Blue Fairy Book* (1889) in "The Story of Prince Ahmed and the Fairy Paribanou" as the majestic daughter of a powerful **genie**. In other versions of the tale she is depicted as a fairy **swan maiden**.

Peris

Benevolent spirits of Persian mythology, in constant battle against the malevolent ***divs.*** In early sources, they are described as capricious spirits, capable of bestowing ill fortune in the form of crop blights and natural catastrophes, as well as exerting a benign influence on the affairs of mortals. As belief in them evolved, however, they came to be regarded as wholly benevolent and depicted as tiny, beautiful females who subsisted only on the choicest fragrances and perfumes.

Perrault, Charles *(1628–1703)*

A French intellectual, poet, writer, and member of the Académie Française, Perrault was a pioneer of the literary fairytale genre of the seventeenth century. He is best known for his collection of fairy tales *Histoire ou Contes de Temps Passé, avec des Moralités: Contes de la Mère l'Oye* (1697), translated into English as *Histories and Stories of Times Past, with Morals: Tales of Mother Goose.* He drew on tales from oral folk tradition as well as the Italian collection of tales by **Giambattista Basile**, and retold and refined them in a literary style. It is his version of many popular tales that we are familiar with today, such as "Cinderella" (*Cendrillon ou La Petite Pantoufle de Verre*), "Little Red Riding Hood" (*Le Petit Chaperon Rouge*), "Blue Beard" (*La Barbe Bleue*), and "The Sleeping Beauty" (*La Belle au Bois Dormant*).

The **Grimm** brothers drew on some of Perrault's stories, reworking them in their famous collections of fairy tales, and Perrault's tales continue to be widely read and adapted today.

PEXY

See **Colepexy**.

PHARISEES

See **Feriers**.

PHENODREE

See **Fenodoree**.

PHOUKA

(Also *pooka, puka.*) Shapeshifting creature of Irish folklore. The *phouka* takes many forms and is described by turns as wild and tricksy, or helpful and benevolent. He is sometimes described as a **bogie** beast taking the form of an eagle, a bat, a dog, a rabbit, a goat, or a sleek black horse and luring humans onto his back then embarking with them on a wild ride. In other tales he takes the form of a creature akin to a **pisky**, or **brownie**, helping with agricultural labors such as threshing. In **Lady Wilde**'s *Ancient Legends, Mystic Charms, and Superstitions of Ireland* (1887), "Fairy Help" tells the story of a farmer's son called Phadrig and a *phouka* of this type.

When Phadrig befriended the *phouka*, the helpful spirit threshed the corn and brought prosperity to the farm. In gratitude, Phadrig made him a gift of a blue silk suit to replace his tatty old clothes.

On donning his new garb, the *phouka* so admired himself he declared that he was now too fine a gentleman for corn threshing and promptly departed from the farm to go and see a little of the world dressed in his fine new clothes.

He never returned to the farm. However, on Phadrig's wedding day, a golden goblet of wine mysteriously appeared in the groom's hand. Guessing it was a gift from his old friend the *phouka*, the bride and groom drank the wine and after that lived out their lives in happiness and prosperity.

Other tales, such as "The *Phooka* of Kildare," mix elements of the bogie beast and the brownie. In the form of a donkey, the *phouka* helps around the home, performing household tasks such as cleaning, but quits his work as soon as he is rewarded for his labors with a new coat.

The name may derive from the Old Norse *pook*, or *puki* for a nature spirit. In English, this became "pook," or "**puck**."

See also the Welsh ***pwcca*** and the Cornish ***bucca***.

Pigseys

Name given to the **pixies** in Devon. *See also* **Pisky**.

Piskey

See **Pisky**.

Piskie

See **Pisky**.

Pisky

(Also piskey, piskie.) The Cornish breed of **pixy**. In *Popular Romances of the West of England* (1865), **Robert Hunt** states that Cornish piskies are different from their cousins the pixies, or **pigseys**, of Devon and Somerset. The pigsey, or pixy, according to Hunt is: "a mischievous, but in all respects a very harmless creation, who appears to live a rollicking life amidst the luxuriant scenes of those beautiful counties." In contrast, the pisky of Cornwall is "a most mischievous and very unsociable sprite. His favourite fun is to entice people into the bogs by appearing like the light from a cottage window, or as a man carrying a lantern." In this guise, piskies are a type of **will o' the wisp**. The little fellows were also known for causing a nuisance to farmers, riding their horses, and chasing their cows, although tales such as that of the **pisky threshers** show that the piskies could be a helpful and hardworking bunch, too, should they choose to be. Hunt conceded that the piskies must have been a merry lot, since "to laugh like a piskie" was a popular saying.

Joan the Wad and **Jack O'Lantern** are sometimes named as the queen and king of the Cornish piskies. **Coleman Grey** was a pisky foundling, brought up by a human family until his own kind came to claim him. In other stories, piskies play the familiar fairy trick of stealing away a human child and replacing it with a pisky **changeling**.

Pisky Threshers

A popular Cornish tale in which a **pisky**, or a group of piskies, depending on the version of the tale, takes on the role of a helpful **agricultural spirit**.

One morning a farmer was astonished to discover a huge pile of freshly threshed corn in his barn. Curious as to who was responsible, that night as the moon came up he crept silently to the barn and put his eye to a chink in the door. To his surprise he spied a pisky dressed in a tattered green suit clutching the *dreshel* (flail) and working so quickly that his little arms were a blur.

The farmer tiptoed back to bed, where lay awake wondering what would be the best way to thank the little fellow for his hard work. Remembering the pisky's tattered clothes, he decided upon the gift of a new green suit.

The next morning the farmer had a little suit made and laid it out in the barn ready for the pisky.

That night, when he crept up to the door, he saw the pisky dress himself in his new suit, look at himself admiringly and exclaim:

"Piskie fine and piskie gay,
Piskie now will fly away."

With that the pisky was gone, never to be seen again.

This is one example of many tales in which fairy helpers depart as a result of being given the gift of a new suit of clothes. Others include the Irish story of Phadrig and the ***phouka***, and the **Cauld Lad of Hilton**.

Pitch Woman

See ***Tah-Tah-Kle-Ah***.

Pixie

See **Pixy**.

Pixy

(Also pixie.) The term "pixy" has come to be widely used for small **elf**-like beings, generally described as no more than a hand span in height. Originally, they were particular to the West Country of England. In Cornwall they went by the name of **piskies** and were said to be a slightly different breed from their cousins in Devon and Somerset. In Devon, they were also known as **pigseys**.

Pixies were particularly fond of leading travelers into bogs or marshes with their bobbing lanterns. To be "pixy-led" was to be led on a wild goose chase through fields or across the moors and cliffs. Throughout the West Country there are many tales of pixy-led travelers arriving home disheveled—often following the revels of the village fair—and insisting that the pixies were to blame for leading them from the path with their flickering lamps. Turning a coat or other item of clothing inside out was the method most often used to break the pixies' enchantment and find one's way back onto the path.

In Devon, Pixy Day is celebrated every June in the town of Ottery St. Mary to mark the day on which, according to legend, the pixies were banished from the town to nearby sandstone caves known as Pixies' Parlour. The poet Samuel Taylor-Coleridge was born in Ottery St. Mary. His poem *Songs of the Pixies* (1793) was inspired by local pixy lore.

See also **Colepexy**.

Plant Annwn, the

Fairies of the Underworld in Welsh folklore. Ruled over by the

Welsh Fairy King of the Underworld, **Gwyn ap Nudd**.

Ponaturi

Sea spirits of Maori mythology. Similar to the land-dwelling ***patupaiarehe***, they were described as pale-skinned with reddish hair and were afraid of sunlight and fire. However, unlike the generally benevolent *patupaiarehe*, these sea-dwelling creatures were hostile to humans and could lash out with their long claws. They spent their days in a land beneath the waves, coming ashore to sleep at night.

One legend tells of the Maori ancestor Tawahaki and the *ponaturi*. When they killed his father and kidnapped his mother, he blocked up all the doors and windows of their land dwelling while they slept, so that when they awoke they were tricked into believing it was still nighttime.

As the sun rose, Tawahaki and his brother opened the doors and windows to let the sun's rays stream in, killing the *ponaturi* and so taking their revenge.

Pontianak

In Malay and Indonesian myths the Pontianak is the malignant spirit of a woman whose death occurred during pregnancy. Her appearance is that of a long-haired, deathly pale woman, clothed in white, whose imminent presence is heralded by the sound of a baby wailing. Intent on revenge for her untimely death, she eviscerates and devours her victims and, when she preys on a male, the only deterrent is to plunge a nail into the back of her neck, for as long as this remains in place she will be a beautiful, good, and dutiful wife.

This legendary spirit is woven into folklore and her story is still told in films and modern tales of the supernatural. There have even been newspaper reports of sightings.

Portunes

Small agricultural fairies in English folklore. The thirteenth-century chronicler **Gervase of Tilbury** described them as very tiny, wizened old men dressed in ragged garments, resembling miniature versions of the agricultural laborers whom they assisted. Like household **brownies**, they worked at night to complete tasks left unfinished by humans during the day.

Although generally helpful, portunes had the mischievous habit of taking the bridle of a traveler's horse at night and leading both horse and rider into a pond or ditch before laughing loudly and making off into the darkness.

They were fond of roasted frog, which they cooked over the coals of the farmhouse hearth.

Potamoi

Male spirits of the rivers and streams in Greek mythology, the sons of Oceanus and Thethys and brothers of the **oceanids**. Oceanus was ruler of the rivers and the seas, the oldest of the Titans, whose mother was Gaea, Mother Earth, and father was Uranus, ruler of the heavens. Thethys was Titaness of the Oceans. According to the ancient Greek poet Hesiod, Oceanus had 6,000 children in total, 3,000 daughters and 3,000 sons. The daughters were known as the oceanids and were **nymphs** of the sea. The sons were spirits of the rivers, often depicted as half-man, half-bull, or half-man with the tail of a fish.

Peg Powler

Malevolent water spirit of the river Tees. Like her Lancashire counterpart, **Jenny Greenteeth**, she lured people into the water in order to drown and devour them, so, as a **nursery bogie**, she was invoked to frighten children into staying a safe distance away from the dangerous waters of the river. Tales of naughty children being dragged down into the depths were designed to keep unruly children from venturing too close to her watery domain. In *Notes on the Folklore of the Northern Counties of England and the Borders* (1866), Henderson describes her as a sort of **Lorelei** with green tresses and an insatiable appetite for human life.

The foam on the River Tees is known as "Peg Powler's suds" and the spongy froth as "Peg Powler's cream."

See also **Grindylow**, **Rawhead and Bloody Bones**.

Powries

(Also dunters.) Spirits of the mills on the Anglo-Scottish border. Described in William Henderson's *Notes on the Folklore of the Northern Counties of England and the Borders* (1866) as inhabiting old forts, peel-towers, castles, and dungeons, they are constantly heard making a noise as if beating flax or barley. If the noise is louder or more prolonged than usual it is said to be an omen that death or disaster is imminent.

Preta

The "hungry ghosts" of Buddhist and Hindu beliefs, the *preta* can never be satisfied, for their hunger is insatiable. Spirits of people who lived their earthly lives full of greed, addiction, and selfishness, or those whose burial ceremonies were neglected thereby condemning their spirits to a perpetual transient state, they are depicted as corpselike entities with bulging bellies and attenuated necks through which no food or drink can pass.

See also ***Gaki***.

Puck

Puck is now synonymous with the merry jester fairy in Shakespeare's *A Midsummer Night's Dream*. However, "pucks" already existed in British folklore before Shakespeare's time as mischievous **hobgoblins**. "Puck" or "pouke" was an old word for devil, and variations of the name are found in various cultures: *puki* in Iceland, *puk* in Friesland and Jutland, ***pixy*** and ***piskie*** in Devon and Cornwall, ***phouka*** in Ireland, ***pwcca*** in Wales

Some say that *Cwm Pwcca*, or Puck Valley, in Wales, part of the romantic glen of the Clydach in Breconshire, was the original inspiration for the setting of *A Midsummer Night's Dream.*

Shakespeare established Puck and **Robin Goodfellow** as names that can be used interchangeably to refer to a rougish yet on the whole benevolent type of fairy. He drew on traditional country folklore in his characterization of Puck, describing him as "sometime a fire." In Worcestershire a "poakeledden" traveler was one who had encountered a mischievous *poake* **sprite** in the form of a flickering light that caused him to stray from the path. Puck took on the form of a **will o' the wisp** to play his midnight pranks and delighted in leading night wanderers on a merry dance.

Puddlefoot

A Scottish **brownie** who dwelled in Altmor Burn, a stream near Cloichfoldich croft (farm).

The brownie was fond of splashing and paddling in the stream before going to the farm to set about the household chores. As he went about his work, he trailed wet footprints through the house. For this reason, the locals called him Puddlefoot, but only when they were sure he was out of earshot.

One evening a man returning from market, emboldened by ale, called to Puddlefoot by name.

"Oh, oh, I have gotten a name. It's Puddlefoot they call me!" exclaimed the brownie, and promptly vanished, never to be seen again.

Puka

See ***Phouka.***

Pwca

Welsh version of the English **puck**, Irish ***phouka***, and Cornish ***bucca.*** Most commonly he is described as a **will o' the wisp**. There are many tales of folk who have been led astray by the light of his flickering lantern.

The story generally goes that a villager loses their way as they are returning home at night. They spy a light up ahead and start to follow it, believing it to be someone carrying a lantern. Curiously, no matter how quickly or slowly they walk, the light always remains the same distance away.

Eventually they are led to the top of a high gorge, where the sound of rushing water can be heard below. As the bearer of the lantern leaps across the chasm, the light blazes brightly, revealing him to be an ugly, tiny, naked man, with long hair and pointed ears.

Seeing that the villager has not been lured into his trap of jumping into the gorge, the little man emits a shrill laugh, puts out the light and scampers off into the night, leaving the terrified villager pinned to the spot until morning.

Cwm Pwca is the name given to the *pwca's* gorge.

In other tales, such as "The *Pwca* of Trywyn Farm," offerings of milk and bread are left out for the *pwca,* presumably in return for helping with agricultural tasks such as herding the cows. When a milkmaid once helped herself to his bread and milk, she received a sound beating from invisible hands and a warning to leave the *pwca*'s food well alone.

An illustration by a Welsh peasant in **Sikes**' *British Goblins* (1880) portrays the *pwca* as a tadpolelike creature with a large head.

Q

Qailertetang

A female companion to **Sedna** in Inuit tradition, living in the depths of the ocean and possessing power over the weather.

Qallupilluk

In the myths of the Inuit, Qallupilluk are humanoid creatures with scaly skin living in the sea, ready with their long fingernails to snatch children into the depths. Tales are told of them to keep children safe on the treacherous ice floes.

Qareen

See ***Qarin***.

Qarin

(Or *qareen.*) A type of ***djinn***, a personal spirit, or constant companion (*qarin*) in Islamic tradition, attached to each individual. It can be persuasive in urging wrongdoing and must be guarded against.

Qutrub

In pre-Islamic Arabian legend the Qutrub is a catlike ***djinn*** created from a fiery wind.

PART 5

Fairies in Literature and Legend

FAIRIES IN LITERATURE AND LEGEND

Today, the image of a fairy that most readily springs to mind is of a delicate, little, winged creature like Tinkerbell from J. M. Barrie's *Peter Pan.* However, this was not how our ancestors envisaged fairies. Through the ages fairies have been through many transformations, shapeshifting via the mouths of storytellers and the quills of playwrights and poets and onto the page, stage, and screen. Every culture has its own story to tell (*see "A Flit through the History of Fairy Tales," p.416, for a look at fairy tales from different countries*). Here we explore the rich history of fairy lore in English literature.

A BRIEF HISTORY OF FAIRIES IN ENGLISH LITERATURE

From the supernatural beings of myth and legend to the knights and ladies of medieval romance, Shakespeare's Oberon and Titania, the fairy godmothers of nursery fairy tales, Tolkien's elves, dwarves, orcs, and beyond, English literature is home to a rich cast of fairy creatures in many guises.

Legends and Medieval Romances

The men and women of Celtic legend are larger-than-life characters, experts in the arts of glamor and enchantment who wield magical powers. The word "fairy" did not come into common usage until later, but these were the magical fairy beings of their time.

The Scottish sagas and Irish hero cycles tell of heroic deeds, such as the feats of the Irish hero Cuchullin, whose strength is pitted against a series of powerful enchantresses and magicians. It is a world in which fairy chiefs possess magical swords, and stones cry out in joy when a true king sets foot upon them. The epic tales of the Welsh *Mabinogion* tell of ancient heroes, and of King Arthur, accompanied in his quests by a band of mighty warriors possessed of magical powers. (*See p.420 to read one of the oldest Celtic fairy tales, "Connla and the Fairy Maiden."*)

Celtic legends mixed with Breton traditions in the *lais* of Marie de France, which were written for the English court in about the twelfth century. In these medieval romances, magical enchantresses were portrayed as ladies, and the heroes as chivalrous knights. In *English Fairy Poetry* (1880), Flores Delattre wrote:

As the Celtic fairies glided away from their popular origins into the province of romantic fancy, and, from a pre-Christian, purely mythological conception of peasant-lore, came to be looked upon as one of the favourite themes of the more enlightened class of lords and ladies, their magic 'amorousness' was made more and more conspicuous, and they soon came into contact with the fays of French romance.

The tale of "Sir Launfal and the Fairy Tryamour" is a popular romance from this period (*see p.422*).

In the fourteenth century, Geoffrey Chaucer was writing tales populated by knights and fairy ladies, such as "The Tale of Sir Thopas," as well as tales inspired by classical Greek and Roman mythology, such as "The Merchant's Tale," featuring Pluto and Prosperine as the King and Queen of the Fairies. In Chaucer's *The Canterbury Tales,* the Wife of Bath lamented the passing of the time of elves and fairies. However, in the world of literature, fairies were far from gone.

In the sixteenth century, Edmund Spenser drew on fairy lore and Arthurian legend to write one of the longest poems in the English language, the epic *Faerie Queene* (1590). The poem consists of six books. Spenser intended the finished work to comprise 12 books, each focusing on the story of a knight and a particular virtue, such as holiness, chastity, and friendship. The Faerie Queene herself, named Gloriana, was based on Queen Elizabeth I, and the poem was written as a commentary on life in Britain in the sixteenth century, but it also contained references to many elements of fairy lore, such as changelings, fairy glamor, and shapeshifting.

A French medieval romance, the *Huon of Bordeaux,* featuring the fairy court of King Oberon and

Queen Mab, was to influence Shakepeare's *A Midsummer Night's Dream*, setting the stage for a new trend in fairies in the Elizabethan era.

Shakespeare and the Poets

In the Elizabethan age, with the spread of literacy, a new generation of poets and writers came from the country to the town, bringing their own traditions with them. These homegrown country beliefs mixed with ideas from the medieval romances to produce a new breed of small, mischievous fairies in literature and on the stage.

Before Shakespeare, John Lyly was one of the first poets to introduce small fairies into drama. In *Endimion* (1591), fairies make an appearance to pinch the villain black and blue and reprimand him for prying into fairy affairs:

"Pinch him, pinch him, blacke and
blue,
Sawcie mortalls must not view
What the Queene of Stars is doing,
Nor pry into our Fairy woing."

But it was Shakespeare's *A Midsummer Night's Dream* (*c.*1595) that fixed the image of little trooping fairies in the public consciousness. Unlike the larger-than-life fairy beings of legend and romance, Shakepeare's fairies were "no larger than an agate stone," as Queen Mab is described in Mercutio's famous speech in *Romeo and Juliet*. But, like the fays of romance, Shakepeare's fairies live in a community, ruled over by the princely Oberon and the fair Titania. And, like mortal monarchs, the fairy ruler has his jester in the form of Puck.

Like the fairies of country folklore, the fairies enjoy dancing, have a penchant for cleanliness, and are wont to steal human children and leave fairy changelings in their place. They are mischievous and tricksy, and despite their diminutive size, still exercise a degree of power over nature; Oberon and Titania's quarrels disrupt the seasons and the weather, causing storms that ruin crops and leave a shortage of food for humans.

Once Shakespeare had placed fairies firmly in the limelight, a new fashion in poetry followed. Poets such as Drayton, Herrick, and Browne delighted in describing fairy courts in ever more minute detail. In Michael Drayton's poem *Nimphidia, The Court of Fayrie* (1627), fairies are tiny enough to hide inside a cowslip bell. William Browne's poems were slightly more rooted in folklore, describing underground fairy palaces that could be seen by the traditional method of looking through a "self-bored stone."

Alexander Pope's *The Rape of the Lock* (1717) is often cited as one of the first references to fairies having wings. The poem is a satirical take on Victorian society, based on a petty squabble that ensued when a gentleman cut a lock of hair from the woman of his fancy. The sylphs or fairies Pope describes are similar to the picture-book fairies that we are familiar with today.

Some to the Sun their Insect-Wings
unfold,
Waft on the Breeze, or sink in Clouds
of Gold,
Transparent Forms, too fine for
mortal sight,
Their fluid Bodies half dissolv'd in
Light.
Loose to the Wind their airy
Garments flew,
Thin glitt'ring Textures of the filmy
Dew;
Dipt in the richest tincture of the
Skies,
Where light disports in ever-mingling
Dies,
While ev'ry Beam new transient
Colours flings,
Colours that change when'er they
wave their Wings.

The Rape of the Lock, Canto II

While the fashion in the Elizabethan and Jacobean ages was for poets to prettify fairies, making them ever-smaller and often the butt of satirical jokes, William Blake took them seriously, famously saying that he had witnessed a fairy funeral procession in his garden, of creatures resembling the size and color of green and gray grasshoppers, carrying a little body laid out on a rose leaf.

The Romantic Revival

Toward the end of the eighteenth century there was a revival of interest in the roots of fairy lore and folklore. In *Reliques of Antiquity* (1765) Thomas Percy collected together an assortment of traditional ballads, including "Tam Lin" and "Thomas the Rhymer." This attracted the attention of the historical novelist and folklorist Walter Scott and sparked an interest among antiquarians and poets in the grassroots of folklore in the British Isles. The term "folklore" was coined in 1846 and the subject became an official field of study.

Romantic poets drew on folk beliefs and fairy lore for inspiration in their work. Keats took up the theme of the serpent wife in the story of Melusine in *La Belle Dame sans Merci* (1820) and again explored the theme in *Lamia* (1820), while Christina Rossetti's *Goblin Market* (1852) drew on traditions of taboos and fairy food, describing the tempting fruits of the goblin men that, once tasted, brought ruin and longing to mortals.

With the Romantic revival there was an unprecedented explosion of interest in fairies in Victorian Britain. During this period many folklore studies of fairies were carried out that form the basis of the traditions of fairy lore in the British Isles today. Thomas Keightley's *The Fairy Mythology* was published in 1828, and folklore studies were carried out across the British Isles.

The Folklorists

Much of the material that forms the basis of what we know about fairy lore in the British Isles today was collected by folklorists during the Victorian era. Further information, including brief biographies and relevant publications, is provided under individual entries in the main A–Z listings.

General

Keightley, Thomas, *The Fairy Mythology* (1828)

The British Isles

Briggs, Katharine, *A Dictionary of Fairies, Hobgoblins, Brownies, Bogies and Other Supernatural Creatures* (1976)

Evans-Wentz, Walter Yeeling, *The Fairy-Faith in Celtic Countries* (1911)

Cornwall

Bottrell, William, *Traditions and Hearthside Stories of West Cornwall* (1870–80)

Hunt, Robert, *Popular Romances of the West of England* (1865)

Ireland

Croker, Thomas Crofton, *Fairy Legends of the South of Ireland* (1825)

Gregory, Lady Augusta, *Gods and Fighting Men* (1904)

Wilde, Lady Jane Frances, *Ancient Legends, Mystic Charms, and Superstitions of Ireland* (1887)

Yeats, William Butler, *Fairy and Folk Tales of the Irish Peasantry* (1888)

The Isle of Man

Rhys, John, *Celtic Folklore: Manx and Welsh* (1901)

Waldron, George, *A Description of the Isle of Man* (1726)

Scotland

Campbell, John Francis, *Popular Tales of the Western Highlands* (1890)

Campbell, John Gregorson, *Superstitions of the Highlands and Islands of Scotland* (1900)

Carmichael, Alexander, *Carmina Gadelica* (1900)

Dennison, Walter Traill, *The Orcadian Sketch-Book* (1880)

Kirk, Robert, *The Secret Commonwealth of Elves, Fauns and Fairies* (1691)

Scott, Sir Walter, *The Minstrely of the Scottish Borders* (1802–1803)

Somerset

Tongue, Ruth, *Forgotten Folk-tales of the English Counties* (1970)

Wales

Sikes, Wirt, *British Goblins* (1880)

FAIRIES IN CHILDREN'S LITERATURE

While folklorists were out collecting tales from oral traditions, in nurseries English translations o fairy tales from the French *salons*, German tales collected by the brothers Grimm, and the Arabian *Thousand and One Nights* were proving popular. These tales were not originally intended for children. In fact, little was produced for children at that time bar dull educational tracts. However, when the popularity of fairy tales from the Continent showed there was a market for children's literature, it quickly led to the birth of a new genre.

At first, fairy tales were put to work to give children a moral education. As Katharine Briggs wrote:

Educationalists were impatient for quick results and wished to turn children into little grown ups as early as possible. Where the value of entertainment was admitted, it was generally as means of sugaring the pill. It was a bad time on the whole for the fairies.

At this time, new versions of the old English tale "Jack and the Beanstalk" included a fairy lady who was introduced into the tale to tell Jack that the giant had stolen his father's treasures, thereby justifying Jack's actions in stealing them back from the giant's castle. The giant's bad behavior was put down to an excess of drink and the ending was changed so that the giant wasn't killed but mended his ways and learned how to be a good husband.

The moralization of fairy tales angered and exasperated many folklorists and writers, including Charles Dickens, who railed against it in "Frauds on the Fairies" in *Household Words* (1853), in which he stated that it was of grave importance that fairy tales should be respected.

By the time the twentieth century arrived, moralizing had given way to a tendency to sentimentalize childhood, resulting in a focus on the saccharine, whimsical aspect of fairies. When J. M. Barrie's Tinkerbell and Peter Pan took the stage in 1904, and the audience clapped their hands to show that they believed in fairies, these fairies looked very different from the fairies of centuries past. Fairies had undergone a metamorphosis from the formidable heroic beings of legend, via the tricksy yet powerful little creatures of Shakespeare's dramas, to gentle creatures with gauzy wings, and would soon grace the screen in Disney versions of classic fairy tales.

GROWN-UP FAIRIES

However, another, earthier, strain of fairies began to emerge to buck the trend of whimsy, championed by the likes of Rudyard Kipling in *Puck of Pook's Hill.* In the twentieth century, Tolkien's *The Hobbit* and *The Lord of the Rings* brought fairies back to their folk roots, while Angela Carter's folksy translation of Charles Perrault's fairy tales provided down-to-earth alternatives to Perrault's "Mother Goose" morals. Carter followed this up with a collection of her own reworkings of fairy tales for adults in *The Bloody Chamber* (1979).

Throughout the twentieth century authors drew inspiration from the rich traditions of folklore to populate their work with creatures that our ancestors might have recognized back in the mists of time of myth and legend. This continues up to the present. Terry Pratchett, A. S. Byatt, Alan Garner, and Neil Gaiman are among the many authors who draw from the deep well of folklore to create characters and fantasy worlds that captivate, scare, delight, or surprise us, just as the storytellers of old held their audiences spellbound with fairy tales many hundreds of years ago.

Whether sparkly, delicate little creatures leaving trails of fairy dust or earthy beings tinged with the scent of the woods, fairies continue to flutter from the pages of our books. Their power over our imaginations remains as strong as ever.

A FLIT THROUGH THE HISTORY OF FAIRY TALES

As we have seen, ideas about fairies—their size, power, appearance—have changed over time and according to literary fashions and tastes. Many of the stories included here don't contain the small, winged fairies found in children's storybooks and films today. They do all contain elements of the magical and marvelous: dwarves and *djinn*, talking animals, a hag who lives in a hut on chicken legs, and a fairy godmother in the shape of a date tree.

There is much scholarly debate over the origins of and relationships between myths, legends, folk tales, and fairy tales, just as there is over the origins of fairies. Are they the echoes of the monstrous and miraculous deeds of ancient gods and heroes? Were they our ancestors' attempts to understand the natural world around them—to make sense of light and dark, sun and moon, stars, clouds and rain? (When you think about the old folk jingle "The Song of Sixpence" in this way, the pie is the Earth, the birds are the 24 hours in a day, the king is the sun, the queen is the moon, and the opening of the pie is daybreak.)

Some believe that fairy tales share a common place of origin, whence they spread across the globe, taking on local variations and character. The fairytale collector George Dasent wrote, "The whole human race has sprung from one stock planted in the East, which has stretched its boughs and branches laden with the fruit of language and bright with the bloom of song and story, by successive shoots to the utmost parts of the earth." Others, however, believe that similar tales sprang up spontaneously in tribes and communities scattered around the world as a universal response to life's challenges and situations.

Whatever their origin, for centuries these ancient tales have captured our imaginations and sparked a sense of wonder—just like the fairies themselves.

ANCIENT TALES, MYTHS, AND LEGENDS

The following is a brief dip into the world of fairy tales, highlighting some of the earliest tales to be written down in various countries. Before this, tales existed in the oral tradition, in the minds and mouths of the people, passed down from generation to generation and spread across the lands by traveling storytellers. Even after the stories were written down, there was still two-way traffic between the oral and the written traditions, each borrowing from and informing the other.

This is by no means an exhaustive list; it is designed to give a taste of the rich history of fairy tales and offer a flavor of those tales to spark further exploration.

Scandinavia: Old Norse Legends

The *Prose Edda* and the *Poetic Edda* comprise the major repository of Old Norse mythology. The Icelandic scholar, poet, historian, and politician Snorri Sturluson is credited with compiling the *Prose Edda* in the twelfth century, but the stories date back to much earlier times. Here we find tales of Odin, the All-father of Norse mythology, Tyr, Thor, and Freyja (after which Tuesday, Thursday, and Friday are named), of dwarves, master smiths, and magical weaponry, and of Loki, the trickster god of fire.

Loki and the Dwarf

One day the mischievous Loki cut off the hair of Sif, wife of Thor. When Thor was told of this wickedness, he was determined to punish Loki most severely. But Loki promised he would get the Svartalfar in the Underworld to make hair of gold for Sif. He went to the Caverns of Svartalfheim and called on the sons of Ivallda, who were dwarves. To demonstrate their skills, they not only made the hair of gold but also crafted a beautiful ship called *Skidbladni,* which always sailed swiftly before the wind, and a spear called Gugner which was unerring against the enemies of its owner.

Loki was so proud of these fine things that he wagered his own head against the dwarf Brock, being certain that Brock and his brother Eitri could not forge three better items.

Eitri the master smith set his fire going and asked Brock to pump the bellows to keep it very hot. A fly settled on Brock's hand and bit him, but Brock never stopped working the bellows until Eitri had taken the work out of the fire. It was the most amazing boar with bristles of gleaming gold.

Eitri put more gold into the furnace and once more Brock set to work with the bellows. Yet again the fly came and bit him, this time on the neck, but still he did not falter in his work. Of course, the fly was Loki in disguise, trying in vain to spoil the work.

Eitri retrieved a gold ring from the fire and it was called Drupner.

Next the smith put iron in the furnace and Brock continued his labors at the bellows. The fly bit him between the eyes and blood ran down his face, so he had to stop pumping long enough to swat away the fly and wipe the blood from his eyes. Eitri berated him for stopping, but the hammer he had forged was nearly perfect. This great hammer was called Miölner.

Eitri gave the three items to his brother, the dwarf Brock, and asked him to take them to Asgard so the wager might be settled.

Loki brought his hair of gold, the ship, *Skidbladni*, and the spear, Gugner, before the appointed judges, Odin, Thor, and Frey, and explained the special qualities of his items.

Brock then gave Odin the ring, Drupner, and said that every ninth night eight more rings would fall from it. He gave the boar to Frey and told him that it would run through air and water by night and by day. At night its golden bristles would light the way. Finally, he gave the hammer, Miölner, to Thor and said that it would hit any target true and would then return to his hand, and that when he chose he could make it small enough to carry on his belt.

When the judgement came, the hammer was deemed the best of all the wondrous items and the dwarf Brock won the wager.

Loki did not want to lose his head, so he ran and ran, through forests and over mountains. Brock demanded that Thor catch him to fulfil the wager. And so he did, but Loki insisted that the dwarf could only have his head and could not cut his neck. So Brock took a knife and a thong to sew up Loki's mouth. The knife was blunt and he had to borrow his brother's awl to finish the job, but when he was done mischievous Loki could open his mouth no more.

In *The Fairy Mythology* (1828), Thomas Keightley interprets this ancient tale as interactions between the forces of nature. Sif is the Earth and Loki the fire god, so when Sif's hair is "cut" it is the trees and forests that are burned. As a punishment Loki has his mouth sewn up to moderate his heat so that the Earth becomes temperate once more, allowing nature to flourish. The boar was a common offering to Frey and Freya, the gods of animal and vegetable fecundity. The forging of Thor's mighty hammer, traditionally the symbol of thunder, in Eitri's fire may point to the origins of thunder being in the earth, wherein are found all the precious metals.

Celtic Myth and Legend

In Celtic regions, Irish, Scottish, and Welsh tales recounted the heroic deeds of magical heroes, often involving a voyage to an Otherworld. In "Connla and the Fairy Maiden," the Otherworld is Moy Mell. Scholars place the tale in the fifth century or earlier, making it one of the earliest fairy tales in modern Europe. It is recorded in the Old Irish *Leabhar na h-Uidhre* (Book of the Dun Cow). As it was passed down the ages, it is likely that Christian scribes added the references to the day of the judgement and the waning power of the druids.

Connla and the Fairy Maiden

Many centuries ago in Ireland, the chief king was Conn of the Hundred Fights. His oldest son had a magnificent mane of flame-red locks and was known as Connla of the Fiery Hair. One day the father and son were standing together on the height of Usna when into Connla's vision drifted a maiden dressed in strange attire.

"Who are you and where have you come from?" he asked.

His father could not see the maiden and was astonished when he heard her words echoing through the mists: "I am come from the Valley of Paradise, the Vale of Eternity, where there is no time and therefore no death, and no sin. Ours is a life of contentment and we live in the round, green hills, so men call us the Hill Folk."

"Whose words are these?" he asked.

The maiden's voice rang out again, pure and true: "Connla speaks to me and I am a fairy maiden. My life is now and forever. I will always be young and fair, never meeting old age or death. And I love your son, and I call him to join me and journey to Moy Mell, where Boadag is king, and there is no sorrow or grief. A fairy crown awaits him there. He, too, can have eternal youth, his hair always as red as the flaming sun, his strength never fading, until Judgement Day."

Conn of the Hundred Fights, who feared no man, found dread in the words of the fairy maiden. He called upon Coran, his druid, saying, "Coran, this fairy's voice has filled me with fear. I know not how to conquer the wiles of this sprite and I do not wish to lose my beloved son to such trickery."

This was a time when the druids had command of all the spirits of the land, and none was more powerful than Coran, who was obedient only to the king. So he came to the height of Usna and cast his spells upon the spot where the maiden's voice had been heard.

Her voice was quieted, but as she dissolved into the mists, she threw an apple to Connla of the Fiery Hair.

The days grew into weeks and the weeks into months, and young Connla would neither eat nor drink except from the apple, which never seemed to diminish in size or substance. And he could not forget the beautiful maiden. Indeed, his longings seemed only to grow greater with the passage of time.

Then came a day when Connla and his father were standing together on the Plain of Arcomin and once more Connla saw the fairy maiden appear before him. In a voice so clear she spoke to him: "Connla of the Fiery Hair, do you not know that of all your people you are the chosen one? It is for you, and only you, to come with me to Moy Mell, the Plain of Pleasure, to be with the folk of life, the ever-living ones."

The king heard these words and cried out, "Where is my druid Coran? He must come and drive away this beguiling spirit!"

Then the maiden spoke directly to the king, without fear.

"Great king, the druids' time is passing swiftly. There comes a Law that will sweep away their dark spells, and your son must come with me to the land where he can live without fear of either sin or death."

Conn turned to his son and said, "Have I truly lost you to this maiden's words? Have I no power to keep you with me?"

"I love you, my father, and my people above all earthly things," replied Connla, "but this fairy's words draw me away as the sun draws away the night, with a power that no man can resist."

The maiden spoke again. "Now you can see it. There is but one true way, so come with me in this gleaming crystal *curragh* to the kingdom of Boadag, which lies where the sun sets and where we can live forever in joyous harmony."

Hearing these words, Connla of the Fiery Hair leaped into the crystal canoe and it glided swiftly toward the setting sun. In sorrow the king and his court watched it until they could see it no more.

Connla and the fairy maiden were never seen again by the people of Ireland and it is said they live now and forever on the Plains of Pleasure.

Medieval Romances

In medieval Europe, heroic legends gave way to courtly romances of knights and lady enchantresses. "Sir Launfal and the Fairy Tryamour" was a popular story from this period. Based on the *lai* "Launval" by Marie de France of Brittany, it was translated into English and adapted by the English bard Thomas Chestre.

Sir Launfal and the Fairy Tryamour

Among the famous knights of King Arthur, none was as generous as Sir Launfal. He became a favorite of the king, who appointed him his steward. This happy arrangement continued for ten years, but when Guinevere came, who was to marry King Arthur, and saw how close Sir Launfal had become to the king, she was filled with envy and jealousy.

At the great wedding ceremony, Guinevere gave gifts to all the knights except Sir Launfal. He was deeply hurt by this and decided to leave the court. King Arthur reluctantly accepted his decision and gave him some money and two young knights, Sir Hugh and Sir John, to accompany him on his travels.

They rode to Carlisle, where Sir Launfal knew the mayor, in the hope of finding accommodation and giving service. But the mayor, seeing that Sir Launfal was out of favor at court, offered him only a small lodging by the orchard.

The three men stayed there, but Sir Launfal was so generous with the money that King Arthur had given him that they were soon living in poverty.

When a year had gone by, Sir Hugh and Sir John asked their master if he would return to the court of King Arthur with them, but he was a proud man and said, "Go with my blessing. You have been good companions. But don't tell anyone of my poverty."

So the young knights returned to King Arthur, who was now at Glastonbury. Queen Guinevere pressed them for news of Sir Launfal, hoping to hear of his downfall. But they would only say, "He is well and happy, but we were homesick and so returned here to court." King Arthur believed them and was pleased, as he still felt affection for Sir Launfal and wished him no harm.

Meanwhile in Carlisle the mayor held a great banquet and lords and ladies came from far and wide. Sir Launfal was not invited, as he was now as ragged and thin as a beggar. He was filled with self-loathing and in his depression he took his poor lean horse and rode into the forest.

It was a hot summer's day and before long, in his weakened condition, Sir Launfal dismounted to rest beneath the shade of a tree. As he contemplated his sorry state, he became aware of two beautiful maidens standing before him.

"Sir Knight," they said, "our Lady Tryamour, the fairy princess, wishes you to come to her. Follow us if you will."

Sir Launfal followed the maidens until they came to a magnificent pavilion, all hung with tapestries on pillars of gold. The maidens bade him enter and when he did, he was all but blinded by the vision of loveliness that lay within. On a soft purple couch there lay the most beautiful lady he had ever seen.

Sir Launfal fell to his knees, "Fair lady, poor as I am, I offer myself to your command."

"Gentle knight," she replied, "I know all about you, as I know of all earthly things. I am Tryamour, the daughter of the King of the Fairies. I am well aware of your true worth and I am in need of such a noble knight to help me in my work with those in difficulty. If you will serve me well, then I will make you happy and you will have this Fortunatus, a purse of inexhaustible gold, and Blanchard, my fairy horse, and my good servant Gyfre. But you must never tell a mortal soul of my existence or you will lose all of these things."

"My lady," said Sir Launfal, "I will do your bidding and will come to you whenever you may call. I am forever in your service."

He kissed her hand and they celebrated their pact with food and wine. He then took his leave and rode back to his lodge in the orchard.

The next morning Gyfre came riding on the white horse Blanchard at the head of a procession of young knights, all laden with fine clothes and armor. When the mayor of Carlisle saw all these riches, he tried to endear himself to Sir Launfal, but the good knight was not interested in his insincere attentions and the major left in shame.

News of Sir Launfal's good fortune soon spread, and lords and knights from miles around came to a great tournament to try the skill of the powerful knight. One after the other, the brave knights jousted against Sir Launfal riding on his noble white steed, Blanchard, but none could defeat him.

There was at this time a notorious knight in Lombardy, Sir Valentyne, who had a reputation as a great fighter but was a mean and cruel man. He challenged Sir Launfal to meet him at a tournament in Lombardy.

The jousting was fierce, but eventually Sir Valentyne was killed and, although his angry knights all came at Sir Launfal to avenge their leader's death, he fought them off and returned to his own land.

King Arthur heard of all these things and wrote a letter to Sir Launfal asking him to return to his court and resume his duties as his steward. Sir Launfal called on his mistress, the Fairy Princess Tryamour, and asked her if he might take up this offer. She granted her permission, but reminded him that he must not betray her existence.

A huge feast was arranged and King Arthur gathered together a multitude of lords and ladies to celebrate the return of his favorite knight. There was much merriment and dancing and everyone was happy to see the good knight after his long absence—everyone, that is, except Queen Guinevere. Her anger and jealousy knew no bounds. She went to Sir Launfal as the feasting grew to a close and said to him, in a voice hard with malice, "If it weren't for the king's affection for you, I would never have had you back in my service. And you would never have found another noble lady to serve, not in all the world!"

This angered Sir Launfal, and without thinking, he said, "I have been serving a nobler and more beautiful princess than you for seven years, and even her lowliest maid is more queenly than you will ever be!"

Queen Guinevere was furious and immediately told King Arthur of Sir Launfal's insult. The king wanted to execute the knight at once, but because of his standing he had the right to trial by his fellow knights. All the court knew of the queen's temper and there were many who sympathized with Sir Launfal. Finally it was agreed that if he could bring forth the princess or the maidens who were fairer than the queen, then he could go free. If he could not do so within a year and a fortnight, then he would be hanged as a traitor.

Sir Launfal was dismayed, as he knew he had betrayed the lovely Lady Tryamour, and Gyfre his fairy servant and Blanchard his fairy steed had vanished.

He traveled the land with Sir Percival and Sir Gawain, searching for the fairy princess, but they searched in vain. As the appointed time grew near, they returned to the palace and Sir Launfal awaited his fate.

Then ten beautiful maidens came riding through the castle gates.

Sir Gawain looked out and said, "Have no fear, my friend. Surely one of these fair damsels must be your princess."

But Sir Launfal, truthful as ever, replied, "No, I do not know these maidens."

The young ladies stood before King Arthur and said, "Your Royal Highness must prepare a chamber for our Princess Tryamour, who is the daughter of the King of Olyroun."

King Arthur commanded that the best chamber in the castle be prepared with rich tapestries and candles. Then a cry went up from the assembled court as a lady on a white horse appeared in the distance. She came among them and a hush fell upon the crowd as they admired this wonderful vision. The Lady Tryamour was clad in a purple robe, trimmed with ermine, and wore a golden crown glittering with rubies and emeralds. Her red-gold hair flowed like sunlit water over her shoulders, and her fair skin and sparkling eyes were almost too beautiful to behold. Her handmaidens helped her to dismount and she stood proudly before King Arthur.

"I cannot deny that my knight Sir Launfal spoke the truth when he told of your incomparable beauty," said the king.

A cheer went up from the courtiers and Sir Launfal stepped forward and mounted the steed Blanchard, which had been brought up by Gyfre. Together, the fairy princess and her noble knight Sir Launfal rode off with their entourage toward the setting sun. They traveled on through the night until they entered Olyroun, the Isle of the Fairies. There they still live in eternal paradise and it is said that every year on the Feast of St. John the horse Blanchard can be heard to neigh and any knight may ride a course with Sir Launfal.

Ancient Arabia: Tales of the Thousand and One Nights

The *Tales of the Thousand and One Nights,* incorporating tales from Arabic, Persian, Indian, and Egyptian folklore, exchanged along the trade routes of the silk road, were first written down in the early 1500s. A French archeologist named Antoine Galland translated them into French and brought them to a European audience as *Les Milles et Une Nuits* in the early 1700s. They were published in France at a time when Charles Perrault's literary fairy tales had recently come into vogue and proved extremely popular throughout Europe, painting a fabulous image in the European mind of magical flying carpets, wish-granting genies, and beautiful princesses inhabiting fragrant and exotic lands. The 1706 English translation, *Arabian Nights Entertainments,* captured the imagination of the English-speaking world and influenced many writers, including Samuel Taylor Coleridge, Thomas de Quincey, Lord Alfred Tennyson, Edgar Allen Poe, and Herman Melville.

The tales are framed by the story of Scheherazade and the Sultan Shahriyar. Shahriyar was the Sultan of the Persian Empire and his brother, Shaw-zummaun, was the King of Tartary. Both princes caught their wives committing adultery. The King of Tartary executed his wife and her lover, but

Sultan Shahriyar took even more extreme measures in retribution: after executing his wife and all of her ladies-in-waiting, he vowed to take a different wife every night and have her executed by his Grand Vizier in the morning.

When Scheherazade, the Grand Vizier's daughter, was called upon to go to the sultan, she used her talent for storytelling to save her life. With the help of her sister, Dinarzade, she wove compelling stories that captivated the sultan's imagination so that each morning he longed to hear more and thus spared her life for one more day.

By their very nature the stories have a continuity within themselves and between them in order to maintain the sultan's interest. The first story Scheherazade narrated was "The Merchant and the *Djinn*."

The Merchant and the Djinn

Once there was a rich merchant who, by way of business, had to travel a great deal. On one particularly long and arduous journey he took biscuits and dates with him for refreshment. On the way home he stopped in the shade of the palms by the cool water of an oasis and ate some of the biscuits and dates, casting the shells carelessly about him. He washed himself in the waters, then knelt to pray.

As he prayed, a great shadow fell across him. Looking up, he saw the vast and terrifying form of a huge *djinn* coming at him with a sharp scimitar raised above his head.

"Arise so I can kill you, as you have killed my son!" said the *djinn*, his voice like thunder.

"But I haven't even seen your son," the merchant said. "How could I have killed him?"

"Didn't you sit here and eat your dates and throw the shells in all directions?" demanded the *djinn*.

"I cannot deny it."

"One of those shells hit my son in the eye and killed him. Therefore I must kill you!"

"Please, I implore you to spare me. If I did kill your son, it wasn't my intention," the merchant pleaded.

"No matter," cried the *djinn*, throwing the merchant on the ground and raising the scimitar to cut off his head, "you must die!"

The merchant continued to protest his innocence. "Will you take my innocent life and take me from my beloved wife and children?" he cried.

At this point Scheherazade stopped relating her story, just as dawn was breaking.

"What a wonderful story," said Dinarzade. "I'd like to hear what happens next."

"The conclusion is even more surprising," said Scheherazade, "and if the sultan will see fit to spare me for one more night, I will continue tomorrow."

Shahriyar was also intrigued as to the outcome, so he agreed, and the Grand Vizier was happy to learn that his daughter was safe for another day.

The following morning Dinarzade woke Scheherazade and the sultan and the story continued.

Lying at the mercy of the *djinn*, the merchant made one final effort to save his life, promising that if he only had time to see his wife and children and settle his affairs, then he would return to meet his fate.

At first the *djinn* didn't believe him, but when the merchant swore a solemn oath in the name of the Prophet, he relented and allowed him one year to complete his arrangements.

The merchant returned home and paid his debts, gave alms to the poor, set his slaves free, divided his property among his children, and gave a generous inheritance to his wife.

As the year came to an end, he said, "My dear family, I must obey my holy oath. You must allow me to do this and you also must be true to yourselves."

And so he traveled back to the oasis and sat by the water awaiting the arrival of the *djinn*.

As he sat there in sorrow, an old man leading a hind appeared and sat with him.

"Why have you come to this place?" he asked. "It may look quite pleasant, but I have heard it harbors evil spirits."

The merchant told him all about the *djinn* and the old man said he would stay to witness what was to transpire.

At this point Scheherazade stopped relating her story once more and once again the sultan postponed her execution so that he could hear the rest of the story.

The next morning, an hour before dawn, Dinarzade woke her sister, but before she could speak, the sultan himself asked that Scheherazade continue the tale of the merchant and the *djinn*. And so she did.

As the old man with the hind was talking with the merchant, another old man came to the oasis, followed by two black dogs. He, too, was told of all that was happening, and he also decided to stay to see what would transpire.

In no time at all, a third old man arrived, leading a mule. Then a thick, dark cloud loomed across the water and swept up to the shore where they were all sitting. With a great roar, the huge *djinn* materialized, clutching his scimitar.

"Get up!" he commanded the merchant. "Prepare to die, for I must kill you as you killed my son!"

The three old men were terrified and filled the air with their lamentations.

Scheherazade broke off once more, just as the sky was turning gray with the first light of a new day. Sultan Shahriyar was intrigued and yet again put off her execution in order to hear more.

Near the end of the next night, Scheherazade told how the old man with the hind persuaded the *djinn* to pardon the merchant one third of his offense, by promising to tell of his own amazing adventures.

These stories filled the next two nights, the old man describing how his wife had transformed his son and his favorite slave into cattle, for she was jealous of the son and his slave-mother. Ultimately, the wife was changed into a hind, once her trickery had been revealed and the son saved. As a result of these stories, the *djinn* forgave the merchant one third of his offense.

Now the second old man, the one with the two black dogs, implored the *djinn* to hear his story and thereby to withdraw a further third of the merchant's punishment.

The sultan also wanted to hear this tale and so Scheherazade passed more nights in safety relating this story.

The old man told the great *djinn* that the two black dogs were in truth his own brothers. They had been careless in their trading activities and despite the old man's generous financial assistance, they had tried to drown him on a long sea voyage. However, the old man had married a wife in a distant land and she was really a fairy, or *djinn*, and had been able to save him from the sea and return him to his home. She wanted to kill the two brothers, but he would not allow it, so instead she changed them into two black dogs. They were condemned to remain as dogs for five years and now that the time was nearly up, the old man was on a quest to find his wife and have his brothers returned to their former selves.

The great *djinn* of the oasis thought this a good story and forgave the merchant another third of his offense.

The third old man, the one with his mule, was about to tell his story when Scheherazade stopped again to preserve her own life.

It was now the eighth night. Dinarzade woke her sister and the sultan at the usual hour. Scheherazade said that the third old man's story was even more astonishing than those of the other two, but all the details had not been made known to her. However, the great *djinn* was suitably impressed and he remitted the final third of the merchant's life.

With that, the *djinn* vanished from sight and the merchant thanked the old men for saving his life and returned to end his days happily with his wife and family.

Scheherazade said to the sultan, "Sir, you have enjoyed these stories so far, but none are as fascinating and full of wonder as that of the poor fisherman."

So the sultan was again persuaded to delay the execution, and Scheherazade embarked on the next of the tales of the *Thousand and One Nights.*

Italy: The Story of Stories

In the mid-1500s Gianfrancesco Straparola published two volumes of collected anecdotes and tales in *Le Piacevoli Notti* or *The Facetious Nights* (also known as *The Pleasant Nights* and *The Delightful Nights*).

Following on from this, in the mid-1600s Giambattista Basile, an Italian soldier, poet, writer, and collector of fairy tales, compiled *La Cunto de la Cunti* (*The Story of Stories*) (1634, 1636), also known as *Il*

Pentamerone, a collection of 50 stories based on traditional Italian folk tales. It was one of the first national collections of fairy tales and influenced later writers and collectors, including Charles Perrault in France and the brothers Grimm in Germany. It includes the earliest recorded versions of many tales that are still familiar to readers today, including *Cenerentola*, or "Cinderella."

Cenerentola

There once was a prince who lived in one of the coastal provinces of Italy. His wife died giving birth to their only daughter who he named Zezolla, in memory of his beloved wife. In her infancy, he was completely devoted to the child. As she grew older, he took a governess to teach her all the skills needed by a young woman, such as chain-stitching and knitting and lace-making. The governess was very kind and loving toward the little princess and Zezolla wished that she could become her mother.

The governess herself began to realize that she could use Zezolla's devotion as a way of becoming the prince's wife, and she encouraged the princess to tell her father how happy she would be if only he would marry the governess. At first, he could not take this seriously, as the governess was older than him and was not of his class. As time passed, however, and his daughter continued to press him on the matter, he came to see that this marriage could bring them all happiness.

So they arranged for a grand wedding ceremony and a great feast. Zezolla was still too young to join in the dancing, but she stood at an open window to watch and listen. Quite suddenly, there was a fluttering of wings and a dove flew down onto the sill beside her. To her surprise, the pretty bird spoke to her, saying, "Zezolla, whenever you are in need, you must send your request to the Dove of the Fairies, who dwells on the Island of Sardinia, and it shall be granted to you."

With that, the dove was gone, flying toward the sun in the south.

For a time following the wedding the new stepmother was devoted to Zezolla and ensured that she had the best of everything—good food and drink, fine clothes to wear, and servants to attend to her every need. But as time went by, she revealed that she had daughters by her previous husband, who had died some time before. These daughters were introduced to the palace one by one, and the stepmother was such a cunning person that she was able to turn her husband's love away from his own Zezolla in favor of these new young women.

Things got worse and worse for the princess until she was reduced to working in the kitchen and became known by a different name: Cenerentola.

One day it happened that the prince had to visit Sardinia to attend to his affairs. He called upon his stepdaughters and asked what gifts he should bring them from the island. They asked for fine clothes, trinkets, rouge, and all manner of pretty, frivolous things. As an afterthought the prince said to Cenerentola, "And what about you, child? What shall I bring for you?"

Nothing, father," she replied. "I ask only that you commend me to the Dove of the Fairies and ask her to send me something. If you forget this, then you will be unable to move back or forth from the island. This I promise."

The prince was puzzled, but sailed across the sea to Sardinia and completed his business. He found many gifts for his stepdaughters, but quite forgot about his own Zezolla.

When he boarded the ship, the captain and crew hoisted the sails, but the ship would not move, no matter what they did. Exhausted, the captain lay down to rest, and as he slept, he dreamed of a fairy who said to him, "The reason you cannot move your ship is because the prince has broken his promise to his own true daughter."

The captain told this dream to the prince, who was ashamed and went to the Grotto of the Fairies. He commended his daughter to them, and a beautiful maiden came to him and asked him to remind Zezolla of the dove. Then she gave him gifts for his daughter: first a date tree, second a hoe, then a bucket made of gold and last a silken napkin to water and clean the tree's leaves.

The prince returned to his ship and they sailed before a fair wind back to their home port.

The stepdaughters received their presents, but their delight was nothing compared to Zezolla's joy when she saw the gifts the fairies had sent. She took the date tree and planted it carefully in a decorated pot. Every morning and evening she watered it from the golden bucket and wiped its leaves with the silken napkin.

The tree grew rapidly and one morning a fairy appeared from within its leaves and asked Zezolla, "What do you wish for?"

Zezolla asked that she might sometimes leave the palace without anyone knowing.

"Very well," said the fairy. "Whenever you wish to leave the palace, come to me and say: 'My little date tree, with my hoe I have tended thee, with my golden can I have watered thee, and with a silken cloth I have wiped thee dry. Now strip thee and dress me speedily.' When you wish to undress say 'Strip me and dress thee.'"

Soon it was announced from the king's palace that there was to be a great feast and a ball. The stepdaughters all dressed in their finery, powdered their faces and filled their hair with ribbons and bows. Zezolla ran to her date tree and said the words as the fairy had instructed. Within moments she was dressed like a princess and seated upon a palfrey, a little white horse, attended by 12 smart footmen all dressed in fine jackets and breeches.

As Zezolla entered the ballroom, all the company were amazed at her beauty, and none more so than the young king himself. No one knew who she was or where she lived, so the king sent his most trusted servant to follow her home. But Zezolla cast gold pieces on the ground to distract him, and in his greed he lost sight of her.

Back at home, Zezolla went to the date tree and became Cenerentola once more. When the stepdaughters came back, they spoke of all the fine things they had seen and done. None of them realized that Cenerentola was the mysterious beauty they had seen.

It wasn't long before the king held another great banquet in the hope that he might see once more the fair lady he had so admired. The sisters fussed and fiddled and put on their feathers and frills and rode off to the palace and Cenerentola went to the date tree and repeated the spell.

This time a number of fairies appeared to dress her. They replaced her rags with a shimmering gown and brushed her hair until it gleamed like gold. She rode to the banquet in a silver coach drawn by six white horses, driven by a handsome coachmen and attended by footmen all clothed in fine livery. When she entered the palace, the stepsisters were filled with envy and jealousy, and the young king was overcome with love. Again he sent his servant to follow Zezolla, but she dropped jewels from the coach and in his desire for rubies and emeralds he lost sight of her.

The sisters still had no idea that Cenerentola was the mysterious beauty who had won the king's heart. The king had no idea either and was furious with his servant for failing in his quest once again. So desperate was he to see the fine lady again that he very soon arranged another great celebration.

Once the sisters had departed for the palace, Cenerentola went to her date tree and again the fairies appeared and in no time she was as bright and glorious as the sun itself. This time she rode in a wonderful golden carriage to the king's palace and she danced with the king, but still she would not reveal her true identity.

When she left the palace, the servant was determined not to lose her this time and ran so fast that the golden coach had to fly like the wind to outpace him. As the carriage sped along, Zezolla lost one of her dancing slippers. The servant, having lost the coach, retrieved the slipper and took it to the king, who was pleased to have at least some clue to his beloved's identity. He took the slipper and said, "If the basement is so beautiful, what must the building be? You were the prison of a gentle white foot and now you are a chain around my heart!"

He sent a proclamation around his kingdom, demanding that all the princes of all the provinces bring their women to a great banquet at the palace. A great feast of pastries and pies, ragouts, stews, and sweetmeats was prepared. Many hundreds of women from throughout the land arrived, noble and ignoble, rich and poor, plain and pretty, and all tried to fit into the slipper, but in vain.

In despair, the king enquired of his princes if they were certain that all of their daughters had been brought before him. And so Zezolla's father had to admit that he had not brought her, as she was but a kitchen maid.

The next day Zezolla was brought before the king. As soon as she sat down and removed her shoe the slipper jumped onto her foot like iron to a magnet. The king was overjoyed and in no time he and Zezolla were married and everyone, including the stepsisters, had to pay homage to their new queen.

The sisters lived out their petty lives with their mother, always filled with spite and envy. The king and his beautiful queen lived happily in splendor and joy for the rest of their lives.

France: Birth of the Modern Fairy Tale

Salons, fashionable gatherings of literary and artistic figures, were all the rage in France in the late 1600s. It was here that the literary fairy tale was born.

French intellectual and writer Charles Perrault was a pioneer of the literary fairytale genre. He is best known for his collection of fairy tales *Histoire ou Contes de Temps Passé, avec des Moralités: Contes de la Mère l'Oye* (1697), translated into English as *Histories and Stories of Times Past, with Morals: Tales of Mother Goose*. He drew on tales from oral folk tradition as well as the Italian collection of tales by Giambattista Basile and retold and refined them in a literary style. It is his version of many popular tales that we are familiar with today, such as "Cinderella" (*Cendrillon ou La Petite Pantoufle de Verre*), "Little Red Riding Hood" (*Le Petit Chaperon Rouge*), "Blue Beard" (*La Barbe Bleue*), and "The Sleeping Beauty" (*La Belle au Bois Dormant*). The Grimm brothers drew on some of the same stories as Perrault, reworking them in their famous collections of fairy tales, and Perrault's tales continue to be widely read and adapted today.

Writing around the same time as Perrault, the countess Madame Marie-Catherine d'Aulnoy was one of the most influential writers in the *salons*. The British fairy-tale collector Andrew Lang has called her "the true mother of the modern fairy tale" and credits her with inventing "the modern Court of Fairyland, with its manners, its fairies, its queens, its amorous, its cruel, its good, its evil, its odious, its friendly *fées*." Madame d'Aulnoy wrote *Les Contes de Fées* (Fairy Tales) in 1697 and

Contes Nouveaux ou les Fées à la Mode (New Tales or Fairies in Fashion) in 1698. Like many of her contemporaries, she drew on tales from oral folk tradition and retold them in a literary style. "The White Cat" is among the best known of her tales, featuring a beautiful talking feline and a troop of performing cats.

The White Cat

Once there was a king who had three sons. Each son had the ambition of reigning and the old king could not decide which should take the throne after him, so he called them together and said, "I wish to give one of you the crown, but in order to make my decision I would like each of you to get me a little dog to keep me company when I retire. The one who gives me the most beautiful little dog will become king. Return to the palace in exactly one year."

The three brothers were soon on their way, and while the two elder ones had adventures, it is the story of the third that is the most extraordinary. He was traveling from town to town, looking for a dog that would please his father and always thinking he would find a nicer one a little further on, when one day his journey took him to a forest. Night was falling and quite suddenly a thunderstorm erupted. The rain was such that he was soon soaked through to the skin but, worse, he lost his way. Fortunately, he could see a light in the distance and aimed to seek shelter there.

As he approached the source of the light, he discovered it was coming from a magnificent palace with a door made of gold. To announce his arrival, he pulled a chain made of diamonds. The door opened and several pairs of hands ushered him into the palace.

Once he was inside, more hands enticed him into a beautiful room, the likes of which he had never seen before. The fire was lit, and the hands took his wet clothes and gave him garments made of the finest fabrics. The hands then guided him to the dining room, where the table was laid for two.

A most unbelievable thing happened next: a troop of cats entered the room and took up places at one end to form an orchestra.

Then a veiled figure entered and sat at the table. When she pulled her veil back, the prince saw a very beautiful white cat.

"Welcome to my castle, prince," said the cat.

"It is an honor to meet you," said the prince. "I can see you are no ordinary cat, for your castle is splendid—and you can talk."

After supper they adjourned to a room decked out as a theater, where more cats performed a show.

The next morning the white cat and her entourage took the prince hunting in the forest. In the evening the prince was once again invited to share the white cat's supper. He soon forgot about his quest for a little dog and the days passed happily, filled with entertainment and fine dining, until one day the white cat said, "In three days' time you must return to your father's palace. My fastest horse will take you there."

The prince despaired of finding a little dog for his father in such a short time, but the white cat assured him she could help. She gave him an acorn and said, "The little dog you want is in the acorn. Crack it open before your father."

Back at the king's palace, the three brothers were reunited with their father and all were filled with anticipation. The king admired the first two little dogs and wondered why his youngest son had brought him an acorn. However, when he cracked it open, he was astonished and delighted to find the tiniest, most loveable dog inside.

There was no doubt in his mind as to the winner of the contest, but he wanted to be doubly sure of his choice and sent his sons away again, this time to find the finest silk thread that could pass through the eye of a needle.

The youngest prince returned to the white cat's palace and once again the days passed pleasurably, filled with merriment, games, hunting, and banqueting.

Soon another year was over and it was time for the prince to return to his father's palace. Again, he had all but forgotten about his mission.

"Don't worry," said the white cat, "I will provide you with the finest silk you have ever seen, hidden in a walnut."

Back at the king's palace the brothers met and presented their father with the fine silks they had found—except for the youngest, who presented him with a walnut. When the king cracked it open, inside was a hazelnut, and inside that was a cherry stone, inside of which was a grain of wheat, inside which was a millet seed. By this time the young prince was beginning to wonder if the white cat had deceived him, but at last the king cracked open the millet seed to reveal the most wonderful thread of them all; it could pass easily though the eye of even the tiniest of needles several times over.

The king informed his sons that he wished his heir to be married and sent them away once more, this time to look for a suitable princess.

The young prince returned to the white cat's palace. Again, the year quickly passed and it was soon time to return to his father's palace. Again, though, he had all but forgotten his quest.

"I have found no bride—how can I return?" he said.

The white cat then made a strange request: she ordered the prince to cut off her head and her tail and throw them in the fire.

"I promise," she said, "that this will bring us both happiness."

At first the prince refused, but the white cat pleaded with him until reluctantly he agreed.

No sooner had the deed been done, however, than he saw, standing before him, the most beautiful princess of all.

"You have broken the spell—I am now myself again," she said. The prince was overawed by her beauty and eager for an explanation, so she continued: "My father ruled over six kingdoms and my mother's passion was to travel. When she was expecting me, she went to a faraway land where a magical fairy palace was said to be. She tried to enter the palace, but to no avail, so she decided to camp nearby. While she was there she fell very ill and her condition worsened until one day an ugly little fairy woman appeared and claimed she could cure her if she promised to give up her child to the fairies. Feeling that she had no other choice, she agreed. The fairy touched her with her magic wand and, being well again, she returned home.

"When I was born the fairies came to my father's palace to demand that I should be handed over to them, but both my parents refused. Then came a great disaster—the fairies sent their dragon to one of my father's kingdoms and it devoured many of his subjects. My father sought advice from a fairy of his acquaintance and she advised that the only way to put an end to the carnage was to give me up. Reluctantly, he did so.

"I was well brought up by the fairies, but when it was time for me to marry, they chose King Dagonnet, an ugly dwarf, to be my husband. When I refused to marry him, one of the fairies touched me with her wand and I became a cat. My courtiers also were transformed into cats and the servants became invisible, save for their hands. But now all is well and we must at once depart for your father's palace."

The prince was amazed by the beautiful princess's story and was overcome with love for her. He was only too glad to accompany her to his father's palace.

The two elder brothers presented their princesses to the king first and they were indeed very beautiful. However, when the youngest brother and his princess entered the room, the king could not stop himself from exclaiming that her beauty was truly matchless and deserving of the crown.

"I have no need of a kingdom," the princess replied, "for I possess six already, inherited from my father. Allow me to offer one to you and one to each of your two elder sons, and you may also keep your own for now. I ask only that I may take this young prince for my husband, with your blessing. Three kingdoms shall be quite enough for us."

The king—who really had no desire to give up his kingdom just yet—and his court and the princes and their princesses were overjoyed at the news. The marriages between all three princes and princesses were immediately arranged and there followed many months of merriment and celebration. Then each couple went to rule happily over their kingdom, and the youngest prince and his princess lived in happiness for the rest of their lives.

Germany: The Brothers Grimm

The Grimms had a major impact on the fairytale genre and their work inspired many similar collections of folklore and fairy tales in various countries. Their first book, *Children and Household Tales*, also known as *Grimms' Fairy Tales*, was published in 1812. The book contained 86 tales and included some stories similar to those recorded by Charles Perrault. The second volume was published two years later, with 70 additional tales. In its final version it would contain more than 200 tales. Over the years the brothers rewrote some of the tales, adding details and often eliminating the violent and sexual content in order to make them suitable for children. Some of the best known are "Rapunzel," "Hansel and Gretel," "Sleeping Beauty," "Cinderella," and "Tom Thumb." These continue to be adapted and recounted around the world. The popularity of the Grimms' work paved the way for an explosion of fairy tales across Europe.

MID-1800S: THE FAIRYTALE CRAZE SWEEPS ACROSS EUROPE

Denmark: Hans Christian Andersen

Danish author Hans Christian Andersen combined traditional tales from his boyhood memories with stories from his imagination. His first book of tales, *Fairy Tales, Told for Children*, was published in 1835. Further books followed and, as their popularity grew, they were translated into numerous languages. "The Little Mermaid" (inspired by the sad love story of the water sprite Undine), remains one of the most popular and best-known fairy stories today. Other famous tales by Andersen include "The Emperor's New Clothes," "The Princess and the Pea," "The Red Shoes," and "The Wild Swans." While many of Andersen's tales are stories of his own invention, "The Wild Swans" is among those whose roots are in Danish folklore.

The Wild Swans

A long time ago in a far-distant land there lived a king and his queen with their 11 sons and one daughter. The queen fell ill and died and the king soon remarried, as he could not look after his children all alone. But their stepmother was unkind and jealous of the children, especially the daughter, Eliza, and sent her to live in the country with a poor peasant and his wife. Meanwhile, the brothers were kept away from their schooling and their stepmother told the king untrue stories of their bad behavior, so he took no more interest in them.

One day the wicked queen lost her temper and cast a spell upon the young princes that turned them into swans. But her magic wasn't strong enough to prevent them becoming men again at night. Nor could she stop Eliza from returning home when she was 15 years old.

When the queen saw how beautiful the girl had become, she decided to make her ugly before the king could see her. She put three toads into the bath: the first to make Eliza stupid, the second to make her ugly, and the third to fill her heart with wickedness. But such was Eliza's purity and innocence that she could not be bewitched and the toads all turned into flowers. So the queen took hold of her and rubbed her skin with walnut juice and dirtied and tangled her hair until the king could not recognize his own daughter. The poor girl was so wretched and ashamed that she ran away.

Day after day, she walked through fields and forests, dreaming of her childhood, when she had lived such a wonderful life with her 11 loving brothers. She came upon a crystal-clear lake and was horrified when she saw her reflection, so she washed herself clean and braided her hair, restoring her beauty. Then she walked deeper into the forest, eating wild berries and fruits and drinking from bubbling springs.

The nights were very dark and Eliza felt lonely and forlorn. Then one morning she met an old woman gathering berries in a basket. Eliza asked her if she had seen 11 princes riding by.

"No, but I have seen 11 white swans, all with crowns upon their heads," replied the old lady.

"Please show me where you saw them." said Eliza, feeling sure she must be getting close to her brothers.

The old woman led her to the banks of a river flowing majestically toward the sea. Eliza followed it all the way to the seashore and there she sat and rested. She observed the rounded pebbles and smooth pieces of glass, all shaped by the unending motion of the waves.

"Just as the waves rise and fall, never tiring, so will I be unwearied in my search," she thought and she thanked the rolling waves for their inspiration.

As the sun was about to dip beneath the horizon, Eliza saw 11 swans, with crowns on their heads, flying toward the land. She was nervous with anticipation and hid behind some bushes as they landed on the shore. The sun disappeared and the swans flapped their wings and the feathers fell to the ground, revealing her long-lost brothers. She ran to greet them and they embraced her, and all shed tears of joy.

The brothers explained that they had to remain as swans during the hours of daylight and these few long summer's days were the only time when they could fly home from the distant land that had become their new home. For if they were still flying as the sun set, they would fall into the sea as men and be drowned.

The brothers wanted to take their sister with them to their fair country, but none of them had the strength to fly such a distance carrying her. So they gathered willow wands and rushes and, working through the night, they wove a large, strong net in which they could carry their sister, sharing the load between them.

When the sun rose, the brothers transformed into white swans and with their beaks they lifted the net with their beloved sister still sleeping soundly in its soft embrace. When she woke, she was amazed to see the towering white clouds around her and the ocean below gleaming like hammered pewter as the gentle summer breezes ruffled its surface.

As the swans were carrying their precious cargo, they flew more slowly than usual, and Eliza grew worried as the evening approached. She feared her brothers might tumble into the sea before they reached the land. But just as the sun was setting, they landed safely on a long, white strand and rested beneath the palms that lined the shore.

The next day the brothers flew on with their sister, over cedar forests and cities and palaces and up into the high, blue mountains. At last they landed in front of a cave and the brothers explained that this would be her home while they went about their business. On the floor of the cave there grew soft, green, creeping plants, like an embroidered carpet.

As another day drew to a close, Eliza fell asleep and dreamed that she was once more flying among the great white clouds, but this time the clouds were like fabulous palaces and out of one came a fairy queen who spoke to her, saying, "Dear Eliza, you have the power to release your brothers from the spell that binds them. But you must remember the lesson you learned from the sea, when you saw that hard rocks could be transformed into smooth pebbles simply by the endless perseverance of the waves. You must show such endurance and also courage in the task that lies ahead." The fairy held a stinging nettle in her hand and said, "You will gather great quantities of these leaves and crush them with your hands and feet to make a flax. Then you must spin and weave 11 coats. When these are thrown over the swans, the spell will be broken. But there is one thing you must remember: despite all the pain you will suffer from these nettles, you must never speak a word to anyone until your task is complete, or your brothers will perish."

With that, the fairy queen vanished into her palace of clouds.

Eliza woke to find herself alone in the cave. She remembered all that the fairy had told her and went into the forest and gathered many nettles. Her hands and arms were soon sore and blistered, but she persevered and crushed the hard stems and spun the flax.

When her brothers returned at the end of the day, they were shocked to see her sore limbs and couldn't understand why she would not speak. The youngest brother said, "This must be some magic task that our sister is performing to release us from the spell." Eliza nodded and the brothers understood.

The following day, they flew away and Eliza continued with her painful work. Suddenly she heard a huntsman's horn and in no time the hunting party arrived at the cave.

The leader of the group was a handsome young man who approached Eliza and said, "Sweet girl, how have you come to this place? I am king of this land but I have never heard tell of such a beauty as you. Pray tell me your name."

But Eliza shook her head and said nothing.

"Well, I cannot leave you here all alone," said the gentle king. "I will take you to my palace and there you can be safe and happy."

He lifted her onto his horse and led his hunting party through the forest to his castle, which stood in the middle of a beautiful city. Eliza still clung to her bundle of flax and the king could see how important it was to her. He was very kind to her: the women of the court dressed her in fine clothes and she was given as much food and drink as she wanted. She was even given her own chamber, where she could continue with her work, weaving the coats for her brothers.

The king was determined to make her his queen. His archbishop warned against it, saying that she must be a witch, as she never spoke and was preoccupied with weaving the strange garments, but the king overruled him and the marriage took place. Eliza was still unable to speak, but she was very happy, as the king was a good and gentle husband.

One night, however, she ran out of flax. She still had more coats to make for her brothers, so she crept out into the graveyard, among the ghosts, to gather more nettles. The archbishop saw her and the next morning he told the king what he had seen and said that this must be evidence of her witchcraft. Even the statues of the saints shook their heads in disagreement, but eventually the king was persuaded that his lovely wife must indeed be a witch.

Poor Eliza was cast into a cell, but was allowed to continue her painful task. She was condemned to be burned at the stake, but the day before her execution she heard a fluttering at the barred window of her cell—the swans had found her.

That night, her brothers in their human form hammered on the gates of the castle, demanding to be allowed in. But none of the royal servants were prepared to wake the king, who had shut himself in his bedchamber, still feeling great sorrow at his queen's fate.

As dawn broke, the brothers were transformed back into swans and flew over the castle walls. They saw their poor, silent sister being loaded onto a cart with her green coats around her, still weaving the eleventh and final garment. The mob crowded around the cart, jeering and howling, and they were about to drag the green coats away when the 11 swans flew down and surrounded Eliza.

The crowd moved back and fell silent at this remarkable spectacle. Eliza threw the coats, one by one, over the swans, and each in turn became the handsome prince he had always been, although the youngest kept a swan's wing, as his coat was not quite finished.

"Now, at last, I can speak and proclaim my innocence!" said Eliza and the people bowed before her. But she was so exhausted that she fainted into her brothers' arms.

The brothers told their story, and as they spoke, the branches that had been laid at the stake took root and formed beautiful flowering bushes. The king plucked the finest rose and placed it on the bosom of his beloved queen.

When she awoke from her faint, the church bells rang and amid a cheering crowd the royal party returned to the castle and this kingdom was the happiest in all the land.

Norway: Asbjørnsen and Moe

Norwegian folktale collectors Asbjørnsen and Moe collected various tales from different parts of Norway. Adopting an approach similar to that of the Grimm brothers, they opted to tell the tales using simple language in place of dialect, while retaining the national uniqueness of the tales. This helped form the basis for the Norwegian language as it is known today. Their first collection of tales, *Norske Folkeeventyr* (Norwegian Folk Tales), was published in 1841 to great acclaim. A further edition, containing additional stories, published in 1852, proved to be equally successful.

Between 1845 and 1848 Asbjørnsen published another collection of tales, *Norwegian Fairy Tales and Folk Legends.* George Dasent, a translator of folk tales and scholar of Norse studies, translated the first volume into English as *East of the Sun and West of the Moon.*

Asbjørnsen and Moe's work is regarded as part of Norway's national heritage and remains popular today. "The Three Billy Goats Gruff" and "East of the Sun, West of the Moon" are two of the best-known tales from the collection. Tales similar to "The Three Billy Goats Gruff" appear in Germany and Poland.

The Three Billy Goats Gruff

Once upon a time there were three billy goat brothers called Gruff: the smallest goat, the middle goat, and the biggest goat.

One day they had eaten all the grass in their valley, so they decided to cross the bridge over the waterfall and eat the grass on the hillside.

Under the bridge there lived an ugly troll, with eyes that gleamed in the dark and teeth as sharp as razors, waiting to eat any unwary travelers who crossed the bridge.

The first, smallest billy goat set off across the bridge. "Clip, clop! Clip, clop!" went his hooves on the old wooden bridge.

"Who's that crossing my bridge?" said the nasty troll.

"It is only me, the smallest Billy Goat Gruff, and I am going to eat the grass on the hillside," said the smallest goat in a very small voice.

"Well, I am going to eat *you* for my dinner!" said the troll.

"No, no! Why don't you wait for my brother? He's much fatter than me," said the youngest Billy Goat Gruff.

"If you say so," said the troll. "Away with you!"

And the little goat ran quickly up the hill.

A few minutes later the second Billy Goat Gruff came across the bridge. "Clip, clop! Clip, clop!" went his hooves on the planks of the bridge.

"Who's that crossing my bridge?" said the wicked troll.

"It's only me, the second Billy Goat Gruff, and I'm going to join my little brother on the hillside," said the second goat.

"Oh no, you're not!" said the troll. "I'm going to eat you for my dinner!"

"Please don't eat me. If you wait just a minute more then you can eat my big, fat brother instead," said the second goat.

"Very well!" said the troll. "Away you go!"

And the second goat scampered up the hill to join his brother.

Before long the oldest, biggest Billy Goat Gruff came across the bridge.

"Clip, clop! Clip, clop!" went his hooves and the bridge shook under his weight.

"Who's that crossing my bridge?" said the hungry troll.

"It is I, the big Billy Goat Gruff!" said the oldest goat, in a voice every bit as deep as the troll's.

"Now I'm going to eat you for my dinner!" said the troll, and he came out from under the bridge.

"Well, come on then," said the goat, "I am going to spear your eyes and crush your bones!"

And that is what he did: he thrust his horns into the troll's eyes and rolled on his body to break his bones. Then he threw the troll into the waterfall and went to join his brothers on the hillside. There they ate the green, green grass and became very fat.

And that was the end of that.

Russia: Aleksandr Afanasyev

Russian folklorist and collector of fairy tales Aleksandr Afanasyev published *Narodnye russkie skazki* (*Russian Fairy Tales*) in eight volumes between 1855 and 1863. Comprising 600 tales from various regions of Russia, it is one of the world's largest collections of folktales gathered by a single collector. Popular tales from the collection include "Baba Yaga and Vasilissa the Beautiful" and "The Frog Tsarevna." Director Aleksandr Rou's 1939 film *Vailisa Prekrasnaya* is based on "The Frog Tsarevna." Afanasyev's collections influenced many writers and composers and are still in print today in numerous languages.

Baba Yaga and Vasilissa the Beautiful

Many years ago, in the days when dark forests hid evil beings and fairies danced among the flowers, there lived a merchant and his wife. They had one daughter, who was called Vasilissa the Beautiful.

For several years the little family lived happily together, but one bitter winter the merchant's wife became ill. Pale and thin, she lay on her deathbed. Vasilissa held her mother's cold hand and was filled with sorrow. Her mother gave her a little wooden doll and with her dying breath, she told her that if she gave the doll a little to eat and drink, it would always help her.

The merchant and Vasilissa

mourned their loss for many months, and eventually the merchant felt so alone that he took another wife. He hoped that this widow would be a good mother to Vasilissa, as she already had two daughters of her own. But the stepmother and her daughters were envious of Vasilissa's beauty and they gave her all the arduous outdoor work in the hope that it would spoil her complexion and her fine figure. But with the help of her little doll, Vasilissa was able to complete all her tasks with ease and grew ever more beautiful.

After a few years, it happened that the merchant had to go far away on a trading mission and he didn't know when he would return. This meant there was little for the stepmother and the girls to live on, so they sold the house and moved to a little cabin on the edge of the forest. This was a forest of fearful reputation, for in it lived Baba Yaga, a wicked hag who ate people as others might eat pork or chicken.

Late one evening, as they sat around sewing and knitting, the stepmother said, "We cannot burn more oil or candles. I must save the last one that we have." And she snuffed out the last remaining candle. "Now, Vasilissa, you must go to Baba Yaga and bring back some light."

Vasilissa entered the dark, forbidding forest and was very afraid. But she fed her doll with a crumb of bread and a drop of water, and the doll reassured her, saying, "Fear not, my dear, I will guide you and protect you." So Vasilissa walked and walked all the long, dark night, directed by the doll.

As the gray light of dawn peered through the dense treetops, Vasilissa heard the thunder of hooves, and a great white stallion passed her by, its rider dressed all in white. Not long afterward, she felt the trembling of the earth as a great red horse came galloping from the east. This rider was clothed in a flowing red cape. As he passed, the first rays of the rising sun shot through the branches of the trees and Vasilissa was encouraged by the light of day to continue her journey. She walked all day, pausing only to drink from the clear, sparkling streams that flowed through the forest.

As evening approached, Vasilissa came upon Baba Yaga's hut. It stood on chicken legs and was surrounded by a fence of human bones which were crowned with the skulls of her victims.

Vasilissa was frozen with fear, and hardly glanced round as a black horse galloped by, its rider shrouded in black robes.

Night fell, and there came a terrible rumbling from the depths of the forest. The eye sockets of the skulls began to glow and a harsh, grating voice cried, "I smell a human! Who are you? Speak up, child!"

Baba Yaga appeared riding in her iron mortar.

Vasilissa could hardly speak, but managed to say, "Vasilissa is my name. My stepmother has sent me to beg you for some light."

"I have heard of you," said Baba Yaga. "You look like a tasty meal to me. But if you work well for me, perhaps I will spare you."

With that, the witch opened the latch of the gate, which was made of human teeth, and they entered the hut. Vasilissa had to lay food and drink before Baba Yaga, and the old hag seemed to have a huge appetite, eating bread and meat and drinking mead and wine far into the night. When the old woman had eaten her fill, she said, "Tomorrow, after I have left, you must clean the house and sweep the yard, wash the linen and cook the supper, and pick out the mildewed grains from the wheat. If these tasks aren't completed by the time I return, I shall have you for my supper."

Vasilissa was sent to bed with just a crust of bread and a cup of water, which she shared with her doll.

In the morning, she awoke early, wondering where to start on the long list of tasks, but to her delight she found the little doll had already completed them; all she had to do was cook the supper.

Early that morning, the white horseman rode by the hut, and as the sun rose, so came the great red stallion. As dusk was falling, the black horse thundered into the dark depths of the forest.

The eyes of the skulls were glowing in the darkness as Baba Yaga returned to the hut in her mortar. The old hag was disappointed when she saw that Vasilissa had completed all her work, as she had been hoping to make a tasty meal of the girl. However, she stuck by her word and said, "Faithful servants, grind my wheat!" and three pairs of hands appeared out of thin air and proceeded to carry away the wheat.

Baba Yaga ate her supper and told Vasilissa that she must do the same work the next day and also clean a sackful of poppy seeds that had been mixed with dirt.

The next day passed much as the first and Vasilissa, with the help of her doll, finished all that the hag had asked her to do. In the evening the old witch came back, and, satisfied that all was done, commanded the three pairs of hands to take away the poppy seeds and press them for oil.

She sat down to her supper and asked Vasilissa if she had anything to say.

Timidly, the girl said, "Well, I was wondering, who are the horsemen who ride past every day?"

"The white stallion is the brightness of my dawn. The red horseman is the sunshine of my day, and the black horse is the darkness of the night. All these are my faithful servants."

Vasilissa decided not to ask about the mysterious hands that materialized every evening, as she did not want to provoke the hag with any more questions.

Instead, Baba Yaga said, "Now I have a question for you. How is it you manage to finish your work every day?"

Vasilissa did not want to betray her little doll, so she said, "It is my mother's blessing that helps me to work so hard."

"I thought some such thing!" said Baba Yaga, "You will have to leave me now, as I cannot have any blessings in this house!"

The hag pushed Vasilissa out of the door, snatched up one of the skulls with the glowing eyes and put it on a stick for her to carry, saying, "Here is the light for your stepmother and her daughters. That is what you came here for, but it may bring them no joy."

And with that the old hag vanished back into her hut, the gate of human teeth locked tightly behind her.

Vasilissa walked through the dark forest all night and all the next day. As darkness fell, she approached her stepmother's cabin

There was still no light at the window, and as soon as Vasilissa opened the door, her stepmother grabbed the glowing skull from her. She set it upon a candlestick and called her daughters to come and see it. But the skull's eyes glimmered like red-hot coals and followed them around the room, all the while growing larger and hotter and brighter, until all that was left of the stepmother and her daughters was three piles of ash on the floor. Only Vasilissa was left unharmed. She dug a hole in the garden and buried the skull, then left the forest behind her to find lodging in the town that she had left so long ago.

Vasilissa found lodging with a kindly woman who made her living spinning flax. She worked with her and soon she was even more skilled than her mistress. The cloth she made was so fine and soft and beautiful that the old lady decided to take it to the Tsar as a gift. He was most impressed and asked his tailor to make some shirts from the cloth, but he declined, saying that the cloth was too fine and delicate for him to handle.

The Tsar recalled the old lady, and she in turn asked Vasilissa to come and make shirts for the Tsar. Over the weeks that followed, the Tsar became captivated by Vasilissa and asked her to become his wife. And so Vasilissa the Beautiful became the new Tsarina, and when Vasilissa's father finally returned from his travels, he was invited to stay in the royal palace, along with the kindly woman who had first brought Vasilissa to the attention of the Tsar.

Vasilissa kept her secret helper, the little wooden doll, in her pocket until the day she died.

Britain: Lang and Jacobs

English translations of fairy tales from France and Germany proved popular in England and the late 1800s saw the publication of fairy tales by collectors such as Andrew Lang and Joseph Jacobs. Andrew

Lang collected, translated, and retold fairy tales from various nations. In many instances, it was the first time the tale had appeared in the English language. The first of his "rainbow" series of books was published in 1897 (*The Pink Fairy Book*) and the last (*The Lilac Fairy Book*) in 1910. Joseph Jacobs published his collections of English, Celtic, and Indian tales from 1892 to 1916. The work of both remains popular today.

Further information on fairytale collectors and authors mentioned here, including brief biographies and relevant publications, is provided under individual entries in the main A–Z listings.

R

Rå

(Also *rådande.*) Wardens of the Earth, *rå* are a type of *löfjerskor*, or tree spirit in the folklore of Sweden. They dwelled in trees known as *boträd*, "abode" or "habitation" trees, and were their guardian spirits. They were generally invisible to humans, but on fine days they were said to hang their washing to dry in the branches of the tree and this took on the appearance of cobwebs. *Rå* rewarded those who cared for their trees with gifts.

Rådande

See **Rå**.

Ralph of Coggeshall

(Active thirteenth century)

Born in the late twelfth century, Ralph of Coggeshall was a monk, and the chronicler at the abbey of Coggeshall in Essex, England. He became abbot in 1207. The abbey already had a *Chronicon Anglicanum*, begun in 1066, and Ralph continued the work from 1187 to 1224. In it he recorded local and national historical events, gave his opinion on the monarchy, and related anecdotes among other things. The writings also contain descriptions of strange happenings and accounts concerning the fairy realm, such as the **green children** and **Malekin**. The manuscript of the *Chronicon Anglicanum* is held at the British Library in London. Ralph of Coggeshall's writings were published in *Radulphi Nigri chronicon ab initio mundi ad A.D 1199* (1851) and *Radulphi de Coggeshall chronicon Anglicanum* (1875)

Raven

Featuring in the fairy lore, myths and legends of many cultures around the world, ravens are often portrayed as shapeshifting beings, representing a bridge between the mortal and otherworldly realms. As carrion birds that feed on the flesh of dead animals, they are frequently seen as gatekeepers between life and death.

In the mythology of the Native American tribes of the northern United States and Canada, commonly known as the First Nation myths of the Pacific Northwest, the raven often appears as both creator—bringing the sun, moon, stars, fresh water, and fire to the Earth—and trickster.

The *kutkh* raven spirit plays a similar role in the folklore of Siberia. In Scandinavian lore, **Odin**, ruler of the Norse Aesir gods of Asgard, had two ravens named Huginn and Muninn, or Thought and Memory. Each day he sent them forth to gather information from the mortal realm of Midgard, and each night they returned to perch on his shoulder and tell of all they had seen.

In Celtic mythology **Nenem, Morrigu**, and **Macha**, three aspects of the shapeshifting war goddess ***Badb***, assumed the form of ravens, croaking encouragement to the champion **Cuchulainn** on the battlefield and perching on his shoulder when he was finally defeated.

In Welsh mythology the *Mabinogion*, a collection of ancient legends, tells of the heroes **Branwen**, "white or sacred raven," and **Bran the Blessèd**, "raven" or "crow." Bran's head is said to be buried beneath the Tower of London, and in British folklore it is said that the country will not fall as long as ravens live in the Tower.

Shapeshifting or transformation is involved in the majority of European and Celtic raven stories. Two of the best known are from the collection made by the Brothers **Grimm**, *Children's and Household Tales* (1812). The first is "The Raven."

Once there was a queen who had a small daughter who could be precocious and disobedient. One day she lost her patience and when she opened a window and saw ravens flying about, she said to the child, "I wish you were a raven and would fly away and leave me in peace!"

As quick as a flash, the child was transformed into a glossy black raven and flew out of the window into the deep, dark forest.

For many years the king and queen heard nothing of their

daughter. Time passed until one day a young man who was traveling through the forest heard the cry of a raven and it was so beguiling he followed the sound until he drew close to the mournful bird.

"I am really a princess by birth," said the sorrowful raven, "but you can set me free, if you do exactly as I tell you."

"I will be your obedient servant. Tell me what I must do," replied the handsome youth.

"You must go deeper into the forest until you find a little house. Inside you will be greeted by an old woman, who will offer you food and drink, but you must refuse, otherwise you will fall asleep and then you cannot set me free. Behind the house is a great heap of tanned leather and that is where you must await my arrival. I will come every day, for three days if necessary, always at two o'clock in the afternoon, in a horse-drawn carriage. But remember, if you are not awake, you cannot set me free."

"I will not sleep, I promise," said the young man. He rode deeper into the forest and eventually came across the little house, just as the raven princess had said.

As he entered the dwelling, the old lady said, "How tired you look. You must eat and drink with me."

"I really must not, although it is true that I am weary, and hungry and thirsty," said the young man. He was determined to keep his word to the raven, but the old lady pestered him until he allowed himself just a sip of water.

Before two o'clock he went into the garden to wait for the raven. He sat on the heap of leather and as he rested, his weariness got the better of him and he fell into a deep sleep.

On the stroke of two, the raven princess came driving up in a black carriage drawn by four white horses. She was already grieving, as she was sure the young man would be asleep. Finding that he was, she stepped down from the carriage and tried to shake him awake, but nothing would rouse him from his deep slumber. She left in despair.

The next day about noon the old woman once more tried to make the young man eat and drink.

"You are becoming thinner and thinner. Soon you will die," she told him. In the end she persuaded him to take just one drink.

Once more he went to wait for the raven on the pile of hides and once more he was sound asleep when she came riding up in her carriage, drawn this time by four brown horses. Try as she might, she could not wake him and had no choice but to drive her team of horses back into the forest.

The next morning the old lady said to the young man, "Tell me why you will not eat or drink. I hate to see you wasting away."

"I made a promise to a raven princess so that I may free her from the spell that binds her," he explained.

"But if you do not eat or drink, you will die before you can free her," said the old woman.

She brought him food and wine, and he was persuaded by her argument and ate and drank. By two o'clock, of course he was sound asleep, so when a black coach drawn by four black horses rattled into the garden, it was once more impossible for the raven princess to rouse him. She was distraught, but there was still one last opportunity for him to free her. Beside him she laid a loaf of bread, a piece of meat, and a bottle of wine, all of which had magical properties and would never grow less, no matter how often they were consumed. Then she took a gold ring from her finger that had her name engraved upon it and placed it on the sleeping man's finger. Finally, she wrote a letter telling him about the magical food and wine and saying that he could no longer free her at this place, but if he still wanted to do so he might try again at the golden castle of Stromberg. Then she drove her horses off to the golden castle.

When the young man awoke, he was saddened to realize that he had missed his last chance to free the raven from her bond. Then he saw the food and drink and read the letter. He determined to find the golden castle of Stromberg, but didn't know where it was. He walked all day until he could walk no more, then he lay down to sleep.

The next day he walked on again until he heard a great howling and crying. He saw a light glowing in the dusk and he went toward it. It came from a lamp shining through the window of a large house, and at the table on which it stood there was a giant.

Seeing the young man, he said, "At last I can eat—I shall devour you for my supper!"

"I'd rather you did not," said the youth. "If you are really hungry, I can provide you with more than enough bread, meat, and wine to satisfy your needs."

"If that is true, then I will spare your life," said the giant.

They sat at the table and the giant ate all he could manage and still there was more.

"I am well pleased," he said. "What can I do for you in return?"

"Can you tell me where to find the golden castle of Stromberg?" asked the young man.

"Let us study my maps," said the giant, drawing a great sheaf of parchments from a cupboard.

The pair spread the finely drawn documents on the table and looked closely at them, but they could find no sign of the castle.

The giant said, "If you wait here for a day or two, my brother will be home and he has his own collection of maps."

The brother duly arrived and produced some very ancient maps. Eventually they found the golden castle, but it was many miles distant.

"Don't worry," said the giant, "I will put on my seven-league boots and carry you most of the way."

And so he did, leaving the young man to complete just the last few miles alone.

When he came to the castle, which stood on a glass mountain, he saw the raven princess in her carriage entering the great golden gates. He rejoiced and wanted to climb up to her, but he could not, for the glass slopes of the mountain were too slippery. He decided to wait until he saw her come out again. But every day for a year he saw her in her carriage but was unable to reach her.

One day he saw three vagabonds fighting with each other, and he shouted at them to stop. They paused when they heard him, but soon continued to beat each other. He went up to them and asked what they were fighting about. One said he had found a stick that would open any door, the second had a cloak that would make him invisible, and the third had a horse that could be ridden anywhere, even up the glass mountain. But they could not decide how to divide up these gifts.

The young man said, "I have something of great value that I could give you in exchange for these three things. But first I must see that you are telling the truth." So he mounted the horse, grasped the stick and threw the cloak around himself. Of course, he was now invisible, so he gave the bonds some blows and cried, "That will teach you a lesson, you thieving rascals!"

Immediately he rode up the glass mountain.

When he reached the golden gates, they were firmly shut, but he struck them with the stick and obediently they opened before him. He rode in and ascended a great stairway.

Eventually he found the raven princess sitting with a glass of wine on a table in front of her. Of course she could not see him, so he removed the ring from his finger and dropped it in the glass. As it became visible, she recognized it and cried, "That is my ring! Where is my savior?"

The young man threw off his cloak and the princess ran to him, freed from the spell. They were soon married and lived a long and happy life in the golden castle of Stromberg.

The second of the raven tales to appear in the Brothers Grimm collection, "The Seven Ravens," concerns the transformation of humans into ravens and the travails of another human to restore them to their original form. Similar tales from other cultures include the Norwegian "Twelve Wild Ducks," the North African "Udea and her Seven Brothers," and the Russian "The Magic Swan Geese." The tale of "The Seven Ravens" runs as follows.

A man and his wife had seven sons and although they were quite happy, they both longed for a daughter. Eventually their wish was granted and a daughter was born. Unfortunately she was weak and sickly and the father was afraid she might die. He knew she might not go to heaven if she died without baptism, so he sent his sons to the well to collect a jug of water for the ritual. But the sons all wanted to be the first to fill the jug and as they struggled with one another, the jug was dropped into the well.

The sons were afraid to go back home to face their parents, and their father cursed them for not bringing the water, saying, "I wish those wicked boys would all turn into ravens!"

Even as he spoke, seven black ravens flew up from the well, and he at once regretted losing his temper.

The years went by and the little daughter grew stronger and more beautiful, and had no idea that she had any brothers. Then one day she was in the village and overheard some old women gossiping, saying, "She may be beautiful, but it's her fault her brothers are cursed forever!"

The girl asked her parents what had happened and they told her she wasn't to blame. Nevertheless, she determined to find her brothers. So her parents gave her one of their wedding rings to remember them by and a loaf of bread, a jug of water, and a little chair upon which she might rest.

For months the girl walked through forests and fields and eventually she came to the end of the world. It was very hot there and she was afraid of the raging sun, so she ran to the other end of the world, but the moon was very cold there and when it said, "I can smell human flesh!" she was frightened and took refuge among the stars. They were good to her and the morning star gave her a chicken bone, saying, "You'll need this to open the door to the glass mountain where your brothers live."

The girl wrapped the bone in a cloth and walked on until she came to the glass mountain, but she couldn't open the door that led into it. She unwrapped the cloth, but realized she must have dropped the chicken bone, for it was nowhere to be seen. Desperate to open the door, she remembered one of the stars had said that a severed finger could be used instead of the chicken bone, so she summoned up all her courage, took the bread knife and cut off her little finger. Immediately she was able to open the door.

Inside a dwarf took her to a dining room where a table had been laid with seven plates of food and seven cups of wine. "Soon your brothers will return," he said, leaving her alone in the room.

She ate a little and drank a little from each of the seven plates and cups before dropping her parents' ring into the last cup.

Then she heard a great whirring of wings and hid behind the door. Seven ravens flew in and took their places at the table.

"Who has been eating from my plate?" cried one.

"And who has been drinking from my cup?" shouted another.

And then the seventh brother found the ring and recognized it at once.

"Can it be that our sister is here?" he said.

The girl came out from behind the door and in an instant the ravens were all restored to their human form. They embraced their long-lost sister and all returned home to live for many joyous years with their parents.

Raviyoyla

A ***vila***, a forest-dwelling nymph, in Serbian folklore, Raviyoyla was a nature spirit who could take the form of a beautiful female. She possessed great knowledge of the healing properties of the flowers, herbs, and berries of the forest.

She featured in a tale concerning the Serbian hero Prince Marko, who according to one tradition was the son of a *vila* and a *zmay*, or dragon. When Raviyoyla accidently wounded Prince Marko's closest kinsman, Milosh, she was able to nurse him back to health using her knowledge of nature.

Rawhead and Bloody Bones

A nursery **bogie** in English folklore, said to live in the cupboard under the stairs. Those brave or foolhardy enough to sneak a peek through the keyhole might catch a glimpse of the dreadful creature squatting on a pile of the bones of naughty children, blood running down his face. He punished children who lied and said bad words—or peeped into his cupboard.

In *Some Thoughts on Education* (1693), John Locke writes:

> *. . . whilst [the child] is young be sure to preserve his tender mind from all impressions and notions of Spirits and Goblins, or any fearful apprehensions in the dark.*

This he will be in danger of from the indiscretion of servants, whose usual method is to awe children, and keep them in subjection, by telling them of Raw-head and Bloody-Bones . . . something terrible and hurtful, which they have reason to be afraid of when alone, especially in the dark . . . such bugbear thoughts . . . sink deep.

In other accounts, particularly in Yorkshire and Lancashire, Rawhead is described as a pond-dwelling water spirit who lies in wait to drag children down into the watery depths. In this guise, he is similar to **Jenny Greenteeth**, **Grindylow**, and **Peg Powler**.

Red Dwarf

See **Nain Rouge**.

Redcaps

Malevolent **goblins** from the Anglo-Scottish border, so-called because they dyed their hats with blood. They were said to haunt ruined castles that had been the site of evil doings. According to popular tradition, the foundation stone of the old castles on the Borders were bathed in blood, which goes some way to account for the bloodthirsty nature of the redcaps. William Henderson, in *Notes on the Folklore of the Northern Counties of England and the Borders* (1866), describes the redcap as cruel and malignant, appearing as a "short, thicket old man, with long prominent teeth, skinny fingers armed with talons like eagles, large eyes of a fiery-red colour, grisly hair streaming down his shoulders, iron boots, a pikestaff in his left hand and a red cap on his head." The sign of the cross was said to keep these malicious creatures at bay.

Henderson identifies Dutch redcaps as altogether different in nature from their Anglo-Scottish counterparts. These are helpful spirits akin to the household **brownie**, who carry out tasks around the home, mill, or farmstead. (*See* ***Kaboutermannekin***.)

Rhys, Sir John *(1840–1915)*

A Celtic scholar born in Wales, Rhys studied there and qualified as a teacher. In 1865 he obtained a scholarship at Jesus College, Oxford, where he studied classics. His main interest was Celtic philology (comparative and historical linguistics), which led him to the study of Celtic, especially Welsh, folklore. He traveled extensively throughout Europe, Britain, and Ireland, recording Celtic inscriptions, particularly those in the ancient script of Ogham. Among his many published books, one of note is *Celtic Folklore: Welsh and Manx* (1901).

River Mumma

A water spirit from Jamaican folk tradition who lives in the depths of rivers. The fish are her children. She emerges from the waters from time to time and sits on a rock to comb her long, black hair, but do not meet her eyes or even glance at her, for it is said that misfortune will befall all those who make contact with the River Mumma.

Roane

Fairy seal people of Scotland. Their name derives from the Gaelic name for "seal." Like the **selkies** of Orkney and Shetland, they were believed to be people in the form of seals, who occasionally came ashore, shed their skins, and resumed human form.

An account in Grant Stewart's *The Popular Superstitions and Festive Amusements of the Highlanders of Scotland* (1823) tells of the peaceful nature of the roane and their lack of animosity toward the humans who hunted them.

When a seal-hunter who lived near John O'Groats lost his knife while trying to kill a large bull seal, a stranger on horseback arrived at the door of his cottage that night, asking him to accompany him.

The two rode to a cliff, whence the stranger plunged them down beneath the waves to a cave, where there were many seal people. The stranger himself resumed the form of a seal, and the seal-catcher felt himself transformed too.

The seal people seemed very sad, and when the seal guide produced the knife that had been lost earlier that day, the seal-catcher felt obliged to admit it was his, despite feeling very uncomfortable in the knowledge that he had probably used it to kill a good many of his host's friends.

Rather than seeking retribution, however, the seal guide led the hunter to the large bull seal he had wounded earlier that day. Following the roane's instructions, he succeeded in healing the seal and was transported home unharmed on the promise that he would never kill a seal again. He readily agreed and was rewarded with a gift of money worth many sealskins.

Robin Goodfellow

A mischievous **hobgoblin** of English folklore, best known as the merry prankster **Puck** in Shakespeare's *A Midsummer Night's Dream*—the epitome of a roguish yet generally benevolent fairy. The names "Puck" and "Robin Goodfellow" are now often used interchangeably.

Traditions connected with Robin Goodfellow as a tricksy but ultimately kind-hearted spirit predate Shakespeare. According to James O. Halliwell-Phillipps in *Illustrations of the Fairy Mythology of A Midsummer Night's Dream* (1845) the thirteenth-century chronicler **Gervase of Tilbury** described the pranks of two kinds of **goblin** in England, Portuni and Grout which are similar to those of Shakespeare's Puck. A thirteenth-century manuscript preserved in the Bodleian Library of Oxford apparently introduced Robin Goodfellow both in name and action in those early times:

Once Robinet was in a certain house in which soldiers were resting for the night, and after having made a great clamour during the better part of the night to their no small annoyance, he was suddenly quiet. Then said the soldiers to each other, "Let us now sleep, for Robinet himself is asleep." To which Robinet made reply, "I am not asleep, but am resting, in order to shout louder after." And the soldiers said, "It seems then we shall have no sleep tonight."

The broadside ballad *Robin Goodfellow; his mad prankes and many jests, full of honest mirth, and is a fit medicine for melancholy* (*c.*1628), contains much of the popular folklore concerning Robin Goodfellow. In it, he is portrayed as a half-fairy whose father was a "hee-fayrie; whether he was their king or no I know not, but surely he had great government and command in their country, as you shall heare," and his mother, a "proper, young wench." The fairy father provided her with rich clothes, food, and wine, and "All praysed this honest fayry for his care, and the child for his beauty, and the mother for a happy woman." It is often speculated that the "fairy father" is **Oberon**.

Even as a child, Robin Goodfellow was full of mischief. When he was six, his mother became so angered by his tricks that he ran away. He was taken in by a kindly tailor and worked for a time with him, but even he tired of his pranks, and Robin Goodfellow left again on his travels. He fell asleep and dreamed of fairies. When he awoke, he found a scroll written in gold that gave him magical powers, especially to transform himself to any shape, "to horse, to hog, to dog, to ape." These powers were to be used to help the good and hinder the bad. Robin Goodfellow soon found he did indeed have these powers and embarked on his career as a hobgoblin. Several short chapters tell of his many pranks, usually ending with his characteristic "Ho! Ho! Ho!" Eventually, Robin Goodfellow is taken to "Fayry Land, where I thinke they yet remain."

Seventeenth-century English literature provides many examples of Robin Goodfellow's antics. In Samuel Rowland's *More Knaves Yet?* (1613), he displays the typical traits of a household **brownie**, cleaning the kitchen at night in return for a bowl of cream or cheese, while unable to resist playfully pinching the "lazy queane" as she slumbers:

Amongst the rest, was a good fellow devill,
So called in kindness, cause he did no evill,
Knowne by the name of Robin (as we heare)
And that his eyes as big as sawcers were,
Who came a nights, and would make kitchins cleane
And in the bed bepinch a lazie queane.

Was much in Milles about the
grinding Meale,
(And sure I take it, taught the Miller
steale,)
Amongst the creame bowles, and
milke pans would be,
And with the country wenches, who
but hee.
To wash their Dishes for some fresh
cheese hier:
Or set their Pots and Kettles about
the fier.

A poem in Carew Hazlitt's *Fairy Tales, Legends and Romances Illustrating Shakespeare* (1875) often attributed to Ben Jonson touches on many of the shapeshifting exploits typically associated with Robin Goodfellow, particularly a delight in leading night wanderers to stray from the path into woods and bogs:

If any wanderers I meet,
That from their night-sport do
trudge home,
With counterfeiting voice I greet,
And cause them on with me to roam;
Through woods, through lakes,
Through bogs, through brakes,
O'er bush and brier, with them I go,
I call upon
Them to come on,
And wend me laughing, ho, ho, ho!

Sometimes I meet them like a man,
Sometimes an ox, sometimes, a hound;
And to a horse I turn me can,
To trip and trot about them round;
But if, to ride,
My back they stride,
More swift than wind away I go;
O'er hedge and lands,
Through pools and ponds,
I whinny laughing, ho, ho, ho!

See also **Gull**.

RUMPELSTILTSKIN

Also *Rumpelstilzchen* in the German spelling. One of the best-known stories collected by the Brothers **Grimm** and published in the 1812 edition of *Children's and Household Tales.* The meaning of the name in German is literally "Little Rattle Stilt." The same basic character is found in many other countries and cultures, for example **Tom Tit Tot** in England, **Whuppity Stoorie** in Scotland, **Peerie Fool** in Orkney, **Terrytop** in Cornwall, Gilitrutt in Iceland, Joaidane in Arabic, Khlamushka in Russia, Rampelnik in the Czech Republic, Martinko Klingáč in Slovakia, Ruidoquedito in South America, Pancimanci in

Hungary, Cvilidreta in Serbia and Croatia, Tremotino in Italy, Ootz-li Gootz-li in Israel, Daiku to Oniroku in Japan, and Myrmidon or Perlimpinpin, at least, in France. The plot runs as follows.

Once upon a time there was a poor miller who paid his taxes once a year to his young king in the form of a single bag of flour. On one occasion the king said, "Hello, there, old miller. Is this paltry gray bag all you can offer your master?"

The miller felt ashamed and in order to impress the king he said, "I am blessed with a beautiful daughter, your Highness, and she has some wondrous skills."

"Really?" said the king, "Tell me more of this fair maiden."

"She has the power to spin golden thread from straw," blurted out the miller.

"I must see this for myself," said the king. "Bring her to me so that she can demonstrate this amazing skill."

So the young woman was brought to the palace and shut in a small tower room with a spinning wheel and a mass of straw.

"You shall stay here all night," said the king, "and by morning I expect to find the room filled with golden thread, otherwise you will be severely punished."

The poor girl was greatly distressed and tears flowed down her cheeks. Then there was a sudden explosive crack as a small, high window flew open and with a rattle and a thump there appeared before her a little impish man, with a wizened face and very bright eyes, dressed in dark clothes and a red hat.

"What ails you, fair maid?" he asked.

"Alas," sobbed the girl, "I have to spin all this straw into gold and I have no idea how to do it."

"Fear not," said the mannikin, "I can complete this task, but you will have to give me a reward."

"I will pay you with my emerald necklace," said the miller's daughter.

The strange little fellow worked quickly, his gnarled fingers deftly spinning the wheel and transforming the straw into reels of golden thread. Within the hour all the straw was gone. Willingly, the girl gave him her beautiful necklace and with a rattle and a bang he vanished through the window into the darkness of the night.

At the break of day the door swung open and the young king stepped into the room. He stood transfixed at the sight of the reels of gold. He had not expected the girl to succeed. But his greed was not yet satisfied and he ordered his serfs to gather even more straw and fill a larger room. He gave the girl food and drink, but in the evening he locked her in the room with the straw and the spinning wheel and once again demanded that she should spin it all into reels of gold.

The miller's daughter was at a loss, as she did not know how to summon her little helper, but soon there was a crack and a rattle and the little man appeared once again.

"I can see I have a lot of work to do tonight," he said. "But how will you pay me?"

"Will you accept my diamond ring?" the girl asked. "It is all I have left."

"Very well," the little man replied and set to his task. This time it took him more than two hours, but the result was more than double the previous night's work. Once he had finished, the girl reluctantly removed her ring from her slender finger and handed it to him. Then with a rattle and a bang he was gone into the night.

Morning came and the heavy, wooden door swung open. As the king stood there, the sun's rays reflected the golden light from the reels of thread, filling the whole room with a wondrous glow. But the king's greed was still not satisfied and he bid his serfs remove the furniture from his great banqueting hall and gather huge quantities of straw to fill every corner. He promised the miller's daughter that if she succeeded in spinning all this into gold, he would marry her and make her his queen, but if she failed, she would be locked in a dungeon for the rest of her life.

In the twilight of the evening the maiden was left locked in the great hall with only the spinning wheel and the piles of straw for company. As darkness fell, there was a bang as a window opened, and with a thump and a rattle, there stood the little old mannikin.

"Well," he said, "once more I can help you, but what can you offer me as a reward?"

"I have given you everything of value that I own," said the miller's daughter. "But I must complete this night's work or the king will have me thrown into a dungeon. If I succeed, however, he will marry me and make me his queen."

The little man scratched his bristly chin and thought for a minute or two, then he said, "Very well, I will complete the task, but when the king marries you, you must promise to give me your first-born child."

This seemed a long way in the future, so the miller's daughter hardly hesitated before agreeing to the bargain.

Once more the spinning wheel whirled and the reels of golden thread multiplied, and by midnight all the straw was gone. "Don't forget our bargain," the little man said, and with a rattle and a bang he was gone too.

When the king appeared in the morning, his craving for gold was finally satisfied and he said, "You have fulfilled my every wish, and though you are but a poor miller's daughter, I will keep to my word and you shall be my queen."

They had a magnificent wedding and the new queen was so happy she forgot all about the mannikin and her promise to him. Before a year was over, she had given birth to a beautiful child.

Within a few more weeks, however, the bright-eyed little man appeared in the nursery and said to her, "Now you must keep your promise and give me your child."

The queen was horrified and burst into tears, crying, "I will give you all the riches in the kingdom if you will allow me to keep my baby."

"I have no need of riches. You must keep to our bargain and give what you promised!" insisted the little man.

Distraught, the queen pleaded with him further.

Finally he said, "Very well, I will give you one more chance. You have three days to find out my name. If you succeed then you shall keep your child."

The queen had no choice but to agree.

She immediately sent her most faithful servants around the city to find as many names as they could. When the mannikin appeared the next morning, she said, "Is your name Caspar, or Benjamin, or Ruben, or Joseph, or James?"

"No, no, no!"

The queen reeled off a further 40 or 50 names.

The impish fellow grinned and laughed, "No, no, and again no!"

The following day the queen and her servants went to every byway and hamlet in the kingdom in search of unusual names, and when the little demon—as the queen now thought of him— reappeared, she tried such outlandish names as Shortribs, Redcap, Sheepshanks,

Laceleg, Stumpy, Chopsticks, Big Ears, and even Man-of-the-Moon. But all were to no avail and the mannikin left, reminding her that she had only one day left.

On the last day one of the queen's men returned from traveling through the forests, up into the high mountains and down into the deep green valleys, and to her dismay he had no new names. But then he said, "Maybe all is not lost. As I came out of the dark forest I happened upon a little cabin, and in front of this dwelling a bonfire was burning, and a ridiculous little man was dancing and singing:

'With joy I can sing,
for tomorrow I know
a child I can bring,
as no one will know
I am Rumpelstiltskin!'"

The young queen was overcome with relief, as she was sure they had stumbled upon the mannikin's real name.

That same evening the little fellow appeared once more, his old wizened face beaming in anticipation of his victory.

"Well, tell me true, my dear queen, have you found out my name?"

Feigning distress, the queen said, "Are you called Will o'the Wisp?"

"Certainly not!" he said.

"Maybe your name is Gobbledegook?"

"Don't be so foolish. I think you must prepare to give up your child."

"Just one more try," said the queen. "Is it possible that your name is . . . Rumpelstiltskin?"

"The Devil has told you that!" shrieked the little man, "The Devil has told you!"

He became so furious and stamped his feet so hard that he plunged his right foot so deeply into the ground that he could not free himself. In a rage, he pulled so hard at his left leg that he tore himself in half, and that was the end of him.

The king and the queen were overjoyed and they lived happily with their family and their servants for many years.

Rumpel-stilzchen

See **Rumpelstiltskin**.

RUSALKA

A Russian spirit of the water and the woods. *Rusalki* (the plural of *rusalka*) are described in **Thomas Keightley**'s *The Fairy Mythology* (1828) as "of beautiful form, with long green hair; they swing and balance themselves on the branches of trees, bathe in lakes and rivers, play on the surface of the water and wring their locks on the green meads at the water's edge." They were said to be most active at the beginning of summer when people sang, danced, and wove garlands for them, which they cast into streams. A *rusalksa* was the inspiration for Antonin Dvorak's opera of the same name, in which a water maiden falls in love with a human prince.

S

Saci

A mischievous spirit in the folklore of Brazil. He is described as a one-legged, pipe-smoking boy wearing a red cap. It is said that he will grant wishes to anyone who manages to capture him and steal his magical red cap. Like the tricksy household spirits of Europe, he delights in playing pranks—hiding objects around the house, souring the milk, spilling salt—but generally is considered to be more playful than seriously dangerous.

Several variations exist, including Saci Saçurá, meaning Saci with Red Eyes.

Saci Saçurá

See **Saci**.

St. Collen and the Fairy King

This story of a seventh-century Welsh saint's encounter with **Gwyn ap Nudd**, fairy king and ruler of the Underworld, is an example of fairy glamor and how all is not always as it seems in fairyland.

St. Collen went to Glastonbury in Somerset, where he became first an abbot and then a hermit. He lived in a cave at the foot of Glastonbury Tor. One day his meditations were interrupted by two men talking about Gwyn ap Nudd, saying that his castle was on top of the tor. Collen told the men that they shouldn't talk about devils and they should be on their way. In turn, they warned him that he would offend the King of the Fairies by talking in that way.

A few days later a messenger came to Collen, inviting him to visit the King of the Fairies. At first he refused, but after repeated invitations, he agreed to come but hid a bottle of holy water under his cassock as protection against the "devils."

When he reached the summit of the tor, Collen saw the most

beautiful castle surrounded by guards, musicians, beautiful maidens, and men on horseback. He was led to a banqueting hall where servants dressed in scarlet and blue were laying out a great feast. The King of the Fairies invited Collen to eat, but Collen refused, proclaiming: "I do not eat the leaves of a tree." A shudder ran through the court at those words, but the king persisted and drew Collen's attention to the beauty of his servants and courtiers and their brightly colored clothes.

But Collen could see through the fairy glamor. He likened the scarlet and blue to the flames and ice of hell, then drew out his bottle and doused the king and his court in holy water.

In an instant, the banqueting hall, the fairy king, his court, and castle vanished and Collen found himself alone in the light of dawn on top of Glastonbury Tor.

Salamander

Elemental spirit of fire, most often depicted as its amphibious lizard-like namesake.

The fifteenth-century alchemist Paracelsus divided fairies into four groups: the **gnomes** of the earth, the **sylphs** of the air, the salamanders of fire, and the **undines** or **nymphs** of water. Each elemental represented the pure form of that elemental energy. Elementals were said to be creatures partway between humans and pure spirits. They were made of flesh and blood, and ate, drank, slept, and procreated like human beings, but they were capable of superhuman speed and movement, lived longer than humans, and did not have immortal souls.

Sandman, The

The sleep fairy in English folklore, he is a nursery fairy who sprinkles sand or dust into children's eyes as they fall asleep at night so that they may enjoy pleasant dreams. Similar to the Scottish Wee Willie Winkie, the French **La Dormette**, and the Danish **Ole Luk Øj**.

Sankchinni

Vindictive tree spirits in Hindu belief. Appearing as women with a pale complexions, they stand beneath their trees in the dead of night.

In one tale a *sankchinni* inhabited a tree near to a Brahaman's house. One day she attacked the Brahaman's wife, thrusting her into a hole in the tree trunk and imprisoning her there.

Burning a piece of turmeric root is said to be a charm to ward off malignant *sankchinni* tree spirits.

Sanna

See **Sedna**.

Scott, Sir Walter *(1771–1832)*

An author, poet, and playwright most famous for his historical novels, Scott was born in Edinburgh, the son of a lawyer. At the age of two he contracted polio, which left him infirm, and he was sent to live with his grandparents and his aunt Jenny in the Scottish Borders to help him recuperate. Here he became acquainted with the many tales and legends of Scotland that were to feature so prominently in his works. After various attempts at finding a cure, both in England and Scotland, he returned to Edinburgh, now able to walk, to begin his formal education.

Scott studied classics at the University of Edinburgh, and later law, but he remained fascinated by the oral traditions of Scotland and began collecting tales and ballads. His first published work, *The Minstrelsy of the Scottish Borders* (three volumes, 1802–1803), is a collection of ballads that includes "**Tam Lin**" and "**Thomas the Rhymer**." He published his first collection of poems in 1805, in a volume entitled *The Lay of the Last Minstrel* (1805), which was very successful and put him firmly on the road to becoming a popular, famous writer. He continued to write poetry, including "The Lady of the Lake" (1810), but also wanted to document his knowledge of oral traditions. In 1814 he published his first novel, *Waverley*, albeit anonymously as, at the time, prose and novels were deemed to be inferior to poetry and he was unwilling to tarnish his reputation as a poet.

All of Scott's novels include Scottish folklore and were instrumental in preserving the traditional tales of Scotland. He met many writers and antiquarians with the same keen interest in folklore and was, in part, to influence **Thomas Keightley**'s *The Fairy Mythology* (1828) and **Thomas Crofton Croker**'s *Fairy Legends and Traditions of the South of Ireland* (1825–1827).

Sir Walter Scott is regarded as the founder of the historical novel genre and has influenced many writers of subsequent generations.

Seal Maidens

Gentle sea spirits in the folklore of Orkney and Shetland. Tales of the seal people are found throughout Scotland, where they are known as the **roane** or **selkies**.

Typically, the seal maidens come ashore and shed their sealskins to dance in the moonlight. A fisherman spies the beautiful maidens dancing and hides one of the skins. When the maidens see him they take fright, pull on their skins, and slip back into the water. The fisherman persuades the one maiden left behind searching for her sealskin to be his wife. She is a good wife, but never stops pining for the sea. Eventually, she discovers where her mortal husband has hidden her sealskin and returns to the sea.

Seal-maiden stories have many similarities to stories of **swan maidens**. In some parts of Scotland families supposed to be descended from seal people are said to be born with a horny growth between their fingers. The MacCoddrums of the Seals are the most famous example of a clan supposed to be descended from the union of a human and a seal maiden.

Sedna

(Or Sanna.) The sea goddess of the underwater kingdom in Inuit mythology, she lives beneath the sea in Adlivun, the realm of human and animal spirits.

There are various legends recounting how she became the guardian of dead souls. Some versions tell of her union with a fulmar bird in a faraway kingdom from which her father came to rescue her but eventually sacrificed her to appease the storm-raising birds. In others she is described as a **giant** who eats the limbs of her parents to satisfy her enormous appetite. Common to all the legends, she is thrown into the sea by her father who, when she tries to cling to his kayak, chops off her fingers, each one becoming a sea creature.

See also **Anguta**.

Seelie Court, the

In Scottish tradition, fairies are generally divided into the **Unseelie Court** and the Seelie Court. The origin of the names is thought to be the Scottish *seilie*, meaning "happy," "lucky," or "blessed"; *unseelie* having the opposite meanings of "unhappy," "unfortunate," or "unholy." So the Seelie Court is a group of fairies that are, on the whole, benevolent and kindly.

If treated with due respect, members of the Seelie Court will help humans by lending a hand in domestic or agricultural tasks. It is only if humans cause insult or injury to the Seelie Court that just retribution is demanded by the fairies, whereas the malevolent Unseelie Court taunts, injures, and brings about misfortune to humans unprovoked.

Selkies

Shapeshifting seal people of Orkney and Shetland folklore, dwelling on small, rocky islands off the coast known as skerries. Some people believed that the selkie folk were actually people disguised in the form of seals, condemned to live in the seas as punishment for their sins.

Occasionally the selkie folk came ashore, shed their sealskins, and resumed their human form. They were more beautiful than ordinary mortals and there were tales of mortal women calling male selkies to their beds by shedding seven tears into the sea. Female selkies, or **seal maidens**, did not seek mortal husbands but when they came ashore to dance by the light of the moon in human form, fishermen became enraptured by their beauty and hid their sealskins, preventing them from returning to the water, and taking them as their brides. The offspring of these unions were said to have webbed hands and feet. It was believed that when a drop of selkie blood was shed in the sea, ships should seek shelter, for it would give rise to a mighty storm.

Seven Whistlers

Harbingers of death in the folklore of the north of England. Similar to the Welsh ***Cwn Annwn*** and **Gabriel Ratchets** hounds of the **wild hunt**, they are spirits that portend death and disaster. Their cry is said to resemble the call of the long-billed curlew; to hear it is an omen of death.

Shag Foal

(Or tatter foal.) Shapeshifting **bogie** beast of Lincolnshire folklore, a phantom animal that appeared at night, taking the form of a fiery-eyed horse, foal, or donkey, and frightened travelers.

In *County Folklore* (1901), Eli Twigg gives an account of the tatter foal as "a shagg'd-looking hoss, and given to all manner of goings-on, far cluzzening hold of a body what is riding home half-screwed with bargain-drink, and pulling him out of the saddle, to scaring a old woman three parts out of her skin, and making her drop her shop-things in the blatter and blash, and run for it."

Shango

In the Yoruba belief system that originated in Nigeria, West Africa, and has spread throughout the Caribbean and South America, Shango is a warrior ***orisha***, the ruler of thunder, lightning, and fire, known for his drumming and dancing.

Shawano

See **Four Winds, the**.

Shedeem

See ***Mazikeen***.

Shedu

Benevolent guardian spirits of Mesopotamian mythology. Their female counterparts were the ***lamassu***. Protective spirits, similar in nature to the Roman ***genii***, they were generally depicted as winged lions or bulls with human heads.

The *shedu* were assigned to a particular human, whom they safeguarded throughout the course of their lifetime, protecting them against the malevolent influence of the ***utukku***.

SHEE

See **Sidhe**.

SHEFRO

(Or *siofra*.) Small **trooping fairies** of Ireland. According to **Crofton Croker**'s *Fairy Legends of the South of Ireland* (1825), they dwell in the hills, wear foxglove caps on their heads, and are fond of mischief-making.

"The Legend of Knocksheogowna" tells of the pranks and activities of a clan of fairies inhabiting one particular hill and of the shapeshifting escapades of their queen. Knocksheogowna means "the Hill of the Fairy Calf."

The fairies of Tipperary once had a playground that lay like a green carpet across the top of the hill known as Knocksheogowna. There they played and danced all through the clear summer nights to their hearts' delight. Then one spring morning came the rumbling and the lowing of a herd of cattle moving slowly up the hillside, and as they came upon the luxuriant pasture of the fairies' playground, their herdsman realized that he had come across the finest grazing for miles around.

When the night threw its star-spangled cape over the hill, the fairies were most distressed to find their land so rudely broken by the clumsy bulls and cows. The queen of the good people decided that something must be done to drive away these invaders.

As the cattle settled contentedly for the night, the herdsman wrapped himself in his warm blanket, feeling glad to have found such a rich and pleasant land. He was woken from his happy reverie by a loud hissing sound and was horrified to see before him a terrible disjointed creature with the body of a horse, the tail of a dragon, and the wings of an eagle, leaping and dancing and spitting fire.

The poor man was scared out of his wits and tried to cover his face, but the blanket was pulled from his grasp and he was forced to watch and listen as the Queen of the Fairies transformed herself from one horrendous shape to another. One moment she was a little lame man with a huge bull's head, the next she became a great ape with a duck's feet and a turkey cock's tail. And accompanying all of these frightening visions was a roaring, hissing, neighing, bellowing, and belching of fire such as no man can imagine.

Despite all his prayers to the saints in heaven, the poor herdsman was frozen in fear and had to endure the hellish night right through to the welcome light of dawn. The cattle were also disturbed by the sights and sounds of the long, dark night and charged about the hillside.

The herdsman left that very day and the landowner had to hire another man, but he, too, lasted for only one terrible night. The cattle became thin and sickly, and many were lost to accidents, falling into pits and rivers. No man could be found to endure the horrors of the nights, even though the farmer offered double, treble, or even quadruple wages.

The fairy queen was happy that she had driven the men away and as only a few cattle remained, her good people resumed their merry dances, drinking dewdrops from acorns and feasting on mushrooms.

The farmer was at a loss as to how to save his few remaining cattle. As he walked along the road, his head hung low in misery, he happened to meet with Larry Hoolahan. Now this Larry was famous as a piper, the best in 15 parishes, and he also had a reputation as a brave and bold young man. When fortified with liquor, he would face a mad bull or tame the wildest horse. He asked the farmer why he was so downcast, and the man explained his problems.

"Don't you worry," said Larry, "I'm sure if there were as many fairies on Knocksheogowna as there are stars in the sky, then Larry Hoolahan could swat them away with one sweep of his hand!"

"You are indeed a bold man, Larry," said the farmer, "and if you can watch my herds for just one week on top of the mountain, then you shall never go hungry or thirsty again."

The farmer took Larry to his home and fed him and plied him with the best liquor that the barley corn can provide. Then, as the sun set, Larry made his way up to the green pasture. He found a comfortable spot where he could watch the cattle and settled down to play his pipes.

The fairies called upon their queen to drive away this insolent invader. Larry was aware of a rising commotion around him and as he looked up, the shadow of a great black cat appeared against the brightness of the moon, rearing up on to the tip of its claws and mewing with the sound of a watermill. Then it fell to the ground only to rise again in the shape of a salmon, with a cravat around its neck and leather boots on its tail.

Larry clapped his hands and cried, "Bravo! If you'll dance for me, I'll play you a tune."

And he picked up his pipes and proceeded to play. The fairy queen transformed into every kind of strange, distorted creature to distract him, but he played on, quite unperturbed.

Finally, the queen turned herself into a milk-white calf with soft, brown eyes. She moved quietly and seductively beside Larry, but he wasn't deceived and leaped upon her back. She immediately sprang from the mountain top and they flew 10 miles (16 kilometers) and more over the mighty river Shannon to the farthest bank.

Larry fell to the ground and, looking into the fair face of the fairy queen, he said, "By heavens, that was quite a leap!"

The queen said, "Laurence, you are a brave fellow, to be sure, and if you wish I will return you to the mountain top." She resumed the shape of the white calf and with Larry on her back she made one great bound to rest again at the peak of Knocksheogowna.

"Laurence," said the queen, "If you will play your pipes for my good people, then you may keep your herds upon the hill and we will molest you no more."

And so it was that Larry had his food and drink from the grateful farmer, and played his pipes at night, never disturbed again by any wild apparitions.

They say that even now if you listen carefully under the light of an

August moon, you will hear the pleasant pipes of Larry Hoolahan and the gay laughter of the good people dancing on top of Knocksheogowna.

Shehireem

See **Mazikeen**.

Shekkasoh

Tree spirits, or ***nats***, of Burmese folklore. The *shekkasoh* resides in tree trunks, while other types of tree-dwelling *nat*, such as the ***akakasoh*** and the ***boomasoh***, make their homes in other parts of the tree.

Shellycoat

A water **bogie** of the Lowlands of Scotland. He took his name from the shells with which he covered himself and could be heard clattering as he moved. He delighted in bewildering humans.

In one tale, two men were walking along the bank of the river Ettrick at night when they heard a plaintive voice calling from the stream: "Lost! Lost!"

They spent all night following the voice and at dawn they eventually arrived, exhausted, at the spring where the voice seemed to be coming from.

Shellycoat leaped out of the spring and ran off down the hill, laughing with glee at his trick.

Like **Robin Goodfellow**, Shellycoat was mischievous and playful rather than actually malicious, and expressed his pleasure at bamboozling his victims with loud bursts of laughter.

See also **Peallaidh**.

*S*HEOQUES, THE

Small land-dwelling fairies in the folklore of Ireland. According to **W. B. Yeats** in *Irish Fairy Tales* (1892), the name derives from the Irish *sidheog*, "a little fairy." Yeats describes the *sheoques* as the spirits that haunt the sacred thorn bushes and the ancient raths, or ringforts, that are found scattered throughout the Irish countryside. The land fairies are said to have enticed many a mortal down into their dim world. Yeats writes:

Many more have listened to their fairy music, till all human cares and joys drifted from their hearts and they became great peasant seers or 'Fairy Doctors,' or great peasant musicians or poets like Carolan, who gathered his tunes while sleeping on a fairy rath; or else they died in a year and a day, to live ever after among the fairies.

Although generally benevolent, *sheoques* were in the habit of stealing human children, or sometimes adult men or women, and leaving a withered fairy **changeling**, "a thousand or maybe two thousand years old," in their place.

In one account from the 1800s, a man wrote to one of the Irish papers, telling of a case in his own village and how the parish priest made the fairies deliver the stolen child up again. In another account, it was said that a woman from the village of Coloney, Sligo, was taken in her youth. Yeats writes:

When she came home at the end of seven years she had no toes, for she had danced them off. Now and then one hears of some real injury being done a person by the land fairies, but then it is nearly always deserved. They are said to have killed two people in the last six months in the County Down district where I am now staying. But then these persons had torn up thorn bushes belonging to the Sheoques.

SHINING ONES, THE

See **Devas**.

*S*HINSEËN

Chinese spirits of the woods and mountains, where, free from the passions and the cares of life, they dwell in a state of blissful ease but still exercise an influence over human affairs. Sometimes they appear as old men with long beards; at other times as young maidens, sauntering amid rocks and woods by moonlight.

Shock, the

Bogie beast of Suffolk. In various accounts shocks were described as dogs, calves, donkeys, and horses, sometimes with huge, saucerlike eyes.

In one tale, the shock was described as a "thing" with a donkey's head and a velvety hide that appeared at a tollgate one night. When the keeper of the tollgate attempted to seize the animal, it bit his hand and then vanished. The tollgate keeper bore the mark of the shock's bite for the rest of his days.

Shony

(Pronounced *shaw nee.*) Sea spirit of the Isle of Lewis. Traditionally, the people of Lewis made offerings to Shony every Halloween to ensure that they had enough seaweed to fertilize the land. They brewed a special batch of ale using a peck of malt from each family. Then one person was chosen who waded out into the sea carrying a cup of ale to ask Shony to send them plenty of seaweed to enrich the ground for a good harvest the following year. After tipping the ale into the sea, he returned to shore and the villagers lit a candle in the church before going into the fields to drink the rest of the ale and spend the night drinking and dancing.

Shoopiltee

Water horse of Shetland. In *The Fairy Mythology* (1828), **Keightley** described it as a pretty little horse that tricked people into mounting it, only to gallop away with them into the water.

See also ***Cabyll Ushtey.***

Si

See **Sidhe**.

Sidh

See **Sidhe**.

Sidhe

(Also *Sidh, Sith, Si, Shee.*) Gaelic name for fairies, from the word *sidhe,* meaning a barrow or a mound where the fairies were said to dwell. *Sidh* or *Sí* in Ireland, *Sith* in Scotland, and *Shee* in the Isle of Man are all variants on the spelling. The fairies are also known in Ireland as ***Daoine Sidh*** or *Aos Sidh,* or "people of the mounds."

Sikes, Wirt *(1836–1883)*

A journalist, poet, and writer with an interest in Welsh folk and fairy lore, Sikes was born in Watertown, New York. Owing to childhood health problems he had little formal education and was mainly self-taught. He started his career in the newspaper trade as a typesetter and later wrote articles for a variety of publications. He married at the age of 19 and had two children, a boy and a girl. His first book, *A Book for the Winter Evening Fireside,* a compilation of poetry and stories, was published in 1858.

In 1876 he was appointed US Consul in Wales and settled in Cardiff. While there he developed a keen interest in local archeology and history as well as folk tales and mythology, and in 1880 published *British Goblins: Welsh Folk-Lore, Fairy Mythology, Legends and Traditions.* It tells of Welsh mountain and lake fairies, **changelings**, and fairy rings, and includes a classification of Welsh fairies.

Sikes died in Cardiff and is buried in the Brookwood American cemetery in Woking, England.

Silkies

Female **brownies** of Northumberland and the Borders. Like the brownie, the silky carried out domestic chores and chided servants who neglected their tasks. The name may come from the dresses of silk that they were said to wear, and which could be heard rustling as they went about their work.

The most famous of the silkies was the Silky of Black Heddon who lived at Heddon Hall. William Henderson describes her in *Notes on the Folklore of the Northern Counties of England and the Borders* (1866) as a mischievous spirit who was more troublesome than helpful. Although she tidied up what was messy, she also caused disarray where there was neatness. In this respect she resembled the **Cauld Lad of Hilton**. At night she liked to sit in a tree by a lake at Heddon Hall, which became known as Silky's Chair. From her tree, she stopped passing carts and horses unless warded off by a cross of rowan. She left abruptly after a ceiling collapsed, revealing a rough skin filled with gold. One theory was that she had been the ghost of someone who had died without disclosing where their hidden treasure was concealed.

Siofra

See **Shefro**.

Sireen

See **Siren**.

Siren

(Also Sireen, Sirene, Syrene.) Beautiful yet deadly **nymphs** of Greek mythology. Depicted as part-woman, part-bird, the sirens lured mariners to their doom with their irresistibly sweet singing. In this respect they were similar to **mermaids**.

According to legend, Odysseus, hero of Homer's epic poem the *Odyssey*, was one of the few mortals who survived hearing the sirens' melodies. Curious to hear the sea maidens' songs, he instructed his men to plug their ears with wax and lash him to the mast of his ship; under no circumstances were they to untie him, even if he requested them to do so. Enchanted by the sirens' melodies, he did demand to be untied, but his men bound him tighter to the mast and thus he lived to tell the tale.

In some accounts it is said that the sirens were fated to die if they failed to lure a mortal into the watery depths with their voices. When the musician **Orpheus**, traveling with Jason and the Argonauts, heard the sirens, he took out his lyre and drowned out their voices by playing music that was sweeter still.

SIRENE

See **Siren**.

SITH

See ***Sidhe***.

SJORA

Scandinavian water and sea spirit, a harbinger of impending storms. Usually described as a female and often manifesting as a hand rising above the water in warning. In some tales she is described as a friend and helper to fishermen, while in others she is a bad luck omen or is actively pernicious. Many tales relate how a fisherman's kindness to a *sjora*, often in the form of a gift of a pair of gloves, is rewarded with protection.

In one such tale, a fisherman was out on a lake in his boat on a calm afternoon when suddenly the *sjora* appeared, saying, "I am so cold, help me."

The fisherman gave her a pair of gloves and she told him: "Steer to the east side of the lake, my glove-friend."

The skipper took her advice and thus avoided an almighty storm.

Olaus Magnus, Swedish writer and folklorist, noted this tale as early as 1555.

Sometimes the *sjora* delivers her advice in verse:

"The wind is shrieking,
rocks are creaking,
go ashore my glove-friend."
"Make for land, mitten-man,
tonight many wives and children will lose their man."

Another account tells of a group of herring fishermen who were out fishing in their boats when one claimed to have seen a hand rising above the crests of the waves, pointing back to land.

"We must go home, I have seen the sign," he told the others.

But they laughed and ignored the warning.

The first fisherman returned to shore and sure enough a storm blew up and all the others perished.

In other accounts, the *sjora* is described as devilish, such as in the case of a crofter who was rowing home after his day's work when suddenly his boat would go neither forward or backward and began to take in water.

Seeing that a pair of hands was pushing down on his boat, he picked up an ax and swung at the hands. At that instant his boat was freed, but a terrible storm was unleashed, which he was lucky to survive.

SKILLYWIDDEN

A Cornish fairy found by a farmer in "A Fairy Caught," an account given in **Robert Hunt**'s *Popular Romances of the West of England* (1865):

I heard last week of three fairies having been seen in Zennor very recently. A man who lived at the foot of Trendreen Hill, in the valley of Treridge, I think, was cutting furze [gorse] on the hill. Near the middle of the day he saw one of the small people, not more than a foot [30 centimeters] long, stretched at full length and fast asleep, on a bank of griglans [heath], surrounded by high brakes of furze. The man took off his furze cuff and slipped the little man into it, without his waking up; went down to the house; took the little fellow out of the cuff on the hearthstone, when he awakened, and seemed quite pleased and at home, beginning to play with the children, who were well pleased with the small body, and called him Bobby Griglans.

The old people were very careful not to let Bob out of the house, or be seen by the neighbours, as he promised to show the man where the crocks of gold were buried on the hill. A few days after he was brought from the hill, all the neighbours came with their horses (according to custom) to bring home the winter's reek of furze, which had to be brought down the bill in trusses on the backs of the horses. That Bob might be safe and out of sight, he and the children were shut up in the barn. Whilst the furze-carriers were in to dinner, the prisoners contrived to get out, to have a "courant" round the furze-reek, when they saw a little man and woman, not much larger than Bob, searching into every hole and corner among the trusses that were dropped round the unfinished reek. The little woman was wringing her hands and crying: "Oh, my dear and tender Skillywidden, wherever canst ah (thou) be gone to? Shall I ever cast eyes on thee again?" "Go 'e back," says Bob to the children; "my father and mother are come here too." He then cried out: "Here I am, mammy!" By the time the words were out of his mouth, the little man and woman, with their precious Skillywidden, were nowhere to be seen, and there has been no sight nor sign of them since. The children got a sound thrashing for letting Skillywidden escape.

Skinwalkers

Supernatural beings in Navajo legends, these spirits were formerly powerful medicine men who chose to use their skills in evil ways and in various animal guises. The only defense against them was reciting their full name to them, whereupon they died.

Skriker

Goblin of Yorkshire and Lancashire. Sometimes he walked invisibly in the woods, making his presence known only by emitting frightful screams. Sometimes he took the form of **Padfoot**, a large dog with big saucerlike eyes.

Sleigh Beggey

(Pronounced *sleigh beargar*). One of the Manx names for the fairies, meaning "the little folk." Other Manx names included ***Ad-hene***, Them That's In, and the ***Ferrishyn***. People often used other terms to talk about the fairies, for they were said to become angered or offended if referred to directly.

Sluagh, the

(Or the Host.) Malevolent spirits of the Scottish Highlands, believed to be the souls of the unforgiven dead. Like a flock of birds, they are said to fly above the Earth, battling one another, shooting arrows at animals and humans on the ground, and sometimes recruiting mortals to their number to do their bidding.

According to an account in **Alexander Carmichael**'s *Carmina Gadelica* (1900), "the spirits fly about in great clouds, up and down the face of the world like the starlings, and come back to the scenes of their earthly transgressions."

Söedrouen

Norwegian sea spirit. According to **Jakob Grimm** in *Teutonic Mythology* (1883), the *söedrouen* appeared in the shape of a headless old man whenever a sailor's life was lost at sea.

Solitary Fairies

In *Fairy and Folk Tales of the Irish Peasantry* (1888), **W. B. Yeats** divided the fairies of British folklore into solitary fairies and **trooping fairies**. As their name suggests, solitary fairies tended to prefer a life of solitude, while trooping fairies lived in groups or communities and traveled in processions.

Yeats' list of solitary fairies included the **leprechaun**, **banshee, fir darrig**, and ***phouka***. Other solitary fairies included the ***caointeach***, **Brown Man of the Muirs**, and the **duergar**. Meanwhile, the trooping fairies encompassed a wide variety of fairy creatures, from the human-sized shining beings of Irish folklore to tiny nature spirits.

Generally speaking, solitary fairies were considered more fearsome and less pleasant than trooping fairies. Whether large, small, friendly, or sinister, trooping fairies were generally thought to share a love of dancing, music, singing, and merrymaking, and were known for their mischief-making and tricksy ways, whereas solitary fairies were not generally playful, and were of a darker, more somber disposition.

In *A Dictionary of Fairies, Hobgoblins, Brownies, Bogies and Other Supernatural Creatures* (1976) **Katharine Briggs** suggested a third division of fairies to include family groups of domestic household fairies such as **hobs**, although she concluded that presumably they would join other fairies at times of merrymaking or at fairy markets, making them an extension of the trooping fairies.

Spenser, Edmund *(c.1552–1599)*

Poet and author of the epic poem *The Faerie Queene* (1590).

Spenser drew on fairylore and Arthurian legend to write one of the longest poems in the English language. It consists of three books published in 1590 and a further three books published in 1596. Spenser indicated that he intended the work to include 12 books, so the poem remains unfinished.

While drawing on folklore of the past, the poem was also written as a commentary on life in Britain in the sixteenth century. The Faerie Queene, named Gloriana, was based on Queen Elizabeth I. The poem contains references to many elements of fairy lore, such as **changelings**, fairy glamor, and shapeshifting. It features magical items, such as a magic mirror, ring, spear and shield, the water of life, and the tree of life.

Spirit of the Van, the

See **Van Pools**.

Spriggans

Cornish fairy creatures, believed to be the guardians of **giants'** gold. They dwelled in places where treasure was buried, such as old ruins, barrows, giant's quoits, and castles. Some said they were the ghosts of giants. Although generally appearing to be small, they could shapeshift and increase their size, and used their enormous stature to frighten away would-be thieves out to steal their treasure. Their shapeshifting abilities are described in an account of "The Spriggans of Trencrom Hill" in **Robert Hunt**'s *Popular Romances of the West of England* (1865):

It is not many years since a man, who thought he was fully informed as to the spot in which a crock of the giant's gold was buried, proceeded on one fine moonlight night to this enchanted hill, and with spade and pick commenced his search. He proceeded with some time without interruption, and it became evident to him that the treasure was not far off. The sky was rapidly covered with the darkest clouds, shutting out the brilliant light of the moon – which had previously gemmed each cairn – and leaving the gold-seeker in total and unearthly darkness. The wind rose, and roared terrifically amidst the rocks; but this was soon drowned amidst the fearful crashes of thunder, which followed in quick succession the flashes of lightning. By its light the man perceived that the spriggans were coming out in swarms from all the rocks. They were in countless numbers; and although they were small at first, they rapidly increased in size, until eventually they assumed an almost giant form, looking all the while, as he afterwards said, "as ugly as if they would eat him." How this poor man escaped is unknown, but he is said to have been so frightened that he took to his bed, and was not able to work for a long time.

Another account, 'The Fairy Revels on the 'Gump' of St. Just," in Hunt's collection of Cornish folklore tells how the spriggans intervened when a miser attempted to steal treasure belonging to a band of fairies who lived inside a hill known as the Gump. They cast threads over the miser that chained him to the earth and thwarted him in his mission. In the tale, they are described as grotesquely ugly.

A further account, "The Old Woman Who Turned Her Shift," tells of an old lady who managed to get her hands on spriggan gold using the traditional method of turning her shift (dress) inside out to confuse the spriggans. However, although she succeeded in winning their spoils, she was punished for her greed and experienced physical pains every time she wore that dress.

Sprites

A general term for fairies, **elves**, or **pixies.** It is also used to refer to nature spirits or spirits of the air such as **sylphs** and **nereids**, but is not generally associated with earthier creatures such as **dwarves**.

Spunkies

A type of **will o' the wisp** in the folklore of Lowland Scotland and Somerset.

Stock

A piece of wood, or bundle of grass and sticks, fashioned in the likeness of a human who has been kidnapped by fairies. In fairy lore throughout Europe and in other parts of the world one of the fairies' favorite tricks was to steal a human child, or sometimes a nursing mother, and take them away to fairyland, replacing the human either with a fairy **changeling** or with a stock or **fetch**, a "doll" representing the stolen child or woman that, by means of fairy glamor, was given the semblance of life.

Strand Varsels

In *Northern Mythology: Comprising the Principal Popular Traditions and Superstitions of Scandinavia, North Germany and the Netherlands* (1852), Benjamin Thorpe gave various accounts of ***kirkegrims*** and *strand varsels*—specters of the corpses that had been driven onto the shore and still lay unburied.

Before seashores were consecrated, it was dangerous to pass by the coast at night on account of the *strand varsels.*

One night as a peasant was going along the strand toward Taarbek, a *strand varsel* sprang upon his back and clung there fast, crying, "Carry me to the church!"

The man, having no alternative, carried him the shortest way to Gientofte.

When they were under the churchyard wall, the *varsel* sprang quickly over it, but instantly the *kirkegrim* approached and an obstinate battle ensued between them.

After fighting for a while, they both sat down to rest.

"Did I stand up well?" the *varsel* asked the peasant.

The peasant answered, "No."

The battle then commenced anew.

When the combatants sat down to rest again, the *varsel* asked, "Did I stand up well that time?"

Again the peasant answered, "No."

The fight then recommenced again.

When *kirkegrim* and *varsel* sat down for a third time, the *varsel* said, "Now! Have I stood up well?"

Finally the peasant answered, "Yes."

"It is well for thee," said the *varsel*, "that thou hast answered so, for otherwise I would surely have broken thy neck."

In another tale of *kirkegrim* and *strand varsel*, a woman was going to milk her cows at Niveröd when she saw that the corpse of a man had been washed up on the sand and noticed that a large money-bag was bound around his body. No one being near, she took the money, to which she had as good a claim as anyone else. But the next night the *strand varsel* came to the village and made a great noise before her window, desiring her to come out and follow him. Supposing that she had no alternative, she bade her children farewell and accompanied him.

When they were outside the village, the *varsel* said to her, "Take me by the leg and draw me to the church."

The nearest church lay three-quarters of a mile distant, but the woman took the *varsel* by the leg and set off.

When the church was finally in sight, the *varsel* said, "Let me go now, then go to the house by the church gate and desire the people to sit up until thou comest again. When thou hast helped me over the churchyard wall, run as fast as thou canst, lest the *kirkegrim* should seize thee."

She did accordingly, and scarcely had the corpse been placed over the wall than the *kirkegrim* came out and seized the woman by the petticoat, which, being old, gave way, and so she slipped into the house by the church gate in safety.

From that time on, all went well with the woman and she lived contented on the money she had found on the *strand varsel.*

STRANGERS, THE

A Lincolnshire term for fairies, one of many euphemistic names given to them. Other Lincolnshire names included **greencoaties**, **tiddy ones**, and **yarthkins**. People often used euphemistic terms to talk about the fairies, for they were said to become angered or offended if referred to directly.

The strangers are described in an account collected by Mrs. Balfour in *Legends of the Carrs* (1891) as no more than a hand-span in height, with arms and legs as thin as threads, large hands and feet, and heads that rolled about on their shoulders. They had long noses and wide mouths with great red tongues poking out. They dressed in grass-green jackets and trousers and yellow bonnets that looked like toadstools. On summer nights they could be seen dancing in the moonlight on great slabs of rock, while on winter evenings they danced in fireplaces while the household slept.

STRAY SOD, THE

See ***Foidin Seachrain****.*

STRÖMKARL

A fish-tailed spirit of the waterfalls in the folklore of Norway. Strömkarl, the River Man, is an accomplished musician, but humans should be wary in choosing which of his tunes to dance to. According to *Brewer's Dictionary of Phrase and Fable* (1898):

Strömkarl has eleven different musical measures, to ten of which people may dance, but the eleventh belongs to the night-spirit, his host. If anyone plays it, tables and benches, cups and cans, old men and women, blind and lame, babies in their cradles, and the sick in their beds, begin to dance.

See also **Nix**.

Sturluson, Snorri *(1179–1241)*

Icelandic scholar, poet, historian, and politician credited with compiling the *Prose Edda*, which, together with the *Poetic Edda*, comprises the major repository of Old Norse mythology.

From the age of three Snorri Sturluson was educated by Jon Loptsson, an influential chieftain related to one of the most important families of Iceland, who passed on his knowledge of Icelandic traditions, in particular belief in the ancient gods.

He married a rich heiress in 1199 and soon acquired land as well as power. He was elected chief magistrate of the Icelandic High Court, but during his political career he made many enemies, and the King of Norway ordered his assassination in 1241.

He is best known for his work on the *Prose Edda* (or *Younger Edda*), which is written in three parts. *Gylfaginning* (The Fooling of Gylfi) deals with Norse mythology and its gods, *Skáldskaparmál* (Language of Poetry), is a dialogue between the Norse gods of the sea and of poetry, and *Háttatal I* (Enumeration of Meters) is an exploration of the verse forms of Old Norse poetry.

Although Snorri Sturluson was a Christian, he showed respect for the traditional gods of Nordic countries. Many of the ancient myths and tales in the *Edda* tell of Odin (the All-father of Norse mythology), Tyr, Thor, and Freyja (after which Tuesday, Thursday, and Friday are named), Ariadne and her beautiful thread (a recurring storyline in so many tales in different cultures), and Loki (the god of fire). These stories are still well known.

Suanggi

Malevolent spirit of the Indonesian Maluku Islands, said to manifest in the form of a person, usually female, possessed of magical powers used to cause illness or disease. As recently as 2004, there were reports of *suanggi* activity in Tobelo on the island of Halmahera. The spirit was said to have taken the form of an attractive young woman who seduced men in order to attack them and devour their genitals.

Subterraneans, the

Wandering fairy tribes of the Scottish Highlands that dwell under fairy mounds. According to **Robert Kirk** in *The Secret Commonwealth of Elves, Fauns and Fairies* (1691), the subterraneans become impatient after staying one place for long and every quarter year, with the changing of the seasons, they move their lodgings from one mound to another.

Surouas, the Southwest Wind

Ruler of the southwest wind in Breton folklore.

See also **Nurouas, the Northwest Wind**.

Swan Maidens

Shapeshifting enchanted maidens. Tales of swan maidens in various guises appear in folklore around the world. Generally the story goes that the swan maidens take off their feather cloaks and assume the form of beautiful human women to dance or bathe. A mortal man sees them, falls in love with the most beautiful maiden, and steals her cloak. Without her cloak, she is unable to transform back into a bird and agrees to marry the man who possess her cloak.

The Adventures of Prince Achmed (1926), based on tales from the *Arabian Nights*, tells the story of Achmed and the swan maiden **Peri Banu**. It is the earliest surviving animated feature film, featuring Lottie Reiniger's hand-cut shadow characters.

There are many variations throughout the world on the swan-maiden theme. The animal form of the maidens differs, but the story remains the same. In Croatia they are she-wolves, in Africa they are buffalos, in East Asia they transform into various species of birds, in Serbia they are peahens, in Micronesia they are porpoises, in the Arctic, foxes, and for the Arapesh people of Papua New Guinea they are the cassowary bird.

In a Japanese tale, a crane, known as *tsuru no ongaeshi*, transforms herself into a woman and marries a man who is unaware of her true identity. In order to make money she plucks her own feathers to make the most beautiful of fabrics, which her husband sells, but this makes her increasingly ill. When her husband discovers her true identity, she disappears.

Such myths may have very ancient roots. In the caves of Pech-Merle in southwest France, paintings from approximately 25,000 years B.C. have been interpreted as a bison transforming into a woman. In more recent times, the ballet *Swan Lake*, by Tchaikovsky, written in 1875–1876, still enjoys popularity.

See also **Indrásan People**, **Seal Maidens**, **Valkyries**.

Swarth

In Cumberland, the apparition of a person portending death. *See also* **Co-walker**, **Fetch**, **Waff**.

Sylph

Elemental spirit of air. The fifteenth-century alchemist Paracelsus divided fairies into four groups: the **gnomes** of the earth, the sylphs of the air, the **salamanders** of fire, and the **undines** or **nymphs** of water. Each elemental represented the pure form of that elemental energy. Elementals were said to be creatures partway between humans and pure spirits. They were made of flesh and blood, and ate, drank, slept, and procreated like human beings, but they were capable of superhuman speed and movement, lived longer than humans, and did not have immortal souls.

Sylphs embodied the air and wind and were portrayed as strong, powerful beings. Over time, the term has come to be more generally used for all types of air fairies, often depicted as small, winged creatures. The ballet *La Sylphide* was inspired by these supernatural creatures of the air.

Syrene

See **Siren**.

T

TAH-TAH-KLE-AH

Predatory women cave-dwellers in Native American mythology. These cannibals were particularly partial to the taste of children, and some stories tell of a Pitch Woman, who carried a basket on her back lined with a sticky black substance that held the captive child fast. She was also known as the Owl Woman Monster, from the legend that owls were created from one of her eyes on her death.

TAM LIN

The triumph of true love over the bewitchment of the fairies is recounted in the ballad from the Scottish Borders in which Tam Lin, a mortal, is taken by the Queen of Fairies to live with her for seven years. Each night he must return to her Otherworld after his daylight task of guarding the nearby woods.

In the woods, Tam Lin meets and falls in love with a girl who plucks a rose. He tells her she can rescue him from his captivity only by seizing him from his white horse as the fairy retinue rides past in the dead of night and she must cling to him steadfastly through all the terrible transformations the queen will visit on him. This she does, remaining steadfast as Tam Lin is transformed into adder, a bear, and finally a burning coal, and so Tam Lin and his mortal love defeat the enchantments of the fairy world.

The story is set in Scotland, but many of the themes and references to fairy beliefs are found in folklore throughout Europe. The rich references it contains to fairy beliefs makes "Tam Lin" one of the most important of the supernatural ballads.

The Queen o' Fairies she caught me,
in yon green hill to dwell,
And pleasant is the fairy-land
But, an eerie tale to tell!

Ay at the end of seven years,
They pay a tiend to hell;
I am sae fair and fu' o flesh
I'm fear'd it be mysel'.

But the night is Halloween, Lady
The morn is Hallowday;
Then win me, win me, an ye will,
For weel I wat ye may.

In this short extract, from Robert Burns' version of the ballad, there are references to the Queen of the Fairies trying to capture Tam Lin in the green hills of fairyland, as well as the "tiend," or "tithe," a tribute that the fairies were believed to have to pay to hell every seven years. The tiend also features in the ballad of "True Thomas and the Queen of Elfland." Halloween, that most sacred time of the fairies, is also mentioned.

Francis James Child's *The English and Scottish Popular Ballads* (1882–1898) provides a full account of the story of Tam Lim's rescue from fairyland.

TANGIE

A water spirit of Orkney and Shetland, covered in seaweed and taking the form of a rough-haired pony.

A Shetland tale tells of the exploits of Black Eric, a thief and all-round blackguard who terrorized local crofters, and whose steed was a magical and malevolent tangie.

TANIWHA

In the Maori folk traditions of New Zealand the *taniwha* is a powerful water monster, capable of both frightening and protective manifestations. Inhabiting the sea, lakes, rivers, and caves, it takes the form of dragons and gigantic serpents, sharks, whales, and other aquatic creatures, and even enchanted logs.

Taniwha are associated with Maori tribes. Each one has a distinct form and characteristics, for example Tuhirangi, whom Kupe, the great Maori voyager and navigator, sent to guard the Cook Strait.

To this day protection of and respect for *taniwha* are cited as objections to the use of their territory. In 2002 a major road-building project on the North Island was partially rerouted due to local tribes' concern for the area.

Tan-Wedd

A Welsh death portent taking the form of lights in the sky, similar to falling stars but moving more slowly. In **W. Sikes**' *British Goblins* (1880) it is described thus: "a fiery apparition which falls on the lands of a freeholder who is about to die. 'It lighteneth all the air and ground where it passeth,'" says "the honest Welshman, Mr. Davis . . ." adding, "it 'lasteth three or four miles or more, for aught is known, because no man seeth the rising or beginning of it; and when it falls to the ground it sparkleth and lighteth all about.'"

Taotie

A huge-mouthed, flesh-eating monster with an insatiable appetite. Ancient ceremonial vessels in China bear his macabre face; his hideous features instilled fear and were a gruesome warning to other clans. Tales of his exploits are found in Chinese mythology.

Tapio

In Finnish mythology Tapio is a spirit of the forest, the guardian of hunters and animals. He is portrayed as an old man whose face consists of leaves, tendrils, and lichen.

See also **the Green Man**.

Taqwus

A *nukatem*, or original spirit, of the Native American Cahuilla tribe of Southern California. It manifests as a streaking meteor or a form emitting dazzling, blue flashes. A stealer of souls in the night, it is a mischief-maker and agent of misfortune.

Tarans

The restless and unhappy spirits of babies who died before being baptized and now inhabit the wild places of northeast Scotland.

Taroo-Ushtey

A water bull in Manx folklore whose only distinguishing feature is his rounded ears. When he is bred with ordinary cattle, his progeny is misshapen and monstrous. If treated with respect and handled by someone with a rowan stick about their person, he will do no harm, but if provoked, he is likely to inflict damage and disaster on crops, or to carry the offender away to a watery grave.

Tarraway

See **Terrytop**.

Tatter Foal

See **Shag Foal**.

Telchines

(Or Telkhines.) In the ancient texts of Greek mythology the Telchines are described as the original inhabitants of the island of Rhodes, where they worked their sorcery through the art of metalsmithing, manufacturing magical weapons for the gods such as the trident with which Poseidon controlled the seas. In other tales they were punished for their life-destroying powers, portrayed as shapeshifting sea demons, and described as having fins instead of hands and the heads of dogs.

Telkhines

See **Telchines**.

Terrytop

(Or Tarraway.) A Cornish spinning demon, with similarities to the European folklore character **Rumpelstiltskin**, Terrytop is described in *Popular Romances of the West of England* (1865) by **Robert Hunt** as "a queer-looking little man, with a remarkable pair of eyes, which seemed to send out flashes of light. There was something uncommonly knowing in the twist of his mouth, and his curved nose had an air of curious intelligence. He was dressed in black."

"Duffy and the Devil" relates the bargain struck between Duffy, an idle country girl (although a diligent liar), who must spin and weave for her husband, the squire, and Terrytop, who promises to take over the onerous task for three years on the understanding she will go with him at the end of that time unless she can discover his name. The years pass and, at the eleventh hour, she learns his name and confronts him, whereupon he promptly disappears in a flash of fire and smoke. All the garments he had spun, which Duffy had carefully collected and stored, fall to ashes, and the squire, in the middle of a hunt, abruptly finds himself unclothed and shivering, at the mercy of the elements.

See also **Habetrot**, **Tom Tit Tot**, **Whuppity Stoorie**.

Thardid Jimbo

In the tales of the Australian Aborigines, Thardid Jimbo was a bloodthirsty, cannibalistic **giant** who captured and killed a local man who was out hunting for food. He took the mangled body back to a cave where the hunter's two wives were waiting for him to return. The enterprising wives tricked the giant into going deep into the cave and quickly built a vast fire at the entrance, which trapped and eventually roasted the monstrous creature.

Thekk

In the thirteenth-century *Prose Edda* by the Icelandic author and collector **Snorri Sturluson**, the Old Norse myths recount the origin of **dwarves** as "quickened in the earth and under the soil like maggots in flesh . . . but by the decree of the gods they acquired human understanding and the appearance of men, although they lived in the earth, and in rocks . . ." Thekk appears in a list of earth-dwellers and is translated as "Pleasant One."

Thomas the Rhymer

A mortal man who lived in the thirteenth century in present-day Earlston in Scotland and so impassioned the Queen of Elfland that she took him to stay with her for seven years. Fearing that he might be taken by the Devil as his payment from the fairies, she eventually returned him to his home, bequeathing him the gift of prophecy and a truthful tongue. Folk tales and ballads refer to him as True Thomas and recount his gifts as a poet and seer. The ruins of

Rhymer's Tower stand today in Earlston.

Thunderbird

A mostly benevolent spirit in the form of a gigantic bird. The myth of the Thunderbird is shared by many Native American tribes. Various tales attribute the sound of thunder to the powerful clap of his wings, while other legends tell of how during a mighty battle he clamped his talons around a marauding whale, soared to a great height, and dropped the monster into the sea, causing a thunderous reverberation.

Tian Xian Pei

A Chinese legend recounting the tale of the seventh fairy daughter of the Jade Emperor and Dong Yong, a humble peasant, who meet when she visits the mortal world to seek her lost feather cloak. They fall in love but are allowed to reunite only once a year. This story is still retold in opera and plays.

Tibicena

A large, black dog with red eyes in legends from the Canary Islands off the northwest coast of Africa. The supposed inhabitants of the islands in prehistoric times were the Guanches, whose legends and artifacts bear testimony to the terrifying presence of these demons in the caves and isolated mountain heights of the islands. In ritual ceremonies, offerings of especially prepared infusions were made to these supernatural beings.

Tiddy Men, the

See **Greencoaties**, **Tiddy Mun**.

Tiddy Ones, the

See **Tiddy Mun**.

Tiddy Mun

In the low-lying fens of Lincolnshire, where the land was once covered with bogs and stagnant pools, stories are told of the Tiddy Men, or Tiddy Ones, evil spirits who infested this dismal watery wasteland before it was reclaimed from the sea. The men of the fens feared these malignant wraiths, but deep down in the criss-crossing streams there lived an almost benevolent spirit with long, white hair and tangled beard whose name was Tiddy Mun and whose presence was heralded by the sound of running water, a gust of wind, and a screeching laugh. Although he was a fearsome spirit, when the land was flooded and people feared for the safety of their homes, they appealed to him and the waters receded. But, as the land was slowly reclaimed over the centuries, his watery domain dwindled and he wreaked havoc in revenge until the people made offerings of fresh water each time the new moon rose. This placated him and hence good fortune returned to the fens.

Tieholtsodi

A water serpent in the Navajo tradition. His children were stolen from him and he flooded the land in retribution until they were returned, whereupon the waters retreated and peace was restored.

Tikbalang

A hybrid half-human monster with the dark head and hooves of a horse, this trickster spirit appears in folk tales from the Philippines as a forest-dweller with a liking for frightening those walking in the woods, causing them confusion in their wanderings.

Titania

When William Shakespeare wrote *A Midsummer Night's Dream* and called his Queen of Fairies Titania, the name entered the language. It has since been popularized in fiction, art, games, and films.

Tlaloques

Magical rainmaker spirits in the Nahua mythology of central Mexico. These water spirits are responsible for the rain, which was thought to have its source in caves, whence it rose into the sky and then descended from the clouds with the encouragement of the *tlaloques*.

Tokoloshe

A malevolent South African demon, a small, hairy entity living near water in remote places. A sexual predator, a familiar of witch-doctors and general causer of mischief and mayhem, he is a potent figure to be feared and blamed for all the evil-doing of society. He features in media reports and in online debates, comic strips, and songs, and some superstitious people still raise their beds high off the floor with bricks to thwart his possible sexual advances.

Tolaeth

A Welsh portent of death, described as an ominous sound always heard before either a funeral or some dreadful catastrophe. **Wirt Sikes**, in *British Goblins* (1880), describes it as being heard before a death as ghostly footsteps, mysterious rapping or knocking, or as the tolling of church bells. Before a coffin is required, carpenters hear the sound of "the sawing of wood, the hammering of nails, and the turning of screws, such as are heard in the usual process of making a coffin." Before a burial, the tolaeth is heard in the singing of psalms, the grieving cries of mourners and the slow beat of their footsteps. It is sometimes also visible to those who look closely on the ground as:

. . . psalm-singers, two abreast, with their hats off and their mouths open, as in the act of singing; the coffin, borne on the shoulders of four men who hold their hats by the side of their heads; the mourners, the men with long black hatbands streaming behind, the women pale and sorrowful, with upheld handkerchiefs; and the rest of the procession stretching away dimly into shadow. Not a sound is heard, either of foot or

voice, although the singers' mouths are open.

It can be heard only when invisible and seen only in silence.

Tom Thumb

The tale of this accident-prone, diminutive **dwarf** was first recorded in the seventeenth century, although the character and his exploits are said to be known long before this.

Tom Thumb was born to a farmer who wished so much for a son that he sent his wife to Merlin the magician for advice, which was duly given and a son was born.

With the Queen of Fairies as his godmother, Tom received good luck charms, which he certainly made full use of during his exceptionally adventurous and perilous existence, which included escaping death by being boiled in a pudding and being swallowed on many occasions by a variety of animals.

After being discovered by King Arthur's cook inside a royal salmon, Tom became a court favorite and astonished all about him, especially the ladies of the court, with his fabulous tales.

Tom's demise is not recorded in the early written story, but there have been many later embellishments in fiction, operas, and artistic portrayals.

Tom Tit Tot

One of the names used in English versions of the **Rumpelstiltskin** tale. Tom Tit Tot is a malicious, leering little **imp** with a long tail who helps a desperate bride with her spinning in return for her promise to belong to him if she cannot discover his name within the month. As in the Cornish version, "Duffy and the Devil," it is the husband who unwittingly divulges the name to his wife.

See also **Terrytop**, **Whuppity Stoorie**.

Tomte

In Scandinavian folk tradition the *tomte* (as he is known in Sweden) is a mostly benevolent and hardworking guardian of farms and houses and is associated with a particular dwelling or plot of land. He is small and can become invisible or change his size, but is portrayed generally as a little old man wearing drab clothes. The welfare of his household is his priority and he is not above a little poaching to supplement the prosperity of his domain. In return, he needs only to be left alone and treated with respect, although he does enjoy a bowl of special Christmas porridge in his more modern manifestation as the *jultomte*, or Christmas spirit. His likeness, with the addition of a long, red hat, is fashioned from salt dough and used as a seasonal decoration in Swedish homes.

See also **Agricultural Spirits**, ***Niagriusar***, ***Nisse***.

TONENILI

In Navajo legends Tonenili is the spirit of all forms of water. Rain, hail, and snow are in his power and, being a mischievous spirit, he takes delight in causing deluges at most unpropitious moments. In more solemn ceremonies he plays the part of the jester dressed in a costume of spruce branches and a mask, dipping his hand into the pot of water he carries to sprinkle around.

TONGUE, RUTH
(1898–1981)

A storyteller, folk singer, and folklorist, Ruth Tongue was born in Somerset, England. She expressed a love the countryside and the people who lived there. Although she was born into a well-off family, she liked to mix with people who worked the land, listening to their folk tales and learning their traditional songs. They believed her to be a "chime child," that is a child born between midnight on a Friday and dawn on Saturday (although this was not the case). Such a child was supposed to be immune to any evil influence and possess much talent for the arts.

When she was still young, Ruth's family moved to Hertfordshire, where she studied drama and art. In the 1950s she returned to Somerset and settled in Crowcombe, where she lived in the company of her cats, dogs, and pony. She gave lively talks and performances to local organizations and entertained many with her tales and songs. She met the folklore scholar **Katharine Briggs**, who encouraged her to put pen to paper and record her knowledge of local lore. Many critics suspected that she embellished quite a number of her stories and changed them to suit her style, but she remained a popular figure.

Her first book was *Somerset Folklore*, published in 1965 and edited by Katharine Briggs, followed by *The Chime Child or Somerset Singers* (1968) and *Forgotten Folktales of the English Counties* (1970), which contained an introduction by Briggs, who had become a good friend.

Tonntu

See ***Haltija***.

Triton

See **Merman**.

Trolls

Scandinavian mythology is full of tales involving mountain-dwelling trolls. Their appearance ranges from hideously ugly monsters with tails and hairy feet to extremely good-looking human forms toward whom one should demonstrate a suspicious wariness.

One characteristic shared by all trolls is a detestation of the sound of church bells and of anything connected with religious belief, therefore a simple and effective deterrent used by troll-fearing folk was to carve crosses into their wooden front doors.

Although living well away from human populations, trolls weren't solitary creatures but lived in small communities who could often be helpful to their distant human neighbors. This benevolent attitude was somewhat blighted by a tendency toward kidnapping young children and solitary walkers, and it was only through the power of church bells and the singing of hymns near the trolls' mountain abodes that their unwilling houseguests were released.

See also **Gryla**, ***Huldra***, ***Illes***, **Trows**.

Trooping Fairies

In *Fairy and Folk Tales of the Irish Peasantry* (1888), **W. B. Yeats** divides the fairies of British folklore into trooping fairies and **solitary fairies**.

Trooping fairies encompass a wide variety of fairy creatures, from the human-sized, shining beings of Irish folklore to tiny nature spirits. They tend to live in groups or communities and travel in processions, as opposed to the solitary fairies who, as their name suggests, prefer a life of solitude.

Generally speaking, solitary fairies were considered more fearsome and less pleasant than trooping fairies. Whether large, small, friendly, or sinister, trooping fairies were generally thought to share a love of dancing, music, singing, and merrymaking, and were known for their mischief-making and tricksy ways.

In *A Dictionary of Fairies, Hobgoblins, Brownies, Bogies and Other Supernatural Creatures* (1976), **Katharine Briggs** suggested a third division of fairies to include family groups of domestic household fairies such as **hobs**, though she concluded that presumably they would join other fairies at times of merrymaking or at fairy markets, making them an extension of the trooping fairies.

Trows

Shetland folklore and its otherworldly creatures have strong connections with those of Scandinavia, and trows are described in *Brewer's Dictionary of Phrase and Fable* (1870) as "Dwarfs of Orkney and Shetland mythology, similar to the Scandinavian **trolls**. There are land-trows and sea-trows. 'Trow tak thee' is a phrase still used by the island women when angry with their children."

The shy, nocturnal trows are subterranean dwellers, living in *trowie knowes*, or earthen mounds, from which they emerge to make mischief and, sometimes, to be helpful. Their love of feasting and music is the cause of much human annoyance, as with their magical trusty arrows the clever trows provide beef and mutton aplenty for their table, while substituting the erstwhile living animals with illusory images, much to the befuddlement of farmers. Musicians, too, beware, for trows are master fiddlers and their sweet music lures mortal players to their underground lairs to entertain at lavish feasts. Their enchanted stay may seem but to pass in the blink of an eye but can last a year or more. Many of the tunes are said to have been passed from the trows to the islanders, and are played to this day. One frailty distinguishing some of the trows that hampers their enjoyment of dancing is a limp, or henk, consequently they are known as henkies.

Sea-trows are described as "great rolling creatures, tumbling in the waters" by Rev. John Brand in *A Brief Description of Orkney, Shetland, Pightland-Firth and Caithness* (1701). He recounts the havoc they caused among the fishermen's nets and how the sailors endeavored to keep them at bay by wielding long, heavy oars.

See also **Gray Neighbors**.

Tsao Chun

See **Zao-Jun**.

Tsonokwa

(Or dzunukwa.) In folklore relating to indigenous tribes of Vancouver Island, BC, the *tsonokwa* is a mountain-dwelling **giant** in both male and female forms: a child-eating, somewhat dozy female version whom children can often outrun and outwit, and a more fearsome male.

Tuatha de Danann

The legendary fairy race of Ireland, descended from ancient royalty and the conquerors of the resident Firbolgs. After fierce battles, they were in turn vanquished by the Milesians and reduced to dwelling in an underground realm

Tulip Fairies

Flower-loving pixies in Dartmoor folklore. The following story is related in W. W. Gibbings' *Folklore and Legends* (1890):

An old woman living on Dartmoor had a very pretty garden where she grew the most beautiful bed of tulips. The pixies loved it so much that they brought their elfin babies there to sing them to sleep. Often, at midnight, a sweet lullaby could be heard, accompanied by the most melodious music, which seemed to come from the tulips themselves. The delicate flowers waved their heads in the night breeze as if dancing to their own song.

As soon as the babies were asleep, the pixies would go to a nearby field, where they would dance in fairy rings. At the first light of dawn, they would return to their babies in the tulips.

So favored by the pixies, the tulips retained their beauty much longer than any of the other flowers in the garden and as the pixies breathed over them they became as fragrant as roses.

The old woman was delighted and would never allow anyone to pick the tulips from her garden. But when she died, her heir destroyed the tulips and replaced them with a bed of parsley. This offended the pixies and they caused the parsley to wither away.

For many years nothing would grow in that bed, or indeed in the whole garden.

The pixies were, however, as capable of rewarding kindness as they were of nursing an injury, and they affectionately tended the spot where the old woman was buried. Every night they could be heard there, lamenting and singing sweet dirges. Though no human hand ever tended the old lady's grave, the prettiest flowers grew there and the grass was forever green.

TÜNDÉR

Fairies of Hungarian folklore. These supernatural females could appear and disappear at will and manifest or vanish objects at their whim.

As in other cultures, Hungarian fairies were fickle-natured, sometimes helping, at other times hindering the lives of humans. Means of fairy enchantment at their disposal included a lake of beautifying milk, tears, saliva, rejuvenating water, healing herbs, sleeping draughts, rods of diamonds and gold, magic wands, and copper and gold whips—the cracking of which invoked dragons and devils.

One of their magical incantations runs as follows:

You are mine, I am thine.
Be there, where you have come from!
Fog before me, smoke behind me.
Hop, hop! Let me be, where I wish to be.
Hop, hop! They shall not know where I have come from, nor where I am going to!
Let me be, where my thoughts are!

In some accounts, their home was a magical isle in the Danube named Csallóköz, meaning "to deceive, to disappear, to disillusion." There they lived with the fairy queen, Ilona, a shapeshifting being who swam in the Danube in the form of a swan.

In other tales, the fairies inhabited castles on lofty mountain peaks bequeathed to them by **giants** or of their own construction. The fairy **Dame Rapson** enlisted the help of a magical cat and cock to build her mountain castle.

As in other cultures, Hungarian fairies were connected with human luck, fate, and destiny; the Hungarian poet Berzsenyi wrote: "*Tündér szerencsénk k´´ye håany vet,*" meaning, "Fickle fortune's whim elevates and destroys us." The Hungarian saying "*Csallóközi szerencse,*" "the luck of Csallóköz," means "vanishing luck."

In Hungary the Milky Way is known as the Fairies' Way, said to mark the path used by fairies to travel around the Earth, and like other fairies, *tündér* were known to kidnap humans—**Dame Hirip** was a child-snatching fairy woman.

Tündér were also fond of singing and dancing in rings. Flowers sprang up where their feet touched the ground. Should a mortal man step into the ring, a *tündér* might choose to take him as her lover, or to dance with him until he died from exhaustion. Those who survived a dance in the ring, or who pleased the *tündér* with their musical skill, could expect to receive a fairy gift. As is often the case with treasures from the fairy realm, the next day the gifts often vanished or transformed into worthless items such as leaves or stones. However, one tale tells of how the fairies enticed a shepherd into Borza-vara cave and kept him there for three days, singing, dancing, and playing music, before sending him away with a hatful of gold.

Named *tündér* include: Firtos, queen of the good fairies, Tartod, queen of the bad fairies, Fairy Elizabeth, Fairy Helena, Tarko and her twin daughters, Olt and Maros (who give their names to two rivers in Transylvania), and Mika, the warrioress fairy.

Tuoni and Tuonetar

In Finnish mythology Tuoni and his wife, Tuonetar, rule over the kingdom of Tuonela, the Land of the Dead, the Underworld.

Tupilak

See ***Tupilaq***.

Tupilaq, the

(Or *tupilak.*) In Inuit culture the *tupilaq* has a variety of manifestations. In some cases it is an invisible and dangerous presence, the restless soul of an avenging ancestor causing harm to individuals, and only the shaman possesses the ability to see it and to defend the people from it. In Greenland a shaman could use it by fashioning a figure from animal and human bones to represent it and then, in utmost secrecy, investing it with destructive powers and launching it into the sea to seek its target. However, the outcome was not a foregone conclusion—if the shaman's enemy possessed greater powers, he would find himself under attack.

Turehu

See ***Patupaiarehe***.

Tuurngait

A collective name for the numerous disembodied spirits in Inuit folklore, ranging from the harmful to the helpful. Their variety attests to the belief that all sentient creatures possess a soul, or spirit, which survives death and has the potential to become a force for good or evil.

Tylwyth Teg

"The Fair Family," or "Fair Folk," the Welsh name for fairies, sometimes called ***Bendith y Mamau***, Mother's Blessing, a euphemism used for protection from their sometimes malicious activities.

U

Uncegila

In many Native American folk tales Uncegila was a gigantic water serpent, a malevolent creature who wrecked crops and brought devastation to the land and people.

One version of the legend tells of the many attempts to kill this monster and the many brave warriors who perished from her terrible gaze, which first blinded and then killed them. However, a courageous discussion took place between twin boys, one of whom was blind, during which they decided to rid the land once and for all of the Uncegila.

Together they concocted a plan, knowing that the only chance of success was to pierce the monster's heart, which lay beneath the seventh spot on her scaly skin. Their weapons were magic arrows that always found their target, and so armed, they set out to wait by the creature's watery lair.

As soon as the depths began to boil and churn, the eyes of the sighted twin turned rapidly away and he called to his brother to shoot. The magic arrows flew through the air and pierced the seventh spot. Struck through the heart, the serpent was killed.

Underjordiske

Earth-dwelling spirits of Norwegian folklore. Literally, "those who live underground," they live in mountains and in ancient burial mounds. Although usually concealed from human sight, there are tales of the *underjordiske* appearing to humans in remote forests or mountains.

In one tale, the *underjordiske* show a young man a wealth of treasures and farmland and promise that he shall have them all if he takes one of their beautiful *huldra* daughters to be his bride. The young man agrees, and sits down to eat with the *underjordiske.* But when he starts to say grace, a scuffle ensues and he is unceremoniously ejected and neither bride nor riches are forthcoming.

Undine

(Or ondine.) German water **nymph** dwelling in forest ponds and waterfalls. According to legend, undines lack a soul, but are able to obtain one by marrying a mortal man and bearing him a child. *Undine* (1811), a novella by Friedrich de la Motte Fouqué, tells the story of Undine, a water nymph who married a knight named Huldebrand in order to gain a soul, but in so doing also gained knowledge of the pain and suffering of the human condition. The storyline resembles that of *The Little Mermaid* by **Hans Christian Andersen**. The story enjoyed widespread popularity, especially during the nineteenth century. It was adapted into operas by Hoffman and Tchaikovsky and has inspired many other works of literature, film, music, and art.

Unseelie Court, the

In Scottish tradition, fairies are generally divided into the Unseelie Court and the **Seelie Court**. The origin of the names is thought to be the Scottish *seilie*, meaning "happy," "lucky," or "blessed"; *unseelie* having the opposite meanings of "unhappy," "unfortunate," or "unholy." So the Unseelie Court is a group of fairies with a dark side to their character.

The ***Sluagh***, or "Host," the souls of the unsanctified dead cursed to hover over the Earth, belong to the Unseelie Court. They like to assault travelers, even unprovoked, beating them or carrying them through the air, and sometimes recruit defenseless humans to their number, forcing them to unleash elf-shot (flint arrows) on people and cattle. Although they are primarily malevolent, on occasion a member of the Unseelie Court may take a liking to a particular human being and treat them as a sort of pet. Generally, though, one would be well-advised to avoid all dealings with them.

Urisk

(Or uruisg.) A solitary Scottish fairy, the urisk is a kind of **brownie**.

He sits by pools, hoping to attract the attention of passersby in order to gain their friendship. However, people are often frightened by his odd looks—he is part-human and part-goat. He is humble and willing to help and often aids farmers with their work, herding cattle and working in the fields, but he is characterized by his loneliness.

Uruisg

See **Urisk**.

Utukku

The ancient Babylonian tradition names a multiplicity of evil spirits as *utukku*, demons responsible for all the ills of the mortal world who, although invisible to humans, were depicted as monstrous hybrids, scorpions, and snakes dwelling in isolated places such as caves and ruins. An evil force in opposition to the benevolent ***lamassu*** and ***shedu*** guardian spirits, they were bent on exorcising their malevolent influence over humans, inciting sinful thoughts and deeds and bringing ruin to mortals who succumbed to their evil machinations. Nowhere and no one was exempt from their malignant attentions as they wreaked havoc and pestilence, appearing as destructive whirlwinds, seizing mortals if they walked in the graveyards where ***ekimmu*** dwelled, and silently invading houses, dreams, and passions to foment hatred and anger and unsatisfied lusts.

Against this vicious throng of ubiquitous spirits, the only defense was the recitation of magical incantations by priests and the performance of rituals specifically related to the class of demon responsible.

V

Valkyries

(Or Valkyrs.) The **nymphs** of Valhalla, hall of fallen battle heroes in Norse mythology. They traveled through the skies on horseback, holding their drawn swords aloft. In battle they selected the bravest Viking soldiers destined for death and took them to the afterlife hall of Valhalla to await Ragnarök—the great battle that would end the world. While the warriors awaited the final battle, the Valkyries waited upon them, serving them with mead and ale. They were also **Odin**'s messengers, and when they rode out on their errands, the flickering light of their armor lit up the skies as the *aurora borealis*, the northern lights. Venturing down to the earthly mortal realm, they disguised themselves as white swans to bathe in secluded lakes. Should they be seen by humans without their swan disguise, they became ordinary mortals and could never return to Valhalla. In modern culture Valkyries have been the subject of works of art, musical works, notably Richard Wagner's opera *Die Walküre*, poetry, and video games.

See also **Swan Maidens**.

Valkyrs

See **Valkyries**.

Van Pools

The Spirit of the Van haunts the Van Pools, a beautiful body of water in the Welsh mountains of Carmarthen. She appears on New Year's Eve, dressed in white, with long, golden hair, sitting in a golden boat that she propels with a golden oar. Her story shows that unions between mortals and fairies do not always run smoothly.

According to legend, many years ago a young farmer heard of the Spirit of the Van's great beauty and went to the lake on New Year' Eve and awaited her arrival. Upon seeing her, he fell in love and asked her to marry him, but she faded away.

Night after night he went back to the lake in the hope of seeing her again. His farm was neglected as a profound melancholy descended on him. At last he sought the help of a Welsh mountain sage, who advised him to leave gifts of cheese and bread by the water's edge.

He did as instructed, but still the spirit would not appear. The following New Year's Eve he took his best cheeses and loaves of bread to the lake. At last the spirit appeared and rowed in his direction. She stepped ashore and, to his delight, consented to become his wife, bringing cattle with her as her dowry. She warned him that he should never strike her. If he did, the third time he did so she would disappear.

The pair lived very happily until one day they were invited to a christening and in the midst of the ceremony the spirit burst into tears. Her husband asked her why she was making such a fool of herself. "The poor babe is entering a world of sin and misery, why should I rejoice?" she replied. Embarrassed and angry, her husband gave her a push and she warned him he had struck her once.

Sometime later they attended the funeral of the very same child. This time the spirit laughed and sang. Her husband asked again why she was making such a fool of herself. "I laugh," she replied, "because the child has now left a world of sin for a world of joy." Her husband pushed her again and she warned him he had struck her twice.

Then they were invited to a wedding where the bride was young and the man of advanced years. Once again the spirit wept and said: "It is the Devil's compact—youth has married age for gold. I see misery for them both." Her husband, forgetting her earlier warnings, pushed her again. This time she vanished forever, taking the herd with her.

VEJA MAHTE

The Mother of the Wind in Latvian folklore. She rules over the winds, the birds, and the woods.

VEJO PATIS

The Master of the Wind in Lithuanian folklore, depicted as a two-faced, bearded man with wings. He held a fish in his left hand, a dish in right hand, and a cockerel perched upon his head. His sons, Rytys, Pietys, Siaurys, and Vakaris, were the lords of the east, south, north, and west winds.

Vejo Patis was a gatekeeper of the heavenly realm of Dausos. He did not allow undeserving souls to enter, and blew them into oblivion with a gust of his breath.

Ventolines

Literally, "little winds," the gentle wind spirits of Cantabria, northern Spain. Unlike fierce **El Nuberu**, the bringer of storms, the *ventolines* are benevolent and bring gentle breezes to steer fishing boats safely back to harbor.

Vila

Slavic **nymphs** said to have power over the wind and to delight in creating storms. In Polish legends they are called *wila.* These fairylike creatures, appearing as beautiful maidens, either naked or dressed in fabulous blue robes or skirts of leaves, live in the wilderness or in the clouds, and are sometimes said to be the spirits of women who have lived frivolous lives. They dwell between this world and the afterlife and their feminine charms belie the fact that they are also fierce warriors whose voices can form gusts of wind powerful enough to lift a house.

Possessing healing powers and the ability to foretell the future, *vila* will sometimes help humans. They have also been said to lure young men to dance with them and, according to their mood, this can go well or badly for the man in question. A thick ring of grass is left where they have danced, but treading upon this brings bad luck.

In Serbian folklore, a *vila* is a forest nymph who dwells in rivers or caves. They are shapeshifters and can appear as swans, horses, falcons, or other animals, as well as beautiful young women dressed in long, white gowns. They are benevolent unless provoked and generally help the poor and needy. But be warned: to cross a *vila* is to incur her wrath, and a glance from an angry *vila* can prove fatal.

See also **Oosood**.

Vivian

One of the names given to the **Lady of the Lake** of Arthurian legend.

Vodyanoy

(Plural: *vodyaniye.*) In Slavic mythology the *vodyanoy* is a malignant water spirit living in the depths of rivers or at the bottom of the sea, preferably where a strong current assists in his favorite pastime of delivering humans to his underwater abode to be his slaves. A shapeshifter, sometimes appearing as a fish or giant frog, or as an ancient man with a green beard and scaly body, he is blamed when flooding occurs or a dam bursts.

W

Wabun

See **Four Winds, the**.

Waff

Yorkshire name for a **wraith** or double. Similar to a **co-walker**, a waff is believed to portend death. However, should you encounter your own waff, it is possible to forestall your fate by giving it a stern talking-to, as described in an account in William Henderson's *Notes on the Folklore of the Northern Counties of England and the Borders* (1866). A local of Guisborough saw his waff in a shop in Whitby, whereupon he addressed it boldly: "What's thou doin' here? What's thou doin' here?" He then ordered it to: "Get thy ways yom with thee!" at which it slunk away and caused no more trouble.

See also **Fetch**, **Swarth**.

Wag-at-the-Wa'

A domestic household spirit of the Scottish border country. This cheerful **brownie**'s favorite seat was in the kitchen on the swinging pot-hook, where he rocked to and fro, enjoying the merriment of the household. He had a pernickety nature when it came to neatness and cleanliness and expressed his disapproval for strong liquor by coughing loudly when anyone went to take a sip of anything more potent than home-brewed ale. He was generally described as wearing a red coat and blue britches, often with a nightcap pulled down over one side of his face to cover his jaw, as he had the misfortune to be afflicted with perpetual toothache. Notwithstanding, he was a convivial spirit of an unfailingly cheery disposition and delighted in the company of children.

In a traditional Scottish song, the wag-at-the-wa' was a clock with a pendulum hanging free beneath it. Its purpose was to remind the revelers of the passage of time, and of their wives, who were watching a similar clock back at home.

WAKANDA

A supernatural or magical life force in the belief of the Sioux.

See also ***Manitou.***

WALDGEISTER

Wood spirits in German and Scandinavian folklore, the guardians of the trees. Some were benign, some were dangerous. They inhabited ancient forests and possessed knowledge of healing and medicinal plants.

Hylde-Moer, the Elder Mother, who resided in the elder tree, was one of the *Waldgeister.*

WALDRON, GEORGE (1690–1730)

An English topographer, author, and poet, Waldron resided in the Isle of Man, where he was commissioner for the British government. During his time there he made many observations of the customs of the Manx people and in 1726 he wrote *A Description of the Isle of Man: Some useful and entertaining reflections on the laws, customs and manners of the inhabitants*, a section of which is devoted to Manx fairy lore. **Sir Walter Scott**, among others, was to make much use of his material.

WATER HORSE

See ***Aughisky***, ***Cabyll Ushtey***, ***Each Uisge***, ***Glastyn***, **Kelpies**, **Nuckelavee**, ***Nikur***.

WATER LEAPER, THE

See ***Llamhigyn y Dwr***.

Water Wraith

Female Scottish water spirit. Water wraiths haunt bodies of water, including rivers and fords, and are wont to lure in travelers and drown them. One particular river wraith is described as a tall, withered woman dressed in green with a malignant scowl. With a bony finger she beckons travelers, drawing them down to their watery fate.

See also ***Boginki***, **Bunyip**, ***Dracs***, **Ezerinis**, ***Fossegrim***, ***Fuathan***, ***Jengu***, **Jenny Greenteeth**, **Grindylow**, ***Llamhigyn y Dwr***, **Lorelei**, **Morgan**, *Näkken*, ***Näkki***, **Nix**, **Oriyu**, **Peg Powler**, **Rawhead and Bloody Bones**, **River Mumma**, **Vodyanoy**, **Zinkibaru**.

Wee Folk

Another term for fairies, notably used in Scotland and Ireland. One of many euphemistic names used to avoid the scorn of the fairies or to draw unwanted attention from them.

White Ladies

"White ladies" can refer to both ghosts and fairies. Folklorist **Evans-Wentz** pointed out that the original meaning of both Gwenhwyvar, or Guinevere, and the Irish *bean fhionn* was "white phantom." Direct descendants of the ***Tuatha de Danann*** have also been referred to as white ladies. The usage indicates the close connection between fairies and the dead.

According to one legend from Normandy, France, white ladies lurk in ravines, fords, and bridges, and ask passersby to dance. If they are answered courteously, all is well, but if the passerby refuses, they fling him into a ditch full of thorns to teach him a lesson in manners.

In more modern times the legend of the white lady has persisted in a different guise. A young woman dressed in white hitches a lift at night. A male driver stops and offers to take her to her destination. Just before a sharp bend the young woman shouts, "Look out!" The driver brakes and turns around, only to find that the young woman has vanished.

The same story is found in many countries throughout the world and, despite being well documented, its origins are not known. Some speculate that these white ladies are ghosts returning to the place of their death, others that they are fairies or sorceresses.

White Lady of Ireland, The

See **Banshee**.

Whuppity Stoorie

The traditional Scottish version of **Rumpelstiltskin**, which runs as follows.

A woman lived in a small cottage on the edge of a wood with her baby. Since her husband, a lazy scoundrel of a farmer, had up and left, she had been very poor. Her only valuable possession was a sow that was about to farrow, and she planned to sell the piglets to support herself and the child.

One morning she went to the pigsty to feed her pig, but found to her dismay that it was very sick and not likely to last much longer. Just as she began to sob, an old woman appeared and asked her what she would give her if she cured the pig.

"Anything you want," the farmer's wife replied.

The old woman rubbed some ointment on the pig, said a few incomprehensible words and, miraculously, it got to its feet and gave a happy oink.

"Now for your part of the bargain," she said. "I'll take your baby as payment."

The farmer's wife screamed out in shock.

The old woman continued, "By the laws of my people, the fair folk, I must make you this offer: I'll return in three days' time to collect him, but if you can tell me my name when I return, I'll allow you to keep him."

The farmer's wife despaired. How could she find out the name of a complete stranger?

On the second day she decided to go for a walk with her baby in the forest. As she approached an old quarry, she heard someone singing. She went nearer and saw it was the old woman.

"My name is Whuppity Stoorie and I live in a quarry," she sang.

The farmer's wife couldn't believe her luck. She left quietly and returned home full of joy.

When the old woman returned the next day to collect the baby, the farmer's wife pleaded first that she take the pig and then herself in place of him.

"What would I do with you?" asked the old woman.

"I see. So I am unworthy of you, Whuppity Stoorie," said the farmer's wife.

Upon hearing her name, the old fairy screamed and ran away, leaving mother and child to live happily together.

See also **Habetrot**, **Terrytop**, **Tom Tit Tot**.

Wila

*See **Vila**.*

Wild Hunt, the

Belief in the wild hunt was once widespread across northern Europe. Led by a supernatural master, the hunt generally comprised a pack of fairy hounds accompanied by spectral huntsmen mounted on horseback. It flew through the air, pounded the earth, or hovered just above the ground as it went in search of its quarry.

Specific beliefs varied from place to place. In Norse lore, **Odin** led the wild hunt in pursuit of the fairy **wood wives** of the forest. In Britain **King Herla** became master of the wild hunt after a visit to the Underworld. In Wales **Gwyn ap Nudd** led a pack of white, red-eared hounds, herding souls of the dead to the Underworld. On the Isle of Man, a band of 13 hunters rode out on frosty, moonlit nights on the Manx Fairy Hunt, as described in **Thomas Keightley**'s *The Fairy Mythology* (1828):

A young sailor returning home from a long voyage came ashore at night at Douglas and set out for his sister's house in Kirk Merlugh. Though he had some miles to travel, it was a bright, frosty moonlit night and his path was well lit.

As he walked up the steep hill between Douglas and Kirk Merlugh, he heard the cry of huntsmen, the thunder of horses' hooves, and the trumpeting of horns. He wondered why the hunt was out at night in such a frost. It crossed his path several times and under the light of the moon, he saw the riders as clear as day. There were 13 huntsmen on horseback, dressed in green. Impressed by the sight, the sailor tried to follow them, but they were too swift for him.

When at last he arrived at his sister's house, he described the strange sight to her.

"Dear brother," she exclaimed, "those were fairies and it is well that you are home safe and they did not take you away with them."

In the Highlands of Scotland the formidable fairy ***Sluagh***, or "host," often described as the souls of the unforgiven dead, would take to the air in a great flock, hunting mortal souls to join their number, and shooting at cats, dogs, sheep, and cattle with poisoned darts, or elf-shot. An account in **Alexander Carmichael**'s *Carmina Gadelica* (1900) describes a sighting of them in the Outer Hebrides:

One night, two cattleherds were in a barn tending to the calves. They were talking beside a blazing fire when two strange dogs rushed in and ran around the barn, much to the terror of the men and the calves. The dogs were tethered together by a silver leash spangled with gold and encrusted with brilliant stones that sparkled in the firelight and bright moonbeams. The men heard a voice call out, though they could see no one:

"Slender fay, slender fay!
Mountain traveller, mountain traveller!
Black fairy, black fairy!
Lucky treasure, lucky treasure!
Grey hound, grey hound!
Seek beyond, seek beyond!"

On hearing the call, the dogs ran outside, and when the men had gathered their wits, they followed. In the bright blue night sky they beheld a multitude of spirits with hounds on leashes and hawks perched on hands. The air was filled with music, like tinkling bells, mingled with the shouts of the sluagh *calling to their hounds . . .*

These were the spirits of the departed on a hunting expedition, travelling westwards beyond the "Isle of the nuns," beyond the "Isle of the monks," beyond the Isle of "Hirt," beyond the Isle of "Rockal," and away and away towards "Tir fo thuinn," the Land under waves; "Tir na h-oige," the Land of youth; and Tir na h-aoise," the Land of age, beneath the great western sea."

With the advent of Christianity, the wild hunt was often associated with demonic spirits and witches. As recently as the 1940s, it was reportedly heard passing by on Halloween near Taunton, Somerset, in the southwest of England.

Wilde, Lady Jane Frances (1826–1896)

A patriotic Irish poet with a special interest in folk and fairy tales, she published poems under the pen name Speranza. She was a friend of **W. B. Yeats** and the mother of the writer Oscar Wilde, and her Irish patriotism led her to study the culture and folklore of her country. In 1857 she published *Ancient Legends, Mystic Charms and Superstitions of Ireland*, which included many of Ireland's fairy legends, such as **Ethna the Bride**, the tale of **Fin Bheara**, fairy king of the ***Daoine Sidhe***, abducting a beautiful mortal woman.

Will o' the Wisp

(Also called **Jack O'Lantern**, Friar's Lantern, or *Ignis Fatuus.*) Small lights seen over marshes or swamps and sometimes in graveyards. It is said that these lights are held by fairies to lure travelers away from a safe route. In Britain there are many regional variations for the name of this phenomenon, including:

Cornwall and Somerset: **Joan the Wad**
East Anglia: The Lantern Man
East Anglia and Hertfordshire: The Hobby Lantern
Lancashire: Peg-a-Lantern
Lowland Scotland: Spunkies
Norfolk: Will o' the Wikes
North Yorkshire and Northumberland: Jenny with the Lantern
Shropshire: Will the Smith
Somerset and Devon: **Hinky Punk**
Wales: **Ellylldan**, ***pwca***
Warwickshire and Gloucestershire: Hobbedy's Lantern
The West Country: Jack-a-Lantern, Jacky Lantern
Worcestershire: Pinket

There are many similar examples to be found in folklore around the world. *See also* **Cyhyraeth**, **Fire**

Drakes, **Kit with the Canstick**, **Mab**, **Puck**.

Wish Hounds

See **Yeth Hound**.

Wokolo

Malevolent spirits in the folklore of the Baramba people of Nigeria, the *wokolo* inhabit trees and riverbanks. Humans passing through this terrain should take care, for these malignant spirits fire arrows at unsuspecting passersby.

Wood Wives

German fairies of the forest. Small and dressed in clothes of leaves, they are kind to those who treat them with respect. Hunters must offer them part of their catch to keep them appeased, and, as they are attracted by the smell of baking bread, cooks are advised to bake an extra loaf in case they pay a visit. They will pay the cook with sticks or woodchips that later turn to gold. Wood wives have a deep connection to the forest, and it is said that for every tree felled, a wood wife dies.

Wraith

In the Scottish tradition, an apparition, a specter supposed to appear at the time of a person's death. Wraiths can also appear as vengeful spirits, jealous of living creatures, feeding off human emotions and strength to fuel their shadowy existence, longing for the mortal life that they remember.

X

Xanthe

An **oceanid** from Greek mythology. Each of the 3,000 oceanids had guardianship of a particular element of nature, such as a sea, lake, pasture, flower, or cloud. They were the daughters of Oceanus and Thethys. Oceanus was ruler of the rivers and the seas, the oldest of the Titans, whose mother was Gaea, Mother Earth, and father was Uranus, ruler of the heavens. Thethys was Titaness of the Oceans. Xanthe was a water **nymph**, patron of the golden clouds of sunsets and sunrises. Her name comes from the Greek, meaning "yellow."

Xantho

A **nereid**, or sea **nymph**, from Greek mythology, the golden-haired Xantho was patron of sailors and fishermen. Her name derives from the Greek *xanthos*, meaning "yellow" or "golden." Her mother, Doris, was an **oceanid** nymph, her father was Nereus, eldest son of the sea god Pontus. Doris and Nereus had 50 daughters, known as the nereids. They all lived with their father in a cavern at the bottom of the Aegean Sea.

Y

Yallery Brown

A mischievous, fairylike creature in an old Yorkshire tale.

Tom was a work-shy lad. One day, while resting during his daily chores, he heard a faint whimper from under a stone. He investigated and found a little creature trapped there, begging him to set it free.

Tom obliged and lifted up the stone to reveal a wizened little man no bigger than a one-year-old child. His skin was wrinkled and he was covered in yellowy-brown hair. He introduced himself as Yallery Brown and told Tom he would grant him a wish. Tom asked for help with his daily chores. Sure enough, the next day all his work was done without him having to lift a finger.

But soon people in the village began to talk and there were rumors that Tom was up to some kind of wizardry. So he called to Yallery Brown. When he came, Tom told him his help was no longer needed.

Yallery Brown was enraged and promised Tom bad luck for the rest of his life. Unfortunately for him, that is exactly what he got.

Yarthkins

Fertility spirits of the Lincolnshire fen country, described by Mrs. Balfour in *Legends of the Carrs* (1891). These spirits of the Earth could be benevolent or malevolent. They expected to receive tribute for their work and could turn dangerous if neglected, or slighted in any way, as with **Yallery Brown**.

Ye Shen

See **Ye Xian**.

Ye Xian

(Or Ye Shen.) The heroine of a traditional Chinese fairy tale that is similar to the *Cinderella* story.

Ye Shen lives with her stepmother and her stepsister, Jun Li, who force her to cook and clean and do all of the household chores. One day she befriends a beautiful 3-yard- (1-meter-) long fish that lives in a lake near their home. Jealous of Ye Shen's apparent happiness, Jun Li follows her to the lake, where she witnesses her talking to the fish, which has a white tuft on its chin. She recounts what she has seen to her mother, who kills the fish and eats it.

An old, white-bearded man appears and tells Ye Shen that if she hides the fish's bones under her bed, she will be granted a wish.

When the New Year festival celebrations arrive, Ye Shen's stepmother orders her to stay at home, but the old man appears once more and Ye Shen finds herself dressed in the most magnificent clothes and golden shoes. She goes to the New Year ball and her beauty is much admired by all. Fearing that she has been recognized, she flees, but loses one of her shoes.

The king, fascinated by the dainty shoe, orders a search for the beautiful maiden, but the shoe fits no one. In despair, the king builds a monument, on which he places the shoe. When Ye Shen tries to retrieve it, she is brought before him as a thief. To prove her innocence, she tries on the shoe. It fits and she and the king are married.

Yeats, W. B. *(1865–1939)*

William Butler Yeats was an Irish poet born in Dublin, the son of a well-known painter, John Butler Yeats. He spent his childhood in Sligo and in London. He returned to Dublin at the age of 15 to study painting, but preferred poetry. From a young age he was fascinated by the Irish fairy and folk tales. He was a firm believer in fairies and became involved with the Celtic Revival, a movement that sought to promote Ireland's own heritage. His writing drew from sources in Irish mythology and folklore and in 1888 he wrote *Fairy and Folk Tales of the Irish Peasantry.*

Yell Hound

See **Yeth Hound**.

Yellow Dwarf

A French tale written by **Marie-Catherine d'Aulnoy** as part of her *Contes de Fées* (Fairy Tales). Yellow Dwarf is a nasty piece of work who blackmails a queen in order to marry her beautiful daughter.

The queen's daughter was very beautiful but very vain, and she refused to marry any of the kings who courted her. Becoming desperate, the queen decided to consult the Fairy of the Desert. The fairy was guarded by a fierce pack of lions. The only way to get past them was to bake them a special cake. So the queen baked the cake and set off.

Along the way, she stopped to rest and fell asleep. When she woke up, the cake had disappeared and she was surrounded by the lions.

A yellow dwarf appeared and told the queen he could save her—on one condition: he must have her daughter's hand in marriage.

Reluctantly, the queen agreed and was transported back to her palace, where she was filled with melancholy.

Not knowing what to do about her mother, the princess decided to consult the Fairy of the Desert. She baked the special cake and set off. On the way she stopped to pick some fruit, but her basket and cake disappeared. The Yellow Dwarf appeared and told the princess about the deal her mother had made. The only way to save herself, he said, was to marry him. Given little choice, the princess agreed.

Back in the palace, however, she made plans to marry the King of the Gold Mines and escape the Yellow Dwarf.

On the day of the wedding, the Fairy of the Desert came to the palace and reminded mother and daughter of their promise. When the Yellow Dwarf arrived, he fought the King of the Gold Mines and kidnapped the princess. The fairy, meanwhile, took the king to her grotto, where she told him the only way to escape death was to marry her.

One day the king was walking along the shore when a mermaid appeared, saying she could save him. Together they went to the steel palace of the Yellow Dwarf, where the king slayed six sphinxes, six dragons, and twenty-four nymphs, the guardians of the steel palace, with a diamond sword the mermaid had given him.

Seeing the king with the beautiful mermaid, the princess thought that he had betrayed her. He comforted her, but in doing so dropped his sword. The Yellow Dwarf pounced on it and plunged it into the king's back, killing him.

Bereft, the princess took her own life.

So, because of his jealousy, the Yellow Dwarf lost his princess. And the moral of the story? Nothing good can come of jealousy. In France, yellow is traditionally the color of jealousy.

Yemaja

A mother spirit, or ***orisha*** from Yoruba mythology. An *orisha* is a spiritual entity with control over the elements of nature. Belief in *orishas* originated with the Yoruba people and spread from their homeland in Nigeria to other parts of Africa and to South America.

Yemaja is the matriarchal ruler of the ocean and guardian of children. She is considered to be mother of the *orishas* and is a patron of women. Her name comes from the Yoruba for "the Mother whose children are fish," symbolic of her fecundity and alluding both to her numerous spirit children and her mortal followers. As stories of the *orishas* were spread through oral tradition throughout Afro-American cultures, her name took on variations according to local dialect and pronunciations, and she appears in other countries, including Cuba and Uruguay, under slightly different names. In Brazil, she is venerated as **Janaína,** the spirit of the sea.

Yeth Hound

(Or Yell Hound.) A black, headless hound of Devon, with fire in his eyes and on his breath, said to be the manifestation of an unbaptized child, the Yeth Hound is one of many examples of black hounds found in British and European folklore—***Cwn Annwn*** in Wales, Black Shuck in Norfolk and Suffolk, ***Cù Sith*** in the Scottish Highlands; Moddey Dhoo on the Isle of Man, Tchico on the island of Guernsey, and Rongeur d'Os (Bone Gnawer) in Normandy, to name but a few. They are generally nocturnal and sometimes headless.

The wailing of the Yeth Hound is said to echo across the moors as it wanders the Devon countryside at night and may have been the inspiration for Arthur Conan Doyle's *The Hound of the Baskervilles.*

Ys

Mythical Breton city, a realm of magical beings said to have been engulfed by the waves in the fourth or fifth century.

King Draglon lived in Cornouaille, south Brittany. He had a large fleet of ships to attack his enemies in faraway countries in the cold north and steal their gold and treasures.

One day his sailors refused to fight, as they had been away from their wives and children for a very long time. They took all the boats and returned home and King Draglon was left alone in the cold winter.

Malgven, the Queen of the North, offered him an alliance. "I know you," she said, "you are a brave fighter, my husband is old and his sword is rusty. You and I will kill him and you will take me to your kingdom."

And so the two returned together to Cornouaille, mounted on Morvac'h, Malgven's magic horse. Morvac'h galloped on the crest of the waves and they soon returned to King Draglon's home where Malgven gave birth to a daughter, Dahut, but died soon after.

Dahut grew into a very pretty young woman. She loved the sea so much that her father agreed to build her a city on the shore. It was surrounded by a high dyke to protect it from the storms and had huge gates, made of bronze, to access the sea. Only one key had been made to open the gates, and the king was its guardian.

Dahut asked the Ocean to bring her handsome sailors and she would take them as her lovers, but she promised the Ocean that she would return them to him. Each night she had a different lover. She would ask them to put on a mask that, in the morning, would tighten around their throat and strangle them. They could then be returned to the Ocean.

One day a handsome knight dressed in red arrived in the city of Ys and Dahut took him, too, as her lover. That night a huge storm broke out. "Let the storm rage," said Dahut, "the city walls are strong and my father guards the only key."

But the handsome knight convinced the princess to steal the key to the gates from her father. She gave the key to him, but in fact he was none other than the Devil, and he opened the gates.

Dahut fled the flooding city and begged her father to let her leave the city with him, riding on Morvac'h as Ys sunk beneath the sea.

Dahut and the king were riding across the waves when a specter appeared, saying, "Shame on you, you stole the key from your father," and urging the king to push his unworthy daughter into the sea.

At first Draglon resisted, but, realizing the crime his daughter had committed, he at last flung her to the Ocean.

The king's horse carried him away and they eventually arrived in a town, Quimper, which he made his capital. A statue of Draglon and Morvac'h can be seen to this day between the two towers of Quimper's cathedral.

It is thought that Dahut, the lover of the Ocean, became a **mermaid**.

Yuki-Onna

The Snow Woman of Japanese legends, who appears as a deathly pale and beautiful woman whose breath freezes unfortunate travelers caught in snowstorms. In older tales she is portrayed as an evil spirit, intent on inflicting an icy death wherever she goes, leaving no footprints in the snow.

In a story from Lafcadio Hearn's *Kwaidan: Stories and Studies of Strange Things* (1904), Yuki-Onna appears when an old man and a boy are sleeping in a hut during a violent snowstorm. She bends over the old man and breathes on him, then, turning to the boy, she is about to do the same when she sees how young and handsome he is. As he gazes at the beautiful, white woman with the strange and frightening eyes bending over him, she whispers that she has taken pity on him, but if he ever tells anyone of their encounter, she will kill him. With those words she disappears and the boy, Minokichi, bars the door of the hut and cannot tell if he has been dreaming. He calls the old man's name and reaches out a hand to touch him, but his face is frozen and still: he is dead.

Minokichi returns to his mother's house and after some time has passed he resumes his work of gathering bundles of wood from the forest to sell. As he walks along the path one day he meets a beautiful young woman named O-Yuki. They talk, they delight each other with their beauty, and eventually they are married. They live contentedly and she bears him ten children but stays as young and beautiful as the day they met.

One evening as they sit beside the fire Minokichi looks at his wife and says he has never seen such a handsome woman, except for a strange and frightening experience in his youth when he could not be sure whether he was awake or dreaming. O-Yuki asks him to tell her the story and he relates the tale of the Snow Woman.

When the tale is done, O-Yuki rises from her chair and shrieks at him that he has broken his promise to stay forever silent and it is only the thought of the children in his care that protects him from her murderous fury. As she berates him, her voice and body fade and twist into a spiraling mist that rises up and out of the roof and she is forever lost to him.

Yule Lads

See **Gryla**.

Yunwitsandsdi

Little people in the folk beliefs of the Cherokee people. These music-loving spirits dwell in the hills of northern Georgia; it is said that the sound of their rattles and drums can sometimes be heard deep in the forests or high in the mountains. They are generally benign but, like most denizens of the fairy realm, they value their privacy and cast spells upon humans who attempt to pry into their affairs.

Z

Zagaz

A Moroccan ***djinn*** of disease, held responsible for the death of infants.

Zână

Romanian fairy, said to give life to fetuses in the womb. Like fairy godmothers or guardian spirits, *zane* (plural of *zână*) bestow kindness, luck, and beauty on a child and watch over them. However, folk tales warn that they also have the power to place curses or bring misfortune if they are upset.

The word *zână* comes from the Romanian for "beauty."

Zao-Jun

(Also known as Tsao Chun, Zao Shen.) Chinese household spirit who watches over the kitchen. Known as "the kitchen god" or "stove god," Zao-Jun is the most important of a host of Chinese household spirits that guard hearth and family.

Zao Shen

See **Zao-Jun**.

Zemi

(Also Ceni.) Christopher Columbus on his voyages in 1492 described these supernatural spirits who were revered by the island Arawak inhabitants of Hispaniola, present-day Haiti. In his account he noted that each village had a building set apart where the people performed ceremonies to this messenger of the gods and spirit of healing and fertility by carefully placing some grains of white powder upon the heads of the carved images around the room, then, with a hollow, forked cane inserted in their nostrils, they inhaled the powder while uttering incantations.

Zenko

See **Kitsune**.

Zeuxo

An oceanid from Greek mythology. One of the 3,000 daughters of Oceanus and Thethys, each of whom presided over a different element of nature.

The Greek poet Hesiod, thought to have been alive around 700 B.C., lists the names of many of the oceanids in *Theogony*, a poem that describes the birth of the Greek gods and goddesses:

They are Peitho, Admete, Ianthe, and Electra, Doris, Prymno, and godlike Ourania, Hippo, Klymene, Rhodeia, and Kallirhoe, Zeuxo, Klytia, Idyia, and Peisithoe, Plexaura, Galaxaura, and lovely Dione, Melobosis, Thoe, and beautiful Polydora, shapely Kerkeis and cow-eyed Plouto, Perseis, Ianeira, Akaste, and Xanthe, lovely Petraia, Menestho, and Europe, Metis, Eurynome, and saffron-robed Telesto, Chryseis, Asia, and enchanting Kalypso, Eudora, Tyche, Amphiro, and Okyrhoe, and Styx, who holds the highest rank. These are the eldest daughters born to Tethys and Okeanos.

See also **Xanthe**.

Zhong Kui

In Chinese legends Zhong Kui is the mythical ghost-catcher and demon-destroyer, a stern-faced ugly man with a full beard whose popularity in folklore was established in the eighth century during the Tang dynasty when the Emperor dreamed of two ghosts, one of whom robbed him while the other, Zhong Kui, caught and ate the offender. His image is used a guardian or "door god" to repel evil spirits.

See also **Lamassu**.

ZINA

A **nymph**-like fairy in the folklore of Moldavia, in present-day Romania. E. C. Grenville Murray's *The National Songs and Legends of Roumania* (1859) relates the tale of Mariora Floriora, the Zina of the Mountains, Sister of the Flowers.

ZINKIBARU

An African spirit of the Songhay people in eastern Mali. Also known as the Blind Master of Fish, he was the water spirit of the Niger river.

Selected Bibliography

Allies, J. 1846. *On the Ignis Fatuus or Will-O'-the-Wisp and the Fairies.* London: Trübner & Co.

Andersen, Hans C., trans. H. P. Paull. 1872. *Fairy Tales and Stories.* London: Frederick Warne & Co.

Ashliman. D. L. 2006. *Fairy Lore: A Handbook.* US: Greenwood

Balfour, C. 1891. "Legends of the Cars." *Folklore,* II

Baring-Gould, S. 1890. *A Book of Folklore.* London: Collins

Batchelor, Rev. J. 1901. *The Ainu and their Folklore.* London: The Religious Tract Society

Beals, K. M. 1917. *Flower Lore and Legend.* New York: Henry Holt & Co.

Blavatsky, H. P. 1877. *Isis Unveiled.* New York: J. W. Bouton

Bottrell, W. 1870–1890 (3 vols). *Traditions and Hearthside Stories of the West of England* (3rd title in the series: *Stories and Folk-lore of West Cornwall*). Penzance: Bottrell

Brand, Rev. J. 1701. *A Brief Description of Orkney, Shetland, Pightland-Firth and Caithness.* Edinburgh: George Mosman

Brewer, E. C. 1898. *Brewer's Dictionary of Phrase and Fable.* Philadelphia: Henry Altemus; Bartleby.com, 2000

Briggs, K. M. 1967. *The Fairies in Tradition and Literature.* London: Routledge & Kegan Paul Ltd.

— 1976. *A Dictionary of Fairies: Hobgoblins, Brownies, Bogies and Other Supernatural Creatures.* London: Penguin Books

— 1978. *The Vanishing People.* London: BT Basford

Broome, D. 1963. *Fairy Tales from the Isle of Man.* Isle of Man: Norris Modern Press

Bulfinch, T. 1913. *The Age of Fable.* New York: Review of Reviews

Campbell, J. F. 1860–1862 (4 vols). *Popular Tales of the West Highlands.* Edinburgh: Edmonston and Douglas

Campbell, J. G. 1900. *Superstitions of the Highlands and Islands of Scotland.* Glasgow: J. MacLehose

— 1902. *Witchcraft and Second Sight in the Highlands and Islands of Scotland.* Glasgow: J. MacLehose

Carmichael, A. 1900. *Carmina Gadelica.* Edinburgh: T. & A. Constable

Carroll, L. 1889. *Silvie and Bruno.* London: Macmillan
Carter, A., and Zipes, J. 2008. *Little Red Riding Hood, Cinderella and Other Fairy Tales of Charles Perrault.* New York: Penguin
Child, F. J. 1882–1898 (5 vols). *The English and Scottish Popular Ballads.* New York: Houghton, Mifflin & Co.
Croker, T. Crofton. 1825–1827 (3 vols). *Fairy Legends and Traditions of the South of Ireland.* London: John Murray
Daniel, N., ed. 2011. *The Fairy Tales of the Brothers Grimm.* London: Taschen
Dasent, G. W. 1904. *Popular Tales from the Norse.* Edinburgh: Constable
Denham, M. 1892–1895 (2 vols). *The Denham Tracts.* London: The Folklore Society
Doyle, A. Conan. 1922. *The Coming of the Fairies.* New York, Toronto, and London: Hodder & Stoughton
Evans, M. A. B. 1895. *Nymphs, Nixies, Naiads: Legends of the Rhine.* New York & London: G. P. Putnam's Sons
Evans-Wentz, W. Y. 1911. *The Fairy-Faith in Celtic Countries.* London & New York: H. Froude
Ewing. J. H. 1871. *The Brownies and Other Tales.* London: J. M. Dent & Sons, Ltd.
Frazer, J. G. 1987. *The Golden Bough.* London: Papermac
Froud, B., 2004. *Good Faeries, Bad Faeries.* London: Pavillion
Froud, B., and Lee. A. 1978. *Faeries.* New York: Peacock Press/Bantam
Garner, A. 2011. *Collected Folk Tales.* London: HarperCollins Children's Books
Gill, Rev. W. Wyatt. 1876. *Myths and Songs from the South Pacific.* London: H. S. King & Co.
Gill, W. 1929. *A Manx Scrapbook.* London: Arrowsmith
Gregory, Lady A. 1904. *Gods and Fighting Men.* London: John Murray
Grey, Sir G. 1855. *Polynesian Mythology and Ancient History of the New Zealand Race.* London: J. Murray
Grice, F. 1944. *Folk-tales of the North Country.* London & Edinburgh: Thomas Nelson & Sons
Grimm, J., trans. Stallybrass, J. S. 1882–1888 (4 vols). *Teutonic*

Mythology. London: G. Bell & Sons

Halliwell-Phillipps, J. O. 1853. *Illustrations of the Fairy Mythology of Shakespeare*. London: the Shakespeare Society

Hartland, E. S. 1891. *The Science of Fairy Tales: An Inquiry into Fairy Mythology*. London: Walter Scott

Hazlitt, W. C. 1875. *Fairy Tales, Legends and Romances Illustrating Shakespeare*. London: F. & W. Kerslake

Hearn, Lafcadio, trans. 1903. *Japanese Fairy Tale Series: Chin Chin Kobakama*. Tokyo: T. Hasegawa

Henderson, W. 1866. *Notes on the Folklore of the Northern Counties of England and the Borders*. London: The Folklore Society

Hunt, R. 1865. *Popular Romances of the West of England*. London: Chatto and Windus

Hyde, D. 1890. *Beside the Fire*. London: Nutt

Ivanits, L. J. 1989. *Russian Folk Belief*. New York: M. E. Sharpe

Jacobs, J. 1890. *English Fairy Tales*. London: Nutt

— 1892. *Celtic Fairy Tales*. London: Nutt

Jones, Rev. H., and Kropf, L., eds. 1889. *The Folk Tales of the Maygars*. London: The Folklore Society

Keightley, T. 1828. *The Fairy Mythology*. London: Bradbury & Evans

Kirby, F. W. 1895. *The Hero of Esthonia: and Other Studies in the Romantic Literature of That Country*. London: John C. Nimmo

Kirk, R. 1691. *The Secret Commonwealth of Elves, Fauns and Fairies*. US: Dover, 2008

Lang, A. 1951. *The Rose Fairy Book*. London: Longmans, Green & Co. Ltd.

Leadbeater, C. W. 1895. *The Astral Plane: Its Scenery, Inhabitants and Phenomena*. London: Theosophical Publishing Society

— 1913. *The Hidden Side of Things: A Treatise on the Occult Realities Behind Ordinary Experiences, Ceremonies, etc. by a Seer*. India: Theosophical Publishing House

Lee, F. H., ed. 1939. *Folk Tales of All Nations*. London: Harrap

Leland, C. G. 1884. *The Algonquin Legends of New*

England. New York: Houghton, Mifflin & Co.
— 1899. *Aradia: or the Gospel of the Witches.* London: Nutt
Macdougall, J.; Calder, G., ed. 1910. *Folk Tales and Fairy Lore in Gaelic and English Collected from Oral Tradition.* Edinburgh: J. Grant
Mackenzie, D. A. 1935. *Scottish Folk-lore and Folk Life.* London: Blackie & Son
MacKillop, J. 2006. *Myths and Legends of the Celts.* London: Penguin
Marriott, S. 2006. *The Ultimate Fairies Handbook.* London: MQ Publications
Moore, A. W. 1891. *The Folklore of the Isle of Man.* Isle of Man: Brown & Son
Porteous, A. 1928. *Forest Folklore, Mythology and Romance.* London: G. Allen & Unwin
Purkiss, D. 2001. *Troublesome Things: A History of Fairies and Fairy Tales.* London: Penguin
Rhys, J. 1901. *Celtic Folklore: Manx and Welsh.* Oxford: Oxford University Press
Ritson, J. 1831. *Fairy Tales.* London: Payne & Foss
Roberts, A. and Montford, C. P. 1969. *The Dawn of Time: Australian Aboriginal Myths in Paintings.* Adelaide: Rigby
Rose, C. 1998. *Spirits, Fairies, Leprechauns, and Goblins: An Encyclopedia.* New York: Norton
Saxby, J. 1932. *Shetland Traditional Lore.* Edinburgh: Grant & Murray
Scott, J. 1883. *Arabian Nights Entertainments.* London: J. C. Nimmo and Bain
Sendak, M. 1981. *Outside Over There.* US: HarperCollins
Sikes, W. 1880. *British Goblins: Welsh Folk-lore, Fairy Mythology, Legends and Traditions.* London: S. Low, Marston, Searle & Rivington
Silver, C. G. 1999. *Strange and Secret Peoples: Fairies and Victorian Consciousness.* New York: Oxford University Press
Spence, L. 1917. *Legends and Romances of Brittany.* New York: Frederick A. Stokes
Stewart, G. 1823. *The Popular Superstitions and Festive Amusements of the Highlanders of Scotland.* Edinburgh: Archibald Constable and Company
Stokes, M., ed. 1880. *Indian Fairy Tales.* London: Ellis & White
Thorpe, B. 1852. *Northern Mythology, Comprising the Principal Popular Traditions and Superstitions of Scandinavia,*

North Germany and the Netherlands. London: Edward Lumley

Tongue, R. 1970. *Forgotten Folktales of the English Counties.* London: Routledge

Werner, T. C. 1922. *Myths and Legends of China.* London: Harrap

Wilde, Lady F. S. 1887. *Ancient Legends, Mystic Charms, and Superstitions of Ireland.* London: Ward & Downey

Wright, E. M. 1913. *Rustic Speech and Folklore.* London & New York: H. Milford

Yeats, W. B. 1888. *Fairy and Folk Tales of the Irish Peasantry.* London: Walter Scott

USEFUL ONLINE RESOURCES

Endicott Studio for the Mythic Arts, endicottstudio.typepad.com

Folktexts: A Library of Folktales, Folklore, Fairy Tales, and Mythology, Professor D. L. Ashliman, University of Pittsburg, www.pitt.edu/~dash/folktexts.html

Hathi Trust Digital Library, www.hathitrust.org

Sacred Texts, www.sacred-texts.com

Sur La Lune Fairy Tales, www.surlalunefairytales.com